INTERSECTIONS

OF MEDIA AND COMMUNICATIONS

CONCEPTS AND CRITICAL FRAMEWORKS

EDITED BY

WILL STRAW   SANDRA GABRIELE   IRA WAGMAN

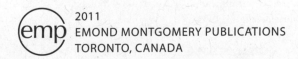
2011
EMOND MONTGOMERY PUBLICATIONS
TORONTO, CANADA

Emond Montgomery Publications Limited
60 Shaftesbury Avenue
Toronto ON M4T 1A3
http://www.emp.ca/university

Printed in Canada on recycled paper.

We acknowledge the financial support of the Government of Canada through the Canada Book Fund for our publishing activities.

Acquisitions and development editor: Mike Thompson
Marketing manager: Christine Davidson
Supervising editor: Jim Lyons
Copy editor: Francine Geraci
Proofreader and indexer: Paula Pike
Text designer and typesetter: Tara Wells
Cover designers: Stephen Cribbin & Simon Evers

Library and Archives Canada Cataloguing in Publication
    Intersections of media and communications : concepts, context, and critical frameworks / editors Will Straw, Sandra Gabriele, Ira Wagman.

Includes index.
ISBN 978-1-55239-464-9

    1. Mass media—Textbooks.   2. Communication—Textbooks.   3. Mass media—Canada—Textbooks.   4. Communication—Canada—Textbooks.
I. Straw, Will, 1954-   II. Gabriele, Sandra, 1972-   III. Wagman, Ira

P90.I58 2011   302.23   C2011-902609-0

Brief Contents

CONTENTS V

PREFACE ix

ABOUT THE AUTHORS xi

MEDIA TIMELINE xiii

PART ONE Studying Media and Communications

1   Why Study Communications? *Kevin Dowler* 3

2   Thinkers and Theories: A Brief Introduction *Stacey Johnson* 21

PART TWO Media Dimensions, Forms, and Functions

3   Dimensions of Media: Time and Space, Storage and Transmission
     Will Straw 37

4   Media Forms, Interfaces, and Formats *Bart Beaty and
     Rebecca Sullivan* 53

5   Media Functions *Ira Wagman* 73

6   Language and Media *Michael Darroch* 89

PART THREE Change and Continuity

7   Media R/Evolutions *Sandra Gabriele and Paul S. Moore* 113

8   The Political Economy of Media *The Editors* 135

9   Regulating the Media *Richard Sutherland* 151

10   Cultural Ownership, Copyright, and Intellectual Property
     Darren Wershler 173

11   Alternative Media *Josh Greenberg and Heather Gilberds* 197

PART FOUR Media, Culture, and Public Life

12   New Media Culture *Michael Strangelove* 219
13   Journalism *Sandra Gabriele and Lisa Lynch* 239
14   Media, Consumption, and Everyday Life *Sonia Bookman* 267
15   Media, Representation, and Identity *Alexandra Boutros* 289
16   Speed, Sensation, and Stimulation *Beverley Best* 309

PART FIVE Researching the Media

17   Thinking About Methods *Kim Sawchuk* 333

INDEX 351

Contents

BRIEF CONTENTS iii

PREFACE ix

ABOUT THE AUTHORS xi

MEDIA TIMELINE xiii

PART ONE Studying Media and Communications

1 Why Study Communications? 3

Kevin Dowler

Introduction 3

Old and New, Same and Different 5

Problems with Pictures 6

Writing and Knowledge 10

Back to the Future 12

Our Media "R" Us 15

Conclusion: The Enduring Questions About Communication 17

Discussion Questions 19

Suggested Resources 19

References 19

2 Thinkers and Theories: A Brief Introduction 21

Stacey Johnson

Some Key Thinkers in Media and Communications 21

References 34

PART TWO Media Dimensions, Forms, and Functions

3 Dimensions of Media: Time and Space, Storage and Transmission 37

Will Straw

Introduction: Time and Space—The Dimensions of Media 37

Media and Time 38

Media and Space 45

Conclusion 51

Discussion Questions 51

Suggested Resources 52

References 52

4 Media Forms, Interfaces, and Formats 53

Bart Beaty and Rebecca Sullivan

Introduction 53

Form: Sound, Print, and Visual Media 55

Interface: Social Networking Media 61

Format: Cultural Industries 63

Conclusion: Intermedia and Transmedia—Pondering the Future 66

Discussion Questions 68

Suggested Resources 69

References 69

5 Media Functions 73
Ira Wagman
Introduction 73
Media Beyond Mass Media 74
Many Media, Many Functions 76
Conclusion 85
Note 86
Discussion Questions 87
Suggested Resources 87
References 87

6 Language and Media 89
Michael Darroch
Introduction: "Voices in the Air" 89
The Semiotic Approach: Language as a
  Symbolic System of Representation 91
Dialogism: Language as an Expression of
  Self and Other 93
Language Through Eyes and Ears: Oral
  and Written Traditions 96
Language in Electronic and Digital
  Culture 101
Humans and Machines: Machine
  Translation and
  Digital Speech Technologies 105
Conclusion 107
Discussion Questions 108
Suggested Resources 108
References 109

**PART THREE Change and
Continuity**

7 Media R/Evolutions 113
Sandra Gabriele and Paul S. Moore
Introduction: What Is Media
  History? 113
The Problem of Doing Media
  History 115

The Dream of Perfect Communication:
  Connectivity 119
Case Study: The Myth of Total
  Cinema 125
Conclusion 131
Discussion Questions 131
Suggested Resources 132
References 132

8 The Political Economy
   of Media 135
The Editors
Introduction 135
The Political Economy Perspective 137
Some Key Concepts in the Political
  Economy of Media 138
New Media for a New Century 143
A Critique of the Political Economy
  Approach 144
Mixed Motives: The Case of the CBC 146
Conclusion: Questions of Political
  Economy in the Digital Era 147
Note 148
Discussion Questions 148
Suggested Resources 149
References 149

9 Regulating the Media 151
Richard Sutherland
Introduction: Power, Policy, and
  the Media 151
Controlling the Message, Controlling
  the Media 157
Policies in Conflict 166
Conclusion: The Limits of Policy 167
Notes 168
Discussion Questions 168
Suggested Resources 169
References 169

10 Cultural Ownership, Copyright, and Intellectual Property 173

Darren Wershler

Introduction: Who Is "Girl Talk," and Why Hasn't He Been Sued? 173

What Is Intellectual Property? 177

A Condensed History of Copyright in North America 178

Other Forms of Cultural Ownership 185

Indigenous Models of Cultural Ownership 186

Public Licensing: The Creative Commons 187

Digital Dilemmas 188

Owning Living Things: Biotechnologies 190

Conclusion 192

Notes 193

Discussion Questions 193

Suggested Resources 194

References 194

11 Alternative Media 197

Josh Greenberg and Heather Gilberds

Introduction 197

What Are "Alternative" Media? 199

Alternative Media as a Tool of Struggle 203

Alternative Media as a Source of Radical Content 206

Alternative Media as a Means of Organizing Cultural Production 209

Alternative Media as a Channel for Expressing Identity and Voice 211

Conclusion 213

Note 214

Discussion Questions 214

Suggested Resources 214

References 215

PART FOUR Media, Culture, and Public Life

12 New Media Culture 219

Michael Strangelove

Introduction 219

Defining Culture 220

Communication and Ways of Thinking 222

The World of Old Media 223

What Is New About the New Media? 225

Factors in the Cultural Shift 226

Shifts in Cultural Production 230

Thinking Critically About New Media Culture 233

Conclusion 235

Discussion Questions 236

Suggested Resources 236

References 237

13 Journalism 239

Sandra Gabriele and Lisa Lynch

Introduction: Journalism's Traditional Role in Public Life 239

What Is News? 240

Forms of Journalism 242

Journalism's Democratic Function: The Ideal 246

Journalism and Democracy? 248

Public Media: Ensuring Journalism's Democratic Role? 254

The Online Transition and the Challenges to Journalism 255

Changing News Presentation and the End of "Fortress Journalism" 257

Conclusion 260

Discussion Questions 261

Suggested Resources 261

References 262

14 Media, Consumption, and Everyday Life 267

Sonia Bookman

Introduction: A Day in the Life 267

Media and Contemporary Consumer Culture 269

Mediating Consumption and Consuming Media 272

Media and Consumption in Everyday Life 277

Conclusion 284

Discussion Questions 284

Suggested Resources 285

References 285

15 Media, Representation, and Identity 289

Alexandra Boutros

Introduction 289

Essentialism 290

Oppositional Identity Formation 291

Ideology 294

Identity and New Media 297

Rise of the Prosumer 298

Participatory Media 300

The Digital Divide 303

Conclusion 304

Notes 305

Discussion Questions 305

Suggested Resources 306

References 306

16 Speed, Sensation, and Stimulation 309

Beverley Best

Introduction: Communicating at the Speed of Light 309

Speed, Commerce, and Communication 310

Media, Globalization, and the Political Economy of Speed 312

Speed and Space 314

The Regime of "Real Time": Immediacy and Instantaneity 317

Stimulation, Distraction, and the Tempo of the City 320

Speed, Spectacle, and the 24-Hour News Cycle 324

Conclusion 327

Discussion Questions 327

Suggested Resources 328

References 328

PART FIVE Researching the Media

17 Thinking About Methods 333

Kim Sawchuk

Introduction 333

Quantitative and Qualitative Methods 334

The Researcher's Toolkit 336

A Methodological Approach 337

Messy Worlds: Seeking Truth, Wisdom, Knowledge, and Understanding 338

Paradigms and Concepts 339

Literature Reviews and Research Problematics: Reading 340

Considerations for Your Study 341

Conclusion: Back to Method 346

Note 348

Discussion Questions 348

Suggested Resources 348

References 349

INDEX 351

Preface

If ever there was a time to reconsider how to approach the key concepts and questions in the study of media and communications, this would likely be it. In the midst of what many see as a revolution in communications technology, students now arrive at universities and colleges having had a different experience of media than generations of students before them. One of the goals of this book is to explore these new experiences of media and consider their significance. For starters, the media with which most of us are engaged are primarily digital in nature. What's more, our connections to media are no longer sporadic, but are becoming more constant, often lasting from morning till night. Meanwhile, the world in which this rapid exchange of information and real-time communicating is taking place seems to be changing in subtle (and not so subtle) ways.

This is not to suggest that this book is strictly *about* digital media; rather, it is about the media we are immersed in *today*, most of which happens to be digital. And, as several chapters in this book point out in various ways, there are many things that remain constant and unchanging about our experience of media, digital or otherwise. Indeed, this book features historical perspectives throughout that provide a vitally important context for understanding today's media, including questions about human communication that were first asked thousands of years ago, and remain relevant today.

Another recurring theme of this book is that rapid changes in communications tend to reinforce an *appearance* of change. It is easy to forget that, alongside the sense of excitement brought by each new development in technology, there is also a sense of déjà vu. The sense of living in the middle of a communications revolution has been a constant in our society for a century or more.

As the title suggests, this book is about the *intersections* that occur among media, communications, technology, culture, and our society. This same sense of intersection marks the involvement of our many fine contributors, whose diverse backgrounds include fields such as sociology, history, journalism, film, English, cultural studies, and, of course, media and communications studies. They were asked to present the key concepts and questions that students need to consider when approaching a particular topic. Our hope is that students will emerge from reading this book with the confidence and knowledge to ask their own critical questions about the media they consume every day.

The authors and publisher wish to thank each of the contributors for their hard work and dedication to this project. They also wish to acknowledge the following people for their input and assistance during its conception and development: Melissa Aronczyk (Carleton University), Beverley Best (Concordia University), Kevin Dowler (York University), Zoë Druick (Simon Fraser University), Herbert Pimlott (Wilfrid Laurier University), Ian Roderick (Wilfrid Laurier University), Myles Ruggles (York University), Chris Russill (Carleton University), Michael Strangelove (University of Ottawa), and the Faculty of Arts and Science, Concordia University.

Please also visit the website for this book for information and additional resources: **www.emp.ca/intersections**.

About the Authors

Bart Beaty is a professor and head of the Department of English at the University of Calgary.

Beverley Best is an assistant professor and graduate program director in the Department of Sociology and Anthropology at Concordia University.

Sonia Bookman is an assistant professor in the Department of Sociology at the University of Manitoba.

Alexandra Boutros is an assistant professor in the Department of Communication Studies and is cross-appointed to the Cultural Studies Program at Wilfrid Laurier University.

Michael Darroch is an assistant professor in the Department of Communication, Media and Film at the University of Windsor.

Kevin Dowler is an associate professor in the Department of Communication Studies at York University.

Sandra Gabriele is an assistant professor in the Department of Communication Studies at Concordia University.

Heather Gilberds is a doctoral student in communication at Carleton University.

Josh Greenberg is an associate professor of communication at Carleton University and is cross-appointed to the Department of Sociology and Anthropology.

Stacey Johnson is a lecturer in the School of Communication, Arts and Design at Seneca College.

Lisa Lynch is an assistant professor and undergraduate program director in the Department of Journalism at Concordia University.

Paul S. Moore is an associate professor of communication and culture at Ryerson University.

Kim Sawchuk is a professor in the Department of Communication Studies at Concordia University and was editor of the *Canadian Journal of Communication* from 2006 to 2011.

Michael Strangelove is a lecturer in the Department of Communication at the University of Ottawa.

Will Straw is a professor of communications at McGill University and director of the McGill Institute for the Study of Canada.

Rebecca Sullivan is an associate professor in the Department of English at the University of Calgary and a fellow at the Calgary Institute for the Humanities.

Richard Sutherland is an instructor in the Department of Communication and Culture at the University of Calgary.

Ira Wagman is an associate professor of communication studies at Carleton University, with a cross-appointment between the School of Journalism and Communication and the Institute for the Comparative Study of Literature, Art, and Culture.

Darren Wershler is an assistant professor in the Department of English at Concordia University.

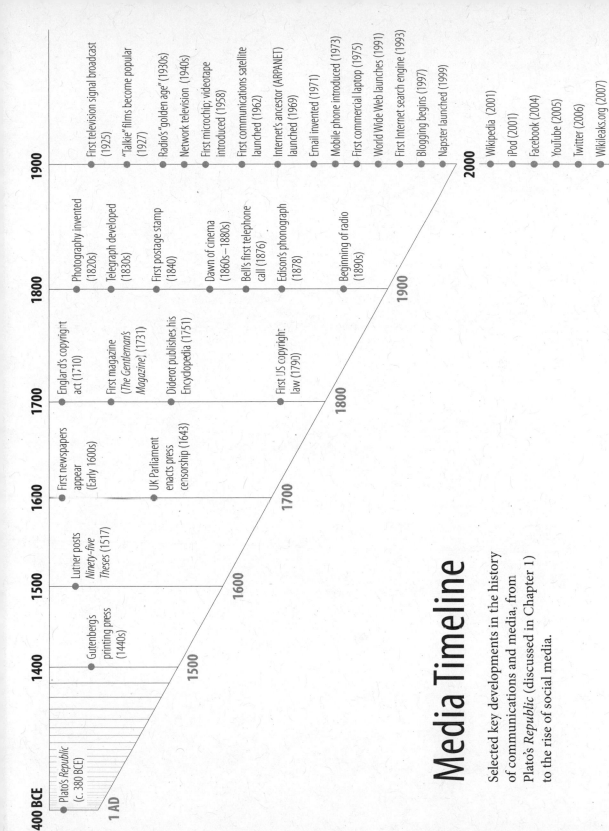

Media Timeline

Selected key developments in the history of communications and media, from Plato's *Republic* (discussed in Chapter 1) to the rise of social media.

Plato's *Republic* (c. 380 BCE)

Gutenberg's printing press (1440s)

Luther posts *Ninety-five Theses* (1517)

First newspapers appear (Early 1600s)

UK Parliament enacts press censorship (1643)

England's copyright act (1710)

First magazine (*The Gentleman's Magazine*) (1731)

Diderot publishes his Encyclopedia (1751)

First US copyright law (1790)

Photography invented (1820s)

Telegraph developed (1830s)

First postage stamp (1840)

Dawn of cinema (1860s–1880s)

Bell's first telephone call (1876)

Edison's phonograph (1878)

Beginning of radio (1890s)

First television signal broadcast (1925)

"Talkie" films become popular (1927)

Radio's "golden age" (1930s)

Network television (1940s)

First microchip; videotape introduced (1958)

First communications satellite launched (1962)

Internet's ancestor (ARPANET) launched (1969)

Email invented (1971)

Mobile phone introduced (1973)

First commercial laptop (1975)

World Wide Web launches (1991)

First Internet search engine (1993)

Blogging begins (1997)

Napster launched (1999)

Wikipedia (2001)

iPod (2001)

Facebook (2004)

YouTube (2005)

Twitter (2006)

Wikileaks.org (2007)

400 BCE · 1 AD · 1400 · 1500 · 1600 · 1700 · 1800 · 1900 · 2000

PART ONE
Studying Media and Communications

Why Study Communications?

How do media help shape our experience of the world, both positively and negatively? In what ways is our connection to media different today than it was in previous decades or centuries? What has stayed the same? How do media help, or hinder, communication among people?

KEY CONCEPTS

1. All media were "new" media at one time or another.
2. Media may reinforce older ways of living or believing, yet at the same time have a modernizing influence.
3. There is no going back after the advent of a new medium.
4. What we know about ourselves as humans arises from the media, which enable us to gather and store information about ourselves.

CHAPTER OUTLINE

Introduction 3

Old and New, Same and Different 5

Problems with Pictures 6

Writing and Knowledge 10

Back to the Future 12

Our Media "R" Us 15

Conclusion: The Enduring Questions About Communication 17

Discussion Questions 19

Suggested Resources 19

References 19

Introduction

The astonishing speed of change in popular culture and media can make keeping up very difficult. "I'm Losing My Edge," a single released in 2002 by the American band LCD Soundsystem, illustrates this quandary. The song is a lament about the loss of prestige, since with the passing of time, the "coolness" the singer once possessed is rapidly slipping away. "I'm losing my edge," he sings, "to the kids from France and from London … to all the kids in Tokyo and Berlin. I'm losing my edge to the art-school Brooklynites in little jackets and borrowed nostalgia for the unremembered eighties." The insider knowledge the singer has about obscure bands and hip clubs, which he displays through his record collection, has become increasingly irrelevant as it is displaced by newer scenes, newer bands, and emerging trends and styles. "I was there," he repeats over and over, as if somehow being *there* mattered anymore, as if anyone cares today. The use of the past tense in this plaintive cry points to the way that being *here* is what really counts, that having an edge means being on the edge, *now*.

The song emphasizes the fragile status of investments in transient forms such as popular music. The labour spent in gaining prestige through insider knowledge of what is on the edge inevitably collides with the speed with which new trends emerge. And the ever-expanding scope of new "scenes" is facilitated by media that have globalized the circulation of cultural goods and attitudes. If, on the one hand, the song is a wry poke at those investments that are ultimately fleeting, on the other hand it contains a kernel of truth about the problem of *relevance*—or, more accurately, the fear of *irrelevance*—that is haunted by the seemingly relentless and endless cycle of the ever-new. Novelty, and the demand to be on the edge, inevitably displaces the past, consigning it with ever-increasing velocity to the junk heap.

Novelty, and the demand to be on the edge, inevitably displaces the past.

This phenomenon, of course, affects us all, as we are constantly exhorted to adopt new styles, new media technologies, and so on, with the promise that each succeeding configuration or device or upgrade will make us somehow both different and better, enable us to "keep our edge." This is why the song resonates with us: we can easily relate our own everyday experience to the problem it raises, and know probably all too well the feelings of anxiety invoked by the possibility of losing one's status and prestige by being behind the times.

We live these days in a fluid environment, where media technologies and the ways we communicate are constantly changing. If keeping pace is often difficult, it is nevertheless important to try and grasp what is different, what has changed with the advent of new media forms and the new practices that accompany them. The recent emergence of social media such as Twitter or Facebook, for example, presumably augur changes in social and cultural formations, attitudes, and practices that demand attention. So when we think about the question posed by the title of this chapter, certainly one answer is that we need to concern ourselves with what is different from conditions that prevailed before these new media forms came along.

But it might also be prudent, as a starting point to the examination of the new, to step back momentarily to reflect on the old. Rather than always asking, "what is different?" or "what is new?," we might dwell instead on the question "what is the *same*?" This question has the virtue of allowing us to see how problems we encounter with new media today echo issues that have surrounded communication and media for centuries, even millennia. By looking back at some older examples, we may find some insights to help us in thinking about present-day media.

One should consider what has changed with the rise of social media, but also, what is the same.

All media, it must be emphasized, were "new" media at one time or another. Thus, in answering the question "why study communications?," we must consider the ways in which, despite the changes that accompany the new, some of the same issues and problems raised long ago continue to be relevant and resonate with us today.

KEY CONCEPT
All media were "new" media at one time or another.

Old and New, Same and Different

Thinking about problems arising from communications media and technologies seems a thoroughly *modern* question. Indeed, some have argued that the idea of thinking about media at all—that is, recognizing something as a medium and calling it that—came about only in the late 19th century, with the advent of recording technologies such as film and the phonograph. This recognition occurs in "response to the proliferation of new technical media … that could not be assimilated to the older system of the arts" (Guillory 2010, 321). This is perhaps the precise modern difference: that we can, thanks to these devices, think about (and in terms of) media, and become able to see the differences media make in our lives.

These differences have not, for the most part it seems, been greeted positively; often, we hear a lament that the introduction of modern media, rather than enhancing our communication, detracts from it. The American media theorist John Durham Peters (1999, 33), for example, notes this tendency in a comment from 20th-century popular culture theorist Leo Lowenthal (1967): "The dehumanization of communication has resulted from its annexation by the media of modern culture—by the newspapers first, and then by radio and television" (336).

This observation appears to be true. Technologies do take over the function of communication from humans—for example, in the way computers conduct trading in the stock market. From this point of view, media do not enhance communication but rather, rob us of "true communication"—which, as Lowenthal remarks, "entails communion, a sharing of inner experience." So, according to Lowenthal, we experience a loss in which media actually take something away: instead of connecting us, they seem to be standing between us, getting in the way of communication. Successive media, it seems, only exacerbate this problem, because they take us farther and farther from true communication.

This perception, in turn, implies a better past in which media did not intrude. Our modern condition, then, is a problem *because* of the media: the media are to blame, so we need to get back to genuine forms of communication. Much commentary, of which Lowenthal's is typical, views our modern situation as lamentable because of media, and yearns for a recovery of a golden past of communication.

Peters (1999, 2) has suggested that what seems our current obsession with the term "communication" implies a sense that something has been lost. In the modern world, then, we find ourselves longing for a truer, more direct kind of communication, one that we imagine our media have taken from us. Lowenthal's comments could be seen as a symptom of that longing. But just because people living before the modern media era didn't use such terms as "media" and "communication" as we do, doesn't mean they weren't thinking about similar problems.

In fact, the very same problems concerning media that make Lowenthal so anxious have their first formulations millennia ago, with the origins of Western religion and classical philosophy. Thus, if we tend to think of problems in communication as a modern condition arising from the changes wrought by contemporary media, a glance back suggests that we are perhaps not so different after all, and that the same problems were also preoccupations for some of the earliest thinkers in Western culture.

Today we may find ourselves longing for a truer kind of communication, which media seem to have taken from us.

Problems with Pictures

Images drawn from Plato's dialogue *The Republic* (written in the 4th century BCE) and the Old Testament of the Bible illustrate humanity's historical problems with pictures. Discussions of pictures are critically important because they reveal some of the earliest thoughts about the trustworthiness of images, and whether they can accurately represent the truth. Such philosophical analysis, coupled with religious taboo, led to a profound skepticism about the truthfulness of pictures, and established attitudes that persist today with regard to what we see on television and on the Internet.

According to 19th-century English philosopher Alfred North Whitehead (1929/1978, 39), Western philosophy "consists of a series of footnotes to Plato." The same might be said for the study of communications today. Indeed, Peters (1999, 52) claims that "Plato's Socrates is our first theorist of communication," and we see this in the way Plato addressed a range of issues about media and communication that continue to be relevant today. These issues arise with Plato's concerns about how paintings and poetry,

Figure 1.1 Plato's Academy

Almost 2,500 years ago, Plato raised issues about communication that remain relevant to us today.

SOURCE: *The School of Athens* by Raphael, 1509–1510. The Yorck Project/The Vatican. Reprinted under Creative Commons agreement.

the media of Plato's time, are a poor substitute for what Lowenthal called true communication.

Plato's Cave Analogy

In the "cave analogy" from Book VII (514a–521b) of *The Republic*, Plato outlines a scenario in which prisoners are, from childhood, shackled in a cave, where all they can see are shadows cast on the wall by the objects and people passing behind them on a road outside the mouth of the cave. In the most general sense, Plato is concerned here with depicting the distinction between appearance and truth—that is, the difference between the image and reality. The shadows, taken by the prisoners to be reality because that is all they have ever seen, are in fact mere representations of real things, and thus are once removed from reality itself. The prisoners, then, are effectively

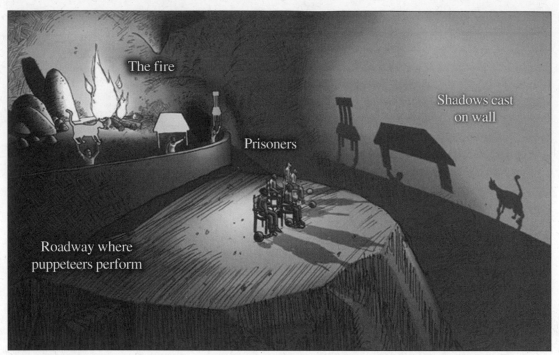

Figure 1.2 Plato's Cave

Plato created his famous "cave analogy" to raise questions about the distinction between appearance and truth, or image and reality. The cave analogy has been compared to an audience watching a film in a modern cinema.

living an illusion, mistaking the image for reality. Plato's point is that without knowing it, most of us live the same way.

Cornford (1941), like some other commentators on Plato who follow, likens the situation of the prisoners in the cave to an audience watching a movie, minus the shackles, of course. In making the parallel to modern media, Cornford raises the question of the degree to which a similar distortion of belief might occur as a consequence of taking movies or television pictures as depictions of reality. Like the prisoners in the cave, we are often faced with the inability to make any distinction between truth and falsehood, because without actually seeing something in reality, we have no basis for comparison. This very issue is the basis of modern communications studies: whether people have distorted views of reality as a consequence of what they see at the movies, on television, or through any other medium. For example, the Payne Fund Studies, the first large-scale analysis of media conducted in the 1930s, sought to discover the effects of movies on children—whether movie viewing would lead to delinquency and undermine traditional moral authorities such as the family and school (Jowett, Jarvie, and Fuller 1996). Those authorities were worried about whether children might confuse what they saw at the movies with what was appropriate in real life. If Plato was concerned with the way that we, like the prisoners, take the shadows to be true, similar questions continue to be raised in our time regarding the influence of media images, from the cinema to television and beyond.

Plato specifically raises the question, later in *The Republic*, of what we today call media when he discusses art, and tries to show how a painting or a poem are far removed from reality and truth. To illustrate, Plato uses the example of a bed. In the dialogue, Socrates says that the "real creator of a real bed" (597d) is a god. Second comes a bed fashioned by a carpenter: "what he produces is not the form of the bed which according to us is what a bed really is, but a particular bed" (597a). The carpenter's bed is therefore a *copy* of the ideal form of a bed. "We shan't be surprised," says Socrates, "if the bed the carpenter makes is a shadowy thing compared to reality." Thus, as a step removed from reality, the carpenter's bed is the same as the shadows on the wall of the cave.

Plato then has Socrates ask his student Glaucon what an artist does, and he replies, "I think we may fairly claim that he represents what the other two make" (597e)—that is, the "real" bed and the one made by a carpenter. Consequently, what an artist does, by copying the other two beds, is at a third remove from reality and truth, a copy of a copy. The status of the image thus becomes obvious in this scheme: because it is so far removed from reality, a painting—or a movie, or a television program—is merely a superficial likeness three times removed from the real world, and thus not to be confused with it, or perceived as an accurate depiction of reality.

The lesson to be drawn from this discussion should be clearer at this point: media, like painting and poetry, have the effect of drawing us away from or distorting reality, because as mere copies of real things, they cannot make any claim to be true. We should therefore, according to Plato, be skeptical about any claims images make to give us the truth about what really exists.

Our Long Tradition of Suspicion Toward Images

The suspicion that images do not represent what is actual certainly persists today, thanks in part not only to the skepticism raised in these early philosophical reflections, but also in the manner in which it is embedded in the Western religious tradition. We are subject to a historical double-whammy, so to speak, as a consequence of the combination of philosophical skepticism and the religious ban on images. In the Old Testament of the Bible, at Exodus 20:4, the lord says to the people camped at the base of Mount Sinai:

Similar questions are raised in our time regarding the influence of media images on people.

According to Plato, we should be skeptical about claims that images can give us the truth about reality.

"You shall not make for yourself an idol, whether in the form of anything that is in heaven above, or that is on the earth beneath, or that is in the water under the earth."

Certainly comprehensive in its scope, this warning appears to encompass virtually everything that can, and perhaps everything that cannot, be seen. This general ban on the image, if interpreted in various ways over time, nevertheless initiated a troubled relationship with depictions of humans and nature that has influenced, alongside classical philosophy, Western thinking ever since.

As we discover in reading on, instead of obeying this injunction, the people cast an image of a calf from the gold melted down from their jewellery (Exodus 32:1–6). Coming down from the mountain, in his rage on witnessing the revelry around the idol, Moses throws the tablets containing the commandments to the ground, and they are broken. This is clearly a moment of major crisis: the manufacture of the **graven image** threatens to undermine the founding principles upon which the emergent culture would rest, at the very moment they are introduced.

The history of the Judaic, Christian, and Islamic worlds has been marked by controversies over whether it is proper to make images of divine or earthly beings. Each culture has seen the periodic emergence of what is called **iconoclasm**—the distrust and deliberate suspicion of religious imagery (Besançon 2000). This persistent hostility toward images can be seen in the 2001 destruction of the two Bamiyan Buddha sculptures by the Taliban in Afghanistan, or in the pulling down of the statue of Saddam Hussein at Firdos Square in Baghdad by US coalition forces in 2003. A more common version of this iconoclasm, perhaps, is the long-standing suspicion that television or other image-based media do not show us the real world. "Kill Your Television," a 1990 song by the English rock band Ned's Atomic Dustbin, expressed something of this sentiment when it told its listeners: "You don't know shit because you've never been there."

What can be derived from all this is an abiding hostility toward the status of images, and perhaps, in a backhanded way—in both Plato's writings and the biblical tradition—the recognition of the power that images possess. In both cases, the concern appears to centre on the *intercession* of the image—that is, the way in which it stands between us and the truth. In both cases, the image threatens to draw us away, or distract us, from the real and the true.

graven image
An idol or representation of a deity used as an object of worship.

iconoclasm
The distrust and deliberate suspicion of religious imagery; the destruction of various types of icons.

Writing and Knowledge

The final example that deserves our attention, and one that speaks directly to the effects of media, is the advent of writing as it is described in Plato's

Phaedrus. Toward the end of this work (which is in the form of a dialogue between Socrates and Phaedrus), Socrates recounts a legend that purports to explain the way writing was given to us. In this legend, the god Theuth displays his various inventions (numbers, astronomy, dice games, and so on) to Thamus, king of Egypt at the time. Theuth comes finally to writing, claiming, "what I have discovered is an elixir of memory and wisdom" (274e). To this, Thamus replies that he has indeed invented a potion, a drug, but one that has the opposite effect to that claimed by Theuth: rather than aiding either memory or wisdom, writing will actually result in forgetfulness. "Through the lack of practice at using their memory," says Thamus, "as through reliance on writing they are reminded from outside by alien marks, not from within, themselves by themselves" (275a).

Like the other media discussed in *The Republic*, writing has only the *appearance* of wisdom or truth. In effect, writing is a sort of dead or inert speech unlike, as Phaedrus says, "the living, animate speech of the man who knows, of which the written speech would be rightly called a kind of phantom" (276a). Put slightly differently, the written word, like the painting to which it is compared, is just an image, inert marks on the page, and thus like the shadows that inhabit the world of appearances. If, as Saint Paul said (2 Corinthians 3:6), "the letter kills, but the Spirit gives life," Plato, too, remarks on and seems disturbed by the inhuman character of writing.

Writing is "dead" speech, then—the ghost of speech—because it circulates without humans to accompany it. Plato was concerned that this absence would lead to people's reading about ideas without really understanding them, because there would be no one to explain what the words might mean. Plato insisted there is only one way to impart knowledge properly, what he describes as "legitimate" writing: "written together with knowledge in the soul of the learner" (276a). By this, he actually meant inscribed in memory via conversation with a teacher or, as Peters (1999, 46) puts it, in "a reciprocal coupling of speaker and hearer, a closed communication circuit." For Plato, only the face-to-face dialogue ensured that ideas were properly understood. Open circuits of communication, on the other hand, like the circulation of written texts or broadcast signals, pose grave risks to the transfer of knowledge, because they raise the possibility of misinterpretation, misunderstanding, or deception. Plato, then, is the first speaker (and critic) to formulate the notion of what Peters (1999, 36) calls the "deprivation of presence"—the way that human contact seems to diminish as we turn more and more to media for our information. And so we end up back with Lowenthal's longing for "true communication" as a communion between souls. While Lowenthal blames mass media for depriving us of this true communication,

Human contact seems to diminish as we turn more and more to media for our information.

he is really taking up a complaint made millennia ago by Plato, one that has echoed across time up to today.

Back to the Future

Creating Spectacles

If we were to look for parallels today, they might be found in contemporary concerns over media as a kind of spectacle, particularly the staging of events for the sole purpose of obtaining public profile. The uncertainties that vexed Plato regarding encounters with writing have their contemporary counterparts in the dramas that have accompanied the rise in popularity of YouTube, for example. High-profile cases include the online video romance between emokid21ohio and emogirl21 which turned out to be a hoax, or that of "16-year-old Bree," lonelygirl15, who was supposedly a teen shut-in blogging about her woes and who became the second most subscribed YouTube channel in mid-2006 before being revealed as an actor working

Figure 1.3 lonelygirl15

This massively popular video series appeared on YouTube regularly for over two years. It was later revealed to be fictional.

from a written script. The creators of lonelygirl15 claimed that she was simply like all of us, and implying, perhaps correctly, that we all "perform" in social situations. The difference, however, might be, as Plato argues in the case of writing, that in direct human interaction we can get at the truth through the give and take of dialogue. In the same way that writing cannot explain itself to us, we do not know what is going on behind the video image on YouTube, which potentially hides as much as it reveals, and which might then mislead us. Indeed, we don't even know whether the consequent out-raged video posts following the revelation of lonelygirl15's actual identity are themselves authentic or staged.

The Separation of Information from Human Interaction

Because *Phaedrus* explores these same issues, this is precisely why Plato's work is relevant today. It provides us with "a checklist of enduring anxieties that arise in response to transformations in the means of communication" (Peters 1999, 47). What Plato had to say about writing has been said again and again with the advent of successive media, from the printing press through to our contemporary digital media technologies. The concern is what recent writers have described as the "uncoupling" of information transmission and human interaction, which was inaugurated by writing and accelerated by the printing press and subsequent distribution technologies. Since the advent of writing (whether given to us by the gods or by more earthly means) and all subsequent media of storage and distribution, the transfer of knowledge no longer requires speech between humans. Infor-mation can be stored in a myriad of ways and recalled when needed, or reproduced and distributed far beyond the physical bounds of those who speak and hear—indeed, via radio waves and space vehicles out into the known universe and beyond. The extent to which this uncoupling reverberates today can be seen in theses on the decline in civic engagement, such as Robert Putnam's (2000) *Bowling Alone*, which blame media such as television and video games for decreasing social interaction.

The Positive Potential of Mass Media

If we begin to see how responses to the emergence of successive media arise from attitudes developed long ago, they have not been uniformly **dystopian** in the manner of Plato. As social theorist Jürgen Habermas (1987, 390) claims, mass media may enable the emergence of broader contexts for de-bate. For example, we can imagine the ways in which media might facilitate discussion of the environment, which is of concern to people across the globe, and thus requires conduits for information dissemination and exchange far

dystopia
A society full of misery and disease; the opposite of utopia.

beyond our local contexts. Certainly, mass media can be centrally controlled, and thus block or distort discussion in a manner that concerned Plato. But they also permit inclusiveness, overcoming the narrow confines of face-to-face interaction. This, as Habermas says, is their "ambivalent potential."

For example, if today we should be concerned about the concentration of social media among a few large corporations such as Google, we could also point to the ways in which these technologies assisted rescue efforts in the aftermath of the earthquake in Haiti, or their instrumental role in organizing protests recently in Tunisia and other North African and Middle Eastern states. As Benedict Anderson (1991) has shown, with the everyday ritual of newspaper reading, we could think of ourselves for the first time as participating vicariously in an "imagined community" along with other readers. This sense of belonging is potentially the same with respect to the virtual communities fostered through Facebook, Twitter, or more recent media forms.

Media can also create large "imagined communities" that lack direct human interaction.

The Paradox of Media

The idea that media have an "ambivalent potential" underlines their somewhat paradoxical character, because media can both *transform* yet also *intensify* an experience at the same time. Elizabeth Eisenstein (1979), charting the transformations wrought by the introduction of the printing press in Europe in 15th century, noted the double-sided character of media when she explained how "even while communal solidarity was diminished, vicarious participation in more distant events was also enhanced; and even while local ties were loosened, links to larger collective units were being forged" (132). In other words, if the need to meet face to face to exchange information decreased after printing began, at the same time newer kinds of community and connections emerged because of printing.

Figure 1.4 Gutenberg's printing press
Media can be paradoxical, destroying some social ties while creating new ones at the same time.

Likewise, John Thompson (1995) has observed the ways that "media enable individuals to experience vicariously events which take place in distant places, thereby stimulating their capacity to imagine alternatives to the ways of life characteristic of their immediate locales" (191). Of course, the notion that such experience is vicarious pulls us back into the very concerns raised by Plato with respect to the distancing effects of media, and the problems that not having direct access to reality seem to entail. But the solidarity of the face-to-face community desired by Plato is not necessarily either diminished or destroyed by media: "trends pointing to modernism and fundamentalism, for example, were both launched by Bible-printing" (Eisenstein 1979, 130). Thus, "communication media can be used not only to challenge and undermine traditional values and beliefs, but also to extend and consolidate traditions" (Thompson 1995, 195). Traditional ways and modern lifestyles are not necessarily exclusive options. We could cite the rise of Christian fundamentalism via tele-evangelism as a phenomenon that corresponds with this claim, or perhaps the rise of Islamic fundamentalism facilitated through the Internet.

New media, then, do not necessarily make all previous ways of life or belief systems disappear, as is sometimes claimed, and as Plato apparently feared. On the contrary, Plato's dialogues have been kept alive by media from the printed book to the Internet. Media may reinforce older ways of living or believing, while paradoxically also having a modernizing influence. They may contribute to the expansion of communities and collective participation and action beyond local face-to-face confines, without—despite Plato's concerns—leading to the disappearance of human interaction and debate. The paradox of media is that they can both preserve the status quo and facilitate change at the same time.

> **KEY CONCEPT**
> Media may reinforce older ways of living or believing, yet at the same time have a modernizing influence.

Our Media "R" Us

Perhaps the most important lesson to be learned from Plato, however, is that there is no going back after the advent of a new medium—a point that lends considerable irony to his gloss on the new medium of writing. As classicist Eric Havelock (1963) demonstrated, Plato could not have accomplished all that he did without writing. It is the arrival of literacy, through the technology of alphabetic writing, that enabled Plato to develop the thoughts explored in the dialogues, because this became possible only after writing released humanity from the need to memorize everything. Once we could jot down our day-to-day concerns, we could then turn to more reflective and abstract thoughts. Because of Plato, wrote Havelock, "we use abstract language in describing or explaining experience" (257). In short, as Walter Ong (1982/2002) wrote: "more than any other single invention, writing has transformed human consciousness" (78).

> **KEY CONCEPT**
> There is no going back after the advent of a new medium.

But according to Friedrich Kittler (2010), these observations about writing overlook the very technology of the medium itself, and the way in which it becomes the basis for making sense of ourselves. Recall that Plato described a kind of writing that was "written on the soul." As Kittler observes, Plato had to be familiar with the technology of writing so that he could invent a model for the way that knowledge might be inscribed onto the surface of what he calls the soul. So, "lo and behold: a definition of the soul was immediately offered by the wax slate, the *tabula rasa* upon which the Greeks etched their notes" (Kittler 2010, 34). Kittler's insight is that media become the means through which we understand and define ourselves: "we know nothing about our senses until media provide models and metaphors" (34). In this case, thanks to writing, we become retrofitted with a soul.

Mind and Memory as Movies

Of course, the description of our inner workings using media as models changes with the advent of new media. As Kittler writes, after cinema arrived, physicians noted the phenomenon, brought on by the possibility of imminent death, of one's life flashing before one's eyes, or better, unwinding like a spool of film. As a consequence of the introduction of cinema, "in 1900, the soul suddenly stopped being a memory in the form of wax slates or books, as Plato describes it; rather, it was technically advanced and transformed into a motion picture" (Kittler 2010, 35).

Insofar as this transformation occurs with successive media (think, for example, of the ways in which our brains have somehow acquired the status of computing machines—what were they before we had computers?), Kittler argues that what we know about ourselves as humans arises from the media with which we gather and store information about ourselves. When all we had was writing, what we knew about ourselves was whatever could be written down; with the advent of film and sound recording, we could capture other data that could not be stored in writing. Thus, how we understand ourselves changes as a consequence. Indeed, as several thinkers have shown, from Marshall McLuhan to Bernard Stiegler (2010, 67), one effect of media is to provide external means (such as notebooks or photographs) with which we can store our memories, starting from the Palaeolithic and Neolithic periods, all the way down to today's computer memory chips. This, in turn, means—following Kittler—that the way we make sense of our interior life is by comparing it with the technologies we have at hand: "the only thing that can be known about the soul or the human are the technical gadgets with which they have been historically measured at any given time" (Kittler 2010, 35).

In summary, if we are different, as moderns, we are different to the degree that newer media technologies reshape the way in which we describe ourselves as humans by providing new metaphors for understanding the workings of our bodies and minds. Indeed, we are often today thought of as information processing devices, a metaphor that arises out of cybernetics and computational sciences on the one side (Wiener 1961) and from models of communication drawn from engineering on the other (Shannon and Weaver 1949). Both views have found their way into biology and are used to describe processes in the human body and mind.

But if these metaphors make differences—if we become different because of transformations in media technologies and what they allow us to understand about ourselves—there is nevertheless a sameness that runs like Ariadne's thread all the way back at least to Plato, and probably beyond, in which we can see precisely how a given media situation is the basis of what it means to be human. We can see this in the current moment, when data "clouds," in which we store our photographs and music collections, serve as metaphors for ideas of collective intelligence and new forms of consciousness. As has been the case throughout the history of media (and as you will see elsewhere in this book), the ways in which we store and access our information have shaped the ways in which we understand what a human being is.

> **KEY CONCEPT**
> What we know about ourselves as humans arises from the media, which enable us to gather and store information about ourselves.

Conclusion: The Enduring Questions About Communication

The idea that media and communications technologies help to make us who we are, and have done so since time immemorial, leads to one possible answer to the question of "why study communications?" From this point of view, what and who we are arises out of an encounter with a historical series of media devices that serve less as tools or extensions of our bodies and more as independent entities that reflect back on us and help us define ourselves.

Sociologist Niklas Luhmann (2000) states that our fate as moderns is that "whatever we know about our society, or indeed about the world in which we live, we know through the mass media" (1). As he is quick to point out, this statement applies to sociologists and media scholars as much as it does to anyone else. After all, scholars and academics read books, and books are media too, just like television and the Internet, although we often forget that fact. It might be appropriate to amend Luhmann's statement to include not only knowing what is out there—the world, society—but what is inside us, as well.

If Luhmann is correct that anything that counts as knowledge today is stored somewhere, whether in a book, or on a tape, disc, or someone's server farm, and if Kittler is correct that technology is our basis for making sense of ourselves, then we are measured and stored there somewhere, too. But as this chapter has argued, this has been the human condition, and dilemma, ever since we started to think about thinking, and about communicating. Any new medium seems to evoke the same questions that attended the rise of the medium that preceded it, and so on, backward to Plato, and forward to our time and beyond. We encounter new media and ask whether they enhance or inhibit communication, and are always astonished at how much we seem to be just like our forebears.

Present-day questions about the implications of new forms of communication have a remarkable tendency to sound the same as they did when first asked, thousands of years ago. Recognition of this sameness may help us to stop worrying about having an "edge." In many ways, despite the changes in media, the same problems about how effectively we communicate continue to haunt our thoughts when we come to ponder how we might make sense of our human condition.

The strange irresolution that prevents us from not communicating also leads us to ask, repeatedly and endlessly, questions about whether our communication is successful. Think of all the times you asked someone: "do you love me?" Then ask yourself (1) was the answer satisfactory and (2) did that stop you from asking the same question again later? As Plato tried to show, the success of the outcome becomes even harder to determine when we ask without the benefit of direct contact, in a world where we increasingly use media to communicate. As a result, the question Plato asked, of whether communication has become "deprived"—that is, inauthentic or incomplete—remains with us today. Any communication, whether near or distant, is fraught with uncertainty. In light of this fact, Peters (1999, 30) suggests that "a cheerful sense of the weirdness of all attempts at communication offers a far saner way to think and live." Undoubtedly, communication is risky, and can fail. Failure is something Plato hoped to avoid, and something we also always hope to avoid. This is the reason we keep studying communications and media.

DISCUSSION QUESTIONS

1. How can examining the ways in which new media were viewed in the past help us understand our present media environment?
2. Give some examples of recent media technologies that have influenced, or provided metaphors for, the understanding of human life.
3. Do new media enhance communication, or do they hinder it? Explain.

SUGGESTED RESOURCES
Books

Chun, Wendy Hui Kyong, and Thomas Keenan. 2006. *New Media/Old Media: A History and Theory Reader*. New York: Routledge.

Gleick, James. 2011. *The Information: A History, A Theory, A Flood*. New York: Pantheon.

Lanier, Jaron. 2010. *You Are Not a Gadget*. New York: Alfred A. Knopf.

Mitchell, W.J.T., and Mark B.N. Hansen. 2010. *Critical Terms for Media Studies*. Chicago: University of Chicago Press.

Sconce, Jeffrey. 2000. *Haunted Media: Electronic Presence from Telegraphy to Television*. Durham, NC: Duke University Press.

Websites

Digital Ethnography. http://mediatedcultures.net/ksudigg.

Variantology: On Deep Time Relations of the Arts, Sciences and Technologies. http://www.variantology.com.

James Gleick: Bits in the Ether. http://around.com.

University of Minnesota Media History Project. http://www.mediahistory.umn.edu.

Theory.org.uk. *Media, Identity, Sources and Products*. http://www.theory.org.uk.

REFERENCES

Anderson, Benedict. 1991. *Imagined Communities: Reflections on the Origin and Spread of Nationalism*. London: Verso.

Besançon, Alain. 2000. *The Forbidden Image: An Intellectual History of Iconoclasm*, translated by Jane Marie Todd. Chicago: University of Chicago Press.

Cornford, Francis MacDonald, trans. 1941. *The Republic of Plato*. Oxford: Clarendon Press.

Eisenstein, Elizabeth. 1979. *The Printing Press as an Agent of Change: Communications and Cultural Transformation in Early Modern Europe*. New York: Cambridge University.

Guillory, John. 2010. "The Genesis of the Media Concept." *Critical Inquiry* 36: 341–62.

Habermas, Jürgen. 1987. *The Theory of Communicative Action* (vol. II). Boston: Beacon Press.

Havelock, Eric Alfred. 1963. *Preface to Plato*. Cambridge, MA: Belknap Press.

Jowett, Garth, Ian Jarvie, and Catherine Fuller. 1996. *Children and the Movies: Media Influence and the Payne Fund Controversy*. Cambridge, UK: Cambridge University.

Kittler, Friedrich. 2010. *Optical Media: Berlin Lectures, 1999*. Cambridge, UK: Polity Press.

Lowenthal, Leo. 1967. "Communication and Humanitas." In *The Human Dialogue: Perspectives on Communication*, edited by Floyd W. Matson and Ashley Montagu, 335–45. New York: Free Press. Quoted in John Durham Peters (1999), *Speaking into the Air: A History of the Idea of Communication*. Chicago: University of Chicago Press.

Luhmann, Niklas. 2000. *The Reality of the Mass Media*. Palo Alto, CA: Stanford University Press.

Ong, Walter. 2002. *Orality and Literacy: The Technologizing of the Word*. London: Routledge.

Peters, John Durham. 1999. *Speaking into the Air: A History of the Idea of Communication*. Chicago: University of Chicago Press.

Plato. 2005. *Phaedrus*, translated by Christopher Rowe. London: Penguin Books.

Plato. 1974. *The Republic*, translated by Desmond Lee. Harmondsworth, UK: Penguin Books.

Putnam, Robert. 2000. *Bowling Alone: The Collapse and Revival of American Community*. New York: Simon and Schuster.

Shannon, Claude, and Warren Weaver. 1949. *The Mathematical Theory of Communication*. Urbana, IL: University of Illinois Press.

Stiegler, Bernard. 2010. "Memory." In *Critical Terms for Media Studies*, edited by W.J.T. Mitchell and Mark B. Hansen, 66–87. Chicago: University of Chicago Press.

Thompson, John B. 1995. *The Media and Modernity: A Social Theory of the Media*. Palo Alto, CA: Stanford University Press.

Whitehead, Alfred North. 1929/1978. *Process and Reality: An Essay in Cosmology*, edited by David Ray Griffin and Donald W. Sherburne. New York: Free Press.

Wiener, Norbert. 1961. *Cybernetics; or, Control and Communication in the Animal and the Machine*. Cambridge, MA: MIT Press.

CHAPTER 2 / STACEY JOHNSON

Thinkers and Theories: A Brief Introduction

Some Key Thinkers in Media and Communications

The following is intended to provide a brief summary of the work of key people discussed in this book. It does not presume to be an exhaustive or authoritative list of thinkers and their theories, but serves to introduce selected writers and their key works in a concise way, noting the concepts, theories, or schools of thought with which they are usually associated. Additional references to these thinkers within this book can be found in the index.

 **Theodor Adorno** was a philosopher and key contributor to the Institute for Social Research at the University of Frankfurt, better known as the Frankfurt School. The Frankfurt School's contribution to philosophy is *critical theory*. Critical theory has close ties to Marxism, but goes beyond economics in an attempt to explain human oppression. Critical theory is of interest to communication studies because it draws attention to social phenomena such as culture, mass entertainment, and education as tools used by the elite to maintain oppression. Adorno's most important work is *Dialectic of Enlightenment* (1944), written in collaboration with Max Horkheimer.

Adorno specifically identified the culture industry as a barrier to human freedom and enlightenment because of its structure as a system that promoted the top-down creation and standardization of culture. This arrangement, Adorno argued, ultimately leads to the transformation and reduction of artistic expression into just another commodity for sale. Hence, media and culture are powerful distortions and distractions that serve to sustain capitalism.

The central criticisms of Adorno's work are that it is elitist in terms of its definition of culture; that it presents a limited expression of the culture industry as a single entity, as opposed to being a diverse collection of interests and practices; and that it overemphasizes the production of culture by making assumptions about the role of the audience as being essentially passive.

Roland Barthes was a prominent mid-20th-century French philosopher whose ideas can be traced directly to the linguistic theory of Ferdinand de Saussure (see below). Barthes borrowed Saussure's tenets of structuralism for the development of modern semiology, or *semiotics* (the study of sign systems).

Barthes was interested in the contemporary world of myths around him, and in particular those myths expressed through media, fashion, art, architecture, and literature. He argued that myths were complex systems of signification that had the power to convey and reinforce ideologies. *Mythologies* (1972), originally published in French in 1957, is a notable collection of essays on contemporary myths. For example, the well-known piece "Soap-powders and Detergents" is an example of how Barthes explored the layers of meaning to be found in the most mundane items, which could themselves be read as "texts."

In his last book, *Camera Lucida* (1981), Barthes described a photograph as a shadow of the frozen moment. In this treatment he developed analytical terminology: the *punctum*—the detail of a photograph that catches the eye, and jogs the memory; and the *studum*—the spectator's attraction to the image.

Walter Benjamin was a philosopher, literary critic, and intellectual collaborator and contemporary of Theodor Adorno. He was also associated with the Frankfurt School and was influenced by Marxism.

Benjamin's most influential work is his essay "The Work of Art in the Age of Mechanical Reproduction," in which he explored shifts in perception that occurred with the growth of photography and film in the early 20th century. Benjamin inquired about authenticity in the mechanical reproduction of a single cultural artifact—for example, a photograph (which is reproducible) taken of a singular work of art such as an original painting. Here he raised the concept of "aura" to distinguish between the status of the original work of art and the technical reproduction.

Many of Benjamin's writings were revived and reassembled many years after they were written, a fact that can be explained by his premature death at the beginning of the Second World War, when it is believed that he took his own life while trying to escape the Nazi regime in France.

 **James Carey** was a distinguished American media theorist whose work explored how communication technologies affect expressions of culture, and how they structure our ways of thinking and feeling. Carey is best known for his book *Communication as Culture: Essays on Media and Society* (1989). This collection includes "Technology and Ideology: The Case of the Telegraph," in which he took a *political economy approach* (emphasizing industry, economics, and history) to the development of media theory.

Carey singled out the telegraph because "it permitted for the first time the separation of transportation and communication" (Carey 1989, 203) and paved the way for reconfiguring expressions of space and time: a message previously only deliverable by physical movement (Pony Express, rail) could be translated into Morse code and sent instantaneously along the "singing wire." As a result, "the telegraph brought about changes in the nature of language, of ordinary knowledge, of the very structures of awareness" (202), and was a watershed in communication because it played a significant role in shaping and modifying the physical areas in which it grew up, "but did not displace existing patterns of connection formed by natural geography" (203).

James Carey's work is connected to that of both Harold Innis and Marshall McLuhan. McLuhan was a contemporary of Carey's, and Carey, like McLuhan, was inspired by Harold Innis's ideas, in particular, the bias of communication and the significance of communication, empire, and monopoly.

 **Noam Chomsky** is a celebrated linguist, political activist, and mass media critic. His ideas about mass media were celebrated in an award-winning documentary, *Manufacturing Consent* (1992). Since the mid-1950s he has been a researcher and educator at the Massachusetts Institute of Technology, where he is now professor emeritus linguistics. His role as an activist developed during the Vietnam War. More recently, he has been a vehement opponent of the War on Terror and US involvement in Afghanistan and Iraq.

A prolific writer, Noam Chomsky's media books include *Manufacturing Consent: The Political Economy of Mass Media* (1988), written with Edward Herman; *Necessary Illusions: Thought Control in Democratic Societies* (1989); and *Media Control: The Spectacular Achievements of Propaganda* (2002).

Chomsky's media work is significant for his contributions to the development of the *propaganda model*. It isolates five propaganda filters: concentration of ownership; advertising; news sourcing; "flak," or interfering with journalists who threaten the status quo; and an uncritical belief in the free market. He challenges the "elites-know-best" perspectives of Lasswell and Lippmann, and sees mainstream media as an agent for distortion. "Propaganda is to democracy what the bludgeon is to a totalitarian state" (Chomsky 2002, 20).

John Dewey was an American philosopher whose influence in communication derives from his ideas about the role of journalism in society. This influence can be traced to Dewey's *The Public and Its Problems* (1927), his response to Walter Lippmann's *The Phantom Public* (1925).

Dewey distinguished between the concepts of the "state," elected officials and policy- and lawmakers, and the "public," a broad and diffuse group of citizens who elect the state. A "public" is not a monolithic group or category, but rather comes into being in an ad hoc way on the basis of its shared interest in any given issue. Dewey not only considered the public quite capable of understanding issues otherwise presumed to be only of elite interest, but he felt that issues that affect the public should be debated and discussed in a public forum.

The role of journalism in this scenario is to provide the most accurate information and analysis based on fact in order to facilitate meaningful public debate and conversation. It is from the voices of the many—and not those of the elite few—that the most effective solutions to problems will ultimately rise. Dewey's ideas have become a foundation for thinking about community journalism.

Susan Douglas is a professor of communication studies at the University of Michigan as well as an author, columnist, and cultural critic. Her research in the areas of media and gender is presented in her respective studies of gender and media messages, radio consumption and identity, and expressions of feminism in media: *Where the Girls Are* (1994); *Listening In: Radio and the American Imagination* (2004); and *Enlightened Sexism: The Seductive Message That Feminism's Work Is Done* (2010).

Douglas's study of radio focuses on how that medium has shaped people's day-to-day lives and conceptions of community identity, starting in the 1920s and leading up to the turn of the 21st century. A scholar whose work embraces feminism, Douglas's contributions draw attention to the role that 20th-century media have played in shaping women's psyches, for better or for worse.

 **Elizabeth Eisenstein** is an American historian with a specialization in the French Revolution but who is best known in communications studies for her two-volume work, *The Printing Press as an Agent of Change* (1979), which also appears in abridged version under the title *The Printing Revolution in Early Modern Europe* (1982). In this work she makes the case for the "unacknowledged revolution" inspired by movable type printing.

Eisenstein's research chronicles the social impact of movable type printing by taking a close look at the quality and character of print culture in early modern Europe. Her work looks at how the printing press's unique functions of knowledge dissemination, standardization, and preservation were key elements in the success of the Protestant Reformation, the Renaissance, and the Scientific Revolution. Paradoxically, movable type solidified existing structures of authority, while providing an opportunity for people to bypass that authority using the new technology of print.

Her work is important for communication studies because it provides a window onto the early impact of media technology in Western society.

 **Michel Foucault** was a French philosopher, historian, and social theorist who was originally influenced by *structuralism*, an intellectual approach in which culture is examined through its sign systems (see Saussure, below). Later, Foucault distanced himself from an exclusive connection to that school of thought. He has been categorized, in terms of intellectual traditions, as a *post-structuralist* for his critiques of power, knowledge, and institutions.

Where structuralism sought to understand the sign system of language, Foucault went one step further to explain its expression with respect to institutions and rules. He introduced the term *discourse*—written and spoken language whose meaningfulness depends on the conditions (political, social, cultural) in which it emerges—to determine how power functions in modern society without threat of force, yet still manages to gain the population's full compliance.

As a historian, his methodology aimed to look for discontinuity in history and then examine such moments for what they reveal about systems of thought, social institutions, and the nature of power. Notable works include *Madness and Civilization* (1961), *The Archaeology of Knowledge* (1969), *Discipline and Punish: The Birth of the Prison* (1975), and *The History of Sexuality* in three volumes (1976–1984).

 **Jürgen Habermas** is a philosopher in the *critical theory* tradition. He is linked to communication studies through his ideas about communicative action and concepts of public space and public engagement. In *The Structural Transformation of the Public Sphere* (1991), his study of 18th-century France, Habermas identifies the origins of a "bourgeois public sphere"—a sphere of engagement where private citizens (that is, moneyed people but *not* aristocrats) participate in rational public debate (through newspapers, literature, and so on) and establish public decision-making clout. He contrasts this new public sphere to former concentrations of public decision-making power and authority that were confined to the closed courts of the aristocracy. The concept of the "public sphere" has been useful for research on public opinion and media, and communication and political culture.

Communication scholars have typically been cautious about directly importing Habermas's ideas into the study of communication and media, saying that his work overlooks, for example, non-bourgeois private citizens (that is, working-class people), who are also part of a public sphere. Other critics suggest that he does not sufficiently consider the possibility for distortion that occurs in the communication act (Calhoun 1992). However, he remains a widely cited and influential figure in communication studies.

 **Stuart Hall** is one of the most recognizable names associated with British cultural studies, a school of thought whose origins can be traced to Raymond Williams (see below). British cultural studies emerged as a school in 1964 as the Centre for Contemporary Cultural Studies at the University of Birmingham, England. During his tenure as director, Hall sought to diversify cultural inquiry by raising questions of race and gender in addition to class.

There is a connection to the ideas of the Frankfurt School in Hall's work. Both were engaged by Italian Marxist Antonio Gramsci's concept of *hegemony*, a term that Gramsci developed to express how the dominant ideology comes to be accepted by the population as the status quo. This acceptance occurs with the public's willing compliance and does not require coercion. In Hall's variation on hegemony, people are regarded as both producers and consumers of culture, who retain the ability for political action. His theory of *encoding* (which refers to meaning created by the producer of text) and *decoding* (the audience's reading of it) examines the audience's active role in the process of interpreting texts. The term "text" was originally used to refer to literary texts, but is now used to refer to other media. In Hall's theory, there are three ways of reading texts. These readings are *dominant* (status quo or elite readings, which reinforce hegemony), *oppositional* (which challenge the dominant reading, and are counter-hegemonic), and *negotiated* (in which the audience mixes dominant and oppositional readings to produce meaning).

Harold Innis was a celebrated Canadian political economist and philosopher. It would not be an exaggeration to credit Innis with providing the foundation for communication studies in Canada, but he has had a great impact on shaping communication inquiry in the United States as well (see James Carey). A political economist by training, Innis sought to understand the relationship between transportation and the distribution and maintenance of power in the establishment of empires. In exploring this relationship, he identified the act and process of communication as an important area of inquiry in its own right.

Innis's historical and economic research on the fur trade, cod fishery, and the Canadian Pacific Railway (also referred to as his "staples thesis") led him to draw conclusions about the interplay between geography, technology, and economy in the creation of empires. But it was in his book *The Bias of Communication* (1951) where Innis set out his theory about the role of media in society. Here he distinguished media as being either *time-binding*—durable over time but not portable (think of a stone tablet); or *space-binding*—more ephemeral, less durable, but easy to send/receive (think of papyrus used for ancient writings, as well as modern media). He concluded that the space/time biases implicit in the dominant form of communication played a direct role in defining the interplay of relationships that were ultimately necessary for maintaining an empire.

In Canadian communication studies, Innis has helped scholars understand the historical significance of communication technologies (the railway, public broadcasting, satellites) and their role in shaping Canadian identity.

Friedrich Kittler is a media theorist whose contributions explore the impact of media on society. His ideas about media technology can be located on the intellectual spectrum as being in opposition to those of Marshall McLuhan, even though Kittler does share a belief in the notion of media bias. Kittler challenges McLuhan's humanist theory that technological media are extensions of people, arguing instead that media are autonomous entities. In this scenario, people, along with written history, are increasingly being left behind by the advance of technology.

Kittler's intellectual origins include post-structuralism, but he is critical of that theory for overlooking the role of the communication medium itself in the production of knowledge in society. In other words, the technology used in writing has an impact on the *practice* of writing, and on the way knowledge is structured. Kittler is critical of post-structuralism precisely because the theory privileges writing as the universal medium of communication, a critique paraphrased in Chapter 1 of this book by Kevin Dowler: "[A]ccording to Friedrich Kittler, these observations about writing overlook the very technology of the medium itself, and the way in which it becomes the basis for making sense of ourselves" (15). Thus, technological media not only have an impact on our society, but, first and foremost, they also configure *how* we think.

Harold Lasswell was an American political scientist as well as communication theorist. Lasswell is considered to be a founding figure in what we call modern communication studies. He was a member of the *Chicago School*, a sociological school of thought of the 1920s and 1930s that combined theory with ethnographic field research to quantify the effects of urban life. Lasswell was interested in the political sphere and how elements such as individual personality and social structure affected it. These themes are referenced in some of his most famous written works, *Propaganda Technique in the World War* (1927); *Psychopathology and Politics* (1930); and *Politics: Who Gets What, When, How* (1935).

Lasswell summarized the communication act as "who says what to whom, in what channel, and to what effect," which forms the basis for communication inquiry. During the Second World War, Lasswell's expertise was engaged to analyze Nazi propaganda, and in particular the way in which it used persuasion to secure the compliance of the German people. Lasswell's research methodologies have been influential in the areas of content analysis and statistical measurement, as well as interviewing techniques.

 **Walter Lippmann** was a central figure in the rise of American journalism and an intellectual of the early to mid-20th century, whose writings promoted liberal democracy. His contributions to American letters include newspaper columns, magazine articles, a credit as one of the creators of *The New Republic* magazine, and several books. Two books in particular stand out: *Public Opinion* (1922), in which he coined the phrase "the manufacture of consent"; and *The Phantom Public* (1925), his cynical take on the notion of a democratically enabled "public" as being merely an illusion.

The term "manufacture of consent" describes how public opinion functions to lead the "bewildered herd" of non-elite citizens. Lippmann argued that it was essential for leaders to define the common interests of society in order to maintain social order, and they could achieve this by using public opinion as a vehicle.

 **Carolyn Marvin** is a communication scholar whose work touches on areas as diverse as technology, media history, literacy, and freedom of speech. Marvin is most closely identified with her rigorous historical work, *When Old Technologies Were New: Thinking About Electric Communication in the Late Nineteenth Century* (1988).

Marvin's methodology departs from a traditional approach (which would embark on a study of the *instrument* of communication) and instead focuses on the social drama that revolves around electric communication. In this scenario, competing social groups constantly negotiate power, authority, and control. In particular, she explores how the telephone and the electric light were publicly imagined as new inventions at the end of the 19th century, both in specialized engineering journals and in the popular media. For all of the scientific and experimental excitement around these new inventions within scientific circles, Marvin also reveals that there were more serious public anxieties that related to how these new media might intervene in, and transform, traditional social relations.

Marvin stands out for her methodological contributions, and for reminding students and scholars of communication that all media were once "new" media.

Karl Marx is one of the most influential philosophers in Western thought. His written works are many and include *The Communist Manifesto* (1848), written with Friedrich Engels; *Contribution to a Critique of Political Economy* (1859); and *Das Kapital* (1867), his main work on economics.

Marx believed that the explanation for all struggle boiled down to economic inequality that was implicit in the capitalist system. Put differently, struggle and inequity were structural problems that required a structural solution, achievable only by overthrowing the capitalist system in its entirety. As a philosopher whose work touched on economics, politics, and history, Marx's contributions are broad and influenced many thinkers in media and communication.

The key elements of his *historical materialism* thesis hold that the quality of productive forces in society (the means of production) helps to explain the nature of the economic structure. The nature of the economic structure, in turn, helps to explain the superstructure or dominant ideology.

Closer to the themes discussed in this book, Marx's ideas laid the foundation for critical theory and its disciples (Adorno, Benjamin), and the work of Raymond Williams, Stuart Hall, and the tradition of British cultural studies. Marx's work also informs the *political economy approach* to communication.

 **Marshall McLuhan** is perhaps Canada's most famous thinker, and "the medium is the message" is likely the most often-quoted phrase in all of communication studies. The idea first appeared in McLuhan's *Understanding Media: The Extensions of Man* (1964), in which he introduced a new way of thinking about how electronic media were profoundly reshaping and restructuring patterns of social interdependence, knowledge, and our relationship to institutions. A communicator well ahead of his time, McLuhan's collaboration with Quentin Fiore in *The Medium Is the Massage: An Inventory of Effects* (1967) is part social theory and part graphic novel.

McLuhan's intellectual connection to his teacher Harold Innis, his background in English literature, and his humanist leanings inspired him to pose questions about the relationship between media and society. McLuhan never lived to see the rise to dominance and prominence of the Internet and social media, but it is in the area of new media that his ideas have experienced a robust revival.

Walter Ong is linked intellectually to Marshall McLuhan, who supervised Ong's master's thesis at St. Louis University in the early 1940s, and therefore to Harold Innis as well. Ong was interested in the cultural impacts resulting in the shift from a predominantly oral society to a society dominated by writing and literacy. In *Orality and Literacy* (1982), his most widely known work, he lay out these arguments and traced the evolution of human consciousness through techniques of communication.

It could be argued that Ong's expertise as a scholar of English literature and as an ordained Jesuit priest informed his ideas. He addressed the role played by the early modern Catholic Church in communication history, and the ways in which the advent of print, with its rules and structure, changed creative expression (for example, poetry and writing styles).

His later research continued to pursue ideas about orality and literacy but with attention to the influence of computers and newly formed patterns of online thinking. See, for example, one of his last writings, "Digitization Ancient and Modern: Beginnings of Writing and Computers" (1998).

John Durham Peters is an American scholar whose contributions cut across media and cultural history, and communication and social theory. He is a big thinker whose broad-reaching theoretical pursuits seek to understand communication in philosophical, historical, legal, religious, and technological context.

Like other thinkers in this book, Peters is interested in the impact of media and communication in society, but instead of looking at media as the object of analysis, he takes the whole of communication theory as his object. In *Speaking into the Air: A History of the Idea of Communication* (1999), he argues that the process of theorizing about communication is influenced, from the outset, by the fact that communication can be seen as either a "bridge" (successful communication) or a problem (distortion).

Plato was a seminal philosopher of ancient Greece who is often discussed in communication and media studies for, among other things, his analogy of "the cave," which was outlined in *The Republic*. In this work Plato describes a group of people who live their whole lives chained to a wall in a way that limits vision. All they are able to see of the material world are shadows cast onto the wall by unseen objects behind them. The shadows (which are *mediated* images) are the closest these people will ever get to the experience of reality. In this scenario, the true philosopher is the one who is freed from the cave by coming to the understanding that the shadows do not make up reality at all, but that they are merely a *representation* of the material world.

Plato is also commonly discussed in communication theory with respect to understanding the origins of *rhetoric*, the art of using language to persuade. Plato explored these ideas in his work, *Phaedrus*.

Edward Said was a literary theorist whose critique of Western colonialism is influential in communication and cultural studies research that focuses on notions of the "other." His intellectual influence was *post-structuralism*, and his contributions form the groundwork for *post-colonial* theory and inquiry.

Orientalism (1978) is Said's influential and critical summary of how Western scholarship frames Eastern cultures as "other" and exotic. He argues that Western knowledge carries a dominant way of thinking about Eastern cultures that hastily positions them as a universal and unified totality. In Said's theory, Eastern cultures are perpetually and falsely defined in terms of prejudice for what they are *not*—that is, Western.

Ferdinand de Saussure was a highly influential figure in linguistics, having developed the school of thought known as *structuralism*. His ideas radically altered the terrain of language and linguistics, where the dominant perspective of his time was that language was handed down through ancestry. Saussure held that language could only be understood through a network of relationships, according to certain rules of selection and combination to produce meaning.

The key concepts of structuralism are the *sign*, *signifier*, and *signified*. The signifier and the signified make up the sign, and the sign in turn is produced in the relationship between signifier and signified. An example of a sign in language is the word "cat," but it is crucial to note that such signs are arbitrary: *cat* in English is *chat* in French and *gatto* in Italian. These words are only meaningful in a specific cultural context, and their relationship to a small mammal is completely arbitrary.

Saussure's concepts in linguistics migrated to the social sciences in the early to mid-20th century, and gained considerable traction in literary theory and cultural studies. His influence on Roland Barthes was profound.

 **Clay Shirky** is a new media expert and critic whose book *Cognitive Surplus: Creativity and Generosity in a Connected Age* (2010) looks at how new forms of collaboration are enabling people to make more constructive use of the free time afforded by contemporary society. The book is a followup to arguments made in Shirky's influential book *Here Comes Everybody: The Power of Organizing Without Organizations* (2008), about the effects of social media. He is professor at New York University's Arthur L. Carter Journalism Institute and the Tisch School of the Arts.

Shirky is a regular contributor to the cutting-edge TED (Technology, Entertainment, Design) lectures. He is important in communication studies for his ideas about the rise of decentralized technologies, peer-to-peer networks, and his thoughts on the evolving state of journalism in society. "Society doesn't need newspapers," Shirky quipped in a 2009 blogpost, "What we need is journalism."

 **Raymond Williams** was a Welsh academic, writer, and critic who is credited with helping to lay the intellectual foundation for the school of thought known as British cultural studies. He was a professor of drama at the University of Cambridge in England.

Williams brought Marxist theory and methodology to the study of literature by effectively making the case for the study of literature and culture on the margins—those works outside the list of the great masters. Notice the connection of his methodology of *cultural materialism* to Marx's *historical materialism*, especially with respect to Williams's focus on working-class culture. Williams broke new ground on the legitimacy of popular culture as a field of academic inquiry, and argued that such inquiry could and should also be politicized. Although Williams arrived at the study of popular culture through literature, he was quick to acknowledge the burgeoning role of popular media (such as television and film) in society.

Williams's key works include *Culture and Society* (1958), *Communications* (1962), *Marxism and Literature* (1977), and *Technology and Cultural Form* (1974), in which he provided a critique of Marshall McLuhan's ideas.

REFERENCES

Calhoun, Craig, ed. 1992. *Habermas and the Public Sphere*. Cambridge, MA: MIT Press.

Carey, James. 1989. *Communication as Culture: Essays on Media and Society*. London: Routledge.

Chomsky, Noam. 2002. *Media Control: The Spectacular Achievements of Propaganda*. New York: Seven Stories Press.

Ong, Walter. 1998. "Digitization Ancient and Modern: Beginnings of Writing and Computers." *Communication Research Trends* 18(2):4–21.

PART TWO
Media Dimensions, Forms, and Functions

Dimensions of Media: Time and Space, Storage and Transmission

How do media connect us to places and times other than our own? Do media strengthen or weaken our attachments to places? Do media control our daily schedules, or do we control media?

KEY CONCEPTS

1. *Temporality:* Media have a strong temporal aspect that shapes our daily rhythms and our understanding of changes in the world, and can also give us a strong connection to the past.

2. *Spatiality:* Media locate and orient us within space, or a particular place, but the speed and reach of new forms of media can also make us lose our sense of distance.

3. *Binding spaces:* Our sense of belonging to communities, regions, or nations has much to do with the role of media in binding us together on the basis of shared cultural reference points or media consumption habits.

CHAPTER OUTLINE

Introduction: Time and Space—
The Dimensions of Media 37

Media and Time 38

Media and Space 45

Conclusion 51

Discussion Questions 51

Suggested Resources 52

References 52

Introduction: Time and Space— The Dimensions of Media

Those who reflect upon the role of media in society often focus on the direct ways in which media might influence our ideas and opinions. It is common to analyze media in terms of the messages they emit, and to look for the immediate effects of these messages. In media studies, the belief that media have the power to make us think particular thoughts or feel specific emotions has a long history. This perspective on the media, which is touched upon in some chapters in this book, is sometimes known as the *media effects paradigm*. Scholars and critics working within this **paradigm** may argue over the degree of the media's power, but they are united in their belief that media affect our ideas and opinions.

paradigm
A framework for understanding a theory, pattern, or model.

There are other, equally valuable approaches to the study of media, however, that do not focus on the individual media message and its effects. Some of these approaches are concerned more broadly with the ways in which media shape our experience and understanding of the world. How do media orient us in the world, for example? How do they connect us to places and times other than those in which we live? Do media expand the spatial horizons of our experience, or shrink them? Do they weaken our attachment to the places in which we live, or strengthen it? Do media dictate the schedules of our lives, or leave us to control when and where we use them?

Questions like these are the key focus of this chapter, which deals with the role of media in orienting us in time and space. Because time and space may be considered "dimensions" of our experience, we might say that these approaches deal with the dimensions of media.

Media and Time

The first of the dimensions of media to be discussed here is that of time. Media help to shape and organize our experience of time at many different levels. In a very basic sense, media play a role in providing "timetables" of sorts for our daily lives. Throughout most of recent human history, such media as newspapers, television programs, and new movies have entered our lives according to regular, predictable schedules. This regularity has given order to our lives. We may welcome this order, appreciating the predictability that comes with it, or bemoan the ways in which media seem to control our use of time.

Media provide a sort of timetable for our daily lives.

At another level, media shape our sense of time by constantly adjusting the "distance" between present and past. Media change so quickly that we might often feel as if they are pulling us quickly into an uncertain future, leaving the past behind to be forgotten. At the same time, media are important tools for preserving history, and through them we are granted access to the words, sounds, and images of the past.

Temporality I: Speed and Rhythm

Media come into our lives in chunks of different sizes and durations. In the course of an evening spent watching television, we may watch a five-minute news summary, a half-hour situation comedy, and a two-hour movie. On our laptop or smartphone, we may read Twitter posts of 140 characters or less and then turn to blog entries that are usually much longer. We may linger over a Sunday morning newspaper or immerse ourselves in a novel, then click our way through YouTube videos, taking in just a few seconds of each. The time we devote to media expands and contracts according to different media formats and in response to our own habits and moods. Our consumption of media involves a range of different speeds and rhythms.

> **KEY CONCEPT**
> *Temporality:* Media have a strong temporal aspect that shapes our daily rhythms and our understanding of changes in the world, and can also give us a strong connection to the past.

For roughly 200 years, since the birth of the modern newspaper, we have expected media to bring certain regular rhythms into our experience of the world. Before the newspaper, news was communicated in a wide variety of ways—through popular songs, on sheets of paper nailed to buildings, or in the newsletters that politicians or clergymen might circulate among their acquaintances. These songs, public notices, or newsletters were made public only when their creators decided that some bit of information was ready for public consumption. Few people assumed that the flow of news was constant enough to justify regular daily or weekly publication schedules.

In the 1800s, the daily newspaper as we now know it emerged in major cities of the Americas and Europe. Some papers, like *The New York Sun* (launched in 1833) or the Parisian *La Presse* (1836), were published every 24 hours, with each issue arriving at newsstands at roughly the same time each day. To be successful, these new daily papers needed to convince their readers that every 24-hour period produced enough news to fill another issue. The modern idea of the reporter stems from this period. News was no longer to be patiently gathered up by a publisher until there was enough to fill another issue of a newsletter or magazine. Rather, news was to be actively sought out, by professional journalists who followed police officers to crime scenes or rushed to the sites of fires. Only in this way could a newspaper be assured of sufficient content to meet its daily needs. The daily newspaper led readers to expect that the world would change, if only a little, every 24 hours. With the daily newspaper, media introduced a distinctive rhythm into the lives of city-dwellers.

By the middle of the 20th century, people expected their local movie theatres to change their programming twice a week and their local radio stations to bring weekly installments of their favourite programs. With the widespread popularization of television in the 1950s, people adapted to the daily rhythms of afternoon soap operas, and to the weekly regularity of nighttime comedy or drama programs. In that same decade, the birth of

Figure 3.1 CHUM Chart, March 1964

Beginning in the 1950s, radio stations such as 1050 CHUM published a weekly "hit parade," allowing listeners to follow musical trends from week to week. By the spring of 1964, The Beatles and their imitators had begun to dominate the charts. Artists from an earlier era of pop music, such as Louis Armstrong, were still having hits, but they were remnants of a fading musical past, quickly being overtaken by new trends.

SOURCE: © Bell Media Inc. Reprinted by permission.

The rhythms of older media usually coexist alongside those of emerging media.

top-40 radio stations, in the United States and other countries, led listeners to expect a new "number one" song every seven days. Companies like the Book-of-the-Month Club brought a best-selling novel or biography into people's homes at the same time each month of the year.

The rhythms of these older media now exist alongside those of newer, digital media, which promise us access to most kinds of media content at the time of our choosing. Indeed, at any given moment in history the rhythms of older media have co-existed alongside those of media that are just emerging.

The reader of one of the new daily newspapers in 1840 might have subscribed to an old-fashioned political newsletter that was still published only when its editor felt enough news had been gathered to justify a new issue. A hundred years later, when instantaneous telephone communication across North America was widely available, people still engaged in the slower, more leisurely process of communicating through handwritten letters.

Media Consumption Habits

It is useful, in this context, to examine your own media habits, paying attention to the speed at which you consume media and the ways in which this consumption organizes your time. Do you prefer to follow the second-by-second updates about celebrities posted on Twitter, or to check in every few hours on the slower flow of your friends' status updates on Facebook? Do you watch television programs at the moment of their official, scheduled showing, or stockpile them in order to view several in a row when it is convenient? Do you consume all your favourite media in brief chunks, or make a clear distinction between those to be glanced at quickly and others to be savoured more slowly? Do the rhythms of older media co-exist comfortably with those of new, digital media in your own life?

We may also look at media products themselves, to see how they organize time in multiple ways by incorporating different rhythms of change. The websites of news organizations such as CNN or the BBC, for example, now contain scrolling "tickers" that run across the top of the screen and update major stories almost as quickly as information flows into their newsrooms. Below these tickers, however, we find headlined stories that are likely to be updated more slowly, usually every few hours or so. Farther down, or to the side of the screen, we may see articles on celebrity scandals or social trends, which may have remained the same for days, with only minor updates. These news sites, we might say, arrange several different temporalities together on a single webpage. They remind us that what we call "news" involves very different kinds of events marked by widely varying rates of change.

Temporality II: Past and Present

The previous section dealt with one aspect of the temporality of media—the way in which media shape our sense of rhythm and change. This section builds on some of these ideas to consider the ways in which media shape our sense of past and present. Have media made the past disappear, erasing the ideas and information of periods gone by? Or, on the contrary, have media provided the technological means by which the past is kept constantly alive and available?

One of the most common criticisms of media is that they serve to erase history—that they have become instruments of forgetting. Media, it is sometimes suggested, are too quick to bury the past in their rush to embrace the new and novel. In a media-saturated age, the argument goes, history survives only in the fragile personal memories of individuals or in lifeless public institutions such as museums.

There is much evidence to support the claim that media induce forgetfulness. After all, each day's newspaper is usually destroyed once it has been read, and for most of the 20th century few people cared to preserve archives of radio broadcasts or popular cultural forms such as comic books. Media styles and formats change so quickly that content from a few decades ago may no longer seem to speak to us in any meaningful way. As a result, it may seem to drop out of public consciousness. In the course of the 20th century, certain genres of media (such as silent, black-and-white films of the 1920s or mystery novels set in upper-class country mansions) came with time to seem antiquated, incomprehensible to newer audiences. It was as if the culture as a whole had forgotten how to enjoy or understand them.

The "forgetfulness" of media is only one side of the story, however. Over the last half-century or more, the forgetfulness of media has been balanced, more and more, by the media's active role in keeping the past alive. It is more and more common for such media as cable television channels or Internet websites to use the films, music, literature, and other cultural forms of the past as a source of content. These media have found new ways to distribute this content and to build audiences for the media products of earlier periods. Media, in this respect, have come to assume a "preservation" role that works to limit the forgetfulness of which they were often accused.

Today, the media are playing an increasingly active role in keeping the past alive.

We may find one of the clearest cases of this move from forgetfulness to preservation in the history of Hollywood cinema. In the first 50 years or so of the cinema's existence (roughly from 1895 to 1945), there were few ways of seeing older films that had finished their commercial run. After playing for a week or two in movie theatres, films disappeared from circulation. Very occasionally, as in the case of big hits like the 1939 film *The Wizard of Oz*, a movie might be revived after a few years and distributed again to theatres. Generally, though, if you missed a film during its initial commercial run, it was almost impossible to see it again. Indeed, movie studios cared so little for the older films they had in their vaults that they took few steps to preserve them. It is partly for this reason that half of all American movies made before 1950 have disappeared, their prints destroyed in fires or simply allowed to deteriorate in warehouses.

In the United States, this situation began to change in the late 1940s, when television entered people's homes and became a significant medium

PRIMARY SOURCES

The Long Tail of Media

Chris Anderson, editor of *Wired* magazine and author of the book *The Long Tail*, explains the concept in this interview excerpt. The "tail of smaller sellers" he refers to includes a massive amount of old, "back-list" music, film, literature, and other cultural artifacts and information, most of which, in the past, would have become completely unavailable.

> It's a measure of how our economy and culture is shifting from mass markets to millions of niches. The rise of distribution methods with unlimited capacity or "infinite shelf space," of which the Internet is the foremost (but not only) example, have made it finally possible to offer consumers an incredible variety of products and other goods that were previously suppressed by the economic and physical limits of traditional retail and broadcast.
>
> The Long Tail refers specifically to the "long tail" of the familiar fast-falling demand curve in economics—we've usually looked just at the high part of the curve on the left, where the hits are. But the tail of smaller-sellers is incredibly long, and when you can offer everything all those niche product[s] can add up to a market that rivals the "head."

SOURCE: I Want Media. 2006 (June 26). "Chris Anderson: 'Peer Production Complements Traditional Media.'" *I Want Media*. Accessed April 14, 2011. http://www.iwantmedia.com/people/people58.html.

of entertainment. Film studios found that they could sell their old films to television stations, which were desperate for cheap programming. Television broadcasters began showing old Hollywood movies during afternoons or late at night. By the 1960s, hundreds of films from earlier decades could be seen on television across North America on any given day. Several generations of present-day filmmakers, such as Martin Scorsese and Quentin Tarantino, received their "education" in film history from television.

The German media theorist Friedrich Kittler (1990) suggests that we ask, about any communications medium, what role it plays in the **storage**, **transmission**, and **processing** of information. Movies carry more than information, of course—they contain spectacle, amusement, and ways of making us laugh or cry. Nevertheless, if we ask what television did to movies, we can see television performing all three of these media functions. Television transmitted movies to viewers who might have missed them at the time of their first release. It sent these movies, many of which had sat for decades on studio warehouse shelves, back into cultural life. Television also processed these

storage
In addition to the literal storing of cultural artifacts (films, music, etc.), *storage* also refers to the media's role in introducing older content to a younger generation.

transmission
The carrying of information or other forms of media content across distances.

processing
The presentation of media content in an altered form for a different medium, such as a film edited for television.

movies, by changing them in numerous ways. Television stations cut them up into 10-minute segments in order to insert commercials. In many cases, they trimmed scenes so that a film (and its commercials) might fit into a prescribed 90-minute or two-hour slot.

In addition to processing and transmitting movies, television also became a means of storing the history of cinema. This is not to suggest that television stations simply collected copies of films and built their own libraries (though many of them did that). Most importantly, television became a primary means by which the history of cinema was gathered up, kept alive, and made familiar to younger generations who had not lived through it.

The ability of new media to give us increased access to the past (rather than leaving the past behind) is just as obvious in the case of the Internet. Since its arrival in the early 1990s, the World Wide Web has brought us radically new kinds of experiences, from navigable maps of the streets on which we live to sites on which we can remix our favourite songs or film clips. Even as it has showered us with new experiences, however, the Web has become a powerful means for granting us access to the past. Some of the most popular Internet sites, such as Facebook or Ancestry.com, have led millions of people to reconnect with old friends or to fill in their family trees. Other popular sites, such as eBay or YouTube, keep objects, images, and sounds from the past in constant circulation, available for instant purchase or viewing. The digitization of older books, movies, and recordings whose copyright has lapsed means that the Internet has become a rich archive of cultural expression dating back hundreds of years.

In the case of any medium of communications, we might ask how it alters our sense of the relationship between past and present. On the one hand, the Internet, like other new media (cellphone messaging, for example) may seem to hold us in what some thinkers call a "perpetual present," characterized by constantly changing content that does not last. The particular media temporality described here is what sociologists would call a "thin" sense of time. A thin sense of time is one in which pieces of information do not accumulate or build up a multilayered sense of history. Rather, thin time is that in which bits of information constantly replace one another, like the Twitter feeds that push each previous tweet down and out of sight.

On the other hand, we may view the Internet and other new media as slowly evolving archives in which the past comes to assume ever greater weight and importance. The sense of time produced here might be called "thick," because of the way in which content from the present overlaps with content from several different layers of the past. In this respect, cable television channels devoted to classic television programs, or Internet sites full of fashion photos from the 1970s, may be seen as helping to build up a thick sense of history. This building up of a sense of history, some argue, gives a stability or "ballast" to our culture (like the weights placed in the hulls of ships to keep them on a steady course). To put it another way, media, rather than teaching us to forget, may serve as tools through which a culture learns to remember.

Media and Space

The previous section discussed the ways in which media shape our experience of time. This section is concerned with the ways in which media locate and orient us in space. It discusses the spatial dimensions of media from two perspectives. The first is concerned with the transmission capabilities of media, their capacity to carry information or other forms of media content across distances. The second has to do with the binding capacity of media—their role in linking together people or communities scattered throughout space.

Spatiality I: Crossing Space

Let us begin our discussion of the spatiality of media with two familiar examples. In the first, you receive a letter sent to you through the mail by a friend living in another country. The letter arrives wrinkled or bent, bearing the traces of the different postal systems that have handled it along its travels. Because of the distance it has travelled, the letter takes several days to arrive. This distance also means that the cost to your friend of mailing the letter was high compared with that of a domestic letter.

> **KEY CONCEPT**
>
> *Spatiality:* Media locate and orient us within space, or a particular place, but the speed and reach of new forms of media can also make us lose our sense of distance.

In the second example, a Facebook message from the same friend arrives at the inbox of your account. You recognize your friend's name, and Facebook tells you how long ago the message arrived, but nothing in the presentation of the message gives you clues as to where your friend is living. You assume, probably correctly, that the message arrived micro-seconds after your friend sent it, since that is usually the case for all Facebook messages, regardless of the distance they have travelled.

Unlike the letter, of course, the Facebook message arrives with no evidence of wear and tear, even though it has travelled thousands of miles. The message is clear and readable, with none of the weakness or distortion that, in an earlier age, might have marked communication over long distances (such as international telephone calls). And while Facebook messaging is not, in a very strict sense, free—if we consider the cost of our Internet service, or of the cafe latte we have purchased in order to get Wi-Fi access, or even of the advertisements that appear on the right side of the Facebook page—there are no additional charges for sending or receiving Facebook messages from far away.

The Abolition of Distance

In the language of media theory, we might see Facebook (or, indeed, the Internet) as the latest in a long line of communications technologies that have resulted in the "abolition of distance." Distance has not been abolished in a physical sense, of course—you and your Facebook friend may still be separated by an ocean and thousands of kilometres. However, this distance no longer adds delays, costs, or physical deterioration to the act of communication. For historians, the notion of an abolition of distance has long been used to describe the ways in which media technologies such as the telegraph or radio have made possible almost-instantaneous communication between distant points. (For a detailed discussion of the telegraph and radio, see Chapter 7, Media R/Evolutions.) Distance has been abolished when it no longer affects the time taken to send a message and when it has little effect on the condition in which the message will arrive.

> *Distance has been abolished when it doesn't affect the time it takes to send a message, or the condition of the message upon arrival.*

Even as we enjoy the speed, convenience, and apparently low costs of Facebook messaging, we should note that the idea of an abolition of distance has not met with unanimous approval. Many critics of the notion argue that distance has never really been abolished. They will point to the persistence of national boundaries that block the movement of people and messages, or argue that not everyone in the world has equal access to media resources. Others will point out that differences of language and culture serve as impediments to communications across distance, even when new technologies seem to make such communication easier. (How many anglophone Canadians read blogs or Facebook posts in more than one or two languages, for example?)

One critic of this idea was the novelist and essayist George Orwell (author of *1984*). In 1944, Orwell noted how the promise of an abolition of distance had been popular among social observers 50 years earlier. History since then proved, Orwell argued, that the promise of instantaneous communication across the world had been rendered hollow. It had been blocked by political events and human prejudices. "Actually," Orwell (1944) wrote, "the effect of modern inventions has been to increase nationalism, to make travel enormously more difficult, to cut down the means of communication between one country and another."

Even among those who agree that communications technologies have "abolished" distance, there is disagreement about whether this is a positive development. When Facebook messages from another continent arrive in our inboxes seconds after being sent, with no indication of the place from which they came, what does this do to our understanding of the world? Does this instantaneous access limit our awareness of the economic, human, and environmental costs of the infrastructure that made this instant communication possible? If we live much of our lives in "virtual" friendships with people thousands of miles away, how does this affect our attachment to the physical places or communities in which we actually live? Or our sense of responsibility to such places?

Many will argue that social media such as Facebook make it easier for us to stay in close contact only with those who are like ourselves in background, language, and culture. They relieve us, these critics argue, of the need to engage with the very different kinds of people who surround us in our daily, non-virtual lives.

Likewise, critics remain skeptical about the effects of our increased access to instantaneous forms of communication. When connections seem so easy, they argue, we lose our respect for distance and for the labour, money, and ingenuity required to overcome it. As our friend's message sits in our inbox alongside a dozen other messages, none of which indicate the place from which they were sent, has the difficulty of communicating across distance been abolished, or simply rendered invisible?

Spatiality II: Binding Spaces

If media allow us to cross distances, linking points and people located far apart, this is not the only way in which they have altered our sense of space. Media may also lead us to identify with certain spaces as key features of our identities. Our sense of belonging to communities, regions, or nations has much to do with the role of media in binding us together on the basis of shared cultural reference points or media consumption habits.

The telegraph was one of several 19th-century technologies that helped to pull scattered populations together into media audiences that were more and more unified at the national and even international levels. Communications theorists often refer to this pulling together as the "space-binding" effect of media. As media travel across large distances, they may act as a cultural steamroller, pushing aside local and regional cultures. At the same time, media may strengthen the culture of regions or nations, by binding people together into audiences for the same cultural products or messages.

The history of media offers us many well-known examples of this space-binding at work. We might think of France, for example, as having a shared language and culture that have existed for a thousand years or more, but

As media travel across large distances, they may act as a cultural steamroller, pushing aside local and regional cultures.

HISTORICAL HIGHLIGHT

Politicians, Audiences, and the Telegraph

In his study of the introduction of the telegraph in the 19th century, Menahem Blondheim (1994) points to some of the ways in which telegraphic communication changed the strategies of politicians running for national office. Prior to the development of telegraphic communication, news travelled slowly (if at all) between places that were far apart. Local reporters covered local stories for local newspapers, and only the most important news items (such as the death of a president) would spread quickly across the country as a whole. Politicians of the pre-telegraph age, Blondheim suggests, could promise different things to people in different regions, tailoring their speeches to the desires and expectations of local audiences. They did so with reasonable certainty that voters in one place would not know about the election goodies promised to voters in another (Blondheim 1994, 193).

The expansion of telegraphic communication made this chicanery more and more difficult. Reporters followed politicians while they campaigned, as they always had, but their news reports were now sent out quickly over telegraph wires. As the same stories were carried by newspapers across the country, promises made to voters in one region were known to those in another, who might demand the same things for themselves or learn that a candidate expressed very different views to one audience than to another. The politician in the modern media age, Blondheim concludes, no longer speaks to a local audience exclusively, but to the country as a whole. Local audiences for political speeches become little more than colourful backdrops for speeches whose real audiences are national in scale.

KEY CONCEPT

Binding spaces: Our sense of belonging to communities, regions, or nations has much to do with the role of media in binding us together on the basis of shared cultural reference points or media consumption habits.

this is not the case. France, like most European countries, consisted for centuries of regional cultures with very different ways of speaking and very few shared cultural reference points. It took the spread of the printing press, after the 1400s, and the distribution of books, magazines, and newspapers across the regions of present-day France to create the modern idea of a unified French culture. Print media helped to standardize the French language by producing vehicles (such as popular books) that carried a particular version of the language out to all regions. Likewise, the popular press sent news and entertainment outward from certain cultural centres

(Paris, in particular) and gave people scattered across many different regions the sense of participating in a shared culture. The printing press, we might say, performed a space-binding function, building a high degree of national unity out of a country that had once been decentralized and fragmented.

Similar processes have happened closer to home. In the 1920s, small-scale, local radio stations in the United States would often broadcast regional musical styles, such as hillbilly music or southern blues, to local audiences familiar with this music. As these stations joined together to form national radio networks in the 1930s, these musical styles were transmitted across the United States as a whole. They became niche tastes for the population overall, rather than regional particularities known only to inhabitants of those regions. As they reached audiences outside the areas in which they were born, these styles fused with others, giving birth to newer musical genres with weaker regional roots, such as country and western or rhythm and blues. In other words, radio, along with the cinema and other media, bound the different regions of the United States into a national audience and turned regional styles into components of a larger national culture. Musical genres such as country music became widely shared tastes, featured on radio stations in big cities such as New York or Los Angeles that were often far from the places in which these styles had emerged.

Quebec Culture

In Canada, the case of Quebec culture provides a striking example of the role of media in space-binding. In the 1960s, Quebec underwent what has come to be known as its Quiet Revolution. Nationalist sentiment in Quebec rose quite noticeably, and the Catholic Church, which had dominated Quebec culture for centuries, lost much of its influence to secular institutions such as the public education system and mass media. People spoke more and more of the distinctiveness of Quebec, of its possible status as a separate nation within the Canadian confederation.

Some critics saw Quebec nationalism as old-fashioned, making little sense in a world of global communications in which, it was said, national differences would disappear. We might understand Quebec nationalism, however, not as the resurgence of an old-fashioned sense of identity, but as an attitude created in important ways by modern communications media.

Beginning in the 1950s, television played a major role in tying together the different parts of Quebec within a shared culture. Some elements of Quebec culture had been widely shared before television, of course—songs, religious festivals, and the literary works of well-known authors such as Gabrielle Roy. The reach of these cultural elements across Quebec was

cultural divide
Occurs when two or more groups within a society have little in common, with few shared values or cultural reference points.

uneven, however, and the **cultural divide** between city and country had remained particularly strong. Television intensified the sharing of cultural experiences and points of reference. Popular television programs, such as the family drama *La famille Plouffe*, reached audiences all across Quebec, cutting through the cultural barriers that had normally divided farmer from city-dweller, or east from west. As hundreds of thousands of people tuned into the same programs at the same time on the same night, they took part in shared rituals with few precedents in Quebec life. Television built a strong, distinctive Québécois culture through the dramatic stories, songs, and personalities it made popular across the territory of Quebec.

We can say, in this sense, that television bound the very distant places of Quebec into a much more unified, shared culture. Today, this sense of a common, distinctive Quebec culture is perhaps just as strong, despite the Internet, cable television, and other forces that might seem to threaten it. One reason for this strength is that the different parts of Quebec media reinforce one another. Stars appear in locally made movies that often are among

Figure 3.2 *La famille Plouffe*

Television played an important role in bridging Quebec's regions during the Quiet Revolution. *La famille Plouffe* was a widely watched family drama from the 1950s that offered a common expression of the province's culture.

SOURCE: Library and Archives Canada. Reprinted by permission.

the top box office successes of the year. Their personal lives are covered in gossipy tabloid newspapers aimed at Quebec readers exclusively, and these stars use their celebrity to endorse consumer products in advertisements seen only in Quebec. Rather than weakening the cultural boundaries of the province, then, modern media have bound the different elements of Quebec culture into a tightly integrated, efficient system. The space of Quebec culture has become more vibrant and distinct.

Conclusion

In 1967, the Canadian media theorist Marshall McLuhan wrote, with characteristic brashness, that modern media had given us a world in which "'Time' has ceased, 'space' has vanished" (McLuhan 1967, 63). Those who study media continue to argue about these claims. As this chapter has suggested, our relationship to media involves an experience of time that operates at many levels, from the rhythms of our daily media consumption to the ways in which we access the sounds and images of the past. Likewise, while space might seem, indeed, to have vanished in an age of instantaneous communication, media still reinforce the spatial boundaries that keep some nations or communities strong and distinct.

We might quibble with McLuhan's pronouncement, arguing that his ideas no longer hold true in an age of social media or rich online archives. At the same time, we may find value in his key insight—that the central impact of media is not to be found in the effects of this or that message, but in the way media shape and transform the dimensions of our lives.

DISCUSSION QUESTIONS

1. Consider the media you have consumed today. Try listing the things you have read, viewed, or listened to, and how much time you spent at each. What patterns or routines are you aware of in your media consumption? Do they differ from those of your friends or your family?

2. Do you seek our news "first hand" online, or do you wait to hear the latest news and gossip more slowly, after the news has been "filtered" by your friends on Facebook? Explain.

3. What sorts of older media do you regularly use or consume? How different is that experience from the new, digital media in your own life?

4. Consider the last 10 messages you have received in your inbox. Do you know where they were sent from? Would you ever communicate with those people in any other medium than social media?

SUGGESTED RESOURCES

Books

Carrol, Michael Thomas. 2000. *Popular Modernity in America: Experience, Technology, Mythohistory*. Albany, NY: State University of New York Press.

Innis, Harold. 1951. *The Bias of Communication*. Toronto: University of Toronto Press.

Websites

Library and Archives Canada. *Old Messengers, New Media: The Legacy of Innis and McLuhan*. http://www.collectionscanada.gc.ca/innis-mcluhan/030003-1030-e.html.

REFERENCES

Blondheim, Menahem. 1994. *News Over the Wires: The Telegraph and the Flow of Public Information in America, 1844–1897*. Cambridge, MA: Harvard University Press.

I Want Media. 2006 (June 26). "Chris Anderson: 'Peer Production Complements Traditional Media.'" *I Want Media*. Accessed April 14, 2011. http://www.iwantmedia.com/people/people58.html.

Kittler, Friedrich A. 1990. *Discourse Networks 1800/1900*, translated by Michael Metteer with Chris Cullens. Stanford, CA: Stanford University Press.

McLuhan, Marshall, with Quentin Fiore. 1967. *The Medium Is the Massage: An Inventory of Effects*. New York: Bantam.

Orwell, George. 1944 (May 12). "As I Please." *The Tribune*. Accessed April 14, 2011. http://orwell.ru/library/articles/As_I_Please/english/eaip_01.

CHAPTER 4 / BART BEATY AND REBECCA SULLIVAN

Media Forms, Interfaces, and Formats

What do we mean when we talk about different media? How do different media emphasize our different senses, and what happens when media cross sensory boundaries? Which is most important—the final product, the systems and structures that constructed it, or the way that we react to it?

KEY CONCEPTS

1. *Form:* the specific tools, technologies, and techniques that distinguish a cultural object (for example, music recorded using particular instruments such as guitars or synthesizers, or in a particular style, such as hip hop or metal).

2. *Interface:* the point of contact between a cultural object and its audience (for example, listening to music on an iPod).

3. *Format:* the industrial and institutional contexts in which cultural products are made and distributed to audiences (for example, the 3-minute pop song).

CHAPTER OUTLINE

Introduction 53

Form: Sound, Print, and Visual Media 55

Interface: Social Networking Media 61

Format: Cultural Industries 63

Conclusion: Intermedia and Transmedia
Pondering the Future 66

Discussion Questions 68

Suggested Resources 69

References 69

Introduction

How do we know what we "know" about media? This chapter takes an *epistemological* approach—one that draws on the theory of knowledge—to explore media in terms of form, format, and interface. Each of these modes is based in a different understanding of media, and all have been shaped by history, politics, and aesthetics.

Some media scholars believe that each medium constitutes a different *form*. According to this view, a medium is the agent, or method of transmission, that allows the expression of an idea, thought, or concept. From this perspective, analysts tend to focus on both the final aesthetic object (the "text") and on the unique techniques and technologies that were used to create that object. For example, film critics usually analyze a movie in terms of its editing, lighting, sound, direction, cinematography, and other technical elements. This is called a *formal analysis* (Bordwell and Thompson 2009). Another useful example of form is the comics inside a newspaper. Comics consist of specific elements that make the form recognizable. Every Saturday you can find them located in the same section of the paper, made up of illustrations, printed in colour, with boxes around each frame, and so on. These specific elements make both the newspapers and the comic page predictable and distinct from other forms or media.

A second school of thought contends that the text is less important than the methods by which it was created, disseminated, and consumed. These writers prefer to study the media in terms of *interface*. They argue that media are not a means to an end—the culmination of techniques and styles used to create a unified, autonomous cultural object—but are an end unto themselves. In other words, the television set and its connection to broadcasting signals is more important than any specific television show or regulatory environment. Cramer and Fuller (2008) further define this concept as a "point of juncture between different bodies, hardware, software, users and what they connect to or are part of" (150). "User interfaces" are one common type of interface. The touch screen on a mobile phone, for example, is a graphic user interface that is a point of contact between the user and the software that tells the phone's processor what to do and how to link to the larger network.

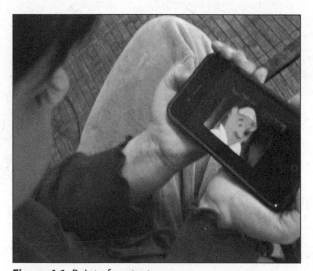

Figure 4.1 Point of contact

User interfaces, such as those on mobile phones, have quickly become one of the most common ways in which people connect with technology.

Critics of both of these approaches claim that media cannot be adequately understood unless they are placed in appropriate context. Such critics use the term *format* to indicate the mechanized, routinized systems by which most media texts are produced, circulated, and ultimately consumed by audiences. For example, a critique of North American media might focus on the organization of different media systems and the standardization of their products to suit the political and economic logics of free-market capitalism. This approach is often informed by the work of Theodor Adorno on "the culture industry" (Adorno 1991).

To explain the differences between these approaches—forms, formats, and interfaces—this chapter will examine five major media categories. The first three—sound, print, and visual media—loosely cohere around the approach of "form." The fourth, social networking, lends itself to the "interface" approach. The last category, cultural industries, illustrates the "format" approach.

Some critics have suggested that sound, print, and visual media are such different forms that each requires specific tools for analysis. Others counter that a medium's form is less important than its interface, as illustrated by new developments in social communication technologies, such as social networking media. This argument suggests that as the technology evolves, the medium—and how users engage with it—has become more important than what is actually said with it. Finally, some scholars suggest that both form and interface are less important than format, and the industrial conditions under which media develop, as in the case of intermedia and transmedia, covered later in this chapter.

It is important to note that each of these media categories could easily be chapters themselves. The goal of this chapter is not to provide a comprehensive overview but to highlight how different ways of conceiving our relationship to media provoke different questions and directions for research. Thus, the emphasis is on the approaches—form, interface, and format—and how the historical and social conditions of media development have informed them.

Form: Sound, Print, and Visual Media

The study of sound media is based on an ancient past of orality/aurality—aural expression in societies where writing and print were unknown or unfamiliar to most of the population. It has also been influenced by contemporary technologies of sound recording and manipulation. Similarly, the study of print media rests on the historical concept of literacy, the bedrock of contemporary cultural values. A modern hybrid of aurality and literacy is the visual media. The rise of visuality, with film and television gaining greater audiences than traditional print media (books, magazines, and newspapers), is an issue that has concerned media scholars for well over half a century.

> ### KEY CONCEPT
> *Form:* the specific tools, technologies, and techniques that distinguish a cultural object (for example, music recorded using particular instruments such as guitars or synthesizers, or in a particular style, such as hip hop or metal).

Sound and Aurality

Do you consider your body a medium of communication? Well, it is—one of our primary means of reaching out to the world. In the days before mechanized technologies, it was the travelling minstrel or town crier who

disseminate
Broadcast, distribute, or widely share any type of news or information.

disseminated news across vast distances. Today, when we think of sound media, we think of audio recording, radio signals, and other forms of tele-communication, like the cellphone. What all these have in common, regardless of their significant historical and technological differences, is a reliance on sound waves for transmitting information.

For Walter Ong, one of the first scholars to discuss sound as a medium, what sets sound apart is its transitory nature. Sound is movement. Even if we pause a recording, or rewind and play it back, the moment that we seek is gone the instant it is heard (Ong 1982, 31). To many, this is the key characteristic that shapes our understanding of sound media. To compensate for its ephemerality, sound relies on identifiable rhythmic patterns including rhymes, repetitive phrasing, standardized or formulaic expressions, and other devices. Thus, when we study sound media, we are interested in the way that sound resonates after it has dissipated. In other words, how is sound—which cannot be stopped—absorbed, deciphered, and remembered?

Before it was possible to capture sound, the body was the primary medium for spoken aural communication. In cultures where print media do not predominate (for example, certain Aboriginal societies), the means of communication are both impermanent and immaterial, and no physical trace of the message is stored for future generations. Consequently, in oral cultures, information spreads slowly and only to small groups of people at a time. The ability of the human mind to recall complex narratives and detailed information is crucial to oral cultures. In our own era of non-stop information, contemplating the amazing human capacity to remember something that may have been heard only once raises questions about media permanence, the body as a communication technology, and the temporal and spatial dimensions of communication. Indeed, as the media scholar Harold Innis argued, the prevalence of orality reflects a culture that is deeply respectful of history and tradition. (For more on Innis, see Chapter 7, Media R/Evolutions.)

When considering sound media as a form, the tendency is to focus on music and musical recordings. Music was a critical mode for recalling and repeating a society's important histories and cultural knowledge. For communications studies, however, music is not only a conduit of social customs and historical knowledge; it is also a set of texts that are consumed for pleasure. According to Jacques Attali (1985), one of the first scholars to ponder the significance of sound as pleasure: "Music, an immaterial pleasure turned commodity, now heralds a society of the sign, of the immaterial up for sale, of the social relation unified in money" (3). Thus, certain aspects of popular music studies seek to address such questions as sound as a semiotic system, the ideology of sound, the economic relationship between musical production

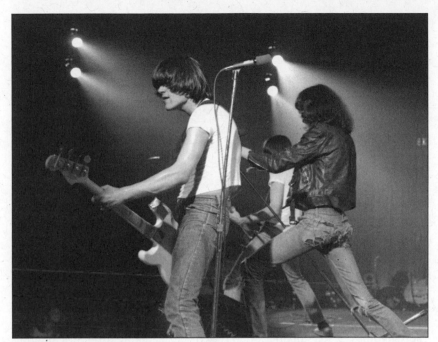

Figure 4.2 The Ramones

In the 1970s, this New York band epitomized classic punk style: three chords, ripped jeans, and black leather jackets. Punk is one musical form that has been a particularly rich starting point for scholars of communications and culture to examine class and gender, as well as performance, semiotics, and style.

SOURCE: Don Pyle/troubleinthecameraclub.com. Reprinted by permission.

Popular music is not only an example of sound media form, and a set of texts consumed for pleasure; it is also a conduit of customs, styles, and historical knowledge that has an ability to organize social groups.

textuality
The quality of containing meaning, which is shared by cultural forms, artifacts, or even mundane daily items, and which can be decoded to reveal underlying values and assumptions.

and consumption, and music's relationship to style and taste. Studies of genre, audience, and performance are linked to popular music's ability to organize social groups, not only by musical preference but also by political practice (Frith and Straw 2001). For example, in Dick Hebdige's landmark book, *Subculture and the Meaning of Style* (1979), musical forms such as punk are offered as launching points to examine a complex system of cultural politics dealing with class and gender oppression.

When musical forms are analyzed as an element of ideology, the ephemerality of sound media is not as pronounced. Instead, the sound moment is anchored as a "text" that can be decoded to reveal specific generic, political, and social organization. This emphasis on **textuality** is very much linked to the dominance of print media in defining complex communication systems. A long-standing, and highly problematic, assumption is that print media and literacy stand as signifiers of civilized cultures. However, a great deal of evidence now exists that challenges such assumptions. For example, the oral cultures of Canadian Aboriginal cultures (Friesen 2000) depend on very sophisticated systems of transmission, while the Inca used the *quipu* (a system of knotted strings) as a means of recording and transmitting information (Ascher and Ascher 1997). The term "literate" has come to imply a double meaning of reading and writing competency, as well as knowledgeability about the world and its affairs. Such assumptions merit considerable scrutiny.

Print and Literacy

Many communication historians suggest that writing became necessary to deal with increasingly complex economic and social systems. The need to keep records and provide proofs of transactions necessitated a more reliable—and impartial—system than human memory. Accounting can be seen as one of the first literate communication systems. The study of print by communication scholars tends to focus on those genres that transmit information, rather than expressive genres such as novels or poetry (Goody 1987, 4). Typical examples are newspapers, magazines, and blogs, but might also include primitive markers such as cave paintings, stone carvings, or hieroglyphics. A key distinction between the academic discipline of communications and, say, English literature or art history, is that the former is interested less in admiring the beauty or eloquence of writing as an art form, focusing instead on the social value of establishing a permanent record for successive generations. Thus, while textual analysis remains a common method used to study communications, as a discipline it is more concerned with social function than aesthetics. Textual analysis includes content analysis, framing, and agenda setting (described below). These methods are all concerned with the way that a printed text is organized to secure different forms of political and social power.

Accounting can be seen as one of the first literate communication systems.

In his landmark study, *The Structural Transformation of the Public Sphere* (1991), Jürgen Habermas argues that the publication of newspapers and political tracts empowered individuals to debate issues and posit arguments that may not have conformed to state or religious authority. The flipside of the association of print with civilization, democracy, and individualism has been the development of sophisticated means of state surveillance and censorship that would have been impossible without the invention of print. Robert Darnton (1982), a notable historian of literacy, has written about state controls over print and limits on freedom of the press. His interest in "illegal literature" links print media to regulatory systems through questions of authorship and ownership. The ability of state and religious authorities to contain ideas and limit information relied as much on printing technologies as did the creators of new ideas. Habermas and Darnton help demonstrate that a form such as print can be both transformative and restrictive, depending on the way that it is used.

The question of how print helps shape public opinion is central to the study of the form. Paul Lazarsfeld and colleagues (1948) argued that newspapers were influential only insofar as their most avid readers became "opinion leaders" in their communities, or citizens who help disseminate knowledge. Scholars of *agenda setting* argued that those in control of the news, including reporters, editors, and publishers, are responsible for determining not only the issues that are important, but also how these will be **framed** in the public debate (McCombs 2004). A primary method by which to reveal these biases is **content analysis**, the detailed coding of news stories according to the specific words and phrases that are used to describe an event (Krippendorff 2009).

Content analyses are often considered a means of quantitative analysis. That is, they provide hard data on the precise language that is used across a wide sample of texts. That data is then applied to critical investigations of how different print forms influence the way that "the public" and "the public sphere" are defined. Such analysis opens up an interesting debate in communication studies over the value of a single text versus a broad sampling of texts. Ironically, while sociological methods such as content analysis have been preferred for the analysis of print media texts, other aspects of communication studies have relied more heavily on methods acquired from literary studies. Visual media, especially film, are arguably the most informed by questions of form.

framing
The way in which an issue or question is presented, based on certain assumptions or biases, which can affect how it is understood by an audience.

content analysis
The study of data collected from investigating, for example, the language used in presenting news stories or other media.

PRIMARY SOURCE

John Stuart Mill, *On Liberty*

John Stuart Mill, in his essay *On Liberty* (1869), decried the role of the newspaper in formulating public opinion:

> Those whose opinions go by the name of public opinion, are not always the same sort of public: in America they are the whole white population; in England, chiefly the middle class. But they are always a mass, that is to say, collective mediocrity. And what is a still greater novelty, the mass do not now take their opinions from dignitaries in Church or State, from ostensible leaders, or from books. Their thinking is done for them by men much like themselves, addressing them or speaking in their name, on the spur of the moment, through the newspapers.

Visual Media: "Signs" of Culture

Visual media are the most dominant media in contemporary society. Encompassing photographs, films, television, and online forms, visual media are distinguished from print and sound—which they often incorporate—by their reliance on representational images. Stuart Hall (1997) has defined **representation** as the relationship between objects, concepts, and signs. Hall argues that representational systems of visual culture are best understood as socially constructed, not only from the immediate experiences of the senders or receivers, but also from the historical and socio-cultural contexts in which the visual image is created. (The concept of representation relies heavily on the functions of language, discussed in greater detail in Chapter 6, Language and Media.)

representation
The relationship between objects, concepts, and signs, best understood as arising from a certain historical or cultural context.

Different forms of visual media have generated different ways to determine the interpretive context of images. The discipline of film studies has stressed the uniqueness of film through *formalist* analyses of its various components: sound, lighting, editing, cinematography, costume and setting design, and most importantly, direction. Some scholars rely on formalism to reveal generic or industrial conventions that have been repeated so often that audiences can instantly recognize and decipher them. For example, westerns are notable for their inclusion of wide vista shots of the landscape, whereas melodramas tend to incorporate more tightly framed shots of interiors. These analyses often go farther, arguing that generic conventions are used not only to ensure visual familiarity but to reflect particular values. For example, the emphasis on exterior spaces in the western and interior spaces in the melodrama can be said to conform to ideological notions of gender that suggest men should roam freely while women belong in the home.

Film scholars such as Christian Metz (1974), Laura Mulvey (1989), and Raymond Bellour (2000) suggest that the visual power of cinema lies in the *cinematic apparatus*. This term refers to the industrial system behind the film, the technologies deployed to show it, and the positioning of the audience in relation to the film screen. From this standpoint, it is the practice of looking at a film, and not the film itself, that is meaningful. These scholars have been highly influenced by psychoanalytic theories about the construction of subjectivity through practices of viewing. They suggest that "the gaze" is not merely the act of looking but refers to the dynamic environment in which looking ascribes power to some while subjugating others to a voyeuristic and sadistic system of control.

Critics of formalist and psychoanalytic theories note their assumption that film viewing takes place within darkened, anonymous public spaces. These critics claim that the most prevalent form of moving images, television, constructs its "apparatus" very differently. As a domestic technology, television is integrated into the home, offering more ready access but also a less immersive experience. Raymond Williams (1974) offered a key concept in understanding the relationship between screen, image, and audience when he characterized television as a "flow." As a never-ending succession of images and sounds pour forth, television cannot be reduced to an event (like sound), a text (like print), or a gaze (like film). It is ubiquitous, perpetual, multisensory, and disruptive. Williams argues that both the socio-technological coordination of television (seasons, schedules, and commercial breaks) and the cultural–textual coordination of television form (the conformity of genres, such as the sitcom, to the dictates of television's structures) mean that television is best understood as a system of structural and modular flows.

Just as the advent of television compromised film scholars' assertions of a static cinematic apparatus, Williams's concept of "flow" has been challenged by the advent of digital media, which disrupt broadcasting's control over structural and modular organization. The advent of blogs, peer-to-peer file sharing, video streaming, digital downloading, and personal video recorders (PVRs) now means that audiences are exerting ever-increasing control over their media. The study of digital media, and what has been called "Web 2.0 technologies," has pushed critical emphasis farther away from the distinctiveness of forms and toward the relationships between technologies and their users. Put another way, interface is a key question for discerning how we relate to new media and, perhaps, how those who produce these media seek to relate to us.

Web 2.0 technologies have led to an increased critical emphasis on technologies and their users, and less emphasis on the distinctiveness of forms.

Interface: Social Networking Media

As this chapter was being written, one of the authors had a video chat with a family member, typed a comment into an online news site, updated her status on Facebook, watched a streaming video episode of *The Daily Show*, and downloaded a Beatles song from iTunes, all on the same interface—her computer. Telephones, newspapers, televisions, postal systems, and CD and DVD players now appear superfluous, their discrete use having been fully integrated into one machine. What does it mean when media technologies are converging as quickly as the possibilities expand for their use? Can this phenomenon be explained by analyzing the form, or can we better understand it by considering the interface? Scholars of new communication technologies suggest that something more important is going on than a mere transition from the oral to the literal to the visual. They suggest that we must consider how media infiltrate our daily lives and implicate our very

KEY CONCEPT
Interface: the point of contact between a cultural text and its audience (for example, listening to music on an iPod).

selves in their construction. In other words, to recall Marshall McLuhan's (1964) famous claim, "The medium is the message."

In her essay, "Fragmented Future" (1999), Darcy DiNucci coined the term Web 2.0 to designate the end to a standardized, flat engagement with the online screen and the rise of new interfaces that would be more like interactive "transport mechanisms," portals through which the line between programmers, designers, and users would be erased (32). Text, images, and video would blend imperceptibly and move easily across multiple platforms—computer screens, televisions, even telephones.

DiNucci's vision took some time to materialize, but when it did, it seemed to herald a society transformed. In 2006, *Time* magazine named "you" its person of the year—that is, the ever-growing number of individuals who are creating and modifying their own mediated environment. It claimed: "It's a story about community and collaboration on a scale never seen before. … It's about the many wresting power from the few and helping one another for nothing and how that will not only change the world, but also change the way the world changes" (Grossman 2006). Furthermore, the agent responsible for this revolution in communications was not an individual, a group, or a government, but a technology: the World Wide Web.

Time's optimism about the potential of technology to transform the world is not unprecedented. Indeed, more than a few scholars have attributed democracy and individual liberty to the invention of the printing press. This argument is known as **technological determinism**, because it presupposes that technology determines its own use and also its use-value. The advent of new technologies has generated new values regarding communication and the role of media in our lives. By shaping our interaction with different media, technology can be seen to produce its own meaning. In this case, the fact that social networking media make it possible for us to enjoy multiple forms of interaction—immediate, asynchronous, anonymous, directed—with other self-designers seems to create unlimited possibilities for media democracy.

technological determinism
The belief that the technologies used in a society will determine that society's values and culture.

At present, analysts of Web 2.0 tend to focus less on the actual content of the new media than on the specifics of the form itself. They suggest that the specific interactions made using these technologies matter very little because they are highly unstable and subject to change. In other words, the technological interface is itself the central concept at issue. Technology, as defined by Jacques Ellul, refers to the totality of all tools and techniques available to structure human experience. In his influential book, *The Technological Society* (1965), he lamented the rise of technologies and the concomitant decline of human beings as the centre of communicative processes. Others,

HISTORICAL HIGHLIGHT

The History of Web 2.0

1999   Darcy DiNucci coins the term

1999   The word "blog" is first used

       Blogger software is released later that year

2001   Wikipedia is launched

2002   Friendster is launched

2003   MySpace is launched

2004   Facebook is launched

2005   YouTube is launched

2006   Twitter is launched

including Marshall McLuhan (1962), lauded the transformations wrought by new technologies, particularly those of "the electronic age" that brought about "a global village" of technological interdependence. More contemporary research into social networking media has contemplated the transformation of literacy (Livingstone 2002), the formation of online communities (Papacharissi 2010), and the reconfiguring of leisure (Wagman 2010).

Despite vast differences in their methods of analysis, or their specific subject matter, what is shared among these scholars is a tendency to focus on the technology and how it transforms the user-audience rather than on its final outcomes (its forms) or its engineering and regulation (its formats). Yet, as the Internet becomes more and more integral to our daily lives, squeezing out such media as film, television, radio, and newspapers, greater attention is being paid to issues of ownership and regulation of its architecture, its transmission signals, and its content. Claims about the revolutionary uniqueness of new media are challenged by the resurrection of familiar problems that have long concerned researchers of other media forms: who profits, who is granted access, and under what conditions? These questions beget a different way of understanding media that sees them not as autonomous phenomena, events, and texts, but as a vast industrial complex.

Format: Cultural Industries

Early in 2011, two rather startling events took place. In Egypt, a popular uprising against a dictatorial leader resulted in that government's effectively "shutting down" the Internet. At the same time, Canadians were confronted with the possibility that major media conglomerates, including Bell and

"Movies and radio need no longer pretend to be art. The truth that they are just business is made into an ideology in order to justify the rubbish they deliberately produce."

—*Theodor Adorno and Max Horkheimer*

"We need approaches that are sensitive to the potential power of the cultural industries, as makers of texts, as systems for the management and marketing of creative work and as agents of change."

—*David Hesmondhalgh*

Rogers, would begin charging their Internet clients based on the amount of data they share. The first example, political repression of the Internet, and the second, capitalist exploitation of the Internet, configure the major issues surrounding the study of media formats and cultural industries: namely, who controls the forms and interfaces of the media, and to what end?

Some media scholars suggest that both form and interface are less important than format and the industrial conditions under which these media develop. Noting the stultifying social effects of mass-produced media, these critics question the political and economic functions of media industries, and the way that different media are structured to provide the illusion of consumer choice and mass appeal.

The study of media as an industry was begun by Theodor Adorno (1991), who argued that culture was losing its character as an aesthetic form of authentic human expression. He believed that culture was becoming no different than any other mass-produced commodity. The result, he lamented, was a uniform system of "culture production" that did nothing to advance the human condition and everything to ensure that systems of political and economic domination would continue. The products of "the culture industry" adhered to instrumental and utilitarian goals that subsumed creativity under systems of generic similarity and comfortable familiarity. In other words, aesthetic innovation is eliminated when culture is shaped to fit conventional formats. Examples include the sitcom, the three-minute pop song, the melodrama, and the tabloid magazine. Regardless of whether the product is sound, print, or visual, the conditions of media production are all highly routinized and numbingly standardized.

From Culture Industry to "Cultural Industries"

Adorno's bleak outlook on culture in an age of mass media has been softened by many scholars re-thinking "the culture industry" as a series of interconnecting "cultural industries." The difference is not merely semantic. As David Hesmondhalgh (2002) argues, the texts produced by cultural industries are different from commodities such as bread and oil. They are at the centre of our practices of making meaning out of the world. He suggests that the question of media power and influence must go farther than the top-down models offered by Adorno. Rather, the question must be posed again whether the commodities produced by cultural industries actually serve the exclusive interests of their owners and regulators (Hesmondhalgh 2002, 3). Certainly, in both examples listed above, state- and corporate-controlled interfaces such as the Internet are being used to circulate texts that challenge

Figure 4.3 The conventional formats of the culture industry

Much of the culture we consume is packaged in standardized formats, with typically very little deviation. In fact, variety in formats is discouraged. When was the last time you heard a 10-minute song on the radio?

the limits of government and business control over the media and the media's messages. Thus, pluralizing the word *industry* and modifying *culture* to become *cultural* is meant to demonstrate the complexity and diversity of industrialized cultural production by mass media systems. While *American Idol* may not be art, neither is it simply a brainwashing tool of an omnipotent capitalist-state machine.

The way that cultural industries format their products illustrates their *industrial* logics as well as how they imagine their audience. Ratings systems, "prime-time" scheduling, distribution channels, regulatory networks, and ownership structures provide important insights not only into mediated forms but also into their interface. For example, one of the arguments made against Internet user fees stresses the fact that Internet providers also own a significant portion of our broadcasting and telecommunication systems. Are these industrial players trying to force audiences away from the "free" Internet and back to the advertising-dominated cable or satellite broadcasting systems? Does Bell want you to get your news about Egypt from a blog it doesn't control, or from CTV News, which it owns?

While Adorno has argued that the ultimate form of the cultural product doesn't matter, scholars of cultural industries see this issue differently. They argue that textual analysis goes hand in hand with industrial critique, connecting those outcomes to the various organizing practices to show how they respond to large economic, political, societal, and technological shifts. Some call this "critical media industry studies," an approach that ties political–economic critique to cultural–textual analysis (Havens, Lotz, and Tinic 2009). In this conception, analysis of industry ownership, regulation, and organization are related to formal and ideological analysis of the specific texts produced under these conditions.

A third element to be considered is the labour of what have been termed "creative workers." This approach rejects the simplistic view of oppressive media owners and either passive-victim or subversive-transgressive media consumers by adding a third social actor to the analysis: the actual people involved at the middle and low levels of media production. It also considers the organizational culture in which media products are made, and the economic and social value that comes with being a part of the cultural industries. Toby Miller, in a nod to Web 2.0, refers to this as Media Studies 3.0. It combines audience-based research such as interviews and focus groups, political–economic analysis of the industry, and the formal critique of texts. It treats communications and media access as a human right that is, on the one hand, being compromised by the increasingly global reach of media conglomerates, but on the other, ameliorated by the accessibility of social networking media (Miller 2010, 6).

Efforts to combine industry studies with audience and textual studies suggest that the divisions between forms, interfaces, and formats no longer hold true in an age of technological and economic convergence, and of user-generated media. Thus, having explored these different tentacles of media studies, it is worth concluding with some thoughts about future directions and how our media-saturated societies are generating whole new lines of questioning.

Conclusion: Intermedia and Transmedia— Pondering the Future

While there can be no doubt that media texts, industries, and interfaces are converging at an increasingly rapid pace, the robustness of media studies offers more than just one way to approach this development. Some scholars have renewed their emphasis on the text and the particular aesthetic strategies that produce hybrid art forms. For others, it is the industry and technology that make possible the transposition of a text across different media. These scholars show us that contemporary forms, formats, and interfaces are inextricably intertwined in our everyday experiences of the media.

Intermedia is not just a comparative approach to the way that different media deal with similar texts—as in, say, a cinematic adaptation of a well-known novel. Rather, it envisions the intersection of sound, print, and screen media as a whole new form. Dick Higgins, a conceptual artist and part of the Fluxus movement in the 1960s, originally conceived of intermedia as a type of genre between genres, so to speak. Referencing Samuel Taylor Coleridge as the first to use the term in 1812, he cited contemporary art forms such as "visual poetry," "happenings," and "abstract calligraphy" as early examples of intermedia (Higgins 2001, 52). In a seminal work, Jay David Bolter and Richard A. Grusin (2000) have offered the concept of "remediation" to describe the ways that the logics of new media forms re-fashion old media forms, such as books or television, which then re-fashion themselves (273). They offer as one example the way that computer animation was influenced by the formal properties of classical animated films, culminating in full-length computer-animated films such as *Shrek* or *Toy Story*. These films, and others like them, take their formal characteristics from both the worlds of computer graphics and of Hollywood cinema.

There is a second way of understanding these computer-animated films, and that is the way that the originating narrative (an ogre who marries a princess, a cowboy puppet who befriends a toy robot) is transposed onto a variety of different media: video games, television series, interactive websites, comic books, even live theatrical performance, as with *Shrek: The Musical*. Henry Jenkins (2008) refers to these media migrations as **transmedia**—the integration of texts across multiple platforms to extend the narrative beyond any one original medium. Thus, in order to get the "whole story" of contemporary media properties, audiences must be prepared not only to see the film, but also to play the game, read the comic, follow a Twitter feed, and so on. The narrative literally transcends formal limitations (Jenkins 2008, 95). The methods for studying forms introduced earlier in this chapter are not entirely appropriate for understanding this series of relationships and transformations from medium to medium.

Intermedia and transmedia are important concepts in media studies not only because of the way they collapse formal boundaries. They also suggest new ways of repurposing both media commodities and audiences. Economic and technological convergence now makes it possible to take a character or story previously linked to a single media form (such as superheroes in comic books) and create vast syndicates of interconnected narratives that transform comic book audiences into film audiences into video game players,

intermedia
The intersection of sound, print, and screen media into a whole new form.

transmedia
The occurrence of a text across multiple platforms, thereby extending its narrative; for example, Batman comic books, movies, cartoons, toys, and so on.

with the same company owning all the different platforms and maximizing its profit accordingly. For example, Batman comic books are published by DC Comics, a subsidiary of Time-Warner, while Batman movies are produced by Warner Brothers, Batman animation by Warner Brothers Animation, and so on. Jenkins calls this "convergence culture," the economic and techno-logical conditions of inter- and transmediality: "Welcome to convergence culture, where old and new media collide, where grassroots and corporate media intersect, where the power of the media producer and the power of the media consumer interact in unpredictable ways" (Jenkins 2008, 2).

Thus it is the job of media studies to explore that unpredictability, precari-ousness, and instability of media in all their forms, formats, and interfaces. It is the task of scholars to consider the political–economic forces of media power that have the textual power of representation, and the human power of audiences who exert their own meanings over their media. This is not to say that form, format, and interface are no longer relevant, but rather, that we need to emphasize their distinctive character as co-dependent and mutually reinforcing. This way of understanding media ultimately stems from the same place as all the other approaches described in this chapter: from the actual conditions of the making, disseminating, and consuming of media at a par-ticular moment in history. With the shift toward intermedia and transmedia, media studies has not reached an ending. Rather, it is a story with no end-ing, only a series of new beginnings.

DISCUSSION QUESTIONS

1. This chapter emphasizes only one approach for sound, print, and visual media: that of form. What would an analysis of these different media that emphasized interface or format look like?

2. What is the difference between intermedia and transmedia studies? What sorts of questions are possible when doing an intermedia an-alysis, and what questions are possible when doing a transmedia analysis?

3. Which is the more important question, in your opinion: the mean-ing of the text, the industrial properties of the text, or the systems of transmitting the text? Explain.

SUGGESTED RESOURCES
Books

Beaty, Bart, Derek Briton, Gloria Filax, and Rebecca Sullivan, eds. 2010. *How Canadians Communicate: Contexts of Popular Culture*. Athabasca, AB: University of Athabasca Press.

Hesmondhalgh, David. 2008. *The Media and Social Theory*. New York: Routledge.

Lewis, Justin, ed. 2003. *Critical Cultural Policy Studies: A Reader*. Cambridge, UK: Blackwell.

Miller, Toby. 2001. *A Companion to Cultural Studies*. Cambridge, UK: Blackwell.

Valdivia, Angharad N. 2003. *A Companion to Media Studies*. Cambridge, UK: Blackwell.

Websites

Confessions of an Aca-Fan: The Official Weblog of Henry Jenkins. http://www.henryjenkins.org.

Media-Studies.ca. http://www.media-studies.ca.

Seize the Media. http://seizethemedia.com.

WorldHistorySite.com: Communication Technologies and World History. http://www.worldhistorysite.com/communication.html.

REFERENCES

Adorno, Theodor. 1991. *The Culture Industry: Selected Essays on Mass Culture*. New York: Routledge.

Ascher, Marcia, and Robert Ascher. 1997. *Mathematics of the Incas: Code of the Quipu*. New York: Dover.

Attali, Jacques. 1985. *Noise: The Political Economy of Music*. Minneapolis: University of Minnesota.

Barthes, Roland. 1973. *Mythologies*. London, Paladin.

Bellour, Raymond. 2000. *The Analysis of Film*. Bloomington, IN: Indiana University Press.

Bolter, Jay David, and Richard A. Grusin. 2000. *Remediation: Understanding New Media*. Boston: MIT Press.

Bordwell, David, and Kristin Thompson. 2010. *Film Art: An Introduction*. New York: McGraw-Hill.

Carey, James W. 1989. *Communication as Culture: Essays on Media and Society*. Boston: Unwin Hyman.

Cramer, Florian, and Matthew Fuller. 2008. "Interface." In *Software Studies: A Lexicon*, edited by Matthew Fuller. Cambridge, MA: MIT Press.

Darnton, Robert. 1982. *The Literary Underground of the Old Regime*. Boston: Harvard University Press.

DiNucci, Darcy. 1999. "Fragmented Future." *Print* 53(4):32.

Ellul, Jacques. 1967. *The Technological Society*. New York: Vintage Books.

Friesen, Gerald. 2000. *Citizens and Nation: An Essay on History, Communication, and Canada*. Toronto: University of Toronto Press.

Frith, Simon, and William Straw, eds. 2001. *The Cambridge Companion to Pop and Rock*. Cambridge, UK: Cambridge University Press.

Goody, Jack. 1987. *The Interface Between the Written and the Oral*. Cambridge, UK: Cambridge University Press.

Grossman, Lev. 2006 (December 13). "Time's Person of the Year: You." *Time*. Accessed February 8, 2011. http://www.time.com/time/magazine/article/0,9171,1569514,00.html.

Habermas, Jürgen. 1991. *The Structural Transformation of the Public Sphere: An Inquiry into a Category of Bourgeois Society*. Boston: MIT Press.

Hall, Stuart. 1997. *Representation: Cultural Representations and Signifying Practices*. London: Open University.

Havens, Timothy, Amanda D. Lotz, and Serra Tinic. 2009. "Critical Media Industry Studies: A Research Approach." *Communication, Culture and Critique* 2:234–53.

Hesmondhalgh, David. 2002. *The Cultural Industries*. London: Sage.

Higgins, Dick. 2001. "Intermedia." *Leonardo* 34(1):49–54.

Horkheimer, Max, and Theodor W. Adorno. 2002. *Dialectic of Enlightenment: Philosophical Fragments*. Palo Alto, CA: Stanford University Press.

Innis, Harold A. 1991. *The Bias of Communication*. Toronto: University of Toronto Press.

Jenkins, Henry. 2006. *Convergence Culture: Where Old and New Media Collide*. New York: New York University Press.

Krippendorff, Klaus. 2009. *The Content Analysis Reader*. Thousand Oaks, CA: Sage.

Lazarsfeld, Paul Felix, Bernard Berelson, and Hazel Gaudet. 1948. *The People's Choice: How the Voter Makes Up His Mind in a Presidential Campaign*. New York: Columbia University Press.

Livingstone, Sonia M. 2002. *Young People and New Media: Childhood and the Changing Media Environment*. London: Sage.

McCombs, Maxwell E. 2004. *Setting the Agenda: The Mass Media and Public Opinion*. London: Polity Press.

McLuhan, Marshall. 1962. *The Gutenberg Galaxy*. Toronto: University of Toronto Press.

McLuhan, Marshall. 1964. *Understanding Media: The Extensions of Man* (2nd ed.). New York: New American Library.

Metz, Christian. 1974. *Film Language: A Semiotics of the Cinema*. Oxford, UK: Oxford University Press.

Mill, John Stuart. 1869. *On Liberty*. Accessed March 9, 2011. http://www.serendipity.li/jsmill/on_lib.html.

Miller, Toby. 2010. "Media Studies 3.0." In *How Canadians Communicate: Contexts of Popular Culture*, edited by Bart Beaty, Derek Briton, Gloria Filax, and Rebecca Sullivan. Athabasca, AB: Athabasca University Press.

Mulvey, Laura. 1989. *Visual and Other Pleasures*. Bloomington, IN: Indiana University Press.

Ong, Walter J. 1982. *Orality and Literacy: The Technologizing of the Word*. London: Methuen.

Papcharissi, Zizi. 2010. *A Networked Self: Identity, Community and Culture on Social Network Sites*. New York: Routledge.

Wagman, Ira. 2010. "Log On, Goof Off, and Look Up: Facebook and the Rhythms of Canadian Internet Use." In *How Canadians Communicate: Contexts of Popular Culture*, edited by Bart Beaty, Derek Briton, Gloria Filax, and Rebecca Sullivan. Athabasca, AB: Athabasca University Press.

Wiliams, Raymond. 1992. *Television: Technology and Cultural Form*. Middletown, CT: Wesleyan University Press.

Media Functions

What do media do? What can't media do? How successful are media in carrying out various functions? How does considering our everyday uses of media help us understand media's functionality?

KEY CONCEPTS

1. Media gain their cultural and social value through our use of them.

2. Limiting our understanding of media to "mass media" causes us to overlook other forms of communication that *mediate*—or come between—different aspects of social life.

3. The raw materials of communication involve a message, a means of delivery, and some combination of senders and receivers.

4. The emergence of new communication technologies multiplies the potential for miscommunication.

CHAPTER OUTLINE

Introduction 73

Media Beyond Mass Media 74

Many Media, Many Functions 76

Conclusion 85

Note 86

Discussion Questions 87

Suggested Resources 87

References 87

Introduction

This chapter examines the functions of media—the roles the media play in our society and in how we live. What do they allow us to do, and not to do? There are many answers to these questions. Indeed, one may be inclined to ask a different question: what *can't* media do? We use media technologies to record moments in our lives, to entertain ourselves, to get information, to spy on people, to buy things, to waste time, to connect with other people, or to express ourselves. Of course, this is only a partial list. Scholars have sought to develop their own list of the functions of media,[1] and many of us could probably add 10 or 20 different roles that media play in our own lives. This is a reflection of the fact that so many media feature in our lives and serve many different functions.

The chapter presents two main arguments: first, that we must consider "media" in the broadest of terms—that is, media should not be restricted to mass media, such as film, television, or radio. Second, media have at least three functions: a *communicative* function, an *empowering and disempowering* function, and a *remedial* function. This list, too, is necessarily partial; readers are thus encouraged to add their own suggestions to what is offered here.

Regardless of the functions that we choose to list, we should remember that questions about the *functionality* of media are fundamentally questions about the *instrumentality* of media. Media help us appreciate the different ways in which the same medium can function when placed in the hands of people as varied as dictators and dilettantes. Those uses are often different from the creators' original intention. For example, although the architecture of the Internet was established to protect sensitive information in the event of a nuclear attack, we use it very differently today. This is so because "the media" actually don't *do* anything on their own. They have been designed by people to do things, and they are used by people to do things. The fact that we tend to talk about media almost as if they were human is very much a reflection of our time: we have come to see technologies as having human characteristics, performing tasks for us without requiring us to think about the people who designed them. The gap between how media are intended to be used and how they are used is also a reminder that what media *can do* is of little relevance if we do not consider the ways in which media *actually do* things when used in real-life situations. It is through our use of media, then, that media gain their cultural and social value.

> **KEY CONCEPT**
> Media gain their cultural and social value through our use of them.

Media Beyond Mass Media

Various Ways of Understanding the Word "Media"

Raymond Williams (1976) once pointed out that the word "media" derives from the word "medium," referring to *the middle* (169). To "mediate," then, refers to the act of "coming between" two or more different parties. In industrial relations—for example, negotiations between a union and an employer—a mediator is an individual who seeks to come between two sides of a debate. The mediator works with both parties in order to arrive at common ground in the hope of producing a resolution that is mutually satisfactory.

The word has other connotations, too. Anyone who has ever attended a séance or played with a Ouija board knows about the medium in the spiritualist sense—something that acts as the "channel" for communicating with the dead or the spirit world. We tend to think of money—cash—as a "medium of exchange." By this we mean that money makes possible the transfer of goods and services from one person to another. The claim that television serves as a medium for advertising (that is, bringing audiences closer to products) is another example of this secondary understanding of media. Here, media represent not only a "coming between," but a means through which communication takes place. We can certainly think of media technologies, such as radio or television, in this sense of the word.

Another way of understanding media is arguably the most common. Here, we tend to think of media as the agencies, organizations, companies, and industries that make media texts for consumption by large groups of people. One can think of newspapers, magazines, television networks, or advertising agencies as "the media," and their activities as acts of "mass communication." Such acts are made possible through the development of broadcasting technologies, such as satellites, cable systems, wireless communication, and networking. This other conceptualization of media, then, is as much technical as it is institutional.

From this discussion we can see that what we normally consider as "media" come in different shapes, sizes, and forms. To restrict our understanding of media to "mass media," then, misses the many different forms of communication that *mediate*—or "come between"—different aspects of social life. These media forms include objects as diverse as clock radios, interpretive dance, and billboards. Even a carton of milk can serve as a medium: the carton transports the milk and acts as a platform for displaying the brand, the kind of milk, and nutritional information. In some cases, the carton serves as a billboard to announce contests or seek the whereabouts of missing children.

KEY CONCEPT

Limiting our understanding of media to "mass media" causes us to overlook other forms of communication that *mediate*— or come between—different aspects of social life.

As many have pointed out (see Chapter 4 in this volume), bodies themselves can serve as media. Talking to people on what we now call a "one-to-one level" (as opposed to broadcasting) involves the use of expressions, gestures, sounds, and smells, all of which play out through the medium of the body itself (for example, see Marvin 2006). It is true that with the rise of digital technologies and the proliferation of new devices, we are in an age of abundant media, but it would be untrue to say that this phenomenon is unprecedented. We have had lots and lots of media in the past; the fact that we have more of it now than ever before is worth noting, but not at the expense of an understanding that we have had many media long before anyone logged on to a computer.

Messages, Senders, and Receivers

Regardless of their number and the variety of functions that media offer users, we can say, following John Durham Peters (2010), that "every medium has a 'what,' a 'how' and a 'by/to whom'" (266). By this, Peters indirectly refers to one of the early scholars in communication, Harold Lasswell (1948), who considered communication as a series of questions: "Who says what to whom in which channel with what effect?" Both conceptualizations of media, themselves separated by 60 years, share the common understanding that the raw materials of communication involve a message, a means of delivery, and some combination of senders and receivers. The tendency with the study of media has been to focus on its technological components; both Peters's and Lasswell's conceptualizations remind us of the primacy of actors—people—in the mediated experience of human communication.

> **KEY CONCEPT**
> The raw materials of communication involve a message, a means of delivery, and some combination of senders and receivers.

To put it a different way, what all media share is that they come between us and a range of social situations and processes. This is what we mean by *mediation*. One has only to go to an automated teller machine (ATM) to remember how the social situation we call "banking" has changed over time, from human to computerized interfaces standing between you and your money. Banking is now less about withdrawal slips, signatures, and tellers and more about personal identification numbers (PINs) and computer terminals. What is true about the example of banking is true about a number of different aspects of contemporary social life; the fact that banking is a mediated experience, however, remains unchanged.

Many Media, Many Functions

If we accept the argument that there are many different media forms, then determining their functions would seem to be an equally complex task. However, a medium's functionality is very particular. For something to have a function means that it performs a specific task or tasks, such as thinking, or has some physical purpose. We associate function with work or class, for example.

> *For something to have a function means that it performs a specific task.*

As another example, one performs one's function as master of ceremonies at a wedding by welcoming the audience, making jokes about the wedding party, introducing the speakers, and leading the group in a celebratory toast. The term also has a particular meaning in the context of computers—functions provide the roadmap for computerized operations. A computer may be able to perform a particular function, such as saving a document, if those responsible for programming have taught it that performing the function

SIDEBAR

Approaches to Media Studies: Media Effects Versus Uses and Gratifications

How may we account for the enjoyment we get when we watch a comedy? How do media make everyday situations—such as listening to an iPod while waiting for the bus—more enjoyable? Different approaches to media studies have sought answers to these questions.

In the "media effects" approach, critics tend to subscribe to one of two possible arguments. The first argument asserts that audiences are passive recipients of media messages (that is, people do what their television tells them to do). We hear this logic all the time, whenever people complain that radio and television give us only "dumbed down" versions of the news. A second argument glorifies the transformative effects of media technologies—witness the current fascination with social media. This argument also views media consumers as fundamentally passive.

Although the media effects approach has some validity, both arguments above rely on weak assumptions about causality. That is, they both rest on the assumption that the media have a direct causal effect on us when in fact, there is little evidence to support claims of a one-to-one relationship between technological change and social change.

The "uses and gratifications" approach, on the other hand, works from the opposite premise: that people are not merely passive consumers, but are generally knowledgeable about the media available to them and selectively make optimal use of them. This approach acknowledges the multiple ways in which media enhance our lives, and plays down the more dubious ways in which we sometimes make use of them (see Katz, Blumler, and Gurevitch 1974).

---

of *control + s* (or *command + s*) activates its "save" function. In both these very different senses, then, the word "function" encapsulates both the action of the thing itself, and those entrusted to perform those tasks. This idea— that function attaches people to things—lies at the heart of the three functional aspects of media that follow.

The function of media is, at its heart, about attaching people to things.

The Communicative Function

In its most basic sense, the primary function of media is communicative. Media serve as the means through which we communicate with one another. We use the word "platforms" to describe the different ways in which people now view movies, television programs, and more. While the use here is intended to draw attention to the different gadgets ("Watch TV on your iPod!"), we can also see a platform in the literal sense, as the place, the jumping-off point, in which communication takes place, where images, messages, and ideas "move" from one person and place to another. Whether in the form of blogs or bodies, televisions or trumpets, each form of media makes possible the production, circulation, and reception of messages from one person to another in a given place and time. Media, then, enable the transfer of ideas, which is the basis of the modern understanding of communication itself.

Media's communicative function is primarily representative in nature.

If media have a communicative function, then we also must accept that the primary nature of that communication is *representative*. Despite our best intentions, we never truly communicate everything that we are thinking in every situation. Our communication is always mediated by many different factors, including our ability with language, social protocols that govern basic situations with rules and cultural codes, or laws that prohibit certain kinds of communication. Of course, acts such as writing, painting, dancing, playing a musical instrument, or shooting a movie are attempts at representation—to talk about joy or pain, to comment about politics, or to tell a story. These acts use representational forms, symbols, images, and ideas to "get the point across." All media forms, then, make possible modes of communication that are representative in nature.

The representative function of media makes it a popular area for scholarly analysis. Some critics are primarily interested in the study of discourse—the form of the message itself, how language is used to communicate meaning and truth in our world. Other approaches seek to make sense of the way images, sounds, or other forms of communication, made possible through media, serve to represent particular ideas, assumptions, moments in time, and so on. Because those representations play an important role in helping us make sense of one another and the world around us, scholars pay close attention to how our media represent the world. The representation of women, the representation of political figures, the depictions of such issues as war, the economy, or technology, are thus important because they are based on an understanding that the way something is represented is also the way in which that thing is communicated and, for the most part, is then understood.

Communication Biases

Many scholars have suggested that communication technologies are *biased* in that they privilege one form of speaking over others. Harold Innis (1952/1991) wrote that folklore, passed orally from generation to generation, was biased in time (passing from one generation to another), while paper and print was biased in space (allowing the message or image to move around from place to place). Although we may not routinely think of media in these terms, we implicitly think about the relationship between the formal aspects of media and the kinds of communication they make possible. Do blogs lend themselves to confrontational discourse? Some people think they do; others note confrontations in situations that lend themselves to confrontation, such as political debates. What about people whom we characterize as being "bad on the phone" because of the tone of their voice or their apparent lack of interactivity? How about people who appear more confident on Twitter than in person? Many students frequently say that they are better at writing essay questions than completing multiple-choice exams. If we take them at their word, then what emerges is that some people feel as though they can communicate in some contexts better than in others.

These examples also underscore the point that despite our quest for better and better communication, acts of communication are never pure, never perfect, never evenly distributed from one person to the next. It is safe to say that the primary feature of communication is how much *miscommunication* or *non-communication* takes place around any communicative act. We routinely miss the message; we did not get the signal, or are not able to communicate back. We routinely misunderstand one another, cannot catch the nuance of someone's words or "body language," or think that someone saying one thing is saying something different entirely.

Acts of communication are never pure and never perfect.

These are the unintended cases, but of course there are other cases where miscommunication is the intended result. For example, we associate the word **spin** with acts of public relations, in which politicians, corporations, or celebrities use the same means of communication as the "gutter press" to recuperate their image or advance their own opinion. Other times we tell lies about people to gain advantage or to impugn someone. In still others, we complain that politicians never give citizens a straight answer on matters of shared concern, using the floor of the House of Commons to engage in "political theatre" or to speak in vague terms that cloud, rather than clarify, our understanding of the topic.

spin
An example of intended miscommunication, in which the audience is given distorted information in order to shape their views.

If we were to keep track of all communication taking place in the world, we would likely find that more people miscommunicate than successfully communicate with one another. As in the video game *Angry Birds*, the messages miss their targets more than they hit them, either on purpose or by accident. Despite the rhetoric that comes with new technologies that they will make communication better and more efficient, it

KEY CONCEPT
The emergence of new communication technologies multiplies the potential for miscommunication.

could also be argued that new technologies simply multiply the opportunities for miscommunication that came with the old technologies. Seen this way, the fact that one fails to "get the point across" in an email or over the telephone is a technical matter. The potential—indeed, the promise—of miscommunication remains a part of communication regardless of the medium.

The Empowering and Disempowering Function

We can also think of the function of media in terms of power. We know the ways in which propaganda campaigns exercised by the state exert power over populations. We talk about how the ownership of media companies that are concentrated in the hands of a few large corporations may inhibit the quality of public discourse. We know about the ways that states can control the flows of communication by monitoring what is said and not said on the Internet, or shutting down the Internet altogether, as some countries have tried to do in order to contain pro-democracy protests. If we see protesters' bodies serving as media, then we are well aware of the role played by protests in bringing about social change, of speaking truth to power.

All these examples point us in the direction of thinking about media as having an **empowering** function. Media, then, serve as the means through which dominant ideas are communicated, and thus are part of the exercise of power by some groups over others. Media also serve to empower those who wish to resist power. The production of "alternative media," from pamphlets to blogs, illustrates how media can communicate over distance, represent the world in different ways, and give expression to people whose voices have not been heard. (See Chapter 11 in this volume.)

Of course, we can also think of the empowering features of media in technical terms. Just look at all those dials, buttons, and "apps." Each of them permits what technology people call "functionality," allowing us to save a document, look up the weather, check on arriving flights, or turn appliances on and off. Much of the debate affecting the television industry today is that—with the rise of personal video recorders (PVRs), the proliferation of television shows available on DVDs, and the rise of on-demand television opportunities through cable providers and services like iTunes and Netflix—people now have the power to skip over commercials. Previously, audiences were exposed to commercials in return for free access to programming, and this understanding drove the economic engine of the entertainment industry for much of the 20th century. The discourse that now customers "have the power" in new ways is, in part, due to the emergence of additional functionality, which has altered the experience of watching television, for good or ill.

empower
A function of media that allows them to exert or confer power; it applies to both dominant media and those who use media to resist power.

We are all aware of the ways in which the empowering function of media by some may well result in a parallel function—the *disempowering* of others. The examples are numerous: the fact that running a broadcasting operation is an expensive venture (and in Canada, a vast bureaucratic one) means that others may find it difficult to participate, and thus some voices may be heard more often than others. The fact that we live in a world with so many media may also have the effect of disempowering people who wish to live "off the grid," people who do not want to have Facebook profiles, hold Twitter accounts, or be available by email seven days a week.

Many people have trumpeted the vast power of social networking in serving as a platform for protest and social organization. This assertion is true; the medium does offer the potential to develop ways to empower people who do not have power in other spheres. However, as people in Burma, China, or, more recently, Egypt are well aware, the Internet can be turned off as quickly as it has been turned on. The same means of empowerment can also be used to monitor people's activities. A media technology can be used to extend the means of surveillance as well as organize protest. The empowering and disempowering functions of media, then, need to be considered in tandem when we examine the functionality of media.

The Public Service Function

Few people have the means to operate a radio station, television network, or newspaper. In the case of broadcasting, bandwidth—frequencies or channels— is a scarce commodity; only a few companies or organizations can broadcast over the air. In Canada, as in most other countries, broadcasting is seen as a privilege; in return for that privilege, the broadcaster is expected to devote some of its time to fulfilling a public service function. Such activity draws attention to the fact that although the main purpose of most media companies is to earn a profit, some operations will be carried out without that objective in mind. This is the principle behind many television news organizations, which rarely make money but exist as a public service, bringing news and information to viewers about events and issues in their communities and globally. Many networks offer public service announcements (PSAs) that notify viewers about matters of shared interest and publicize social issues

Figure 5.1 CBC Radio

The creation of public broadcasters in Britain, Canada, and elsewhere in the 1920s and 1930s reflected the belief that the then new medium of radio had a vital public service function.

SOURCE: CBC.

such as problem gambling or alcoholism. The existence of public broadcasting, such as the CBC in Canada, exemplifies the belief that media should act in the service of the public.

The notion that some media, such as broadcasting, should perform a public service function has been one of the most powerful ways of thinking about the media. The establishment of public broadcasting in Britain and Canada was based on the belief that the new medium of radio offered the potential to serve the public interest, providing entertainment, news and information, and cultural enrichment such as theatre, opera, and literature. Although the public service function does not necessarily increase a broadcaster's profit, many countries have decided that broadcasting should be free of commercial content in order to allow public broadcasting to develop and flourish.

The Lack of Access to Means of Communication

If media permit participation in new ways, they also make it more difficult for people who choose not to participate or, for a variety of reasons, cannot participate. One fact about Internet access that is often overlooked is the requirement of a certain level of income to afford a computer and a monthly access fee, not to mention the technological literacy needed to power computers, to surf the Internet, to compose sentences, to distinguish between a legitimate message and one with nefarious intent, and so on.

One of the striking features of many new media technologies is that they appear to prevent the user from fixing them when they break, largely because they obscure the means by which they are manufactured. A quick look under the hood of your car is a case in point; whereas previously one could act on one's car through the use of hand tools, such as wrenches and screwdrivers, to address "that pinging sound," such tools are effectively useless now, when many machines largely function behind "black boxes" understood only by highly specialized mechanics. In other cases, we call a customer service representative to ask for something, only to learn that "the computer won't let us do that." Leaving aside the issue that many of us would have needed help even with the screwdriver, and that there are plenty of instances where requests are ignored for other reasons, the principle here is the same. The same media, whether computers or people, that enable and empower us to accomplish tasks we could not conceivably do on our own, now actively frustrate our plans.

remediation
An evolutionary process in which newer media remind us of, and are intertwined with, older media.

The Remedial Function

The third function that media perform is **remedial**. That is, our newest media remind us about the older technologies and ways of communication that came before them. Drawing attention to the remedial function of media has the effect of driving us toward an understanding of the *historicity* of mediated experience.

Marshall McLuhan (1964) famously observed that the content of one medium is effectively another medium. In their book *Remediation* (1999), Jay David Bolter and Richard Grusin note the ways in which older media forms adapt to the emergence of newer media forms in order to ensure their own continued existence. This has, for Bolter and Grusin, a double effect: it both blends together old media forms in new ways, and at the same time promotes a mode of communication that is closer to the "real thing" than that which preceded it:

> Many web sites are riots of diverse media forms—graphics, digitized photographs, animation, and video—all set up in pages whose graphic design principles recall the psychedelic 1960s or Dada in the 1910s and 20s. Hollywood films, such as *Natural Born Killers* and *Strange Days*, mix media and styles unabashedly. Televised news programs feature multiple video streams, split-screen displays, composites of graphics and text—a welter of media that is somehow meant to make the news more perspicuous [easy to understand]. Even webcams, which operate under the logic of immediacy, can be embedded into a hypermediate web site where the user can select from a "jukebox" of webcam images to generate her own paneled display. (Bolter and Grusin 1999, 9)

One can see how Bolter and Grusin's analysis can easily be applied to the current media landscape. The social networking site Facebook is an amazing achievement, one mythologized in articles hailing the genius of its creator, Mark Zuckerberg. Perhaps its greatest accomplishment is in bringing together a whole range of old media. Facebook combines the mail (the written letter, the email, the text, and the "tweet") along with the address book, the desk calendar (in which we used to write friends' birthdays), the phonebook, the professional directory, the music video, the video game, instant messaging, and so on. The now passé practice of throwing werewolf bites at our friends reminds us of the gestural or embodied practices of communication by touch. Writing on one's "wall" testifies to some of the earliest surfaces of communication itself (Wagman 2010). Finally, is there anything more prominent on Facebook than the photograph, a medium that is nearly 200 years old?

If we want to go back even further, we could say, as Carolyn Marvin does, that the computer is simply the telegraph with a lot of memory (1988, 3). Such a claim is not as far-fetched as it may initially appear; one can easily

Figure 5.2 The "news crawl"
The leftward-running scroll of breaking news at the bottom of cable news broadcasts reminds us of older media forms, like the telegraph.

recognize things as diverse as the Facebook status update, the tweet and the "news crawl" that runs across the bottom third of cable television news channels as hearkening back to the tickertape of the telegraph systems (Carey 1989, 201–30). That reference is itself a nod to the way a practice like "the news" has been subjected to remediation, reminding us of the once-dominant means by which news (business, then current events) travelled across time and space, and the companies (wire services) that offered it (for example, see Read 1992). On the backs of new technologies, then, rest a lot of remediated media, technologies that themselves were the processes of individual and cultural innovation and adaptation. The fact that Facebook makes communication clean and instantaneous is one worth noting; the fact that it reshuffles and remediates old media in new and interesting ways is something different entirely. While certainly not its intention, what Facebook makes possible, through its remediation of "older" media, is to make those very old media present and visible, even in the context that we refer to as "new."

Thinking of media as serving a remedial function has another effect: it challenges the way we talk about "new" media and technologies. Indeed, our culture has tended to privilege the *newness* of new media, as when we talk about the ways in which new media forms displace old ones. Although computers have been with us, in some shape or form (as calculating machines, and now as machines for "surfing"), since the mid-1800s, we tend to talk about computing as "new media." Even the Internet is called "new," although it too has been around for over 20 years. As Benjamin Peters (2009) notes, such arguments are arguments about history, about the tension between the continuity of human societies over time and the rates and means by which humans change their society.

Thinking of the remedial function of media, then, allows us to follow Peters's suggestion to "push beyond the commonsense fact that history is past and that new media is now" (2009, 15). If we are reminded that old and new media forms co-exist, and that there remains considerable "residue" of old media in the makeup of new media, we are more likely to consider the social, cultural, legal, economic, and aesthetic developments that make our new media seem new. BlackBerry devices and iPhones rely on 3G networks and wireless communication, but they also rely on typewriters, or touchpads that have the features of typewriters (the QWERTY keyboard), to make them the commodities that they are today. The existence of wireless networks themselves is a reminder of those that came before, taking us back to the use of networking in telegraphy and radio, and more importantly, to the invention that has made it all possible—electricity.

Conclusion

This chapter has argued that media serve three basic functions: they communicate, they empower, and they historicize. Choosing these three functions was intended to draw attention to three aspects present in all media forms: the power to represent, the power to bring about or frustrate action, and the power to remember and re-remember.

What ties these three functions together is that regardless of the medium, an appreciation of the function of media is an appreciation of the ways in which media are used in many different elements of daily life. The new media of the 21st century are technological marvels; they do many things, they store a considerable amount of memory, they make communication instantaneous and efficient, they allow us to produce, distribute, and engage with popular culture in new and interesting ways. But such capabilities in and of themselves tell us little unless we can appreciate the different ways in which people use media in their daily lives. Roger Silverstone (1994, 2–4) wrote that it is the "dailiness" of television—the fact that it is always on, the fact that we watch it on a daily basis, the fact that it remains the primary way in which much of the world gets information about the rest of the world—that gives the medium its meaning.

While indeed television may be changing for those of us with access to a multimedia world, the point of Silverstone's observation remains that an understanding of media is an understanding of the *social contexts in which they are used*. A function without someone to utilize that function is like a call unanswered, present but ignored. Thinking about the ways in which people put media "into play," the varied ways in which media come to be used, and which may differ from or extend their original intention, help us to remember that they serve primarily as *tools* that we use to make sense of the world around us.

Media serve primarily as tools that we use to make sense of the world around us.

It is also the case that in describing all that media "do," we can consider their flipside, all that these same media allow *not* to happen. While media technologies make some things possible, they also make it possible for things not to be done. The proliferation of media technologies with recording capabilities now enable many ordinary people to serve as journalists, documenting and reporting on what others say and do. Those same media also make it difficult for people to live in privacy, without having to worry that their activities will be recorded or disseminated without their permission. Thinking of the function of media in terms of their uses and misuses helps us to consider, in broad terms, the complex and contradictory roles they play within society at large.

NOTE

1. For example, communication theorist Denis McQuail (2000, 79–80) has identified five different functions of media. The first is *informational*. Media can provide information about events and conditions in society and the world. The second function is *correlational*. Here McQuail means that media can offer explanations of events, provide support for established forms of authority, coordinate activities, and contribute to consensus building. The third function of media is to provide *continuity*. Here media can express the opinions of the dominant culture and can determine the extent to which that culture may recognize subcultures or marginal groups. The fourth function is *entertainment*. Here media serve to provide diversion and relaxation and reduce social tension. Finally, the fifth function is *mobilization*, in that media can serve to organize groups of people in the spheres of politics, war, or religion in pursuit of a shared set of goals.

DISCUSSION QUESTIONS

1. Although this chapter focuses on three key functions of media, the author acknowledges in the introduction that there are others, and suggests that the reader add his or her own. Having read this chapter, what other media functions can you think of?
2. Can you think of examples in which acts of communication can be discouraged as well as encouraged? Explain.
3. We tend to focus most of our attention on the impact of new technologies on the way we live. What are some ways in which "old media" still remain important?

SUGGESTED RESOURCES

Acland, Charles, ed. 2007. *Residual Media*. Minnesota: University of Minnesota Press.

Couldry, Nick. 2002. *The Place of Media Power*. London: Routledge.

Curran, James. 2002. *Media and Power*. London: Routledge.

Edgerton, David. 2006. *The Shock of the Old*. Oxford, UK: Oxford University Press.

Gitelman, Lisa. 2008. *Always Already New*. Cambridge, MA: MIT Press.

Peters, John Durham. 1999. *Speaking into the Air*. Chicago: University of Chicago Press.

REFERENCES

Bolter, Jay David, and Richard Grusin. 1999. *Remediation*. Cambridge, MA: MIT Press.

Carey, James. 1989. *Communication as Culture*. New York: Routledge.

Innis, Harold. 1952/1991. *The Bias of Communication*. Toronto: University of Toronto Press.

Katz, E., J.G. Blumler, and M. Gurevitch. 1974. "Utilization of Mass Communication by the Individual." In *The Uses of Mass Communications: Current Perspectives of Gratifications Research*, edited by J.G. Blumler and E. Katz, 19–32. Beverly Hills, CA: Sage.

Lasswell, Harold. 1948. "The Structure and Function of Communication in Society." In *The Communication of Ideas*, edited by Lyman Bryson, 37–51. New York: Harper and Row.

Marvin, Carolyn. 1988. *When Old Technologies Were New*. Oxford, UK: Oxford University Press.

Marvin, Carolyn. 2006. "Communication as Embodiment." In *Communication as ... Perspectives on Theory*, edited by Gregory Shepherd, Jeffrey St. John, and Ted Striphas, 67–74. Thousand Oaks, CA: Sage.

McLuhan, Marshall. 1964. *Understanding Media: The Extensions of Man*. New York: McGraw-Hill.

McQuail, Denis. 2000. *McQuail's Mass Communication Theory*. Thousand Oaks, CA: Sage.

Peters, Benjamin. 2009. "And Lead Us Not into Thinking the New Is New: A Bibliographic Case for New Media History." *New Media and Society* 11(1&2):13–30.

Peters, John Durham. 2010. "Mass Media." In *Critical Terms for Media Studies*, edited by W.J.T. Mitchell and Mark B.N. Hansen, 266–79. Chicago: University of Chicago Press.

Read, Donald. 1992. *The Power of News: The History of Reuters*. Oxford, UK: Oxford University Press.

Silverstone, Roger. 1994. *Television and Everyday Life*. London: Routledge.

Wagman, Ira. 2010. "Log On, Goof Off, and Look Up: Facebook and the Rhythms of Canadian Internet Use." In *How Canadians Communicate* (3rd ed.), edited by Bart Beaty, Derek Briton, Gloria Filax, and Rebecca Sullivan, 55–77. Athabasca, AB: Athabasca University Press.

Williams, Raymond. 1976. *Keywords*. London: Croom Helm/Fontana.

CHAPTER 6 / MICHAEL DARROCH
Language and Media

How is language a medium for representing and operating in our world? Should we consider language a technology? How do new media technologies affect how we speak, read, and write?

KEY CONCEPTS

1. *Semiotics* is the study of signs and symbols, especially as means of language or communication.

2. *Dialogism* is the theory that linguistic meaning is produced only through dialogue between speakers of a language.

3. *Orality*—spoken communication—has fundamentally different characteristics than written language.

4. Electronic and digital media have transformed the ways in which we speak, read, and write.

CHAPTER OUTLINE

Introduction: "Voices in the Air" 89

The Semiotic Approach: Language as a Symbolic System of Representation 91

Dialogism: Language as an Expression of Self and Other 93

Language Through Eyes and Ears: Oral and Written Traditions 96

Language in Electronic and Digital Culture 101

Humans and Machines: Machine Translation and Digital Speech Technologies 105

Conclusion 107

Discussion Questions 108

Suggested Resources 108

References 109

Introduction: "Voices in the Air"

Today, many people feel that we should be able to speak to our communications devices as often as we type or punch in commands. There is a long history to the technical research that has led to the development of machines that can both understand our human languages and even speak back to us. However, only in the late 20th and early 21st centuries has listening to or interacting with automated voices and speech technologies become a familiar, everyday event. In a June 2006 commentary for the *New York Times*, entitled "Voices in the Air," writer Mark Allen cheerfully recounted how familiar the electronic voice of the New York subway announcement system had become for him:

> My first relationship started more than a decade ago. We met at the Delancey Street subway stop, where I used to take the F train to work every morning. It was after I had entered the turnstile and walked down the platform, out of the view of watching eyes, that I heard her crackling, sputtering voice come through the overhead speakers. Her words thundered throughout the entire station, and her voice seemed goddesslike, but the often-failing technology that voice was coming through made her seem vulnerable. I don't know who the real person was; it was the voice I became friends with. It seemed to live within the very metal and concrete walls of the subway station that greeted me every morning, a maternal voice beating within the heart of the city itself. (Allen 2006)

In recent decades, recorded voices and automated voice assistants have proliferated in many navigational routines of everyday life: elevators announce our arrival at a floor; bank ATMs offer the option of vocal instructions; city buses, subways, and streetcars remind us of the next stop on our route; GPS systems direct drivers to precise destinations; Bluetooth-enabled technologies allow us to interact with automobile dashboards; audio tours guide us through museums and galleries; and voice assistants steer us through mobile phone applications or commercial call centres. "Live" human voices have been displaced from many everyday experiences and routines. Are our human voices now merely one node on a much larger network of speaking things?

One question we need to ask is: Does it matter that language and voices are no longer the domain only of human beings? Prior to electronic and digital voices, language was understood as a uniquely human activity, something that only humans could produce. The human voice was thought to represent a direct connection to the human soul, and language was considered a "channel" into the human mind: the place where rational thought is produced. At the same time, language also represents a clear connection to a community of other human beings. In this sense, language is frequently understood as a defining characteristic of a shared culture. Thus, language has been understood as both an individual activity and a communal activity. In either case, language has clearly been considered fundamentally and uniquely human.

Language has been understood as both an individual activity and a communal activity. But does it matter that it is no longer the domain only of human beings?

But today, we perhaps take for granted that language is also a way of connecting to our non-human media technologies. Is there a relationship between language and media? Writing about new media technologies in the age of electricity, Marshall McLuhan (1954) claimed: "All media, especially languages, are mass media" (6). What does it mean to consider language, that uniquely human faculty of speech, as a medium similar to other technical media? Can we consider (oral and written) language itself to be a kind of technology? Have electronic and digital technologies altered how we speak and write, or how we represent our world through language? How is language connected to other media technologies or systems? This chapter will address these questions. To begin, let us consider two ways in which language has been studied as a human capacity to operate in and represent our world: semiotics and dialogism.

The Semiotic Approach: Language as a Symbolic System of Representation

One theory that seeks to explain how we use language to represent our world is the *semiotic* approach, sometimes called a social constructionist approach to language and representation. This approach was developed principally by Ferdinand de Saussure (1857–1913), a Swiss linguist known as the founder of modern linguistics. Semiotics, or the "science of signs," seeks to describe how we use language to create meaning about our world. Language is a system of representation, and as a system it is governed by certain rules or conventions. The idea of a language system can be extended beyond speech and writing to include images, other sounds, cinema, and more. Does a system of representation— for example, a language system like English—simply reflect the world around us like a mirror? Or rather, do we make meanings about our world only by deploying this system of representation? This latter view is the one adopted by semioticians: our material world is meaningful to us only when we use a language system. According to this understanding, reality is not external to language, but is in part *shaped* by the language that we use. By extension, then, we can perhaps offer a first argument for considering language as a kind of medium: language does not simply mirror, but rather **mediates** (stands between, or is in the middle of) the external world and our interpretations of that world.

> **KEY CONCEPT**
> *Semiotics* is the study of signs and symbols, especially as a means of language or communication.

mediate
To stand between two positions or parties, and convey messages between them.

Langue and Parole

According to Saussure (1916/1966), then, language is most certainly a communal phenomenon. Language is communal because all its users must share certain rules and codes—the basic codes we learn in order to speak that language and to share understandings about our external world. For example,

Noam Chomsky

Noam Chomsky, a linguist as well as a political theorist, developed an approach to language similar to the semiotic approach. He argued that mastering the rules of a language system constitutes a kind of *linguistic competence*, whereas when we produce individual utterances in a given moment, we are engaging in *linguistic performance*. Linguistic performance is determined in part by linguistic competence, but also by psychological and cognitive factors such as memory (Chomsky 1967, 397–442).

English sentences follow the sequence subject–verb–object ("John drank his milk"), but in German many verbs come at the end of a sentence ("*Johann hat seinen Milch getrunken*," or literally, "John has his milk drunk"). Saussure used the term *langue* to refer to this basic structure of language, the communal language system—or the grammar—that all of us use to generate sentences in our languages. He distinguished *langue* from what he called *parole*, or speech. *Parole* is the individual act of using language—that is, any instance in which an actual speaker or writer makes use of *langue* to produce a recognizable linguistic utterance.

Signified, Signifier, Sign

To understand how the system of rules or conventions that constitute language serves to produce meanings, Saussure proposed that language is a system of "signs." A linguistic *sign*, according to Saussure, consists of a union of two elements: on the one hand, there is a form—an image, sound, or word—and on the other hand there is a concept in your mind to which that form refers. You could say that the form, what Saussure called the *signifier*, triggers in your head a corresponding concept, or *signified*. Both these elements are needed to produce a sign; in fact, it is this relationship between the signifier and the signified—the sign—that produces meaning. What is important here is that the sign is entirely *arbitrary* in nature: Saussure wanted us to understand that there is no natural or predetermined relationship between the signifier (form) and the signified (concept). For example, when you read a signifier consisting of the three letters C–A–T, why should it necessarily prompt you to conjure up the mental concept of a small, domesticated, furry pet? Rather, Saussure's point is that the three letters C–A–T are arbitrarily related to that mental concept; their relationship to the "small furry pet" is only the result of our collective cultural and linguistic heritage. One way that we know this relationship is arbitrary, Saussure argued, is that different languages have different signifiers to represent the same or similar mental concepts: the French word *chat* or the German word *Katze* also conjure up the signified concept "cat."

Saussure made several further points about the nature of the sign. First, because there is only an arbitrary relationship between signifier and signified, between the form and the concept, then the sign itself can have no fixed, essential, or ultimate meaning. In fact, Saussure reasoned that language produces meaning only through *difference*: words and images do not signify on their own, because of some intrinsic character, but rather only in distinction to other things. CAT therefore does not signify "small furry pet" of its own accord, but rather through the difference between CAT and DOG, CAT and BIRD, and so on. Distinctions between the sounds of words also mark differences in meaning: thus in English, we are able to make a distinction between the meaning of CAT and CAP based on the difference of one sound. This point can be summed up by stating that it is not signifiers themselves, but rather the *differences between signifiers*, that produce meaning.

Second, signs are therefore elements of a symbolic system of representation, and are defined in relation to other elements of that system. This idea alone tells us that language is a social or communal phenomenon, for here again is the idea of *langue*, the linguistic system or conventions that we all share. "If the relationship between a signifier and its signified is the result of a system of social conventions specific to each society and to specific historical moments—then all meanings are produced within history and culture. They can never be finally fixed but are always subject to change, both from one cultural context and from one period to another" (Hall 1997, 32).

Dialogism: Language as an Expression of Self and Other

Saussure treated language as a system of laws (*langue*) over which speakers have no control (Holquist 1990, 42). Other scholars, such as the Russian literary critic Mikhail Bakhtin (1895–1975), have opposed this point of view. Bakhtin (1975/1981) developed a different theory of language, which he called *dialogism*. He opposed the idea that language resides solely outside the individual as a symbolic system of representation. By the same token, he also opposed the idea that the individual, the self, uniquely controls language and meaning. For Bakhtin, meanings are produced in *dialogue*, when different speakers of language speak to one another.

Speaking as a Social Activity

Like Saussure, Bakhtin did believe that language is both individual and social. However, Saussure placed the emphasis on the social system of language—*langue*—rather than on the individual act of speaking—*parole*. He did not believe that we could study *parole* effectively. In contrast, Bakhtin considered the individual act of speaking itself to be an inescapably *social* activity. In his view, every linguistic

> **KEY CONCEPT**
> *Dialogism* is the theory that linguistic meaning is produced only through dialogue between speakers of a language.

utterance (spoken or written) presumes there is someone out there listening or reading, someone else who can interpret what was said. Thus, every linguistic utterance is a dialogue: all speech and written texts are created with an *audience* or *addressee* in mind.

Bakhtin's emphasis on the diversity of speakers has several implications. On the one hand, he suggests that all meaning is generated through the differences between speakers, who enter a kind of struggle over meaning. Everything we say is potentially adapted and modified by other speakers. This may be a positive implication if we believe that a diversity of opinions is generally beneficial. On the other hand, the fact that meaning resides between speakers suggests that meaning is never finally fixed. If we accept these assumptions, then no one person, group, or nation can ever assert a certain or fixed identity: what it "means" to be Canadian or Québécois, North American or European, can be understood only in the context of dialogue between these various groups.

PRIMARY SOURCE

Dialogism

According to Bakhtin (1981, 293–94):

> The word in language is half someone else's. It becomes "one's own" only when the speaker populates it with his own intention, his own accent, when he appropriates the word, adapting it to his own semantic and expressive intention. Prior to this moment of appropriation, the word does not exist in a neutral and impersonal language (it is not, after all, out of a dictionary that the speaker gets his words!), but rather it exists in other people's mouths, in other people's contexts, serving other people's intentions: it is from there that one must take the word, and make it one's own.

Power and Resistance

Another important implication of Bakhtin's theory of dialogism is the idea that speakers stand in different relationships of power to one another. These relationships are represented through the positions that speakers hold in the course of dialogue. If linguistic interactions involve a struggle over meaning, then the different perspectives of speakers can also come into conflict in this struggle. Bakhtin used the term *heteroglossia*—the presence of two or more voices or viewpoints—to describe these different registers of language and power found in our everyday world. Speakers with greater social power may be in a position to impose certain perspectives on others. The imposition of a dominant perspective might seem to diminish dialogue and create a condition of monologue or *monoglossia*, where one dominant viewpoint prevails. Yet, Bakhtin's point is that no one person or group can ever fundamentally control the production of meaning. Even if a disparity in power allows the voices of the powerful to prevail at one moment in time, the voices of others will always seek to resist this domination. In some notable cases, cultural communities facing discrimination from mainstream society have reappropriated (reclaimed) negative labels in a newer, positive sense. For example, consider how today the word *queer*, at one time a pejorative term for homosexuality, has been reclaimed by gay-lesbian-bisexual-transgendered communities in a positive sense, such as when we speak of *queer rights*. Such an act of reappropriation demonstrates community solidarity through language use and serves to deprive the term of its previously negative connotations.

Figure 6.1 Reclaiming language

Perhaps the most notable example of a formerly pejorative term that has been reclaimed is the radically altered use of the word "queer." Nowadays, people speak of queer rights, there are queer film festivals, and even queer studies programs at some universities.

SOURCE: Lunamania.org.

· Bakhtin's studies of language also have broad implications for understanding the values we attribute to differences between individual ways of speaking, local dialects, or national languages. In one sense, each speaker possesses an *idiolect*, a form of language unique to the person speaking in a given historical context (only you speak the way you do at any given time). At the same time, by recognizing that all meaning in the world is made through dialogue with others, we recognize that language has social characteristics that take shape at many complex and competing levels. For example, slangs and other local vernaculars of certain communities, subcultures, and racial groups have historically been rejected as legitimate or acceptable forms of language. To counter this belief, the socio-linguist William Labov (1972) famously demonstrated that speakers of inner-city Black English Vernacular have just as well developed a vocabulary, and are just as capable of conceptual learning, as any other speaker of English.

Where Saussure had described a linguistic utterance as taking one of two discrete forms, either spoken or written, Bakhtin conceived an utterance as

Language has social characteristics that take shape at many complex and competing levels—slang, for example.

a complex whole comprising both these activities. The next section discusses other scholars who have maintained that spoken and written traditions of language have very different attributes.

Language Through Eyes and Ears: Oral and Written Traditions

Orality and Literacy

Another approach to language (often associated with Marshall McLuhan) is the notion that orality—spoken communication—has fundamentally differ-ent characteristics from those of written language. Some have argued that the introduction of written language transformed the ways in which we speak, and that human cultures enjoyed a "primary orality" before the technology of writing was intro-duced (Ong 1982). But once introduced, writing transforms an oral culture into a literate culture. A literate person, Walter Ong (1982) has argued, is a human being "whose thought pro-cesses do not grow out of simply natural powers but out of these powers as structured, directly or indirectly, by the technology of writing" (77). In other words, writing is first and foremost a media technology—one that requires tools and equipment (whether pens or keypads) to represent the active, spoken sounds of oral language in the passive space of a page or screen (80–81). For Ong, the technology of writing deeply penetrates the inner workings of a literate human being's mind, even to the point of how this person speaks: "Without writing, the literate mind would not and could not think as it does, not only when it is engaged in writing, but normally even when it is composing its thoughts in oral form" (77). Ong's under-standing of written language as a visual medium contrasts to Saussure's contention above, that written language is merely a substitution for auditory signifiers: "Because [writing] moves speech from the oral–aural to a new sensory world, that of vision, it transforms speech and thought as well" (Ong 1982, 84).

> **KEY CONCEPT**
>
> *Orality*—spoken communi-cation—has fundamentally different characteristics from those of written language.

Phonetic Alphabet

Scholars such as Ong and Eric Havelock, a scholar of Classics, have argued that in Western history, a major shift toward a written tradition occurred in ancient Greece: the development of the basic alphabet that we use today. While previous civilizations, such as the Sumerians in ancient Mesopotamia, had developed sophisticated writing systems, these systems lacked one im-portant characteristic that has allowed the modern alphabet to persist in its basic form for thousands of years: the representation of *vowels*, or what we know today as our *phonetic alphabet*. Hebrew and Arabic, and other Semitic languages, to this day do not have letters to represent vowel sounds, only consonants. Such written languages require a reader to know how to speak the language in order to pronounce written words—that is, in order to be able to fill in the unrepresented vowels. With the Greek introduction of vowels, the alphabet became more flexible: it was not tied to a specific language, but rather could represent the spectrum of sounds of any language system (Ong 1982, 89). As McLuhan (1964) summed up, "the phonetic alphabet, by a few letters only, was able to encompass all languages. Such an achievement, however, involved the separation of both signs and sounds from their semantic and dramatic meanings. No other system of writing had accomplished this feat" (90).

On the one hand, then, the phonetic alphabet presented a remarkably flexible power: the capacity to **transliterate**, or translate, the languages of oral societies that had never developed an accompanying written language. On the other hand, this power has not always been welcomed. For example, some attempts to transliterate First Nations languages into the English alphabet have resulted in controversy about who speaks for these societies. Here again, we face an example where language has become the contested space of power relations between cultures and groups.

transliterate
To adapt or convert languages that have different alphabets or systems, including oral languages and sign languages.

The Resilient Power of Orality

Different writing systems are thus sometimes described as something like "downloaded" forms of primary oral languages. From this point of view, written languages made it possible to record all those spoken utterances that disappear once uttered. From another point of view, however, certain forms of oral language—such as epic storytelling—never simply disappeared in the first place. Rather, epic stories were structured in specific ways so that they could be memorized. Many *ways of speaking* are passed from generation to generation without ever, or rarely, entering into the world of written communication. Another example is children's rhymes. Many common rhymes repeated today on the playground have been passed down for centuries, but are recorded in writing only in specialized volumes such as indexes of nursery rhymes.

SIDEBAR

Children's Rhymes

One example of a common form of oral storytelling that is not typically written down are the games and rhymes that children pass on to one another on the playground, such as:

> It's raining, it's pouring,
> The old man is snoring.
> He got into bed
> And bumped his head
> And couldn't get up in the morning.

In a famous study, Opie and Opie (1959) tracked how certain children's rhymes can even follow a remarkable "speed of oral transmission" while rarely entering the adult world. Can you remember such rhymes from your own schoolyard days?

Linearity and Non-Linearity

This discussion has come some way in considering relationships between speaking and writing. One further aspect of orality differentiates McLuhan and Ong's perspectives from those of Ferdinand de Saussure, whose work is discussed earlier in this chapter. Saussure suggested that written language, as a linear pattern of successive marks or notations across a page, mimics spoken language as a succession of sounds across time (Saussure 1966, 24–25; Ong 1982, 17). In contrast, McLuhan (like his student, Walter Ong) argued that written forms of language—including handwriting and printed text—had a fundamentally different structure than oral forms of language. McLuhan believed that oral communication involved a simultaneous exchange of viewpoints. The back-and-forth nature of oral communication—its non-linear nature—is similar to the idea of dialogism discussed previously. In contrast to the non-linear nature of orality, McLuhan thought that print was linear and sequential: one letter comes after another, one word after another, one line after another on a page or screen. For McLuhan, and other scholars like Ong, the sequential format of written language has served to restructure the ways in which human thought, and social patterns, are organized.

Writing, McLuhan claimed, tends to emphasize greater detachment from our emotions and senses. For example, think about all the ways in which you might pronounce the word "tonight" on a mobile phone to indicate emotion, which cannot be so easily represented in writing or a text message. According to McLuhan and Ong, writing gave priority to our sense of vision at the expense of our other senses. **Oral–aural** cultures, or societies organized around speaking and listening, tend to foster greater intimacy and connectivity between people. In contrast, literate cultures, or societies organized around visual and linear written traditions (for example, cultures with complex legal systems, bureaucratic governments, and corporations), tend to foster greater cultural uniformity and individualism.

oral–aural
Oral refers to the voice, and thus speaking; *aural* refers to the ear, or hearing.

Print Technologies and Print Culture

The discussion in this section has focused on differences between speaking and writing. The thesis that powerful social transitions took place, first from orality to cultures of writing, and second from handwriting to cultures of print, has enjoyed great influence. This thesis places a strong emphasis on print technologies, starting with the development of the first printing press by Johannes Gutenberg around the year 1440. Following this line of thinking, the printing press shifted the act of writing from the handwriting of an individual to a mechanism containing movable pieces of type. Ong

PRIMARY SOURCE

Edmund Carpenter

Another colleague of McLuhan, the anthropologist Edmund Carpenter, summed up arguments about orality and literacy in an essay about early mass media entitled "The New Languages" (1957, 4–6):

> Writing, for example, didn't record oral language; it was a new language, which the spoken word came to imitate. Writing encouraged an analytical mode of thinking with emphasis on lineality. Oral languages tended to be polysynthetic, composed of great, tight conglomerates, like twisted knots, within which images were juxtaposed, inseparably fused; written communications consisted of little words chronologically ordered. Subject became distinct from verb, adjective from noun, thus separating actor from action, essence from form. Where preliterate man imposed form diffidently, temporarily—for such transitory forms lived but temporarily on the tip of his tongue, in the living situation—the printed word was inflexible, permanent, in touch with eternity: it embalmed truth for posterity. ...
>
> Gutenberg completed the process. The manuscript page with pictures, colors, correlation between symbol and space, gave way to uniform type, the black-and-white page, read silently, alone. The format of the book favored lineal expression, for the argument ran like a thread. from cover to cover: subject to verb to object, sentence to sentence, paragraph to paragraph, chapter to chapter, carefully structured from beginning to end, with value embedded in the climax. This was not true of great poetry and drama, which retained multi-perspective, but it was true of books, particularly texts, histories, autobiographies, novels. Events were arranged chronologically and hence, it was assumed, causally; relationship, not being, was valued. The author became an *authority*; his data were serious, that is, *serially* organized. Such data, if sequentially ordered and printed, conveyed value and truth; arranged any other way, they were suspect.

(1982) describes this shift as turning writing into a manufacturing process: "Alphabetic letterpress printing, in which each letter was cast on a separate piece of metal, or type, marked a psychological breakthrough of the first order. It embedded the word itself deeply in the manufacturing process and made it into a kind of commodity" (116). Another historian of print, Elizabeth

PRIMARY SOURCE

"An Eye for an Ear"

Marshall McLuhan claimed time and again that writing emphasized vision—the eye—while orality emphasized hearing—the ear:

> The dominant organ of sensory and social orientation in pre-alphabet societies was the ear—"hearing was believing." The phonetic alphabet forced the magic world of the ear to yield to the neutral world of the eye. Man was given an eye for an ear.
>
> Western history was shaped for some three thousand years by the introduction of the phonetic alephbet [*sic*], a medium that depends solely on the eye for comprehension. The alphabet is a construct of fragmented bits and parts which have no semantic meaning in themselves, and which must be strung together in a line, bead-like, and in a prescribed order. Its use fostered and encouraged the habit of perceiving all environment in visual and spatial terms—particularly in terms of a space and of a time that are uniform,
>
> c,o,n,t,i,n,u,o,u,s
>
> and
>
> c-o-n-n-e-c-t-e-d.
>
> The line, the continuum
>
> —this sentence is a prime example—
>
> became the organizing principle of life. "As we begin, so shall we go." "Rationality" and logic came to depend on the presentation of connected and sequential facts or concepts. ...
>
> Rationality and visuality have long been interchangeable terms, but we do not live in a primarily visual world any more. (McLuhan and Fiore 1967/2001, 44–45)

Eisenstein (1979), has described the printing press as a technological "agent of change" that introduced *standardized* usages of language, such as standard ways of spelling words and using punctuation.

However, other scholars of print culture disagree that printing technologies simply standardized the practices of reading and writing, and by extension determined the meanings we make of texts. One criticism of McLuhan and Ong's work is that, ultimately, they privileged speaking over writing: orality, they felt, represented communication that binds people together, whereas writing and other print technologies separated us into individual readers and writers. Scholars of book history, such as Leslie Howsam, challenge the notion that printed texts are "fixed" forms of transmitting knowledge, whereas oral and manuscript forms of transmission are more fluid and adaptable forms of human communication. On the contrary, there is now a consensus "that print does not necessarily serve to fix a text, now or in the past—that print is only relatively less malleable and unstable a form than the computer screen or the copyist's script" (Howsam 2006, 51). From early manuscript culture right through to the print culture of today's screen technologies, human agents have always been involved with producing, distributing, reading, translating, and adapting texts and the meanings they carry. In this sense, print might be viewed more as a catalyst that *assists* social changes, rather than single-handedly producing or determining them (Briggs and Burke 2002, 22).

Eisenstein states that the printing press led to standardized usages of language, while Howsam asserts that printed texts are less "fixed" than they may appear.

Language in Electronic and Digital Culture

Language: One Medium Among Many Channels?

In his books *Discourse Networks 1800/1900* (1990) and *Gramophone, Film, Typewriter* (1999), the German media philosopher Friedrich Kittler argued that another technological shift took place between the 19th and 20th centuries. Up to about the year 1800, print and writing represented the only significant mass medium. Kittler describes the alphabet as a kind of "bottleneck" through which all information flowed. However, the idea of writing as a bottleneck of information was not obvious to the people of this era. For this reason, language and literature were understood to be a mysterious medium in which ancient, pre-linguistic truths were recorded. People's experiences of sights or sounds had to be squeezed through this alphabetic bottleneck—26 letters in different combinations—and deciphered (or in Kittler's view, hallucinated) by readers.

Kittler perceived a shift in people's understanding of media, which occurred in the early 20th century.

By the year 1900, however, a number of new technologies had been developed that broke print's stranglehold on information. These technologies included new ways of recording sound (the gramophone) and images (film). Sounds and sights were now given their own media channels. Written language was no longer the only medium to transmit pictures or sounds. In other words, where language and writing once formed the only medium that could record our experience of the world, by the turn of the 20th century, the world could be recorded through different media streams. As a result, Kittler believes, writers and readers after 1900 became acutely aware of the differences between these media of communication, and language and literature became just one medium among all these others.

The Wonderful Writing Machine

Most of us are so familiar with the so-called QWERTY layout of our computer keyboards that we take for granted the ability to type. But for prior generations, learning to type words, like learning to handwrite, was a matter of serious study. What was the experience of typing for the first generation to use the QWERTY keyboard? An answer to this question is recorded in the book *The Wonderful Writing Machine* by Bruce Bliven (1954, 111–12), a popular history of the typewriter:

> The phrase "learning to type," as it is now used, means learning to type by touch using all eight fingers and both thumbs, although many non-professionals manage to operate the machine successfully with inferior techniques. The prolific writer Irwin Ross, for instance, goes like a bat out of a cave using only one finger of one hand, as if testing to see whether the keys are red hot. His is a most unusual method, for the average hunt-and-peck operator employs at least two fingers, or four, and many, from time to time, sneak in a fifth. Modern touch-typists are modest about their abilities, however, and say, when questioned, "I don't really know how to type; I just use my own system."
>
> By today's standards, no one knew how to type for fifteen years after the typewriter came onto the market. Ten-finger touch technique was not thought of until 1882, and it didn't catch on until 1888. An "expert" or "trained" operator, during all that time, was simply one familiar enough with the arrangement of the keys to go fairly fast, who understood what the various buttons, levers and keys were for, and who could change a ribbon or disengage a jammed type bar.

Figure 6.2 QWERTY

Language and New Media

Since the beginning of the electric age in the mid-19th century, numerous technologies have affected how we use spoken and written language, including the telegraph, telephone, radio, gramophone, typewriter, television, Walkman and MP3 players, digital and other mobile media, as well as speech recognition technologies. For example, communications scholar James Carey has studied how the telegraph, the first electronic medium, also influenced written language:

> The telegraph reworked the nature of written language and finally the nature of awareness itself [demanding] a form of language stripped of the local, the regional, and colloquial. They demanded something closer to a "scientific" language, a language of strict denotation in which the connotative features of utterance were under rigid control. ... [L]anguage had to be flattened out and standardized. The telegraph, therefore, led to the disappearance of forms of speech and styles of journalism and story telling—the tall story, the hoax, much humor, irony, and satire ... . (Carey 1989, 210)

The effect of the telegraph in the 19th century—a flattening out of language into condensed written statements—is comparable to ways that Internet and mobile media have affected written language today. For example, consider the ways in which you abridge your own thoughts when using Twitter, sending SMS messages, or posting status updates on social media platforms.

Similarly, in the early 20th century, radio was initially interpreted as a mass medium with awesome linguistic and acoustic power—the power of one voice to reach and potentially persuade or control the many. For Eric Havelock, the scholar of the ancient Greek alphabet and oral culture mentioned above, the radio promised to change how we think about speaking in today's context:

> The limits of the powers of the human voice from time immemorial had been set by the size of an audience physically present. These were now simply removed. A single voice addressing a single audience on a single occasion could at least theoretically address the entire population of the earth. ... As we now probe orality in history we are probing its partial resurrection in ourselves. (Havelock 1986, 30)

For historians studying orality, such as Ong and Havelock, the radio suggested that we were about to enter a new kind of oral culture.

Today, mobile and smart phones are recognized as technologies with multiple implications for future shifts in language use. Just as oral cultures

The telegraph in the 19th century had an effect on language not unlike the one we are experiencing with digital communication formats today.

persisted historically despite the onset of print culture, so has print consistently been transformed by new media, especially contemporary mobile media. Indeed, in the case of mobile phones, we increasingly write and text using media primarily oriented to speaking. Think, for example, of the casual language we tend to use when posting on social media platforms such as Facebook, the abbreviated forms of language we use when texting or tweeting, or the ability to switch between chatting by typing and speaking by Internet video through a software application such as Skype. As with other auditory technologies, mobile media have produced a new kind of technologically mediated conversation, new ways of speaking and writing through which social life and cultural identities (especially among youth and teenagers) are constructed. In the densely interconnected communities of many multicultural societies, for example, mobile phones have created a new context for mixing languages and **code-switching** (the act of shifting between different languages or dialects). In their study of mobile youth culture, Caron and Caronia (2007, 125) note that

code-switching
Occurs when a person switches between different languages or dialects.

> the mobile phone has transformed spaces (e.g., the street and bus) and times (e.g., before class or after school) into unprecedented opportunities to talk on the phone, and thus increased the number of communicative events available for displays of identity. As the number of routine exchanges increases, new scenarios arise in which everyday language takes on crucial roles such as constructing identity and membership in a cultural community.

How have Internet and mobile technologies affected our writing skills and habits? As students, you may have heard the assertion that young people today write less well than in previous generations, and that new technologies have something to do with this declining ability. New technologies have long been blamed for reducing the standards of language use. As scholars such as Kittler have argued, technologies such as radio, film, and television have consistently threatened to displace written language from the centre of cultural attention. Have today's Internet and mobile media brought about a resurgence of writing through new formats such as email, texting, and posting? Even if we are all writing more often using these different media platforms, do we perhaps now pay less attention to how we write in these everyday activities than previous generations? In what circumstances do we even rely on our technologies to write for us—for example, when we expect word processors to correct our spelling and grammar?

With Internet-based technological changes in the last decades, such as the rise of podcasting and RSS news feeds, or the introduction of ebook readers such as Kindle, one important area of study is the influence of the Internet on languages worldwide. By standardizing written language, the printing press has been credited with promoting linguistic sameness and thereby contributing to the rise of national cultures (Eisenstein 1979; Anderson 1991). From one perspective, the Internet works to standardize language further—for example, by promoting English as an international *lingua franca*. At the same time, the Internet has facilitated the dissemination of histories and perspectives of non-anglophone cultures and also served to promote the preservation of endangered languages. The Internet's influence on local and regional linguistic cultures is perhaps most evident in the growth of national broadcasting systems that operate in different languages, such as the BBC's world radio service that broadcasts in multiple European, Asian, and Middle Eastern languages.

Humans and Machines: Machine Translation and Digital Speech Technologies

In all of the approaches to language and media reviewed so far in this chapter, human beings have occupied a central position: media may affect how humans speak or write about our world, but ultimately it is still humans who do the talking or typing. Today, however, we have witnessed a proliferation of technologies that understand certain linguistic commands, and which can speak back at (and sometimes even for) us.

Machine Translation

Recall that in the approaches of both Saussure (1916/1966) and Bakhtin (1981), meaning is based on difference. For Saussure, differences between signifiers produced meaning; for Bakhtin, meaning was produced only in dialogue between speakers. In the early years of computing technologies, some scientific researchers and philosophers expressed a belief that digital computers would achieve *linguistic universality* by overcoming differences within and between languages. In 1949, the mathematician Warren Weaver outlined his hope for linguistic universality in a memorandum that became the stimulus for machine translation research in the United States (Hutchins 2000, 17). Weaver expected computers to resolve the unending diversity of languages by locating a universal substructure on which all human languages are built. Computing machines, he predicted, would be able to translate between all languages, to build a bridge between different forms of human communication. Weaver's "common base of human communication" (1955, 23) predicts a *universal set of rules* by which all languages must work. However, anyone who has tested online translation applications will know that

Weaver's dream has remained an unfulfilled promise. Sixty years of research and development in the areas of language and speech recognition have taught us one certain thing: designing computer software that can recognize human speech is famously difficult.

Speech Recognition Technologies

While the promise of machine translation has long informed research into speech recognition technologies, by the 1970s speech science began to abandon the search for Weaver's undiscovered universal language. Instead, speech scientists have focused on developing two general approaches to speech recognition: models based on *rules* (similar to a grammar) and models based on *probability*—that is, the most likely or statistically probable match in a database. When a person speaks into a telephone, for example, the speech is recorded. Typically, this recorded speech is broken into smaller sequences of perhaps as little as five milliseconds. These segments are then "filtered"— cleared of any background noise that falls outside the typical bandwidth of human speech, a frequency range of 500 Hz to 2800 Hz. Speech software filters out the information that our ears would isolate as relevant data: human speech versus background noise.

Most of the speech recognition applications that you are familiar with— "apps" on an iPhone, for example, or recognizers in your car—take a hybrid approach: they draw upon both *rule-based* and *statistical* versions of language processing. Rule-based grammars are most accurate when the likelihood of a particular word or phrase is very high, but statistical models are better at dealing with unforeseen or messy input (for example, when a speaker says something unexpected). In either case, speech recognition science accepts that 100 percent recognition is an unachievable goal. (No human recognizes the speech of others 100 percent of the time, either!)

To think about the ways in which computers "recognize" commands or construe meaning, consider the example of a voice-operated iTunes song library. In a rule-based model, the speech recognizer applies a series of preset categories handcrafted by humans: we are asked to choose a genre, an artist, an album, to run shuffle, and so on. In a statistical model, on the other hand, the speech recognizer employs algorithms (finite sequences of instructions) to learn new categories. For example, one could show a computer 100 sentences in which the word "Feist" triggers a certain action (such as "play a song by Feist"). Based on these statistical examples, the recognizer is able to infer that a new use of "Feist" should trigger the same action. In some ways, the hybrid nature of rule-based and statistical models in speech recognition technologies mirrors how humans themselves understand spoken

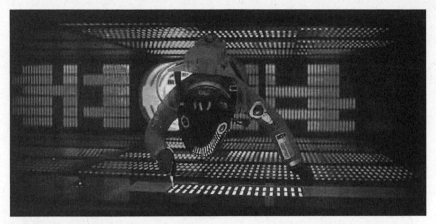

Figure 6.3 HAL 9000

Astronaut "Dave" turns off the talking computer in *2001: A Space Odyssey*.

SOURCE: Moviestore.

language: we can all apply our language's underlying grammar (what Saussure called *langue*), but we can also make reasoned guesses about meaning based on likelihood if we are unsure of what we have heard, or if words sound the same or similar.

A final observation about the relationship between human language and media technologies: because the dream of a universal language facilitated by machines is now perceived to be unattainable (machines will never speak like the infamous sentient HAL 9000 computer of Arthur C. Clarke's *2001: A Space Odyssey*), we have come to recognize that only in selective circumstances do we humans, in fact, wish to talk to our machines. In many cases, spoken language is simply not the most effective way of communicating with technical devices: human speech is noisy and much more ambiguous than commands sent by typing or using a touchpad. Even when we speak, we often apply the rules of grammar clumsily, using frequent repetitions or redundancies. Thus, it is perhaps not surprising that with all the progress in developing technologies to recognize speech, we still typically use them only for specific applications in niche markets: automated voice assistants that lead us to make one or another statement, or mobile phone applications that guide us through a series of specific actions. Ultimately, we don't always want to talk to machines.

Human speech is noisy and much more ambiguous than commands sent by typing or using a touchpad.

Conclusion

This chapter began by asking whether it matters that language and voices are no longer the domain only of human beings. Connections between language and media systems are by no means a recent occurrence; language has long been connected to and influenced by prevailing media technologies and systems.

This chapter has compared and contrasted a range of perspectives about language and media: the semiotic theory of linguistic representation; the dialogic understanding of making meaning and forms of power and resistance; differences between the characteristics of orality and literacy, between writing and print; opinions about the variety of electronic and digital media that have influenced or transformed the ways in which we speak, read, and write; and the possibilities of human–machine interaction through language and speech.

DISCUSSION QUESTIONS

1. In what ways do the technologies you use every day affect how you write or read?
2. In addition to schoolyard rhymes, what other ways of speaking are never, or rarely, written down?
3. Do you agree or disagree with the opinion that young people write less well today? Are there circumstances in which you have chosen to write in a formal way? Explain.
4. Are you comfortable using voice-activated software and applications, or do you prefer typing or using a touchpad? What aspects of speaking or writing influence your choice?

SUGGESTED RESOURCES

Books

Clark, Katerina, and Michael Holquist. 1984. *Mikhail Bakhtin*. Cambridge, MA: Harvard University Press.

Culler, Jonathan. 1986. *Ferdinand de Saussure* (rev. ed.). Ithaca, NY: Cornell University Press.

Hall, Stuart, ed. 1997. *Representation: Cultural Representations and Signifying Practices*. London: Sage Publications.

Jurafksy, Daniel, and James H. Martin. 2009. *Speech and Language Processing: An Introduction to Natural Language Processing, Computational Linguistics, and Speech Recognition*. Upper Saddle River, NJ: Prentice Hall.

Marchessault, Janine. 2005. *Marshall McLuhan: Cosmic Media*. London: Sage.

Wershler-Henry, Darren. 2005. *The Iron Whim: A Fragmented History of Typewriting*. Ithaca, NY: Cornell University Press.

Winthrop-Young, Geoffrey. 2010. *Kittler and the Media*. Cambridge, UK: Polity Press.

Websites

Centre for Oral History and Digital Storytelling. Concordia University History
Department, Montreal. http://storytelling.concordia.ca/oralhistory/index.html.
Our Voices, Our Stories: First Nations, Métis and Inuit Stories. Library and
Archives Canada, Ottawa. http://www.collectionscanada.gc.ca/stories/
index-e.html.

REFERENCES

Allen, Mark. 2006 (January 11). "Voices in the Air." *The New York Times*. Accessed
March 3, 2011. http://www.nytimes.com/2006/06/11/nyregion/
thecity/11voic.html.
Anderson, Benedict. 1991. *Imagined Communities: Reflections on the Origin and
Spread of Nationalism*. London: Verso.
Bakhtin, Mikhail. 1975/1981. *The Dialogic Imagination*. Translated by Caryl
Emerson and Michael Holquist. Austin, TX: University of Texas Press.
Bliven, Bruce, Jr. 1954. *The Wonderful Writing Machine*. New York: Random House.
Briggs, Asa, and Peter Burke. 2002. *A Social History of the Media*. Cambridge, UK:
Polity Press.
Carey, James W. 1989. "Technology and Ideology: The Case of the Telegraph."
Communication as Culture, 201–30. Winchester, UK: Unwin Hyman.
Caron, André H., and Letizia Caronia. 2007. *Moving Cultures: Mobile
Communication in Everyday Life*. Montreal and Kingston, ON:
McGill–Queen's University Press.
Carpenter, Edmund. 1957. "The New Languages." *Explorations* 7:4–21. Toronto:
University of Toronto Press.
Chomsky, Noam. 1967. "The Formal Nature of Language." In *Biological Foundations
of Language*, edited by E. Lenneberg, 397–442. New York: Wiley.
Eisenstein, Elizabeth. 1979. *The Printing Press as an Agent of Change*. Cambridge,
UK: Cambridge University Press.
Hall, Stuart. 1997. "The Work of Representation." In *Representation: Cultural
Representations and Signifying Practices*, 13–64. London: Sage.
Havelock, Eric A. 1986. *The Muse Learns to Write: Reflections on Orality and
Literacy from Antiquity to the Present*. New Haven, CT: Yale University Press.
Holquist, Michael. 1990. *Dialogism: Bakhtin and His World*. London: Routledge.
Howsam, Leslie. 2006. *Old Books and New Histories: An Orientation to Studies in
Book and Print Culture*. Toronto: University of Toronto Press.
Hutchins, John. 2000. "Warren Weaver and the Launching of MT: Brief
Biographical Note." In *Early Years in Machine Translation*, 17–21.
Amsterdam: John Benjamins.
Kittler, Friedrich. 1990. *Discourse Network 1800/1900*. Translated by Michael
Metteer, with Chris Cullens. Stanford, CA: Stanford University Press.
Kittler, Friedrich. 1999. *Gramophone, Film, Typewriter*. Translated by Geoffrey
Winthrop-Young and Michael Wutz. Stanford, CA: Stanford University Press.

Labov, William. 1972. *Language in the Inner City: Studies in Black English Vernacular*. Philadelphia: University of Pennsylvania Press.

McLuhan, Marshall. 1954. "Notes on the Media as Art Forms." *Explorations* 2:6–13. Toronto: University of Toronto Press.

McLuhan, Marshall. 1964. *Understanding Media: The Extensions of Man*. New York: McGraw-Hill.

McLuhan, Marshall, and Quentin Fiore. 1967/2001. *The Medium Is the Message*. New York: Bantam.

Ong, Walter. 1982. *Orality and Literacy*. London: Routledge.

Opie, Iona, and Peter Opie. 1959. *The Lore and Language of Schoolchildren*. Oxford, UK: Oxford University Press.

Saussure, Ferdinand de. 1916/1966. *Course in General Linguistics*, edited by Charles Bally and Albert Sechehay. Translated by Wade Baskin. New York: McGraw-Hill.

Weaver, Warren. 1955. "Translation." *Machine Translation of Languages: Fourteen Essays*, edited by William N. Locke and A. Donald Booth, 15–23. Cambridge, MA: Massachusetts Institute of Technology.

PART THREE
Change and Continuity

CHAPTER 7 / SANDRA GABRIELE AND PAUL S. MOORE
Media R/Evolutions

Why does media history matter? What is the relationship between old and new media? How can we assess the effects of new technologies?

KEY CONCEPTS

1. The awe and wonder we feel about our new technologies have also been experienced by previous generations.

2. Changes in media technologies are more accurately viewed as evolutions rather than revolutions.

3. A dominant technology often has a "blinding effect," making it hard for people to recognize the patterns of which they are a part.

CHAPTER OUTLINE

Introduction: What Is Media History? 113

The Problem of Doing Media History 115

The Dream of Perfect Communication: Connectivity 119

Case Study: The Myth of Total Cinema 125

Conclusion 131

Discussion Questions 131

Suggested Resources 132

References 132

Introduction: What Is Media History?

Grebe Tone—as natural as Nature itself. There is no difference in timbre or pitch between the tone of voice or instrument as put on the air and as the Grebe Synchrophase Radio delivers it to you. (Grebe radio advertisement, circa 1926)

[The iPad] makes surfing the web, checking email, watching movies, and reading books so natural, you might forget there's incredible technology under your fingers. (Apple advertisement, 2011)

As these two advertisements—from different periods showcasing differing technologies—suggest, we have long-standing ideas about the relationship of technologies to our everyday lives. Advertisements offer us a unique window on the enduring ways we imagine technology, the interventions it makes in our lives, and our expectations for it. In the examples above, the creators of both these devices stress that technologies can fit seamlessly into our everyday lives, suggesting that they are as natural as—what, exactly?

These ads are hoping you won't ask that question. The naturalization of technologies—the point at which they become so taken for granted that they seem a natural, and expected, part of our lives—is a moment when we can recognize the ideological work that technologies do. Often, just the act of contrasting something new (like an Apple iPad) with something that seems so antiquated (like a Grebe radio) helps to *de-familiarize* our contemporary ways of thinking about media. Exposing the **ideologies** about these everyday items—specifically, the ways in which we take media for granted—is important, because it reminds us that there are other ways of thinking about technology.

ideology
A set or system of concepts and ideals that shape a society or a particular community.

This process of de-familiarization is one effect of studying *media history*. By examining the ways in which we have interacted with communications technologies over time, media historians have drawn upon key concepts from media, communication, and cultural theory in order to identify recurrent themes. Another key insight media history can provide is that our experiences of "new" technology aren't really that new. By looking to history, and by reviewing the emergence of technological innovations and our interaction with them over time, we can see that experiences of awe, hope, fear, and wonder have accompanied the introduction of almost every new communication technology. Studying media over time also demonstrates that "old" media do not simply disappear because a new technology performs a task faster or more efficiently. Old technologies influence how new technologies are understood and are often "remediated," or given new life, by new technologies (Bolter and Grusin 2000). Media history can also help us to reconsider the typical perception that all new technologies are "revolutionary." Although new media have many new effects, the character and extent of those effects is open to debate. Media historians have looked to the past to explore how technologies affect us as individuals—our practices, beliefs, even our individual psyches and ways of thinking—and how they have affected our society and culture.

KEY CONCEPT
The awe and wonder we feel about our new technologies have also been experienced by previous generations.

In the broadest sense, media history reveals how people make their experience meaningful through media. How we perceive the world and communicate with one another is deeply tied to how we describe the past and identify culture (Gitelman 2006, 1). But what do we mean by both "media" and "communication"?

This chapter treats *media* as "socially realized structures of communication" that include technological forms and their associated protocols (that is, the rules and norms about how they are used) (Gitelman 2006, 7). It explores *communication* as a cultural practice, a set of rituals performed by people who share similar ways of representing the world (Carey 1989). Thus, when we "do" media history we are simultaneously asking two different questions: we inquire after the nature of the technologies themselves (their qualities and tendencies, such as being printed on paper or projected on a screen, having sound or not) and the habits organizing the conditions that influence how we use these technologies (their rules and norms, such as being available for free or costing money, being censored or licensed by government). Thus, this chapter shows how technologies have **mediated** our social relations and modes of communication over time.

mediate
To stand between two positions or parties and exchange information between them.

This is a very different approach to media history than just studying the history of big inventions, the genius of inventors, or building a timeline of media innovations. Although these are all part of media history, this chapter instead compares media over time to illustrate more gradual evolutions in the social understanding of media. It will thus focus on the complex relationship between technologies and the societies and individuals who adopt, modify, reject, and use them in varying degrees and with varying commitments. Media historians and theorists refer to this approach as the *social construction of technology*.

The chapter also addresses the problems of bias and ideology in viewing media, and suggests that changes in technology are more accurately viewed as evolutions rather than revolutions. The discussion examines how we tend to mythologize media and the notion of inevitable "progress" toward "perfect communication." It unpacks how communications technologies become invested with the hope of overcoming the problem of individuals' spatial and temporal separation from one another.

KEY CONCEPT
Changes in media technologies are more accurately viewed as evolutions rather than revolutions.

The chapter concludes with a case study of one medium, moving pictures. Examining "the myth of total cinema," the discussion demonstrates how the study of history helps us understand media and the idealizations that we invest in them.

The Problem of Doing Media History

As Elizabeth Eisenstein (1983) and Lisa Gitelman (2006) have both recognized, doing media history is complicated. Media and history have a difficult relationship, much like an uncomfortable handshake with a "distant, disliked relative" at a family reunion (Zelizer 2008, 5). The problem with doing media history is that we can access the past only through the very technologies we aim to study. How do you tell the story of the devices that we use to tell stories? Is there a history before history was recorded? How could you access that history, if not through some media form? For that matter, what gets recorded, and which records persist over time? What happens when old media forms vanish (floppy disks) or new ones appear (YouTube)? We can learn about the influence of the printing press only through printed historical documents; even when we're studying a more recent technology like television, we can access records about its development only through other media such as print, radio, and television itself. This means that media work as a kind of "veil" through which to see the past (Eisenstein 1983). Although getting at the "truth" of the past is perhaps impossible, media are always at work influencing our view of history.

Media are always influencing our view of history.

Several factors here need a bit of unpacking. First, according to some theorists and historians, media change our very ways of being in the world. For thinkers like Harold Innis, Marshall McLuhan, Joshua Meyrowitz, Walter Ong, Elizabeth Eisenstein, and others, the specific characteristics of a given medium of communication (whether it uses paper, screens, or sound waves) greatly affect the ways a civilization organizes itself and develops over time. Every medium encourages certain interactions and organizations among people, cultures, and institutions, while discouraging others (Meyrowitz 2008).

McLuhan (1964) condensed this argument into the pithy phrase, "the medium is the message," which means that we must pay attention to the *form* of a medium (its characteristics) rather than the *content*, or "message" that it carries. McLuhan suggested that media are extensions of ourselves—cars are our extended feet, pens are extensions of our hands—and thus, they introduce a "new scale … into our affairs" (7): "What we are considering here … are the psychic and social consequences of the designs or patterns as they amplify or accelerate existing processes. For the 'message' of any medium or technology is the change of scale or pace or pattern that it introduces into human affairs" (8).

McLuhan argues that the content of new media is always old media (1964, 32): oral narratives become the contents of books; novels, plays, or operas become the contents of film; film becomes the content of television, and so on. Thus, to understand the effects of a medium, rather than study its content, we must study its characteristics and how it reorganizes social, psychic, and cultural conditions. For example, what McLuhan found most interesting about television is how it connects audiences, creating new rituals. The television set was introduced as a piece of household furniture that created new spaces in homes—living rooms—that could bring families together in new ways (Spigel 1992).

Because media have such an influence on how we organize ourselves and how we think, they often operate in ways that aren't immediately obvious. According to Innis (1951/1991), these patterns are not discernible to the people living in a given culture at the time. In other words, dominant technologies have a blinding effect: "We are perhaps too much a part of the civilization which followed the printing industry to be able to detect its characteristics" (139). Innis developed the idea of *bias* to explain the ways that media favour particular organizations of society over others.

> **KEY CONCEPT**
> A dominant technology often has a "blinding effect," making it hard for people to recognize the patterns of which they are a part.

Bias and Ideology

In *The Bias of Communication* (1951/1991), Innis argued that media work to organize our societies, biasing them either toward preserving the traditions of the past (time-biased media) or toward greater flexibility to change (space-biased media). But Innis also believed that we develop media communications in ways that reflect the bias that already exists in a society. Societies that privilege the newest and greatest innovation over the past, or that value mobility over stability, will build and use communication tools that fulfill those preferences.

Time-biased media are better at preserving and disseminating knowledge over many generations because power is centralized. These media tend to be heavy or durable; they are not easily transported but tend to last a long time, such as hieroglyphics carved into stone. According to Innis, societies based on such media tend to have centralized power in small communities.

Space-biased media, on the other hand, are better at disseminating knowledge over great distances, but at the cost of its durability over time. Societies based on these media tend to be secular, militaristic, and territorial. Space-binding media make it easier to form empires and encourage commercialism across distances, because it's easy to move around the information needed to organize these activities. Print, and the papyrus that was used before it, is a space-biased medium compared with stone. Both papyrus and paper are lightweight and easy to move around, but are not as durable as stone. Although Innis did not live to see wireless devices, we can see how the trend toward space-biased media has continued and is heightened today, with cellphones a standard personal accessory.

Innis argued that in order for a society to expand, power and authority need to be decentralized, requiring mobile media systems. He identified papyrus, law, and the alphabet as examples of moving information around more efficiently by standardizing the communication tools used. Ensuring that everyone is using similar systems—that people are "on the same page" (literally, in this case)—is key to asserting unity and uniformity when people are not all in the same location. Thus, Innis argued, the space-biased media that favoured the expansion of a society over greater distances also encouraged monopolies of knowledge. We can see this bias in our contemporary world. You have access to vast amounts of information, but if you aren't "literate" in understanding that information, you must rely on "experts" to explain it to you—or worse, you may give up interest in understanding such complex information at all.

Bias, in this sense, is another way of describing ideology. *Ideology* is a perspective on the world that is shared among many people and is so commonplace that it seems obvious or presumed (taken for granted). Ideology is more than just ideas, however. It affects how we behave, organize ourselves, and interact with one another in the world. A classic Marxist view suggests that because ideologies are presumptive ways of seeing the world, we don't notice the ways in which they work, and thus fail to question them. Louis Althusser (1971) pushes this notion even further. He argues that all our activities are lived out in ideology (158); we are never outside ideology, and thus, central ideologies that are widely shared across a large group of people strike at the heart of the way our societies are built—just as Innis explained with the concept of bias. Although we may not be able to get outside ideology, with careful study we can see how it works, and with vast changes in society, we can also replace some ideologies with others. As is discussed in Chapter 15, the division of human bodies into gendered categories is an ideological system that we don't often question. But we can also recognize that the discourses surrounding motherhood, for example, have changed a great deal since women in North America have entered the workforce in greater numbers.

All this discussion about bias and ideology might lead you to believe that media wield great effects and are consequently determining factors in society. This way of thinking is called **technological determinism**. It is a mistake to think of either McLuhan or Innis in this way, although some people have. Nonetheless, the approaches outlined above focus our attention on the "big picture." In these approaches, media are examined in order to understand society as a whole, and thus commonalities of media are highlighted (Allen and Robinson 2009, 4). In order to understand a given medium, however, we must pay attention to more than its physical characteristics; we also have to understand how a given society employs and institutionalizes that medium. Culture and technology (including communications media) influence each other: social forms and situations encourage the development of new media, which act on society in turn, producing a new cycle of change.

technological determinism
The belief that media wield great effects, and are determining factors in society.

The Dream of Perfect Communication: Connectivity

In his book, *Speaking into the Air* (1999), theorist John Durham Peters traces how the idea of communication has been conceptualized and changed over time. This might seem strange to us—communication seems obvious—but Peters unpacks how the dream of "perfect communication," of bridging the gap between my private experiences of the world and yours, is a fundamental ideology that drives how we think about our communication tools. Think, for example, about the common metaphors we use today to express the "communion of souls" that embodies perfect communication: "we are of like mind"; "we finish each other's sentences"; "she/he is my soul mate." We have built our culture around the idea that we should aim for this impossible ideal of perfect communication, and that our tools, especially communication technologies, can help us overcome the barriers of space and time (Peters 1999, 4). As the following discussion will show, the application of electricity to our means of communication with the telegraph radically transformed what it meant to "stay in touch." As Peters writes, "The mistake is to think that communications [systems] will solve the problems of communication, that better wiring will eliminate the ghosts" (9). Faith that technology can solve this problem has led to the development of a central ideology within our culture: the ideology of technological progress.

The dream of "perfect communication" is an ideology that drives how we think about our communication tools.

The Ideology of Progress

What is progress? In everyday parlance, progress implies a movement toward a goal. It often expresses a belief in the advancement of humanity toward a perfect society. Generally speaking, progress means "the good life": family, community, happiness, leisure, wealth (Slack and Wise 2007). This leads to constantly striving to make material improvements, to make life better and better in ways that match the cultural goals of a given historical time. In the 19th century, we imagined that our technologies could help society achieve greater progress by relieving the strain of physical labour (for example, the steam engine). Sometime in the early 20th century, we began looking to our technologies to help us achieve greater efficiencies (for example, the assembly line). This idea is especially prevalent today, as we expect our communications tools to help us get our work done more easily; being able to connect anywhere, anytime is assumed to be the essential condition for achieving efficiency.

Of course, in many ways this idea is true. New technologies have made many activities easier and faster—just imagine having to send a letter (or fax), or make a phone call every time you needed to be in touch with someone! A common problem with this way of thinking, though, is that we often mistake the merely "new" with progress (Slack and Wise 2007). We privilege newer technologies over old ones, and confuse the newness of a technology with actual progress, even though sometimes an older technology does a better job. Think, for example, how sometimes a telephone conversation with someone is more effective than sending several emails. Moreover, this way of thinking confuses the ends with the means—that is, it equates the new technology with a better society, assuming that new technologies will always make our lives better. Consider how a software update for your computer or your mobile phone can often slow down the way it works. In this case, such interventions by technology, which are "sold" to us as a way of making things better, are actually about trying to sell you something else: the faster processor or the newer model mobile phone. In other words, progress is a central tenet of the modern world (Frisby 1988; Mosco 2004; Slack and Wise 2007).

North America has always associated technological innovation with general cultural progress. For example, the historical treatment of Aboriginal peoples in North America was often justified in the name of "progress." This powerful example also demonstrates to us that progress, like all ideologies, is never innocent. The articulation (linking together) of certain ideas of progress with certain actions (such as the policies of forced residential schools) always serves the interests of a select group of people over others (Althusser 1971; Slack and Wise 2007).

The Telegraph and the Radio

Many historians studying communications technologies have explored the idea of technological progress and the dream of perfect communication as central organizing ideologies in our culture. In the interest of brevity, just two technologies—telegraphy and radio—will be discussed before turning to the detailed case study that will bring all these ideas together. In his book *Communication as Culture* (1989), James W. Carey discusses the effect of the spread of telegraphy. It not only reorganized commerce; it also reorganized what Carey calls "ordinary thought." The telegraph had somewhat contradictory effects on everyday experience. It both shrunk space and expanded it, privileging places connected to the telegraph wire but allowing trading and communication between distant marketplaces. It both consolidated and dispersed power, privileging financial trading and speculation about future prices, but allowing wider access to information, especially as news written in a standardized, generic style.

Telegraphy was an especially important technology because, for the first time, communication could be separated from its physical transportation.

Prior to messages travelling electronically through a telegraph wire, letters had to be physically transported by horses, boats, or people. Floods or other natural disasters could cause messages to go astray. The need to cross the landscape also meant that transporting messages was limited by where the transportation could go and the length of time it would take to get there. A letter travelling overseas took weeks or months to arrive. Delivering letters quickly in the United States could be done using the Pony Express, which relied on a horse-and-rider relay system. An urgent letter travelling between St. Joseph, Missouri and Sacramento, California took about 10 days to arrive (Standage 1998, 61). Imagine how extraordinary it was to reduce the delivery time of a message to mere minutes!

Telegraphy quickly expanded as telegraph lines were strung up across North America. Though it greatly reduced the amount of time it took to send messages, the telegraph still relied on a physical network of wires and relays; messages could go only as far as the lines extended. As the telegraph network expanded, its value also expanded because it could reach more and more people (Standage 1998). Although the telegraph finally separated the message from its mode of transport, the system still relied on older models of transportation. The distance that a message travelled influenced how expensive that telegram would be, much like a railway ticket. Communications destined for places beyond the reach of the telegraph system were simply "faithfully written out at the last station and put into the Mail" (Figure 7.1).

Two points may be made here. First, old technologies, and the associated ways of thinking, don't suddenly disappear when a new technology is introduced. New technologies are always made understandable through practices and routines established with the old ones (Marvin 1990; Gitelman 2006; Bolter and Grusin 2000). Second, if we consider that the cost of a letter is the same no matter where it goes in one country, we can see another example of how a new technology can offer some advantages, but often at the cost of others.

Telegraphy was deeply tied to ideas of progress and radically shifted the way that North American society was organized. It was also a technology that was a bit mystifying to its users. For example, people sending telegrams had trouble distinguishing the medium from its predecessor, the letter. They sometimes insisted on neatly rewriting their messages, as if the receiver would see their handwriting, instead of the handwriting of the telegraph operator on the other end of the line. One woman even went so far as to think someone was trying to trick her into sending money, when she received a telegram from her son—written not in her son's handwriting, but in the telegraph operator's hand (Standage 1998, 68). Congestion in the lines also

TELEGRAPH PRICES.

ALL COMMUNICATIONS ARE STRICTLY CONFIDENTIAL.

Prices of the New-York & Boston Telegraph.

From BOSTON, or from NEW-YORK, to WORCESTER, SPRINGFIELD, HARTFORD, or NEW HAVEN, or from either station intermediate of BOSTON and NEW-YORK, to any other station of the Line, 25 cts., for the first *Ten Words or Numbers*, exclusive of address and signature; and *Two Cents* for every additional word or number. From Boston to New-York, or New York to Boston, FIFY CENTS for the first *Ten Words, or Numbers*, and THREE CENTS for every additional word, or number.

Prices of the New-York & Buffalo Telegraph Line.

From New-York to	NUMBER OF WORDS.																	
	15	20	25	30	35	40	45	50	55	60	65	70	75	80	85	90	95	100
Poughkeepsie, Hudson, Albany, Troy,	$.25	35	45	55	65	75	85	95	1 05	1 15	1 25	1 35	1 45	1 55	1 65	1 75	1 85	1 95
Utica, Rome, Syracuse,	35	50	65	80	95	1 10	1 25	1 40	1 55	1 70	1 85	2 00	2 15	2 30	2 45	2 60	2 75	2 90
Auburn, Geneva, Rochester, Buffalo, Ithaca,	50	70	90	1 10	1 30	1 50	1 70	1 90	2 10	2 30	2 50	2 70	2 90	3 10	3 30	3 50	3 70	3 90
Oswego, Lockport,	75	1 05	1 35	1 65	1 95	2 25	2 55	2 85	3 15	3 45	3 75	4 05	4 35	4 65	4 95	5 25	5 55	5 85

Prices of Canada Junction Line, and Toronto Line, Canada.

From Buffalo to Lockport or Queenston, 35 cts. for the first Fifteen Words.
Do.   "   St. Catharine, Canada, 35 "   "   "   "
Do.   "   Hamilton or Toronto, 50 "   "   "   "
For each additional *Five Words*, or under, to either of the above stations, TEN CENTS.

Prices of the Philadelphia & Pittsburg Telegraph Line.

From PHILADELPHIA TO	NUMBER OF WORDS.									
	10	20	30	40	50	60	70	80	90	100
LANCASTER, . . .	20	40	60	80	1 00	1 20	1 40	1 60	1 80	2 00
HARISBURG, . . .	25	50	75	1 00	1 25	1 50	1 75	2 00	2 25	2 50
CHAMBERSBURG, .	30	60	90	1 20	1 50	1 80	2 10	2 40	2 70	3 00

Figure 7.1 Telegraph rate card, 1846

The telegraph cut communication time from weeks to mere minutes. Note how the rates rise as distances increase. Why might that have been the case?

SOURCE: Courtesy American Antiquarian Society.

meant delays in sending messages, and this became a common complaint in the business world especially. Some telegraph companies reverted to using boys to carry messages back and forth between telegraph stations that were close together (some only a few hundred metres apart). Many lost confidence in the system and complained that the telegraph was just a more expensive postal system (Standage 1998, 94–95).

Although the telegraph was fast, it was disembodied. Much as the earlier telephone had been, radio was heralded because it reconnected bodies in a way that more closely resembled physical contact across space, even if that connection was still fraught with anxiety and confusion (Sconce 2000). What made radio so exciting was the way that it could convey the *sound* of a person's voice, not just the words. Radio was often described in magical, even supernatural, terms when it was first introduced (Citzrom 1983, 65). Much like the telegraph, electricity, and the telephone, radio was seen and discussed as a powerful means toward social cohesion and world peace (Mosco 2004, 128). People believed that the ability to access information from great distances would spread intercultural understanding and help maintain world peace. Peters (1999) points out that the key call used when DXing is "CQ," which translates into "seek you"—a phrase that perfectly captures the desire to be in touch (212). As Susan Douglas (1987) has written, radio was heralded as "an autonomous force, capable of revolutionizing American culture" (xv).

When early radio users searched the airwaves, they were often uncertain and anxious about making the connection—weather conditions and static could interfere with the signal. If radio expressed the dream of perfect communication, it promised more than it could ever deliver. As Jeffrey Sconce (2000) has noted, despite the hopefulness and anticipation associated with radio, popular sentiment also expressed pessimism and melancholy too (61–62). Although radio could connect people from afar and fill a listener's ears with the sound of another person's voice, it also simultaneously reminded the listener of the distance that still remained. As much as it was exciting, radio was also eerie, even sinister (Sconce 2000, 88–91). The uses of radio were also highly contested, with amateurs and commercial interests conflicting in the 1920s, and educational enterprises conflicting with networks into the 1930s, all while the industry itself struggled internally with competing visions for its future (Hilmes 1997, 13).

Eventually, radio became a step closer to the ideal of perfect communication because it brought a mass audience together all at once, in time if not in space. It also perfected the ideal of *individuated purposes*—that is, different types of listeners tuned in for different programming. So radio was something of a paradox, bringing people together yet enabling each to "do his

SIDEBAR

Radio

Radio began as a person-to-person mode of communication, especially useful between ships. In fact, until the early 1920s, radio broadcasting was a popular *amateur* activity. Many popular magazines and newspapers offered helpful advice for making a receiving set with a crystal and other commonly found materials. Radio enthusiasts practised what was called "DXing," listening for distant radio signals, also sometimes referred to as "fishing" in the ether (Hilmes 1997, 43). In the 1920s when programming was established, listeners would tune in with individual headsets, using a crystal set, or a set using vacuum tubes. In either case, the apparatus was cumbersome. Radio listening became much easier after 1925, especially as a family activity, when speakers became standard on sets, and even more so after 1927, with one-knob tuning (Douglas 1999, 78).

The *Titanic* disaster in April 1912 radically changed the amateur climate. After amateurs broadcast much confusing and erroneous information during the rescue efforts, the *Radio Act of 1912* was eventually passed. It required all radio operators to be licensed, and banished amateurs to the least desirable ends of the wireless spectrum (Douglas 1987, 233–39). In Canada, the first commercial licences were issued in 1922. Throughout the 1920s, newspapers, universities, and churches owned many of them (Vipond 1992). The Aird Commission, set up in 1928 after complaints were made about the nature of some broadcasts and allocation of wavelengths, eventually recommended forming a national network with federal subsidies (Vipond 1992, 195). In 1932, with the passing of the *Canadian Broadcasting Act*, the CRBC was formed. The more familiar CBC eventually replaced it in 1936 (see Vipond 1992, 225–80).

Figure 7.2
Children taking turns listening to the radio

SOURCE: Courtesy Glenbow Archives (NA-2903-55).

own thing." For example, in 1922 the *Des Moines Register* printed the bold headline, "All Iowa 'Tuning In' on the Radio," but qualified what that meant in practice: "Father plugs in for weather reports, grandmother gets sermons, mother hears opera in New York, and son and daughter 'jazz it up' to band music in Denver." Similarly, when the *Winnipeg Tribune* launched its own radio station that same year, it published a full-page illustration showing how radio could be heard on the farm, in the home, at the summer camp, and at the sick bed of an ill child, used for dancing, or for education ("Radio Edition" 1922, 1). Nonetheless, the vast "invisible audience" was just as important as specially purposed individual listeners. The *Tribune* later wrote about how a "radio story-teller sings 100,000 children to sleep—all at once!" ("Radio Department" 1922, 6).

One of the reasons the mass radio audience was so easily understood as sharing a common experience was that movie-going had already been understood the same way, despite the fact that disparate audiences watched different movies at distinct times and in far-flung places. One of the attractions of cinema was what Walter Benjamin (2008), in a 1939 essay that remains a classic for many media and communications scholars, called its "technological reproducibility." Two copies of a film could be seen at different times by different audiences, but everyone still felt that they were seeing the same movie. Radio transmitted the sounds of music and stories instantaneously and at great distances, but the idea of connecting through communications predates both forms of mass media. This point raises another myth of media revolutions and leads to our in-depth case study of technological change in relation to cinema in particular.

Case Study: The Myth of Total Cinema

Ever more faithful representation of reality is another key impetus for the continual evolution of communication technologies, and for casting new media as revolutionary. Cinema is most associated with this quest for the perfect reproduction of experience through media. Indeed, André Bazin (2009) called striving for complete realism "the myth of total cinema" in a brief essay from 1946 that, like Benjamin's, remains essential reading in film and media studies. Bazin proposed that the *idea* of cinema as a perfect illusion was inspiring its inventors in the 1890s to create a technology that could reproduce the world through sound, colour, and three-dimensionality. They produced only a first step toward that ideal when cinema became available to audiences in 1896. It took decades for sound and colour films to become standard in the industry, and 3D movies have only recently become common. Bazin famously wrote that "cinema has not yet been invented!" Movies are always experienced partly by imagining their improvement through some future new technology. By the turn of the 20th century, already, moving pictures were discussed in terms foreshadowing radio and television.

The goal of reproducing reality is so strongly associated with moving pictures that a wide range of 19th-century optical devices and spectacles has since been lumped together under the term "pre-cinema." Today they seem merely toys, but most of them have romantically obscure, pseudo-scientific names. In 1825, John Paris introduced a thaumatrope ("magical turner"), which fused two static images on either side of a paper disk when spun quickly. In the early 1830s, Joseph Plateau constructed a phenakistoscope ("deceptive view"), which turned a series of still images on a spinning pinwheel into a single moving image. In 1834, George Horner created the zoetrope ("live turning"), which wrapped the series of still pictures inside a cylinder with viewing slots to allow more than one spectator at once.

These optical devices foreshadow cinema, at least in hindsight. They all use a series of still pictures to create moving pictures, although not movies as we would come to understand and enjoy them in the 1900s. Toys based on these and many other inventions were common pastimes for the rest of the 1800s, culminating in 1893 with Thomas Edison's peepshow viewer, the Kinetoscope ("moving view"), which used a celluloid strip of sequential photographs to show a brief moving picture to a solitary viewer, once he or she paid a penny in the slot of the machine. To add a projector seems an obvious improvement of the kinetoscope, as it would allow a large audience to watch the film together, but Edison was satisfied with the peepshow version of moving pictures until two years later, when he faced imminent competition from projecting moving picture machines. By the late 1890s, Edison Manufacturing was a major industrial and marketing force for all types of modern conveniences and pastimes (Collins and Gitelman 2002). Yet despite Edison's reputation as a consummate inventor, his marketing team simply purchased the best competing picture machine, Armat and Jenkins' Phantoscope ("ghostly view"), and renamed it Edison's Vitascope ("living view"). By the time it debuted to the public—a paying audience in New York on April 23, 1896—the Vitascope had already had a press screening, resulting in promotional newspaper stories all across North

Figure 7.3 Kinetoscope

Thomas Edison's peepshow viewer showed a brief moving picture to a solitary viewer.

PRIMARY SOURCE

THE "VITASCOPE"
Edison's Latest Invention—An Improvement on the Kinetoscope
(By Associated Press)

New York, April 4—*The World* this morning says:

Thomas Edison was in a very happy mood when seen by a reporter in his laboratory in West Orange last night. The great inventor had about completed another machine, which he called the "vitascope." It is an improvement on the kinetoscope, and Mr. Edison says he has no doubt that it will prove to be a success.

The vitascope throws upon a screen, by means of bright lights and powerful lenses, the moving life sized figures of human beings and animals. Last night in the big foundry building adjacent to the laboratory, the machine was rigged up and a very satisfactory exhibition was made.

The first picture shown last night on the screen was a colored panorama of a serpentine dance by Anabelle, who posed before the kinetoscope last summer. The film roll on which the photographs were attached was arranged over a half dozen spools and pulleys, and when the machine was set in motion the dancer's image appeared upon the screen as in life.

The original photographs, as taken by the kinetoscope and developed on the rollers, are about the size of a special delivery postage stamp, and produces a picture life-sized, and hence are magnified about 600 times.

Mr. Edison expects to shortly be able to so improve the phonograph that he will be able to take records much longer than now and the vitascope and phonograph will then be so combined that it will be possible for audiences to watch a photographic reproduction of an opera and hear the music at the same time.

Source: New Orleans *Times–Picayune*, April 4, 1896, 2.

Figure 7.4 Vitascope

America to prime the mass audience for the new medium. At the press screening, before any audience had even seen the Vitascope, Edison already promised an improvement that would combine the pictures with a phonograph to reproduce an opera for an audience sitting anywhere.

By 1898, a revolutionary improvement on cinema was imagined that would go beyond simply adding a phonograph sound recording. The emerging technology of "visual telegraphy" could simulcast a performance from one stage to screens before audiences sitting in theatres elsewhere. A story published in the *Detroit Free Press* in 1898 ("Moving Pictures by Wire") explained the benefits of visual telegraphy with futuristic imagination: "Moving images may readily be seen hundreds of miles away from the initial point of transmission, and that their colors are also reproduced very naturally. It really partakes of the spirit of that wonderful mirror of fairyland, which had to be breathed upon merely in order to produce any wished-for scene."

The terms should sound familiar—they resemble the enthusiasm, and echo the theme of naturalization, found in the advertisements for the Grebe radio and the Apple iPad at the beginning of this chapter. In the early days of cinema, the very term "moving pictures" had already been redefined through a media revolution in which the pictures "moved" across space and were projected on the screen. Of course, when it first became available as radio in the 1920s, telegraphic broadcasting did not replace the movies; a further couple of decades were required to make the visual telegraph commercially viable as television.

By 1927, Hollywood had become a major economic industry, and commercial radio had been licensed for just a few years. Nonetheless, experiments with "radio movies" (already also known as television) led to proclamations that the future of cinema would again involve instantaneous broadcast—except now the audience would be made up of families viewing at home. Even at the experimental stage in 1927, the *New York Times* claimed "radio photography" as an established fact, and speculated about the practical uses for visual newspapers and movies watched at home ("Radio Movies in Home" 1927). These visions of what cinema might become assumed that improving the authenticity of the representation would always require a media revolution, a new medium. The myth of progress supposed by technological determinism continued, even as the descriptions of the new media relied heavily on hybrid inter-medial terms that merely combined two existing media (RADIO + MOVIES = TELEVISION)—and thus a new and supposedly revolutionary medium was instantly understood as an evolution of existing media.

Note that all these examples continued to imagine cinema as pure, escapist entertainment—the epitome of mass culture. The notion of improving the entertainment, too, went hand in hand with removing the mass of viewers from public gatherings to ever-more private spaces. The audience for radio-movies was isolated at home in their living rooms, but they got to take a more active role in their own amusement. The future of movies was thus already imagined in the 1920s as something like the personal entertainment devices of today. Compared to these futuristic media daydreams, Hollywood's switch to sound movies between 1927 and 1929 simply put into action what Edison promised back at the press preview of cinema: add a phonograph.

Hollywood's transition to "talkies," begun in 1927, continues to be viewed as a media revolution, with "silent" and "sound" treated as two distinct eras in the public's imagination, among cinephiles who madly appreciate silent movies with piano accompaniment, and in the conventions of film studies in the academy. But thinking of sound film as a technological revolution ignores the many continuities with silent film production, especially in the economic organization of the industry. After all, sound movies were made by the same movie studios that made silent films, and played in the same movie palaces. The myth is that sound film killed off the expensive live performance of accompanying vaudeville. Here too, however, continuities are forgotten—only the change is remembered, because big-time vaudeville in metropolitan cities continued for decades, just as local stage shows were used strategically by many movie theatres (Stober 2007).

Hollywood needed to pitch the transition to sound as a revolution because of the immense coordination and costs incurred by local showmen to wire their thousands of theatres with speakers. Local theatre owners needed to be assured of a steady supply of sound films in order to front the money to install new equipment. Thus, the transition to sound films happened gradually between 1926 and the early 1930s (depending on where you lived), although somehow a specific film, Warner Brothers' *The Jazz Singer*, is commonly cited as the first talkie. In other words, sound film was essentially an industrial strategy, not a media revolution (O'Brien 2005, 66–77). The idea of sound synchronized to film had been Edison's ideal years before cinema was publicly available. Before 1927, however, earlier versions of sound film had been cast as mere fads, used as a competitive strategy by a small minority of theatres just to distinguish themselves among dozens of competing showmen nearby (Altman 2004). Not until the entire industry decided to coordinate to change the technological norm did talkies become a media "revolution" instead of a novelty (Gomery 2005).

Sound film was essentially an industrial strategy, not a media revolution.

3D Cinema: A Case of Déjà Vu?

The historic shift to talkies in the late 1920s is strikingly similar to the wide-scale adoption of 3D cinema between 2008 and 2010, centred on the immense box office success of *Avatar*, a story told via a "futuristic" technology that perpetuates the myth of total cinema (Stanley 2010). Again, local and competing theatre chains and independent theatre owners needed to invest money to install 3D, and did so only when assured a steady supply of potential blockbuster films (Barnes 2009). The change was less about improvements in cinema technology as it was about a coordinated, industry-wide decision to change the industrial norm of what movie audiences should expect to see (and, with a premium surcharge on ticket prices, expect to pay).

Hollywood had twice before "hyped" 3D as a novelty—in the 1950s in the face of competition from television, and in the early 1980s with the widespread availability of home videocassette recorders (VCRs) and video home system (VHS) movies on videotape (Mitchell 2004). Unlike the earlier adoption of sound films, neither of those dabbling moments in 3D cinema required much investment on the part of local theatre owners, and studios did not produce high-quality films or even a steady supply of 3D films (Belton 1992). In the 1950s, the temporary equipment, the cheapness of its cardboard glasses, and the decision not to charge more for a ticket were all factors that contributed to the perception of 3D as a gimmick, a toy, rather than a new way of experiencing cinema (Paul 1993).

Like the transition to sound movies, the more recent shift to digital 3D (and especially 3D IMAX) came at a significant cost to theatre owners for projection, as well as to studios for production. Even then, charging an extra few dollars for a 3D ticket was a marketing decision and a sign of added value and desirability. Digital 3D required mutual trust and coordination throughout the industry. The result, at least after its first several years, has been a steady supply of relatively good-quality 3D films that studios, local owners, and mass audiences alike have come to appreciate, at least for children's animated films and adolescent action movies.

Ironically, the most revolutionary recent technological change in cinema is hidden from the audience—digital projection. For the first time since the beginning of moving pictures, many theatres are showing movies without using reels of film—and yet audiences pay the same prices to see the same movies at the same theatres, and most do not even notice or care that the projection, like much of the production, is digital (Dargis 2010). Digital projection is a media revolution that audiences are meant to ignore, except when it allows them to watch live events such as the Metropolitan Opera cheaply and from a distance (Heyer 2008). The expectation is to have the *same* experience, not an improved progress toward an ideal. The impetus is to take advantage of new technologies for efficiency and flexibility in production and distribution. The industry's downplaying its transition to digital contrasts with its similarly gradual transition to colour beginning in the 1930s (*Gone with the Wind* and *The Wizard of Oz* were two of the first colour blockbusters, both released in 1939). Although the switch to colour entirely changed the experience for viewers, it is rarely considered a media revolution because it took decades to become standard and involved no technological change in the projectors used to show films in theatres. Sometimes, you're not in Kansas anymore—but you don't even know it.

Conclusion

This chapter has demonstrated how various actors—the press, industry, and the public at large—invest technologies with certain promises and ideals. If we desire perfect communication, through instantaneous connectivity, through the virtual reality of total cinema, then media become imbued with those desires. These beliefs about media are by definition ideological, but the assumptions and consequences are often difficult to identify because we are submerged in the ideology ourselves. Ideologies about media shape our use and experience of them, and always benefit some people more than others. Studying media in the long view of history—as things develop over time and across a multitude of conditions—allows us to glimpse just how these ideologies become established, how they are replicated, and those whom they advantage.

Most historians believe that looking back in time gives us a better understanding of our own contemporary, technologically mediated world. Of course, as Innis and McLuhan warned us, this happens only when we pay close attention.

DISCUSSION QUESTIONS

1. Examine several advertisements for cellphones or for laptop computers. What myths are repeated across the advertisements? What promises are made about this new technology? Now, try finding several old advertisements for "new" media online. What similarities and differences do you notice?

2. Take a close look at Figure 7.1. Why do you think the New York and Boston Magnetic Telegraph company would note, right at the very top of its rate card, that "All communications are strictly confidential"? How do you think this point influenced the way messages were written?

3. This chapter has explained how myths of "perfect communication" have driven thinking about media change in terms of progress. Think of a specific media technology, historic or contemporary, and explain another myth apparent in its design. Can you think of a way some people use it that contradicts or circumvents this ideology?

4. Re-read the news item about Edison's unveiling of the Vitascope to reporters in his laboratory (page 127). How are ideologies of media revolutions employed to explain the importance of the new machine? Consider the photograph of the Kinetoscope (Figure 7.3), the precursor to projected movies mentioned in the news article. Why is the Vitascope a step closer to "total cinema"?

SUGGESTED RESOURCES
Books

Beniger, James R. 1986. *The Control Revolution: Technological and Economic Origins of the Information Society*. Cambridge, MA: Harvard University Press.

Crowley, David, and Paul Heyer, eds. 2011. *Communication in History: Technology, Culture and Society* (6th ed.). Boston: Allyn and Bacon.

Gitelman, Lisa, and Geoffrey B. Pingree, eds. 2003. *New Media: 1740–1915*. Cambridge, MA: MIT Press.

Innis, Harold. 1950. *Empire and Communications*. Oxford: Clarendon Press.

McLuhan, Marshall. 1962. *The Gutenberg Galaxy: The Making of Typographic Man*. Toronto: University of Toronto Press.

Thorburn, David, and Henry Jenkins, eds. 2004. *Rethinking Media Change: The Aesthetics of Transition*. Cambridge, MA: MIT Press.

Websites

Burns, Paul. 2011. *The History of the Discovery of Cinematography*. http://www.precinemahistory.net.

Media History in Canada. http://www.mediahistory.ca.

Prelinger, Rick. *Panorama Ephemera*. http://vectors.usc.edu/projects/index.php?project=58.

Virtual Vaudeville. http://www.virtualvaudeville.com.

REFERENCES

"All Iowa 'Tuning In' on the Radio." 1922 (April 2). *The Des Moines Register* (magazine), 3.

Allen, Gene, and Daniel Robinson. 2009. "Introduction: Media History as Concept and Practice." In *Communicating in Canada's Past: Essays in Media History*, edited by Gene Allen and Daniel J. Robinson, 3–26. Toronto: University of Toronto Press.

Althusser, Louis. 1971. "Ideology and Ideological State Apparatuses." In *Lenin and Philosophy*, 123–65. London: New Left Books.

Altman, Rick. 2004. *Silent Film Sound*. New York: Columbia University Press.

Barnes, Brooks. 2009 (January 11). "Hollywood Finds Headaches in Its Big Bet on 3-D." *The New York Times*, B1.

Bazin, André. 2009. "The Myth of Total Cinema." In *What Is Cinema?*, translated by Timothy Barnard, 13–19. Montreal: Caboose Books.

Belton, John. 1992. *Widescreen Cinema*. Cambridge, MA: Harvard University Press.

Benjamin, Walter. 2008. *The Work of Art in the Age of Its Technological Reproducibility, and Other Writings on Media*, edited by Michael W. Jennings, Brigid Doherty, and Thomas Y. Levin. Cambridge, MA: Belknap Press/Harvard University Press.

Bolter, Jay David, and Richard Grusin. 2000. *Remediation: Understanding New Media*. Cambridge, MA: MIT Press.

Carey, James W. 1989. *Communication as Culture*. Boston: Unwin Hyman.

Citzrom, Daniel. 1983. *Media and the American Mind: From Morse to McLuhan*. Chapel Hill, NC: University of North Carolina Press.

Collins, Theresa M., and Lisa Gitelman, eds. 2002. *Thomas Edison and Modern America: A Brief History with Documents*. New York: Palgrave Macmillan.

Dargis, Manohla. 2010 (December 17). "The Revolution Is Being Shot on Digital Video." *The New York Times*, Arts, 8.

Douglas, Susan J. 1987. *Inventing American Broadcasting, 1899–1922*. Baltimore: Johns Hopkins University Press.

Douglas, Susan J. 1999. *Listening In: Radio and the American Imagination, from Amos 'n' Andy and Edward R. Murrow to Wolfman Jack and Howard Stern*. New York: Times Books.

Eisenstein, Elizabeth. 1983. *The Printing Revolution in Early Modern Europe*. New York: Cambridge University Press.

Frisby, David. 1988. *Fragments of Modernity*. Cambridge, MA: MIT Press.

Gitelman, Lisa. 2006. *Always Already New: Media, History and the Data of Culture*. Cambridge, MA: MIT Press.

Gomery, Douglas. 2005. *The Coming of Sound: A History*. New York: Routledge.

Heyer, Paul. 2008. "Live from the Met: Digital Broadcast Cinema, Medium Theory, and Opera for the Masses." *Canadian Journal of Communication* 33(4): 591–604.

Hilmes, Michele. 1997. *Radio Voices: American Broadcasting, 1922–1952*. Minneapolis: University of Minnesota Press.

Innis, Harold. 1951/1991. *The Bias of Communication*, 34–44. Toronto: University of Toronto Press.

Marvin, Carolyn. 1990. *When Old Technologies Were New: Thinking About Electric Communication in the Late Nineteenth Century*. New York: Oxford University Press.

McLuhan, Marshall. 1964. *Understanding Media: The Extensions of Man*. New York: McGraw-Hill.

Meyrowitz, Joshua. 2008. "Medium Theory." In *The International Encyclopedia of Communication Online*, edited by Wolfgang Donsbach. Accessed April 9, 2011. http://www.communicationencyclopedia.com/public/.

Mitchell, Rick. 2004. "The Tragedy of 3-D Cinema." *Film History* 16(3):208–15.

Mosco, Vincent. 2004. *The Digital Sublime: Myth, Power and Cyberspace*. Cambridge, MA: MIT Press.

"Moving Pictures by Wire." 1898 (April 3). *Detroit Free Press*, 34.

O'Brien, Charles. 2005. *Cinema's Conversion to Sound: Technology and Film Style in France and the United States*. Bloomington, IN: Indiana University Press.

Paul, William. 1993 (September). "The Aesthetics of Emergence." *Film History* 5(3): 321–55.

Peters, John Durham. 1999. *Speaking into the Air: A History of the Idea of Communication*. Chicago: University of Chicago Press.

"Radio Department." 1922 (May 9). *Winnipeg Tribune*, 6.

"Radio Edition." 1922 (April 20). *Winnipeg Tribune*, 1.

"Radio Movies in Home." 1927 (January 11). *The New York Times*, 1.

Sconce, Jeffrey. 2000. *Haunted Media: Electronic Presence from Telegraphy to Television*. Durham, NC: Duke University Press.

Slack, Jennifer Daryl, and J. Macgregor Wise. 2007. *Culture+Technology: A Primer*. New York: Peter Lang.

Spigel, Lynn. 1992. *Make Room for TV: Television and the Family Ideal in Postwar America*. Chicago: University of Chicago Press.

Standage, Tom. 1998. *The Victorian Internet*. New York: Berkeley Books.

Stanley, T.L. 2010 (June 7). "Avatar Era Raises Stakes for Movie Marketing." *MediaWeek* 20(23):13–16.

Stober, JoAnne. 2007. "Vaudeville: The Incarnation, Transformation, and Resilience of an Entertainment Form." In *Residual Media*, edited by Charles Acland, 133–55. Minneapolis: University of Minnesota Press.

Vipond, Mary. 1992. *Listening In: The First Decade of Canadian Broadcasting, 1922–1932*. Montreal and Kingston, ON: McGill–Queen's University Press.

Zelizer, Barbie. 2008. "When Disciplines Engage." In *Explorations in Communication and History*, edited by Barbie Zelizer, 1–12. London and New York: Routledge.

The Political Economy of Media

What economic forces influence the media we consume? Are the business goals of media corporations at odds with their role as important institutions in a democracy? Do new media represent a shift in the business models for media businesses?

KEY CONCEPTS

1. The political economy of media approach sees the profit motive that drives corporate media as being incompatible with a healthy democracy.

2. The public interest is best served by having access to a wide range of journalism sources, both mainstream and alternative.

3. The shift to digital platforms has meant a huge drop in advertising revenue for media companies, leading to uncertainty and change within the media industry.

CHAPTER OUTLINE

Introduction 135

The Political Economy Perspective 137

Some Key Concepts in the Political Economy of Media 138

New Media for a New Century 143

A Critique of the Political Economy Approach 144

Mixed Motives: The Case of the CBC 146

Conclusion: Questions of Political Economy in the Digital Era 147

Note 148

Discussion Questions 148

Suggested Resources 149

References 149

Introduction

"If you agree that Facebook doesn't respect you, your personal data or the future of the web, you may want to join us." This statement greets visitors to the website www.quitfacebookday.com. Despite the massive success of Facebook in a few short years, there are clearly those who object to the way the social media titan does business. For these users, Facebook is—or was—an important aspect of their personal lives, and a vital connection to the world, but they began to feel the bargain they had made was no longer in their own best interest.

However, for the owners and shareholders of Facebook, it is a *business*. And not just any business; it has been a disruptive new force in the world of media and communications. Its value has been estimated at US $50 billion, despite the fact that its actual revenues are far lower than that, in the range of $2 billion (Gandel 2011). What has made Facebook so valuable is, in part, its future potential to generate revenue in various ways by using the personal information of Facebook users. While some of these users may balk at this trade-off, the vast majority seem willing to go along for the ride and enjoy Facebook's benefits; they care little about the company's business model. This is just one example of the economic forces that underpin much of today's media, and define the nature of our connections to them.

Much of this book is devoted to discussing the ways in which we, as individuals, now receive, consume, and interact with the virtual tsunami of information now available to us. A still broader vantage point from which to view the information universe is to examine the economic, political, and industrial dynamics that work "behind the scenes" and play a significant role in shaping the media we consume.

The Media as an Industry

We typically use the word "media" in different senses. The term refers not only to the broadcasting or distribution of information and entertainment on various platforms, but also to an entire industry. The media industry continues to grow, and in some cities—such as Los Angeles, New York, Vancouver, Montreal, and Toronto—it represents a significant share of the local economy. The various media sectors—including news organizations, television and radio broadcasters, magazines, and yes, textbook publishers—are typically dominated by large corporations whose primary goal is to generate a profit for shareholders. This is true of both traditional and new media.

In our capitalist economic model, which emphasizes competition as the driving force behind innovation and business growth, the media and communication industry has proven to be one of the most successful of our time. Currently, the CEOs of media companies, such as Steve Jobs (Apple), Bill Gates (Microsoft), and Mark Zuckerberg (Facebook), are among the richest people on the planet, and they have helped usher in a revolution in human communications. The intense competition in this industry has led to innovations that were unthinkable only a decade or two ago. But this is only one aspect of the communication industry. Those who produce the *content* of mass media—in particular, the news networks and newspaper and magazine publishers—are also in competition, fighting for audiences and for advertising dollars, and in some cases, to promote (explicitly or implicitly) a particular political agenda or party.

This business dynamic has far-reaching implications for determining the content that reaches us through the filter of the mass media every day. There are various ways to analyze and interpret the motives and imperatives that drive media organizations, and the forces that shape their content. This chapter explores some of them.

Mass media producers are in competition with one another for audiences and advertising dollars.

The Political Economy Perspective

As you will see in the next chapter (Chapter 9, Regulating the Media), the media are a critically important institution in modern society because they are so intimately connected with the exercise of power, whether political, economic, or otherwise. The media also largely define how each of us is connected to society.

Put simply, the political economy approach to media is a critical perspective that views the corporate ownership of the media—in particular, the larger, mainstream media outlets—as incompatible with the wider public interest and a healthy democracy. For these critics, the profit motive and related political concerns and agendas are constantly undermining the media's ability to present information fairly. Noted American media critic Robert McChesney (2008, 12) articulates this perspective:

KEY CONCEPT
The political economy of media approach sees the profit motive that drives corporate media as being incompatible with a healthy democracy.

> Political economists of media do not believe the existing media system is natural or inevitable or impervious to change. They believe the media system is the result of policies made in the public's name but often without the public's informed consent. They believe the nature of the media systems established by these policies goes a long way toward explaining the content produced by these media systems. … The central question for media political economists is whether, on balance, the media system serves to promote or undermine democratic institutions and practices.

The dominant media, therefore, are not simply functioning as businesses, generating revenue while they entertain and inform us; rather, critics assert that they are central players in reinforcing the values and ethos of capitalism, using their unique position as media conglomerates and their ability to shape public opinion in order to pursue their own political and economic ends.

The political economy approach has three defining aspects:

- It examines how the economic structures of the media industry, and related government policies and regulations, influence media content.
- It examines these power structures and the ways in which media content enforces or influences existing social relations in society at large—that is, it examines questions of class, private versus public property, minority rights, and so on.
- It often has a "prescriptive" component, based on the belief that the public interest is best served by a media environment in which media corporations do not have free rein; instead, the free market is subject to reasonable regulations.

Some Key Concepts in the Political Economy of Media

The notion of examining media through the wider lens of their political and economic context, and examining the social forces that shape them, drew its inspiration initially from Karl Marx's critique of capitalist society. Marx argued that economic and political concerns could not be divorced from an examination of the power relationships within a society. This Marxist perspective views the economic structure of media industries as the most important factor in determining the nature of the media that dominate a society. Because the major advances in communications and related technology over the last century have been highly lucrative for the owners of these media, granting them great political control, the political economy perspective has, not surprisingly, become a common approach in analyzing media. In 1944, German philosophers (and members of the Frankfurt School) Theodor Adorno and Max Horkheimer wrote an influential book, *Dialectic of Enlightenment*, which argued that mass-produced culture cultivated only "false needs"—that is, needs created and satisfied by capitalism. Other notable thinkers who have helped define this field include Canadians Harold Innis (whose work is discussed in greater detail elsewhere in this book) and Dallas Smythe.

Several key concepts that typically arise in discussions of the political economy of media include *spectacle*, *convergence*, *concentration*, and *globalization*.

Convergence

The ongoing move to digital delivery of information has given momentum to a phenomenon that had already begun prior to the current era of rampant

PRIMARY SOURCE

Spectacle

Douglas Kellner (2005) defines *spectacle* and its role in media culture:

> During the past decades, the culture industries have multiplied media spectacles in novel spaces and sites, and spectacle itself is becoming one of the organizing principles of the economy, polity, society, and everyday life. The Internet-based economy deploys spectacle as a means of promotion, reproduction, and the circulation and selling of commodities. Media culture itself proliferates ever more technologically sophisticated spectacles to seize audiences and increase their power and profit. The forms of entertainment permeate news and information, and a tabloidized infotainment culture is increasingly popular. New multimedia that synthesize forms of radio, film, TV news and entertainment, and the mushrooming domain of cyberspace, become spectacles of technoculture, generating expanding sites of information and entertainment, while intensifying the spectacle-form of media culture.

digitization: that of **convergence**. This term refers to the merging of previously separate media types, platforms, or companies under a single umbrella. For example, Bell Media owns a raft of television, radio, and Web-based media outlets, as well as a share of *The Globe and Mail*. This ownership model is designed to provide economic efficiency through the sharing and parceling of content among the corporate divisions. In the case of CTV and *The Globe and Mail*, the two news organizations have frequently conducted political polling that both could then use in their reportage. Larger media entities enjoy **economies of scale** because, for example, they can afford to offer advertisers a package deal to reach audiences via multiple outlets.

Given this blurring among media formats, media companies can more easily share content across platforms. They can also streamline the branding of their corporate holdings. For example, in early 2011, Rogers Media re-branded its extensive sports broadcasting concerns to reflect the fact that much of the content was being presented across radio, television, and the Web, often simultaneously (in the case of high-profile shows such as *Prime Time Sports*). The new branding strategy saw the old radio name "The FAN 590" replaced with "Sportsnet Radio."

convergence
The merging of previously separate media content, platforms, or companies, to achieve greater efficiency or profit.

economies of scale
The efficiency or advantage enjoyed by companies when production costs are spread across a larger number of products or services.

Concentration

concentration
The degree of competition that exists within an industry, and the centralization of control.

Media **concentration** refers to the degree of competition that exists within an industry, and how centralized the control and power is. Naturally, corporations prefer to have less competition for advertisers and audiences. Thus, they often employ strategies to purchase other (usually smaller) players in their field in order to increase their market share, thereby concentrating media power into fewer hands. For example, CHUM began in the 1950s in Toronto as a modest radio station, but by the time it was sold in 2007 (to CTVglobemedia, now Bell Media), it was known as "The CHUM Group." Its holdings included more than 30 radio stations across Canada, as well as several television stations. This concentration of media can at times lead to quizzical situations, as in the case of Vancouver's two rival daily newspapers—the *Sun* and the *Province*—which are both owned by the same company.

The explosion of Internet media in recent years has given rise to the hope that the Internet would offer alternatives to the most negative aspect of media concentration: the dwindling number of sources of information and opinion. Particularly in the area of journalism, wide-ranging alternatives to mainstream sources can benefit the public interest.

KEY CONCEPT
The public interest is best served by having access to a wide range of journalism sources, both mainstream and alternative.

Whether the Internet can live up to this promise remains to be seen. News and information on the Internet are often repeated from other sources; audiences unfamiliar with the myriad new information sources may be less trustful of them. Economically, the advertising revenues that have driven traditional media have not, in the new online media environment, been able to support large, in-house reporting staffs on Internet news sites.

What is certain is that over the course of the last century, the number of independently owned newspapers has dropped significantly. The Canadian Newspaper Association (2011) lists 95 daily newspapers currently being published in Canada; of these, only four are independent.

Meanwhile, after two decades of accelerated acquisitions, global media companies have continued to grow into ever-larger corporate entities. (One of the more noteworthy recent business developments was the merger of the *Huffington Post* with AOL in 2011, which demonstrated how online media have begun to mature as business properties.) Today, the vast majority of media products consumed in the world are produced by a relatively small number of companies. With such large advertising revenues and profits at stake, there is always a concern that these media outlets—and their sponsors—may wield influence over content. Although Robert McChesney and others concede that global media conglomerates can be forces for social

Figure 8.1 Monitoring the media

Researchers at the Global Media Monitoring and Analysis Laboratory in the School of Communication at Simon Fraser University monitor how TV news around the world reflects shifts in the rapidly transforming global order.

SOURCE: GMMA Lab/Dr. Yuezhi Zhao. Reprinted by permission.

progress, he maintains that corporations are inherently conservative, ultimately preferring the status quo: "By any standard of democracy, such a concentration of media power is troubling, if not unacceptable" (McChesney 2003).

Globalization: Questions for Canada

On a larger scale, concentration leads to questions about maintaining national identities in an increasingly global media marketplace. Many fear that uniquely Canadian voices may be greatly diminished by the onslaught of foreign media now available via the Internet, and by the inability of some sectors of the Canadian media (such as magazines and book publishing) to weather the migration to digital platforms.

Questions inevitably arise: in a highly competitive, **globalized** marketplace, in which the geographic limits of old media broadcast technology have been forever altered by digital delivery, can Canada retain its distinctive media, and a distinctive culture? It's an old question, but it remains pertinent. Ian Morrison (2004), head of the group Friends of Canadian Broadcasting, describes the situation:

globalization
The tendency for markets in goods, labour, media content, etc. to transcend borders; often seen as adversely affecting regional cultures and employment.

Canadian private broadcasters would be dead in the water if they had to face the full force of competition from American broadcasters. They don't face that dim prospect largely because the federal government holds an economic regulatory umbrella over their heads, affording them ongoing protection from the American competition. And yet, those same private broadcasters, Global, CTV, Corus, CHUM and Craig have reduced their investment in Canadian drama TV programs in recent years after convincing the CRTC that it should reduce its regulatory requirements. In 2000 there were 12 drama series on English-language Canadian TV. This year, there are four.

Fair and Balanced?

In recent years, perhaps the most widely discussed example of the convergence of political and economic interests in a single media outlet has been that of the Fox News Network in the United States. Fox News is a division of News Corporation, which is owned by Australian billionaire Rupert Murdoch. Although the network promotes itself as "fair and balanced," it has also provided a high-profile platform for several staunchly partisan Republicans such as Sarah Palin. Many critics have pointed to a pronounced right-wing bias in the network's news and commentary. One recent example involved a leaked memo outlining a directive from Fox senior management to reporters and newscasters, stating that they should refer to Democratic President Barack Obama's health-care reform proposals, which Republicans loudly denounced, as "the government-run health-care option" instead of "the public option," because the former term was shown to be interpreted more negatively by the general public. Fox's general antagonism toward Obama and his policies led him to quip during the 2008 election campaign: "If I were watching Fox News, I wouldn't vote for me" (Bai 2008).

Accusations of bias run both ways; the "liberal media" are also frequently accused of demonstrating a bias in their coverage. In the 2011 Canadian federal election campaign, the *Toronto Sun*, a politically conservative newspaper, ran a front-page story that pointed to bias on the part of the CBC. (The public broadcaster is often accused by conservative critics of having a left-wing bias.) The story concerned a study of the CBC's "Vote Compass" online survey tool, which a Queen's University professor had demonstrated as having a clear bias toward the Liberal Party (Butler 2011).

The interconnections between media—particularly news organizations—and their audiences, shareholders, regulators, and even their own reporters and staff, are of course very complex. Critics such as Robert McChesney would not assert that economic interests are the only determining factor at play in this dynamic, but they do maintain that these are central to any

PRIMARY SOURCE

Naomi Klein on Brands and Multinational Corporations

All aspects of mass media—not just journalism and broadcast media—can be viewed through the lens of political economy, including the marketing and branding of consumer goods. (See also Chapter 14 in this book.)

Canadian author Naomi Klein's widely discussed book, *No Logo: Taking Aim at the Brand Bullies* (2000), articulated a growing dissatisfaction (particularly among poorly treated workers around the world, and many young Western consumers) with the excessive power wielded by multinational corporations. Looking around our streets, malls, and campuses today, it may seem that brands are at least as pervasive now as they were when *No Logo* was published. But Klein has been perhaps the most popular and successful critic yet at opening the eyes of a new generation and leading them to question the economic power structures at play all around them:

> Successful multinational corporations are increasingly finding themselves under attack, whether it's a cream pie in Bill Gates's face or the incessant parodying of the Nike swoosh—what are the forces pushing more and more people to become suspicious of or even downright enraged at multinational corporations, the very engines of our global growth? Perhaps more pertinently, what is liberating so many people—particularly young people—to act on that rage and suspicion?
>
> These questions may seem obvious, and certainly some obvious answers are kicking around. That corporations have grown so big they have superseded government. That unlike governments, they are accountable only to their shareholders; that we lack the mechanisms to make them answer to a broader public. (Klein 2000, xxi)

understanding of the media's role in society, and the ways in which the media function.

New Media for a New Century

The tragic events of September 11, 2001, and the global political chaos that unfolded in its aftermath, coincided with the burgeoning use of digital media by the public. Indeed, many observers have identified 9/11 as a "coming of age" moment for new media, in particular the then-new medium of blogging

KEY CONCEPT
The shift to digital platforms has meant a huge drop in advertising revenue for media companies, leading to uncertainty and change within the media industry.

(Srivastava 2010). This shift to digital delivery has had a profound impact on the business models of many traditional media outlets as they have attempted to adjust to these new realities. For example, advertising revenues, which media companies have relied on, have dropped significantly in the migration to online delivery of media content. This is a primary factor in the "net neutrality" debate (discussed in more detail in Chapter 9, Regulating the Media).

But in addition to online media representing a threat to the revenues of major media corporations, the early years of online media showed that the Web was also offering a far wider range of opinion than had previously been expressed through the limited number of traditional media available to the public.

In the winter and spring of 2003, as the US invasion of Iraq became a reality, many people found a wider range of opinion and analysis on what was happening—and often, facts about the war not being reported elsewhere—from online sources, as opposed to traditional news sources. Critics at the time voiced disapproval of what they saw as "cheerleading" by American news networks (most of whom had "embedded" reporters with US troops on the ground, raising many questions about journalistic ethics). Several studies of US media coverage of the war confirmed that journalists and news organizations were largely repeating the US government's claims that "weapons of mass destruction" existed in Iraq, without digging further. These serious allegations were the reason given for going to war, and they turned out to be false (Boisset 2004).

Most mainstream media did not question the reasons given by the US government for invading Iraq.

Seeking alternative viewpoints, many in the public migrated to online news sources, including the online Arab news agency, Al Jazeera. Because it offered a very different perspective on the Iraq war than that offered by the Pentagon and US networks, Al Jazeera became embroiled in serious and even violent disputes with the administration of President George W. Bush and the US military (Scahill 2005).

A Critique of the Political Economy Approach

Many scholars and media analysts would dispute the arguments of media critics such as Robert McChesney, pointing out that an analysis predominantly based on the economic and political structures that support our mass media is too narrow and reductive. Paul Nesbitt-Larking (2007, 126) counters the political economy approach:

> [T]here are those who argue that capitalism, industrialism, corporate control, or money "explain" everything important about the workings of

HISTORICAL HIGHLIGHT

The Iraq War: Mainstream Media Versus Online Activism

In his book *The New Media Monopoly* (2004, 260), professor and journalist Ben H. Bagdikian states:

> The large media conglomerates do not want greater political and social diversity because it would dilute their audiences and thereby reduce the fees they can demand for the commercials that produce their unprecedented profit levels. ... They have been a most powerful force in shifting the political spectrum of the United States to the right.
>
> The artificial control over the country's political spectrum was demonstrated in 2001 by large-scale protests against the United States' invasion of Iraq. The protests were organized almost entirely via the Internet, the one important medium not yet controlled by the media monopolies. Initially, the standard media owned by conglomerates systematically underreported most of the thousands of protesters who took to the streets across the country and the world. Only after foreign news agencies reported the numbers more accurately—and many Americans used access to these foreign news agencies by Internet—did the American conglomerates alter their earlier inaccurate reporting.

the world. Economics and political economy do not, in fact, explain everything. ... Culture and ideology are more than simply an expression of the forces and relations of production, and although they are related to the workings of the economy, they cannot be reduced to them.

While it is not possible here to examine all the debates surrounding the political economy approach, it may be useful to choose one particular concept as an example, to provide a sense of the form that such debates take.

One of the most widely read books on the topic of the mass media is Edward S. Herman and Noam Chomsky's *Manufacturing Consent: The Political Economy of the Mass Media*, which was also the basis for an award-winning Canadian documentary film. In their book, Herman and Chomsky (1988, 2002, 1–2) advance a "propaganda model" of the mass media:

> The mass media serve as a system for communicating messages and symbols to the general populace. It is their function to amuse, entertain, and

inform, and to inculcate individuals with the values, beliefs, and codes of behavior that will integrate them into the institutional structures of the larger society. In a world of concentrated wealth and major conflicts of class interest, to fulfil this role requires systematic propaganda. ... A propaganda model focuses on this inequality of wealth and power and its multilevel effects on mass-media interests and choices. It traces the routes by which money and power are able to filter out the news fit to print, marginalize dissent, and allow the government and dominant private interests to get their messages across to the public.

A number of objections to the propaganda model have been itemized by Jeffrey Klaehn (2002). Critics see the model as far too deterministic, verging on conspiracy theory. It suggests that the interests of the elites are uniform and do not conflict with one another. Furthermore, the propaganda model makes many presumptions about how news editors and journalists make decisions—unconsciously or inadvertently in many cases, because their political views likely concur with those of the media outlets that hired them. The model also makes presumptions about the effects that news stories have on the public:

The most glaring criticism of the propaganda model that may be voiced in this context is that the model can be seen to take for granted yet still presume intervening processes. While it does not theorize audience effects, it presumes that news content is framed so as to (re)produce "privileged" interpretations of the news which are ideologically serviceable to corporate and state monied interests. If one assumes that "ideologically serviceable" means that the interpretations can and typically do propagandize and/or mislead audiences, then on logical grounds one can infer that the propaganda model does in fact presume and expect that media do have consequential influence and effects. ... [T]he model focuses exclusively on media content, rather than expanding its scope to studying media effects directly. Nor does it "test" actual beliefs and motivations of media personnel or seek to investigate the possible range of effects on government officials, lower-tier media or audiences. (Klaehn 2002, 6)

Mixed Motives: The Case of the CBC

Although analyzing the political economy of private media corporations is by no means a straightforward task, it might seem relatively simple when compared to a public broadcaster, such as the CBC. Canada's public broadcaster is in a unique position: it competes with private television broadcasters for ratings and advertising revenue yet receives government funding and is tasked with "representing Canada to Canadians." (Unlike the television division, CBC-Radio operates without advertising.)

The CBC often finds itself in a dilemma. On the one hand, it can aim to be "popular" and compete for a mass audience, leaving it open to criticism of "selling out" and ignoring its mandate as a public broadcaster. This approach also leaves the CBC vulnerable to critics who wonder why a public broadcaster uses taxpayers' money to produce expensive dramas and other programming that put it in competition with private broadcasters. On the other hand, it can choose to produce programs that may have less mass appeal—documentaries, regional coverage, and public-interest programming—yet would result in lower advertising revenues, and thus less funding for future programming.

In fact, one of the CBC's most lucrative assets is *Hockey Night in Canada*, one of the country's iconic shows, which generates millions of dollars of revenue each year. These funds are then funnelled into other types of less lucrative programming that might otherwise not be produced. Even this valuable property is at risk; many observers expect that in the near future, the CBC will be unable to match the bidding for ever-more expensive sports broadcasting rights. And in 2008, the CBC had to drop out of the bidding for the rights to the signature theme song for *Hockey Night in Canada*. The song can now be heard regularly on TSN's hockey broadcasts.

One of the more ironic sights on the CBC is hockey analyst Don Cherry (who is paid handsomely by Canadian taxpayers) as he consistently ruffles the feathers of any left-leaning audience members with his verbal jabs ("pinkos" and "tree huggers"). Yet, one can imagine the outcry if the CBC were to drop him from its roster of on-air personalities—a move that would no doubt elicit cries of "elitism" and left-wing bias.

The ongoing struggles of the CBC to define itself, and to succeed in the media marketplace while fulfilling its mandate as a public broadcaster, raise important questions. What is the role of a public broadcaster in an age of digital media? Could the CBC one day be the target of an attack from the political right, like the one that America's NPR (National Public Radio) experienced in 2011?[1]

Conclusion: Questions of Political Economy in the Digital Era

What potential do new media hold for increased democratization in our society? Some parts of the world, such as North Africa and the Middle East, have recently shown that the new media have great power to undermine existing authority structures. (The extent to which new media *themselves* create resistance among citizens of authoritarian regimes, and are not simply a *tool* used for political means, is a hotly debated issue.) Do new media have a fundamentally different connection, or relationship, to society's power

Do new media have a fundamentally different relationship to power, or do they just represent the appearance of change?

structures? Or do they simply reinforce those structures in the same way as old media, but with an outward *appearance* of change?

The major technological shifts currently underway in the world of media have, not surprisingly, gained a good deal of attention from scholars of political economy. Vincent Mosco (2008) has assessed recent trends in this field, and finds several different schools of thought. These range from those who see old patterns enduring, to those who see the new and disruptive connections that technology now makes possible.

On the one hand, the enormous capacity the media now have to reach gigantic, worldwide audiences suggests that new media may simply serve as a very useful new way for "old media" to expand its audience base significantly, and thereby reinforce its economic and political clout. As a result, rich nations would continue to dominate the economies and cultures of poorer nations, exert military power over them, and so on.

On the other hand, new media create problems for capitalism. "What was once a largely national market for film and video products and audiences is now a global one, posing serious challenges for coordination" (Mosco 2008). Moreover, the Internet has the potential to create a brand-new "network economy," raising important questions for our traditional concepts of economic power.

Amid the chaos of the current revolution in media technology, there are proving to be many ways of defining its causes and effects, and assessing the benefits and drawbacks for citizens of democratic societies.

NOTE

1. In March 2011 a conservative political commentator, James O'Keefe, had two accomplices clandestinely record a conversation with two of NPR's senior management in which the latter made disparaging remarks about political conservatives, as well as other controversial comments. When these remarks were made public, NPR CEO Vivian Schiller resigned.

DISCUSSION QUESTIONS

1. In the weeks leading up to the Iraq war, demonstrators were able to organize themselves "under the radar," using the Internet, which at that time (2002–2003) had not yet been fully adopted by the major news corporations. How might similar events unfold differently today, now that the Internet is widely used by citizens and corporations alike?

2. Consider the people who work in media industries today. How is their work different from that of similar workers in the 20th century?
3. Do new media have the capacity to fundamentally change how power is wielded in our society? Or are such claims wishful thinking? Explain.

SUGGESTED RESOURCES
Books

Adorno, Theodor, and Max Horkheimer. 1944/2002. "The Culture Industry: Enlightenment as Mass Deception." In *Dialectic of Enlightenment*, translated by Edmund Jephcott. Palo Alto, CA: Stanford University Press.

Hazen, Don, and Julie Winokur. 1997. *We the Media: A Citizens' Guide to Fighting for Media Democracy*. New York: The New Press.

Mosco, Vincent. 2009. *The Political Economy of Communication* (2nd ed.). London: Sage.

Website

Friends of Canadian Broadcasting. http://www.friends.ca.

REFERENCES

Bagdikian, Ben H. 2004. *The New Media Monopoly*. Boston: Beacon Press.

Bai, Matt. 2008 (October 15). "Working for the Working-Class Vote." *The New York Times*. Accessed April 20, 2011. http://www.nytimes.com/2008/10/19/magazine/19obama-t.html.

Boisset, Yves, director. 2004. *U.S. Media Blues*. Documentary film.

Butler, Samantha. 2011 (March 29). "CBC's Voter Quiz Tool Flawed, Prof Says." *Toronto Sun*. Accessed April 20, 2011. http://www.torontosun.com/news/decision2011/2011/03/29/17798821.html.

Canadian Newspaper Association. 2011. Accessed April 20. http://www.newspaperscanada.ca/about-newspapers/faq-about-newspapers/faq.

Gandel, Stephen. 2011. "Is Facebook Really Worth $50 Billion?" *Time*. Accessed April 20. http://curiouscapitalist.blogs.time.com/2011/01/03/is-facebook-really-worth-50-billion.

Herman, Edward S., and Noam Chomsky. 1988/2002. *Manufacturing Consent: The Political Economy of the Mass Media*. New York: Pantheon Books.

Kellner, Douglas. 2005. *Media Culture and the Triumph of the Spectacle*. Accessed April 20, 2011. http://gseis.ucla.edu/faculty/kellner/essays/mediaculturetriumphspectacle.pdf.

Klaehn, Jeffrey. 2002. "A Critical Review and Assessment of Herman and Chomsky's 'Propaganda Model.'" *European Journal of Communication* 17(2):147–82.

Klein, Naomi. 2000. *No Logo: Taking Aim at the Brand Bullies*. Toronto: Knopf Canada.

McChesney, Robert W. 2003. "The Nine Firms That Dominate the World." *Information Clearing House*. Accessed April 20, 2011. http://www.informationclearinghouse.info/article4424.htm.

McChesney, Robert W. 2008. *The Political Economy of Media: Enduring Issues, Emerging Dilemmas*, 12. New York: Monthly Review Press.

Morrison, Ian. 2004 (March 14). "Issues on the Canadian Media Landscape." Remarks at the University of Manitioba. Accessed April 20, 2011. http://www.friends.ca/speech/272.

Mosco, Vincent. 2008. "Current Trends in the Political Economy of Communication." *Global Media Journal—Canadian Edition* 1(1).

Nesbitt-Larking, Paul. 2007. *Politics, Society, and the Media* (2nd ed.). Peterborough, ON: Broadview Press.

Scahill, Jeremy. 2005. "The War on Al Jazeera." Accessed April 20, 2011. http://www.alternet.org/world/28975.

Srivastava, Vinita. 2010. "Blog to the Future." In *The New Journalist: Roles, Skills, and Critical Thinking*, 243. Toronto: Emond Montgomery.

Regulating the Media

Why govern the media? What kinds of power are governments, and other actors, trying to exercise? What are the limits to control in the 21st century?

KEY CONCEPTS

1. Communication technologies are integral to the exercise of power, and are therefore of concern to governments.

2. *Why* societies govern communication is inextricably linked with *how* they govern.

3. There are many reasons for governing the media because media are complex and serve to connect, and often influence, virtually every element of our society.

CHAPTER OUTLINE

Introduction: Power, Policy, and the Media 151

Controlling the Message, Controlling the Media 157

Policies in Conflict 166

Conclusion: The Limits of Policy 167

Notes 168

Discussion Questions 168

Suggested Resources 169

References 169

Introduction: Power, Policy, and the Media

Why Govern the Media?

In late September 2010, Iranian-Canadian blogger Hossein Derakhshan was sentenced to 19 years in prison by Iranian authorities for creating "anti-government propaganda" in his Internet blog (CBC Newsworld 2010). For those Canadians aware of the story of his arrest, trial, and sentencing, this may be one of the few times we actually notice how the media are governed: a repressive foreign government stifles dissension to secure its grip on power. We are, for the most part, far less aware of the other, far less sinister ways in which media may be governed in our own country, or why our government might wish to do so.

To offer a very general answer to the question, "why govern the media?": the media are governed because, as the means of communication, they are

Figure 9.1 Hossein Derakhshan

The arrest in Iran of Iranian-Canadian blogger Hossein Derakhshan offers an extreme example of how some authorities are threatened by the power of the blogosphere, and the lengths to which they will go in attempting to control it.

SOURCE: IranNewsNow.com.

inextricably associated with power. We may define communication in its more instrumental form—exchanging or circulating information (Lasswell 1948/1960), or in its ritual form of associating—as being with others, or as the way in which we collectively shape our reality (Carey 1989). Either way, it is clear that power exists through communication, and that power is a key concept in many theories of media and communication.

One of Canadian philosopher Harold Innis's (1950/1986) main insights was the degree to which communications media shaped the extent and duration of power throughout history. For example, he noted that light, portable media (such as paper or electronic communication) have played a vital role in the exercise of power over extensive empires. Such media permitted the rapid conveyance of commands and edicts from a capital to the outermost limits of the empire and, conversely, information and intelligence back to the centre (94, 103). Norbert Wiener's (1954) work on cybernetics makes an even closer connection between the two: for Wiener, communication is essentially the exercise of power or control in a theory that takes in not only human beings but also machines and even nature (24–25).

KEY CONCEPT
Communication technologies are integral to the exercise of power, and are therefore of concern to governments.

If such a broad answer were all that was required, our work would be done. However, we are after a more focused response. As French philosopher Michel Foucault (1980) has written, power is an extraordinarily various concept and perhaps best examined in its details (115–16). In fact, power over the media is exercised by any number of actors, from those who own and operate media outlets to those who consume media. In this case, we are looking more specifically at the state and the particular kinds of power it exercises over the media. We are concerned with **policy**, encompassing both the means of and the reasons for governing.

The biggest challenge in answering this question may be that there are potentially so many such reasons. This is not to say that media demand strict supervision in every detail; in fact, as with much of society, many aspects of media seem not to be governed at all, nor to need such intervention. For example, unlike teachers, lawyers, or medical doctors, journalists require no specific training or certification in order to practise their trade. Certainly, there are specific skills necessary to be a competent journalist but in Canada, as in most western countries, governments don't concern themselves with how these skills are acquired or assessed. Nonetheless, there are a great many ways in which media are governed, some of which are more obvious than others, but all of which have fairly specific reasons. As this chapter will show, it is almost impossible to answer the question of *why* the media are governed without also examining *how* they are governed.

Governing Media in a Democracy

At first glance, state controls over media might, as John Street (1997) comments, convey an Orwellian picture of authoritarian or even totalitarian governments using censorship and **propaganda** to rule over the populace (77). But power is not absent in democracies; it is just configured differently (77). Not only are such techniques known in Western liberal democracies but, more importantly, they are not the only manner in which media are governed. A government in which the power, at least nominally, rests with the population requires different techniques of governance—a different kind of exercise of power, and different reasons for doing so. Media governance in its various forms is at least as integral to the exercise of democracy as for authoritarian forms of government, because the media are the public's major resource for information. For this reason, various notions and aspects of the public are frequently invoked in Western democracies with regard to media policy. The media, we are told, are there to serve us. The term "public interest" has been a central concept in forming American media policy since the 1920s; the government insists that broadcasters act to benefit the people,

policy
Media policy and cultural policy (often intertwined) are the decisions and strategies that governments make "in the public interest," and are intended to cultivate or control the media industry and cultural institutions.

propaganda
Information intended to influence the public's beliefs about something; can be true to varying degrees, but is often deceptive and sometimes entirely false.

even if the definition of public interest is remarkably vague. Likewise in Canada, our *Broadcasting Act* explicitly refers to broadcasting as a "public service" (*Broadcasting Act*, s. 3(1)(b)).

Such terms outline what is still a very general concept of media policy and its rationale. There are many ways of defining the public interest, perhaps too many (Fly 1941, 102). There are also many ways in which the media might be said to serve the public—as a means of receiving or conveying information, as a means of entertainment or instruction, as a means of expressing ourselves. All these and more could be comfortably contained within the term "public service." But these terms refer mainly to one type of media (broadcasting) and to the policies of one level of government (federal). Media policy concerns not only national governments, but also a number of international bodies, as well as many local and regional governments. The nature and scope of their involvement with media vary widely according to their powers, interests, and ideologies.

Governments do not act alone in the policy process.

Nor do governments act alone in the policy process. In the formulation and exercise of policy, governments are assisted and supplemented by private groups and even individuals. Industry associations, such as the now-defunct Canadian Association of Broadcasters, played an enormous role in developing broadcasting policy in Canada from the 1950s to the 1990s, as government sought their input on many policy matters. Private copyright collectives such as Access Copyright or SOCAN are responsible for collecting payments from users of copyrighted works. These actors have their own sets of motives that overlap, accord with, or even diverge from the government's own. Clearly, any single explanation for the rationale of all these actors is likely an oversimplification.

Even if we look only at Canada, where policy has loomed large in the discussion of media, we might have a lot of explaining to do. Politicians, journalists, and academics are willing to concede that policy plays an enormous role in relation to our media, both in positive and negative ways— media policies have been credited with, among other things, creating a Canadian music industry (Copps 1998) or failing to support the growth of a Canadian national cinema (Magder 1993). Whether such assessments are justified is another matter, but in any case, government is deeply involved in our media and cultural industries.

While some scholars have tried to subject Canadian media policy to a single logic, such as that of national security (Dowler 1996), such attempts tend to ignore the broad concerns that various policy actors bring to the policy-making process, and the diversity of sites where this process takes place. For example, developments in economic policy areas, such as trade and finance, clearly have consequences for media. Media are industries, and as such are subject to taxes, the effects of fiscal policy, and trade agreements. When Canada pressed for the specific exemption of culture, including the media, from the terms of the 1987 Canada–US Free Trade Agreement and, later, the North American Free Trade Agreement (which added Mexico), this was an acknowledgment of how trade practices and policies in goods and services affect Canada's media and cultural industries. The point is not simply that media are caught up in these sweeping and powerful policy formations; media are also connected with many, more local and limited, policies that also have considerable implications.

Local Policies

Some of the policies concerning the music industry in Canada illustrate the complexity of such connections. Federal broadcast regulations require most commercial radio stations to devote 35 percent of their programming to Canadian music selections ("Canadian content").[1] This policy has been credited with stimulating production of Canadian recordings, which can benefit from the promotion that airplay provides (Yorke 1971, cited in Lorimer, Gasher, and Skinner 2008, 176). Federal subsidies such as the Canada Music Fund, which provides a number of programs that benefit Canada's music industry, as well as a number of provincial programs (which have more limited, regional aims), have supported Canadian content. These programs are meant to ensure the supply and development of new and emerging musical artists.

Figure 9.2 Arcade Fire

In their early years as a band, Montreal's Arcade Fire benefited from affordable rents and municipal regulations in that city, which, quite indirectly, allowed the local music scene to explode into international prominence.

SOURCE: Flickr/ManAlive! Reproduced under Creative Commons licence.

Turn over a copy of a CD by Broken Social Scene or Metric, and you will see a logo for the Canadian government. This indicates that the record companies (Arts & Crafts Productions and Last Gang Records, respectively) received government grants or loans for the production of these recordings through FACTOR, a private foundation that administers part of the Canada Music Fund in English Canada. In addition, these companies received strategic business development grants through another part of the Canada Music Fund, the Music Entrepreneur Program.

But these programs and policies (and even provincial policies) operate at a level that most musical artists never reach—that of recording and obtaining airplay on commercial radio. To get to this level, most musical artists must develop their careers initially through local, smaller-scale activities such as playing live at local venues, allowing them to learn their craft, develop a following, and perhaps even make a little money. Although federal policy has little to say about such activities, municipal policy can shape the context in which these activities take place. Bylaws and regulations concerning zoning, liquor licensing, and noise affect the number and profitability of possible venues and, by extension, the opportunities of local bands to play live. Will Straw (2005) has suggested that Montreal's emergence as a centre for disco in the 1970s and beyond was based on a complex mixture of municipal bylaws, regulations concerning the use of recorded music, and a host of other factors (190–91). Similar policies may take the credit for the blossoming of that city's live music scene over the past decade. These policies govern the media, although for the most part on different grounds than promoting the careers of musicians, let alone helping to develop a distinctive Canadian culture. Municipal policies are more likely to be aimed at preventing noise that disturbs residents or other businesses, limiting the consumption of liquor, or ensuring the collection of certain taxes. But these municipal policy measures have consequences for the supply of artists and the sustainability of Canadian content regulation. They also govern media, such as recordings, by limiting the ways and contexts in which audiences can use them—in conjunction with other activities, such as eating, drinking, or dancing; permissible venues; and hours of operation.

The reasons to govern the media may also vary with the media concerned. Media theorists such as Innis (1950/1986) and McLuhan (1964) have taught us to be attentive to *differences among* various media and the way those media affect human interaction, and this attention clearly has implications for media policy. There are obvious differences among, say, television, newspapers, and radio—not to mention other media forms, such as cinema, books, or sound recordings—in terms of how we use them and the kinds of communication they facilitate or enhance. Likewise, the "new media" associated with digital technologies are distinguished from older media in terms of their accessibility and **interactivity**. For these reasons, different media are not all governed equally.

For example, Canadian broadcasting (radio and television) is subject to many regulations and controls concerning who may operate such undertakings and the kinds of programming they provide, whereas newspapers are hardly regulated at all (the reasons for this are discussed below). The Internet is governed by telecommunications to some extent, in terms of how the service is provided to users, but hardly at all in terms of its content (with this latter kind of governance restricted to those few communications that violate criminal law). Such differences are rooted in the distinctive characteristics and histories of these media—the different possibilities that each provides for communication. Thus, each medium exhibits differences in relation to the powers of the state, institutions, and individuals.

interactivity
The capacity for users not simply to receive information but to shape, customize, or share it, and to provide feedback or commentary.

Controlling the Message, Controlling the Media

We can highlight these differences by looking at particular ways of governing the media, such as placing restrictions on communication. Restrictions can be determined on the basis of content—as long as media have existed, governments have tried to prevent the circulation of content that they judge to be obscene, blasphemous, libelous, or seditious. There are different reasons for exercising such powers. Preventing a group from calling for violent overthrow of the government (in the case of sedition) is different from banning a book because its graphic sexual content might offend readers' sensibilities or corrupt public morals (in the case of obscenity).

Media may also be governed very differently in terms of how they are allowed to circulate certain kinds of messages. Sexually explicit material that is permissible in print form might not be allowed for broadcast over radio, which prohibits such use. People reading sexually explicit content in a book or magazine rarely do so by accident, but children may inadvertently be exposed to such content if it is broadcast over the air. Radio and television are regarded as more public media than a book, both in terms of the public resource they utilize (the airwaves) and in their diffusion to their audience, which is more widespread and diverse. This different standard was on display, so to speak, in the debates and hearings that followed the brief flash of Janet Jackson's breast during the Super Bowl XXXVIII half-time show—a "wardrobe malfunction" that resulted in the imposition of a fine on the broadcaster, CBS, by the Federal Communications Commission, the US broadcast regulator (FCC 2004b).

Copyright Laws

Copyright laws offer another excellent example of the ways in which various media are governed differently. Recently, the US Department of Homeland Security shut down a number of websites it claimed were infringing copyright by posting music selections on their sites (Sisario 2010). This action was not unusual, given the many lawsuits aimed at preventing the distribution of copyrighted content over websites (such as MP3.com) and peer-to-peer networks (such as Napster). In this case, however, it was the government and not copyright owners who took action against infringers. The American government is moving to protect the **intellectual property** of record labels by restricting the circulation of that content. But a radio station could have played these songs over the air without the express permission of the record company, as long as it paid a blanket tariff to the appropriate copyright collective, such as ASCAP, BMI, or SESAC. The difference is that the targeted sites were offering the material in a different manner than a radio station. Unlike a radio station, where a song is played at a particular passing moment, the users of the targeted sites could determine for themselves when, and how many times, they listened to a song. The level of interactivity is one of the differences that determine how particular media are governed, a provision that is articulated in copyright legislation such as that before the Canadian Parliament at the time of writing.[2]

As Sheryl Hamilton (2007) has noted, one of the effects of the Internet has been to focus attention on the individual user with regard to intellectual property rights. The proposed copyright legislation spells out consumer rights in detail—what we may and may not do with the content we obtain over the Internet or other interactive media technologies, such as personal video recorders. This concern with the individual and the flow of information works both ways: Canada's Privacy Commissioner recently required the social-networking site Facebook to revise practices with regard to the information its users provided, to allow individuals greater control over the personal data that they were sharing and the people with whom they shared it (Office of the Privacy Commissioner 2009).

Spectrum Scarcity

In some cases, governments also control who gets to circulate information. Here, too, the media are governed unequally. Perhaps the clearest example of how the state governs who may circulate information is found in broadcasting. The broadcast spectrum is limited—there are only so many radio and television stations that can occupy the airwaves. This **scarcity** at least

---

intellectual property
The legal ownership and rights held by a creator of a musical, literary, or artistic work.

spectrum scarcity
Restrictions on the number of possible media outlets arising from the limited number of radio or television channels, Internet bandwidth, etc.

partly justifies the creation of a number of kinds of broadcasting policy. Broadcasters' privileged access to what is deemed a scarce public resource has helped the Canadian government justify its broadcasting regulations (such as Canadian content) under the auspices of the *Broadcasting Act.* Similarly, attempts by government regulators to manage the diversity of offerings on broadcasting systems (not only over the air, but also through cable and satellite distribution) are based on the idea of a scarce resource. For broadcasting, at least, scarcity has played a fundamental role in policy-making. The scarcity of the broadcast spectrum means that broadcasting requires some form of intervention to make it workable. Without some agreement over who gets to occupy which frequency, the airspace would quickly become chaotic.

Throughout the 1920s, the US federal government made several attempts to impose some order on this situation, impeded by challenges to its authority. Susan Douglas (1999, 63) provides a colourful description of the situation after one court decision overturned the government's right to regulate:

> Etheric hell broke loose. Over seven hundred stations, many of which boosted their power, jumped frequencies, and broadcast when they weren't supposed to, battling over ninety-six channels. ... Interference, often in the form of cross talk, overlapping voices and music, or noise, became so bad that in many areas listeners couldn't receive a consistent broadcast signal and sales began to falter.

The last sentence in this quotation suggests that at least part of the American government's rationale for broadcast regulation was economic. Even with its ideological commitment to free markets and competition, the US government had to restrict entry into the market for trade to be orderly enough to be viable.

Such restrictions do not necessarily apply to other media. For example, no policies in Canada (beyond national ownership) restrict entry into the field of newspaper ownership. As with most Western democracies, the government does not license newspapers, and although there may be significant barriers to entry into this field, these difficulties are not the deliberate result of government policy. The means to produce and distribute newspapers are not limited for technical reasons such as spectrum scarcity. Also, the lack of government control is bound up with notions of the freedom of an independent press as an integral element of a functioning democracy, and with the long-standing role that newspapers have played in articulating and spreading democratic ideas. In the United States, freedom of the press is guaranteed under the First Amendment to the Constitution respecting freedom of expression. Canada takes a similar view. This does not mean that newspapers lie wholly outside policy, but the question of ownership is far less restrictive than has been the case in the broadcasting industry. In Canada, the federal government simply requires that ownership of newspapers remain in Canadian hands.

Net Neutrality

Questions of access and scarcity also play out differently with regard to the Internet. Rather than restricting access for producers of content, as in the case of broadcasting, or more or less ignoring it, as with newspapers, Canadian government policy is concerned with promoting the widest possible access to the medium for both producers and users. This is partly because the whole question of access on the Internet is different from that in the traditional mass media, which are more top-down forms of communication. For broadcast, this means that while government regulators imposed necessary limits on producers of communication over the air, they were simultaneously attempting to make these messages available to as wide an audience as possible. On the Internet, the distinction between producers and consumers of communication is blurry, at least in theory, although most people consume more information than they produce. People value the Internet partly because they value its openness and interactivity—the qualities that many would claim were integral to its conception (Castells 2001, 36ff.) and which make it difficult (but not impossible) to control. This is not simply a concern with freedom of expression or the Internet's potential as a vehicle for a renewed public sphere, but a recognition of the medium's utility for commerce and industry.

> *People value the Internet partly because they value its openness and interactivity.*

Government policy debates are focused on ensuring that the Internet's qualities are not compromised. Regulation of scarcity relates to the telecommunications companies' ability to manage traffic and to ensure that bandwidth is adequate for demand, but at the same time to ensure that control over the infrastructure does not impinge on the free flow of information over the network (**net neutrality**). Theoretically, there is no limit on the number of users who can access the Internet, and so there is little justification for requirements to provide specific kinds of content. In 1999 (partly driven by concern over the Internet's status as an "electronic public commons"), Canada's broadcast and telecommunications regulator, the Canadian Radio-television and Telecommunications Commission, elected not to impose any content regulation on the Internet (CRTC 1999, 56).

net neutrality
The principle that Internet service providers should ensure equal treatment to all users and all content.

SIDEBAR

Net Neutrality

On December 23, 2010 the Federal Communications Commission of the United States released its long-anticipated ruling on Internet governance. In its ruling, the FCC announced that it was acting to "preserve Internet freedom and openness" (FCC 2010). The issue that the FCC was dealing with was "net neutrality"—a term that refers to the principle that Internet service providers (ISPs) must offer equal treatment to all users and all content. Debates over control of the Internet have been a concern for many pundits and Internet developers for some time (see Weitzner 2006). The debate came to prominence in 2004, when FCC Chairman Michael Powell called on American ISPs to adopt the principles of "Net Freedom" (FCC 2004a). Powell specified four specific principles:

- Freedom to access content.
- Freedom to use applications.
- Freedom to attach personal devices.
- Freedom to obtain service plan information.

Powell's remarks were made in response to growing pressure from the major telecommunications companies that ultimately control access to broadband Internet services. These companies may have been seeking to favour some business clients over others for strategic reasons, to restrict or even refuse access to applications (such as Skype) that might compete with their other services (long-distance telephone), or to block certain kinds of content altogether. In many cases, the ISPs claimed they needed the ability to restrict certain content in order to manage the available bandwidth of their services more effectively. This practice is called "traffic shaping" by its proponents and "throttling" by its opponents. While Powell's remarks were largely concerned with consumers' rights, the debate over net neutrality also concerned other users of the Internet, such as application developers or resellers of Internet access. In its 2010 ruling, the FCC required ISPs to adhere to principles of transparency in how they manage the network and not to engage in "unreasonable discrimination" regarding content or applications. They were allowed some degree of control in managing bandwidth, but not to allow some users to "pay for priority."

Previously, the FCC's Canadian counterpart, the CRTC, had allowed major Canadian ISPs, such as Rogers and Bell, to engage in limited "traffic shaping," but only where absolutely necessary and only with full transparency (CRTC 2008). There may be some irony in government regulators' exerting their authority to ensure freedom and openness in the public sphere. In any case, the episode suggests that at least some of the threats to the openness and freedom of the Internet come not from government regulators but from the private sector companies that own the infrastructure by which the Internet runs.

Governing Through the Media

Governments do not just control the media by setting restrictions and limits on expression and circulation. If anything, the examples above show a disinclination to use these means. There are also reasons *not* to govern the media, given the view—enshrined in the Canadian Constitution (see below), as well as those of other countries—that freedom of expression is fundamental to democracy. According to many scholars of communication and politics, without the public sphere that the media provide, the concept of rule by the people would have been more difficult to articulate and diffuse widely, and its practice might never have come about (Habermas 1964/1974).

Furthermore, governments also govern *through* the media as a useful means of achieving certain policy aims. In some cases, governments attempt to inform the public; in others, to influence the public's beliefs, attitudes, or behaviours through persuasion or, perhaps, propaganda (although sometimes the line between the two is unclear). Government ads about the dangers of smoking may be true, but they are meant not just to inform but to influence people's behaviour. Likewise, public health bulletins that encourage people to get flu shots, or government campaigns promoting traffic safety, could be considered propaganda of a sort.

PRIMARY SOURCE

The Canadian Charter of Rights and Freedoms

The rights to free expression and a free press are enshrined among Canadians' "fundamental freedoms" in the Charter:

Guarantee of Rights and Freedoms

Rights and freedoms in Canada

1. The *Canadian Charter of Rights and Freedoms* guarantees the rights and freedoms set out in it subject only to such reasonable limits prescribed by law as can be demonstrably justified in a free and democratic society.

Fundamental Freedoms

Fundamental freedoms

2. Everyone has the following fundamental freedoms:
   (a) freedom of conscience and religion;
   (b) freedom of thought, belief, opinion and expression, including freedom of the press and other media of communication;
   (c) freedom of peaceful assembly; and
   (d) freedom of association.

The First World War was a watershed moment in understanding such methods of government. Propaganda played an important role in the war and was accorded considerable credit for the outcome (Mattelart 1996/2000, 36). Exaggerations of success on one's own side and of the enemy's atrocities and setbacks encouraged enlistment and helped strengthen the resolve of the general population. In the wake of the war, some American scholars reflected on the implications of the efficacy of propaganda for large, increasingly pluralist states. The work of Walter Lippmann (1922/1965) and Harold Lasswell (1948/1960) on propaganda recognized media as integral to communication in mass society and, as such, an extremely powerful tool (Czitrom 1982, 123). In these authors' view, the public was vulnerable to the media's influence and could be exploited by governments. Lippmann's work, in particular, questioned whether the vast majority of the public was capable of discerning the truth or value of the information they received via the media. In his view, media could best serve as a means of conveying to the public the well-informed and well-reasoned opinions of the small elite capable of formulating them. Such reflections were significant at a time when the number of media through which one might govern was expanding considerably. Governments on both sides during the war had already taken note of new media forms such as cinema, and had moved to incorporate them into their information strategies (Kracauer 1947/2004, 35).

To Lippmann and Lasswell, the public was vulnerable to the media's influence and could be exploited by governments.

The legacy of the First World War was still being felt as another new medium, radio broadcasting, first emerged in the years immediately following the conflict. During the war, radio (which was then used for person-to-person communication, prior to becoming a tool for broadcasting) had been under military control, with its uses tightly restricted. After the war and the transition back to civilian authority, this new form of radio broadcasting—together with the potential mass audience of newspapers and the speed of the telegraph and telephone—presented both threats and opportunities for governments. Threats arose from the difficulty of controlling information circulated by radio; opportunities included using the medium for educational functions similar to those of museums or schools. Taken together, these grounds were enough to convince many national governments of the necessity of creating a state monopoly over broadcasting. For example, in the United Kingdom, the British Broadcasting Corporation (BBC) was established as the sole purveyor of radio broadcasting.

Defending and Asserting Canadian Culture

The BBC was established partly as a means of asserting a British national identity against the growing influence of American mass culture (Frith

1988). This rationale may strike a chord in Canada, where cultural sovereignty underpins our cultural policy (including much of media policy). Thus, the media in Canada are governed to preserve our distinctiveness and unity as a country in the face of American popular culture. This is particularly true for Canadian content regulations and programs that fund production in the media and cultural industries, as well as for policies limiting foreign investment in broadcasting, film distribution, and book retailing. Although much Canadian broadcast regulation depends on the assumption of scarcity, how we choose to deploy this limited resource has often been based on the aim of preserving or enhancing Canadian sovereignty. This was the case with the 1929 Aird Commission, which the government called in response to concerns about the erosion of Canadian nationalism in regard to broadcasting, and which resulted in the creation of the CBC. This was arguably

HISTORICAL HIGHLIGHT

Banned on the BBC

Not only authoritarian countries such as Iran or China have imposed bans on what their citizens can see or hear. In recent decades, broadcasters in Western countries have often felt the need to clamp down on what many might consider harmless pop music. In 1982, the jaunty pop song "Six Months in a Leaky Boat" by New Zealand band Split Enz was targeted by the BBC—not officially banned, but "discouraged from airplay"—because of concerns that it would undermine public morale during the Falklands War, then raging between Great Britain and Argentina. That the song was recorded and released *before* the outbreak of the war, and its lyrics make no reference to the Royal Navy or Great Britain, was considered beside the point.

A much more provocative song, "God Save the Queen," by pioneering punk band The Sex Pistols, was banned in the UK when it was released in 1977. That year, England was also celebrating the 25th anniversary of the reign of Queen Elizabeth II. Despite the ban, the song reached the top of the charts, and decades later, the Sex Pistols are hailed as rock music legends, while their only album, *Never Mind the Bollocks, Here's the Sex Pistols*, is regarded as one of the most influential of all time.

Not surprisingly, the context in which a song, movie, or book appears can have a great impact on how the public, broadcasters, and the authorities respond to it. Still, it is important to note that free expression in a democracy is undoubtedly compromised if it is only allowed at times when it is considered "safe" to do so, and when it presents no challenge to authority.

Canada's first fully developed cultural policy, although it was not described as such. Likewise, the institution of Canadian content, first in television in the 1960s and subsequently in radio in the 1970s, is also based on Canadian cultural sovereignty (Edwardson 2008).

Yet, the function of these institutions and policies is not solely defensive. Canadian (and, for that matter, British) identity cannot be defined simply in terms of not being American. The assertion of national identity has to include the positive characteristics that are desirable in the population. In the case of the BBC, from its initial conception it was hoped that it would, as its commissioner John Reith wrote, address the listener as an individual "capable of growth and discernment" (quoted in Frith 1988, 28). The cultivation of such active listeners positioned broadcasting as a public service that would, according to Reith, bring "happier homes, broader culture, and truer citizenship" (Frith 1988, 29). This "public service" model of broadcasting would prove widely influential, as Canada's CBC and the use of the term in our *Broadcasting Act* attest. Similarly, Canadian cultural sovereignty involves not only distinguishing ourselves from Americans but a positive identification with Canada and the dissemination of a set of values (however vague) that we associate with our country. Another assessment of the media's role in government—less gloomy than Lippmann's and Lasswell's—appears in the work of their contemporary and fellow American, John Dewey (1924). While acknowledging the enormous influence of the media and the vulnerability of the public, Dewey proposed that the media might be a means of educating people to become competent in the duties of citizenship, and thus help create the conditions for an engaged and active citizenry.

> *Dewey proposed that the media might be a means of educating people to become competent in the duties of citizenship.*

Even in Dewey's time this was hardly a new idea. The use of various means for cultivating people's capacities to equip them for citizenship existed at least as early as the 18th-century Enlightenment (Miller 1993, 14ff.). The **elitist** view of the policy implications of culture held by the BBC's John Reith was based on Matthew Arnold's definition of culture as "the best of that which has been thought or said." It stands in contrast to Dewey's more broadly democratic view of the media's role.

elitist
The tendency to ascribe greater value to the opinions and actions of the wealthiest and most intellectual people in society.

The point here is that various kinds of media are being used to cultivate certain kinds of individuals, to create citizens with the necessary equipment both to exercise power and to be subject to it. It would be fair to say that in our society, the media carry out this very function (Miller 1998, 12). This is one of the fundamental ways in which power, as Foucault suggests, is not simply repressive but productive of "forms of knowledge" and "discourses" (1980, 119). In the context of this discussion,

KEY CONCEPT
Why societies govern communication is inextricably linked with *how* they govern.

though, we see that our ability to answer *why* we govern the media depends, to some extent, on *how* the media are governed.

Policies in Conflict

Given the diverse reasons for governing the media and the means for doing so, it is hardly surprising that policies sometimes interact or interfere with one another in unexpected ways. Media policies are always changing, along with the rationale behind them. And even as new policies are created, older policies (sometimes with conflicting aims) may persist—a situation known as policy "layering" (Parker and Parenta 2008). Policies may also conflict because they start from different principles and areas. So while they govern the media, they rarely do so exactly as intended. Resolving such conflicts is seldom straightforward.

Wikileaks and Conflicting Rationales

The recent controversy over Wikileaks and its release of sensitive, classified documents from the United States and other governments provides an example of the conflicting rationales for media policy in Western liberal democracies. These documents could potentially disrupt the foreign policy and security aims of many states. It is understandable that governments would wish to exercise control over the media in this case, whether to prevent compromising intelligence operations or simply to avoid embarrassment, and many politicians and media experts would agree. But the laws that forbid releasing such information apply mainly to those who are directly involved in obtaining it, not to Wikileaks itself, which is merely publishing information it was given. Some news outlets, such as the *New York Times* (2010), consulted with the US government before publishing portions of this material and voluntarily agreed to withhold some of the documents. At the time of writing, the United States government has taken no action (apart from moral suasion) to prevent the circulation of these documents in the media. It would seem that First Amendment rights[3]—and the interests of powerful media corporations such as the *New York Times*—trump the interests of state secrecy, at least in this particular case.

More generally, we may see a conflict at the heart of much media policy. This arises from the characterization of the media as cultural or creative industries, which places them on the fence between the two rationales of culture and economics. If culture and economy are uneasy bedfellows—as Horkheimer and Adorno's (1941) original coining of the term "culture industry" was meant to suggest—this does not diminish the fact that they are closely bound up with each other. The economics of cultural commodities may differ from other kinds (see Caves 2000; Grant and Wood 2004), but the fact that we consume culture in commodity form whenever we go to a movie or download a song is inescapably true (Miller and Yúdice 2002, 73). As these authors point out, cultural policy is generally developed in response to cultural industries and their dominance (72). This is the case for Canadian cultural policy, such as the establishment of the CBC. The report of the Massey Commission (Royal Commission 1951) also positioned Canadian cultural policy as essentially in opposition to economic or industrial manifestations of culture. In Canada until the 1980s, the government regarded copyright as generally not part of cultural policy, a position that is almost unthinkable now. Yet even before this, Canada—along with many other countries—had long recognized that cultural industries are central to cultural policy, and that there is a need to make these industries a part of policy rather than excluding them from the discussion.

Conclusion: The Limits of Policy

This chapter has explored a number of reasons for governing the media, but these are by no means exhaustive. A full enumeration of the reasons for governance would not be possible, because these are not always clear. This does not mean that media policies are invalid or useless. The problem lies in detailing the complexity of how these policies actually play out. As in the case of municipal policy and popular music, the effects of policy are often far more wide-ranging than policy-makers intend. Besides the policies cited in this chapter, Straw (2005) adds provincial educational policies that established four universities in Montreal (and, hence, a large student population) and political policies—most notably, the pursuit of Quebec sovereignty that, arguably, brought about a decline in the city's economy but made it an inexpensive locale for artists. Such policies were not designed with the health of Montreal's various music scenes in mind (Straw 2005, 191).

The examples of policy conflicts also show that the effects and interactions of policy cannot be completely anticipated. Both policy-makers and academics try to link policy measures with particular outcomes, but this is often difficult to do. It is not just that policies fail to effect the desired outcome, nor that they result in undesirable outcomes. Policies rarely, if ever, succeed or fail just on their own, but rather do so as a result of interacting with many other factors. This is true of all public policy, but particularly so where media policy is concerned. The media themselves are complex and heterogeneous entities, with many different components and aspects, among them

KEY CONCEPT
There are many different reasons for governing the media because media are so complex and serve to connect, and often influence, virtually every element of our society.

content, audiences, producers, institutions—and, incidentally, policy. All these factors share numerous points of contact with other entities. We have also seen that media policies have consequences in other fields—indeed, most of the reasons for governing the media would stem from such consequences, whether these are political, economic, cultural, or moral. The media are governed for many reasons that we know, but also in ways of which we are, at best, only partially aware. This is because the media are interconnected with so many other fields and activities. We can't help governing the media, even if we don't try.

By their very nature, the media are in the middle—intersecting with countless other activities and entities in many different ways: politically, socially, economically, and culturally. This is the media's relationship to power, as well as the basis on which they are governed.

NOTES

1. The details of Canadian content regulations for television and radio, as well as media ownership, the "MAPL" system for assessing Canadian music, and more, can be found at http://www.crtc.gc.ca/eng/cancon.htm.

2. "For the purposes of this Act, communication of a work or other subject-matter to the public by telecommunication includes making it available to the public by telecommunication in a way that allows a member of the public to have access to it from a place and at a time individually chosen by that member of the public." (Bill C-32, *An Act to Amend the Copyright Act*, s. 3(1.1).)

3. The First Amendment to the United States Constitution reads: "Congress shall make no law respecting an establishment of religion, or prohibiting the free exercise thereof; or abridging the freedom of speech, or of the press; or the right of the people peaceably to assemble, and to petition the Government for a redress of grievances."

DISCUSSION QUESTIONS

1. Would it be possible for the Canadian government to enact content regulations for the Internet? Suggest some ways that the government might do this.

2. With the example of Wikileaks in mind, do you think there are situations in which governments should intervene to prevent the circulation of certain messages? When are such measures justified?

3. Unlike its Canadian counterpart, the CRTC, the US broadcasting regulator, the Federal Communications Commission (FCC), has not imposed content regulation on broadcasters. Why not?

4. Despite measures to preserve net neutrality, are there ways in which access to the Internet might be limited for some users? How might governments intervene to address this issue? Should governments intervene in this case?

SUGGESTED RESOURCES

Books

Armstrong, Robert. 2010. *Broadcasting Policy in Canada*. Toronto: University of Toronto Press.

Miller, Toby, and George Yúdice. 2002. *Cultural Policy*. Thousand Oaks, CA: Sage.

Raboy, Marc. 2006. "Making Media: Creating the Conditions for Communication in the Public Good (the 2005 Graham Spry Memorial Lecture)." *Canadian Journal of Communication* 31:290–91.

Websites

Canadian Radio-television and Telecommunications Commission (CRTC). http://www.crtc.gc.ca.

Federal Communications Commission. http://www.fcc.gov.

Michael Geist (Canada Research Chair in Internet and e-commerce law, University of Ottawa). *Michael Geist's Blog*. http://www.michaelgeist.ca.

SOCAN (Society of Composers, Authors, and Music Publishers of Canada). http://www.socan.ca.

UNESCO, Communication and Information Sector. http://www.unesco.org/webworld.

REFERENCES

Bill C-32, *An Act to Amend the Copyright Act*. First reading June 2, 2010.

Broadcasting Act. SC 1991, c. 11.

Canadian Charter of Rights and Freedoms. Part I of the *Constitution Act, 1982*, being Schedule B to the *Canada Act 1982* (UK), 1982, c. 11.

Canadian Radio-television and Telecommunications Commission (CRTC). 1999 (May 17). *Broadcasting Public Notice 1999–84/Telecom Public Notice 99-14, New Media*. Ottawa: Government of Canada.

Canadian Radio-television and Telecommunications Commission (CRTC). 2008 (November 20). *Telecom Decision 2008-108. The Canadian Association of Internet Providers' Application Regarding Bell Canada's Traffic Shaping of Its Wholesale Gateway Access Service*. Ottawa: Government of Canada.

Carey, James. 1989. "A Cultural Approach to Communication." In *Communication as Culture: Essays on Media and Society*, 13–36. New York: Routledge.

Castells, Manuel. 2001. *The Internet Galaxy*. Oxford, UK: Oxford University Press.

Caves, Richard. 2000. *Creative Industries*. Cambridge, MA: Harvard University Press.

CBC Newsworld. 2010 (September 28). "Blogger Sentenced in Iran to 19 Years." Accessed February 17, 2011. http://www.cbc.ca/world/story/2010/09/28/iran-blogger-hossein-prison.html.

Copps, Sheila. 1998 (Fall). "Celine Dion: Made in Canada." *New Perspectives Quarterly* 15(5):17.

Czitrom, Daniel. 1982. *Media and the American Mind: From Morse to McLuhan*. Chapel Hill, NC: University of North Carolina Press.

Dewey, John. 1924. *The Public and Its Problems*. New York: Henry Holt.

Douglas, Susan. 1999. *Listening In: Radio and the American Imagination*. New York: Times Books.

Dowler, Kevin. 1996. "The Cultural Industries Policy Apparatus." In *The Cultural Industries in Canada*, edited by Michael Dorland, 328–46. Toronto: James Lorimer.

Edwardson, Ryan. 2008. *Canadian Content*. Toronto: University of Toronto Press.

Federal Communications Commission (FCC). 2004a (February 9). "Powell Urges Industry to Adopt 'Net Freedom' Principles." Accessed February 17, 2011. http://hraunfoss.fcc.gov/edocs_public/attachmatch/DOC-243689A1.pdf.

Federal Communications Commission (FCC). 2004b (September 22). "FCC Proposes Statutory Maximum Fine of $550,000 Against Viacom-owned CBS Affiliates for Apparent Violation of Indecency Rules During Broadcast of Super Bowl Halftime Show." Accessed February 17, 2011. http://hraunfoss.fcc.gov/edocs_public/attachmatch/DOC-252384A1.pdf.

Federal Communications Commission (FCC). 2010 (December 21). "FCC Acts to Preserve Internet Freedom and Openness." Accessed February 17, 2011. http://www.fcc.gov/Daily_Releases/Daily_Business/2010/db1221/DOC-303745A1.pdf.

Fly, James Lawrence. 1941 (January). "Regulation of Radio Broadcasting in the Public Interest." *Annals of the American Academy of Political and Social Science* 213:102–8.

Foucault, Michel. 1980. "Truth and Power." In *Power/Knowledge*, 109–33. New York: Pantheon.

Frith, Simon. 1988. "The Pleasures of the Hearth: The Making of BBC Light Entertainment." In *Music for Pleasure*, 24–44. London: Routledge.

Grant, Peter, and Chris Wood. 2004. *Blockbusters and Trade Wars*. Vancouver: Douglas & McIntyre.

Habermas, Jürgen. 1964/1974. "The Public Sphere: An Encyclopedia Article." *New German Critique* 3:49–55.

Hamilton, Sheryl. 2007. "Now It's Personal." In *How Canadians Communicate II*, edited by David Taras, Maria Bakardjieva, and Frits Pannekoek, 217–38. Calgary: University of Calgary Press.

Horkheimer, Max, and Theodor Adorno. 1941. *Dialectic of the Enlightenment*. London: Continuum.

Innis, Harold. 1950/1986. *Empire and Communication*. Victoria, BC: Press Porcépic.

Kracauer, Siegfried. 1947/2004. *From Caligari to Hitler: A Psychological History of German Film*. Princeton, NJ: Princeton University Press.

Lasswell, Harold. 1948/1960. The Structure and Function of Communication in Society. In *Mass Communication*, edited by Wilbur Schramm, 117–30. Urbana, IL: University of Illinois Press.

Lippmann, Walter. 1922/1965. *Public Opinion*. Glencoe, IL: Free Press.

Lorimer, Rowland, Mike Gasher, and David Skinner. 2008. *Mass Communication in Canada* (6th ed.). Toronto: Oxford University Press.

Magder, Ted. 1993. *Canada's Hollywood: The Canadian State and Feature Films*. Toronto: University of Toronto Press.

Mattelart, Armand. 1996/2000. *Networking the World: 1794–2000*. Minneapolis: University of Minnesota Press.

McLuhan, Marshall. 1964. *Understanding Media: The Extensions of Man*. New York: McGraw-Hill.

Miller, Toby. 1993. *The Well-Tempered Self: Citizenship, Culture and the Postmodern Subject*. Baltimore, MD: Johns Hopkins Press.

Miller, Toby. 1998. *Technologies of Truth: Cultural Citizenship and the Popular Media*. Minneapolis: University of Minnesota Press.

Miller, Toby, and George Yúdice. 2002. *Cultural Policy*. Thousand Oaks, CA: Sage.

New York Times. 2010 (November 28). "A Note to Readers: The Decision to Publish Diplomatic Documents." Accessed February 17, 2011. http://www.nytimes.com/2010/11/29/world/29editornote.html.

Office of the Privacy Commissioner of Canada. 2009 (July 16). "Facebook Needs to Improve Privacy Practices, Investigation Finds." Accessed December 19, 2010. http://www.priv.gc.ca/media/nr-c/2009/nr-c_090716_e.cfm.

Parker, Rachel, and Oleg Parenta. 2008. "Explaining Contradictions in Film and Television Industry Policy: Ideas and Incremental Policy Change Through Layering and Drift." *Media, Culture and Society* 30(5):609–22.

Royal Commission on National Development in the Arts, Letters and Sciences (Massey Commission). 1951. *Report of the Royal Commission on National Development in the Arts, Letters and Sciences*. Ottawa: King's Printer.

Sisario, Ben. 2010 (December 13). "Piracy Fight Shuts Down Music Blogs." *New York Times*. Accessed February 17, 2011. http://www.nytimes.com/2010/12/14/business/media/14music.html?_r=1&hpw=&pagewanted=print.

Straw, W. 2005. "Pathways of Cultural Movement." In *Accounting for Culture: Thinking Through Cultural Citizenship*, edited by C. Andrew, M. Gattinger, M.S. Jeannotte, and W. Straw, 183–97. Ottawa: University of Ottawa Press.

Street, John. 1997. *Politics and Popular Culture*. Philadelphia: Temple University Press.

Weitzner, Daniel J. 2006. "The Neutral Net." Accessed February 17, 2011. http://dig.csail.mit.edu/2006/06/neutralnet.html.

Wiener, Norbert. 1954. *The Human Use of Human Beings*. New York: Avon Books.

Yorke, Ritchie. 1971. *Axes, Chops and Hot Licks: The Canadian Rock Music Scene*. Edmonton: Mel Hurtig Publishers.

CHAPTER 10 / DARREN WERSHLER

Cultural Ownership, Copyright, and Intellectual Property

What does it mean to own culture? Whose rights should prevail—those of the creators, or those of the public? Should culture be owned at all?

KEY CONCEPTS

1. The laws that govern copyright and intellectual property can evolve over time in response to changes in culture and technology, as well as lobbying from industries and artists.

2. The *commons* consists of those things and places that are owned collectively by a society, not by any single individual, organization, or corporation.

3. New tools for using copyright to ensure the circulation of cultural objects, such as Creative Commons licences, have recently arisen in opposition to traditional uses of copyright laws to restrict the uses of cultural objects.

CHAPTER OUTLINE

Introduction: Who Is "Girl Talk," and Why Hasn't He Been Sued? 173

What Is Intellectual Property? 177

A Condensed History of Copyright in North America 178

Other Forms of Cultural Ownership 185

Indigenous Models of Cultural Ownership 186

Public Licensing: The Creative Commons 187

Digital Dilemmas 188

Owning Living Things: Biotechnologies 190

Conclusion 192

Notes 193

Discussion Questions 193

Suggested Resources 194

References 194

Introduction: Who Is "Girl Talk," and Why Hasn't He Been Sued?

In November 2010, audio artist Gregg Gillis, also known as Girl Talk, released his fifth album, *All Day*. The album, which is available as a free download from the website of the Illegal Art label, is constructed entirely from brief samples of 373 different songs. The Illegal Art website lists all the tracks and thanks the artists by name (Illegal Art 2010), but neither Girl Talk nor his label bothered to obtain official permission from the sampled artists or labels

Figure 10.1 Girl Talk

Gregg Gillis's music raises questions about artistic ownership that will likely become more common in the years to come as the mashup form gains popularity.

SOURCE: © mekuria getinet (www.mekuriageti.net).

before making use of their work on *All Day*. The result is that opinions about both the legality and aesthetic merits of Girl Talk's music are sharply divided.

The most common name for the sort of music that Girl Talk produces is the *mashup*, although these tracks are sometimes referred to as *bastard pop* or *bootlegs*,[1] especially in England, where they began attracting popular attention late in 2000 (McGranahan 2010, 11). Typically, a mashup consists of the vocal track from one pop song matched to the instrumental tracks from another. Girl Talk's tracks are a series of short samples with matched beats, strung together one after the other with a slight overlap (oddly similar to the middle-of-the-road *Hooked on Classics* disco albums of the early 1980s). Terms like "bootleg" and "bastard" were deliberately chosen for the same reason that Girl Talk's label calls itself Illegal Art: to evoke the clandestine, the subversive, and the illicit. Pop music has always used such connotations to sell itself, but is it literally true that Girl Talk's music is somehow illegal?

A Case of Copyright Infringement?

Some legal scholars believe that under current Canadian (Reynolds 2009, 667) and US (Herreman 2009) copyright laws, the creation of mashups in general—and Girl Talk's kind of mashups in particular—probably constitutes copyright infringement. One of the conditions for copyright infringement to occur when making any new work (there are several) is that a sampler has to incorporate a "substantial" part of someone else's work in its creation. In both Canada and the United States, "substantial" means any amount that enables the average person to recognize the source of a sample, so a "substantial" amount can be quite small (Herreman 2009; Reynolds 2009, 649). In an interview in the *Village Voice*, Gillis says, "I like to use [the bands I sample] in a way that everything is recognizable. That's a part of the fun where you recognize the sample and you hear how it can be manipulated" (Village Voice Contributor 2008). By this standard alone, then, it's certainly possible to make an argument that Girl Talk's music infringes on the copyrights of others.

> **KEY CONCEPT**
> The laws that govern copyright and intellectual property can evolve over time in response to changes in culture and technology, as well as lobbying from industries and artists.

The question, though, is what would happen if a copyright infringement case against Gillis ever made it to court. Copyright law is interpreted by *case law*—that is, the terms of what does or doesn't constitute infringement or legitimate use of someone else's creations change constantly, as lawsuits are lost, won, overturned by higher courts, and argued yet again. Are cultural norms changing to the extent that Gillis might actually *win* a copyright infringement lawsuit brought against him?

Lawrence Lessig, a noted American lawyer, author, and a figurehead of the *Free Culture* movement—which takes its name from one of his books (2004)—interviews Gillis in a book called *Remix* (2008). He concludes that even though music like Girl Talk's very likely constitutes infringement right now, the compositional practices of the current generation of musicians will eventually require changes to copyright law. He writes, "For the thing that Gillis does well, Gillis explained to me, everyone will soon do. Everyone, at least, who is passionate about music. Or, at least, everyone passionate about music and under the age of 30" (Lessig 2008, 13–14). As if to underline Lessig's contention, a recent study by the Rockwool Foundation Research Unit in Denmark found that 70 percent of its respondents considered unauthorized downloading for personal use to be a socially acceptable act (Golijan 2011). Meanwhile, the acclaim that Gillis is receiving continues to grow. His *Feed the Animals* was one of *Time* magazine's top 10 albums of 2008 (Tyrangiel 2008) and 24th on *Rolling Stone*'s top 50 of the same year (dsussman 2008). In Pittsburgh, Girl Talk's hometown, city council declared December 7, 2010 to be "Gregg Gillis Day" (Manganaro 2010).

Unauthorized downloading for personal use is becoming a socially acceptable act.

The fact that Girl Talk's music generates so much controversy and uncertainty is a strong indicator that something interesting is taking place with regard to both the creative and consumptive practices common to contemporary culture. In his book *Copyrights and Copywrongs*, Siva Vaidhyanathan (2001) has noted how the advent of hip hop culture and the sudden proliferation of sampling in the late 1980s "revealed gaping flaws in the premises of how copyright law gets applied to music and shown the law to be inadequate for emerging communication technologies, techniques, and aesthetics" (133). In other words, the questions that sampling raises are not just limited to music, but in a digital milieu, are relevant for the entire cultural sphere.

Lev Manovich (2001) argues that if we were to look for a figure to represent the overall logic of digital culture, the DJ—not the writer or visual artist—would be the best choice. The DJ makes new tracks through the selection and combination of pre-existent elements—what we commonly describe as "cut-and-paste," a process we do dozens of times a day on our own computers. Manovich (2001, 135) points out that selection is not an end in and of itself: the DJ innovates, creates, and circulates elements of culture, which might otherwise have been forgotten, for appreciative new audiences.

KEY CONCEPT

The *commons* consists of those things and places that are owned collectively by a society, not by any single individual, organization, or corporation.

The issue that we now have to face is that there is a direct conflict between our current major mode of cultural composition, which is based on a sampling or collage aesthetic, and the last several centuries of copyright law, which has inexorably extended the duration of copyright and expanded the range of materials that fall under it. The way forward is to remember that cultural values and laws can and do change. But practices alone are not enough. We need to give some thought to how our society might produce a culture we can all live with, which means thinking about not just private possessions, but what we hold in common as a society.

For centuries, the very idea of culture has been based on the process of re-conceptualizing that which came before. At the same time, individual creators hope to live off their creations, and industry hopes to profit from the objects to which it holds rights (or at the very least, to recuperate expenses). Creators and producers need some protection for their works so that they can make a living. Without viable and healthy industries that produce and circulate cultural products of all sorts, culture will suffer. Take, for example, the textbook you are holding, and ask yourself why the publisher might want to retain copyright on its materials for as long as possible.

This chapter asks you to consider what conditions best negotiate the sometimes-competing interests of the public, who deserve the right of fair use and a healthy public domain, and creators, who deserve to be rewarded for their creations. What follows is a discussion of the key ideas that inform

---

SIDEBAR

The Changing Commons

The *commons* is "a resource to which anyone within the relevant community has a right without obtaining the permission of anyone else" (Lessig 2001, 19). It is not private, but public property. Most public squares, parks, and streets are part of the commons, which is why citizens have the right to assemble, speak, and debate in them. The *public domain* (see below) is also a part of the commons, as are ideas and theories. What is and is not part of the commons at a given time and place is subject to change.

The questions that every society has to ask itself, writes Lawrence Lessig (2001, 19–21), are *which* resources should be held in common, and *how* should we relate to those resources? Today, though, argues Jeremy Rifkin (2000), among others, public space is being enclosed by spaces that *look* like the commons (such as shopping malls and gated communities) but end up repackaging cultural activities as commodities for sale. He argues that these new spaces have rules and regulations that actually change how they operate. Cultural activities in such places are not an end in themselves, but a means toward commodifying all of lived experience (154–55).

---

how the law has historically overseen the distribution of rights in terms of cultural ownership, and how the notion of cultural ownership has changed. What does it mean to own culture, and whose interests are at stake?

What Is Intellectual Property?

One of the most common definitions of **intellectual property** is that it is "non-physical property that is the product of original thought." The most familiar aspects of its domain include the laws that define copyrights and moral rights, patents and trademarks, and trade secrets. The major characteristic of intellectual property law is that it doesn't protect ideas themselves, because no one owns ideas. Instead, it protects the fixed physical forms that those ideas take by limiting who has the right to produce and control them (Moore 2011).

The term "intellectual property" is relatively new; it appears in US legal records only twice before 1900. Since then, it has become increasingly common (Lessig 2001, 293–94). In the 18th century, notes William Fisher (2003), "lawyers and politicians were more likely to refer to patents and copyrights as 'monopolies' than they were to refer to them as forms of 'property'" (20).

intellectual property
Non-physical property that is the product of original thought.

In other words, in its conception, intellectual property was different in an important respect from possessions or other types of physical property. Like other forms of monopoly, patents and copyrights were seen as potentially subject to abuse, so were granted by the state to people only as a short-term, temporary measure when it was in the public interest to do so. The purpose of the short-term monopoly on intellectual property that is granted to creators is to provide them with just enough funds to be able to create *more* work for the benefit of the whole society, not to reward them for that work in perpetuity, which would likely result in the end of their innovations. As Wendy J. Gordon (1992) observes, a long series of legal precedents recognizes that "the law must grant something less than a right to all the benefits one's work generates" (158) in order to keep intellectual property laws from stifling creativity instead of encouraging it.

The increasing use of the term "intellectual property" is problematic because we tend to pay attention only to the "property" part, and forget that it was designed to serve the public interest. Unlike other forms of property, it's a given that intellectual property will, at some point, pass out of its creators' hands and into the hands of the public. Gordon reminds us that this isn't simply a matter of lazy people appropriating the work of the industrious and innovative:

> After all, the potential free riders—the users, copyists, and adapters—are not mere parasites. Many are creators themselves. They may reach markets different than those reached by the original creators, or they may bring new perspective, reduced cost, special expertise, deeper insights, or innovative technology to the exploitation and adaptation of established works. (1992, 157)

We should therefore strive to balance the rights that we assign to individual creators against the need to create the best possible environment for both vigorous economic development, and individuals and cultures to express themselves (Gordon 1992, 158)—but we don't. The easiest way to see how intellectual property has become more and more like other kinds of property in the eyes of both the courts and the public is to look at the history of its most familiar form: copyright. Over the course of its existence, copyright terms have become longer and longer, and more and more rights have been assigned to creators.

Over the course of copyright's existence, more and more rights have been assigned to creators.

A Condensed History of Copyright in North America

Although the suffix "-right" in the word "copyright" makes many people think of "human rights," those inalienable rights to which every person is entitled simply by virtue of being human, copyright law was designed according to different principles. In both the Canadian (Murray and Trosow 2007, 11) and US legal traditions, copyright is a set of artificial rights created by the state and granted to the creator—actually, more of a privilege or a deal than a right (Vaidhyanathan 2001, 20–21). Copyright law is national, not global, which means that although many countries have treaties and other arrangements with one another to protect the works of their own citizens as these works circulate around the world, copyright law varies in significant respects from country to country.

Most legal scholars point to Britain's *Statute of Anne*, passed in 1710, as the common origin of Canadian and US copyright law. The primary purpose of the *Statute of Anne*, however, was not to enshrine the rights of authors, but to attempt to regulate the use of a new form of media technology that threatened to change the traditional balance of power: movable lead type and the printing press. The duration of protection that authors received for works they published after the *Statute of Anne* was 14 years, with an option to renew for another 14-year term. This is where the notion that it's actually a good idea to grant limited copyright terms comes from—the belief that a culture is richer if its writers and artists are continually producing new work, disseminating new ideas, and creating new commodities to sell.

The *Statute of Anne* marks the first time that the notion of a **public domain** is officially codified into law (Vaidhyanathan 2001, 40). The public domain is the body of works that are outside copyright, either because they have not been turned into fixed forms and copyrighted, because they already have passed out of copyright, or because they are things that cannot be copyrighted, such as ideas, facts, methods, and systems. The public domain also includes the uses for creative works that are not covered by copyright (Litman 1990, 974). What *can* be copyrighted is the fixed form or *work* (for example, a novel, a song, a sculpture, a video) that someone creates from a particular idea, *not* the idea itself. This means that there will always be aspects of any particular work that cannot and should not be controlled.

The United States Congress passed its first *Copyright Act* in 1790. Like the *Statute of Anne*, it also had a term of 14 years, renewable for another 14. The duration of the copyright term remained short to ensure that works flowed back into the public domain quickly, where other creators could make use of them, driving the development of a new culture for a new country. Since the establishment of this law, Congress has extended the duration of US copyright many times, with increasing frequency. In 1831, the initial term increased to 28 years, renewable for another 14, for a maximum of 42 years. In 1909, the renewal term was increased to 28 years, for a maximum of 56 years. In the latter half of the 20th century, Congress again extended the term of US copyright many times, to its current length: the

public domain
The body of works that are outside of copyright, or were never subject to it.

life of the author plus 70 years for individual people, and 95 years for corporate authors. Because of this expansion, copyrighted materials take longer and longer to re-enter the public domain, and the amount of material currently under copyright keeps expanding. As Lawrence Lessig (2004) notes, "now that copyrights can be just about a century long, the inability to know what is protected and what is not protected becomes a huge and obvious burden on the creative process" (252).

The history of copyright in Canada is very different. Canadian Parliament was nominally given control over copyright by the *British North America Act* of 1867, but copyright in Canada was governed by the British *Imperial Copyright Act* of 1842 until 1911. This was due, in large part, to political and economic tensions between Britain and the United States. Although the United States is now the chief global advocate of expanding intellectual property rights, "[u]ntil approximately the middle of the nineteenth century, more Americans had an interest in 'pirating' copyrighted or patented materials produced by foreigners than [they] had an interest in protecting copyrights or patents against 'piracy' by foreigners" (Fisher 2003, 11). After the United States seceded from the British Empire, its printers and publishers routinely produced cheap bootleg copies of European books, many of which found their way into Canada. Like the *Statute of Anne*, the *Imperial Copyright Act*, which made it illegal to import reprints into Britain and its colonies, and added a 35 percent duty to US publications, was conceived of by the British as a means to protect both the economic interests of British publishers and to ward off seditious American ideas from the minds of Canadian citizens.

In the latter half of the 19th century, the Canadian government tried several times to pass its own copyright legislation, but because any such law required British approval, and Britain was more concerned with protecting its own interests than those of its colonies, the legislation was not approved. The Canadian *Copyright Act*, finally passed into law in 1924, remained largely unchanged until 1988. However, the duration of copyright under the *Copyright Act* has also been extended to its current length—the life of the author plus 50 years after his or her death.

New Canadian Copyright Laws

As of this writing,[2] there have been several failed attempts by different governments to change Canadian copyright law to implement some of the provisions of the World Intellectual Property Organization (WIPO) treaties that Canada signed in 1992. The United States implemented these treaties as its *Digital Millennium Copyright Act* (DMCA) in 1998. Copyright law needs to adapt to the changes in the creative environment that have accompanied the widening popularity of the Internet, but attempts to modernize the law in both Canada and the United States have created considerable controversy, especially around the issue of technical protection measures (TPMs), or digital locks. Under the DMCA and the last proposed set of changes to Canadian copyright, even if a person has the legal right to use the content protected by a digital lock, breaking that lock is deemed an infringement of the law.

Critics of TPMs have voiced several concerns. Engineers and academics need to take apart objects in order to study them. Some critics worry that the prohibition on breaking TPMs would prevent such everyday activities from occurring. Others are concerned about companies gathering up large swaths of public domain material and then rendering them less useful to the public by placing them on digital storage media and then making them uncopyable. What will happen in Canada on this issue remains to be seen.

Other proposed changes to Canadian copyright, if they pass into law, will provide explicit protection for some of the uses of copyrighted material in Canada that are currently allowable under US copyright law, such as parody and satire, and provisions for educational use. Again, there is some contention regarding what these exemptions will mean, in practice, for authors, publishers, and the public.

Even without such changes, Canadian copyright law differs from US copyright law in several significant ways other than its duration. One is the inclusion in Canadian law of provisions to protect the **moral rights** of the author. Moral rights include the right to be associated with a work as its author; the right to remain anonymous or use a pseudonym; the right to prevent changes to a work if it has been altered in a way that negatively affects the author's reputation; and the right to prevent a work from being associated with a product, service, cause, or institution. Many European countries also have moral rights as part of their copyright laws. To many creators, the concept of moral rights sounds like a very good idea; the only problem is that many publishers include a clause in their contracts demanding that creators must waive those rights before publication.

moral rights
A series of rights accorded to an author relating to his or her association with a work, or the integrity of the work.

Another important difference between Canadian and US copyright laws is the manner in which each country describes the limits to copyright. The US principle is called *fair use*, and the Canadian principle is called *fair dealing*. Fair use, which became part of US copyright law in 1976, allows anyone to quote a limited amount from a copyrighted object for purposes such as news reporting, academic research or teaching, criticism, commentary, or parody. As Murray and Trosow (2007) note, the "such as" means that these

HISTORICAL HIGHLIGHT

Michael Snow and Moral Rights

In 1979, the Toronto Eaton Centre commissioned the internationally acclaimed Canadian artist, Michael Snow, to build a sculpture for the mall's atrium. Snow's work, *Flight Stop*, consists of a flock of 60 life-size Canada Geese suspended from the rafters. In 1982, as part of its Christmas decorations, the centre hung red ribbons around the geese's necks and used the image in its advertising campaign without asking the artist's permission. Snow asked the centre to remove the ribbons, but was ignored, so he invoked his moral rights, and the court ruled in his favour.

In his article on the *Snow v. The Eaton Centre* case, David Vaver (1983) notes that until this point, very few Canadian creators had ever used moral rights as an occasion to launch litigation (90). The irony is that in some respects, the notion of moral rights was more powerful as a *threat* than it was after it had been used successfully. Once it became obvious that artists could and would invoke their moral rights in court, and could actually win such cases, it became common practice in contracts with artists to include a clause asking them to waive their moral rights as part of the deal, and this very specifically Canadian bit of copyright law began to fade into the background.

Figure 10.2 Michael Snow's *Flight Stop*

are illustrations of some of the uses that might be fair; US copyright law is thus more open-ended than Canadian copyright law, and eventually allowed parody as a fair use because of this openness (75). The notion of how much of any given copyrighted object may be quoted is deliberately fuzzy; in some cases, it might include the whole object, but it is usually limited to a small fraction, such as a few lines of a poem or a few pages of a novel. When doubt arises about whether someone has quoted more than what is fair, copyright holders may launch a court case for copyright infringement.

As mentioned earlier in this chapter, copyright law is interpreted by case law—that is, what counts as fair use at a given time and place is decided in court. On the one hand, this means that copyright law can be adapted to suit the mores and needs of the time, but it also means that it is subject to abuse by wealthy copyright holders. Sending creators a *cease and desist* letter threatening to drag them through the courts if they don't stop quoting from your copyrighted object (no matter how large or small the amount quoted) can be enough to intimidate most people, because copyright cases can take years and cost hundreds of thousands of dollars to defend. This is called the **chilling effect**, and it is a major strategy for the legal divisions of many corporations and the estates of many prominent authors and artists. For example, Paul Zukofsky (2009), the son of American poet Louis Zukofsky, maintains this notice on his website:

chilling effect
A legal strategy used by copyright holders, in which the threat of long, costly legal action tends to dissuade others from using a work.

> Despite what you may have been told, you may not use LZ's words as you see fit, as if you owned them, while you hide behind the rubric of "fair use." "Fair use" is a very-broadly defined doctrine, of which I take a very narrow interpretation, and I expect my views to be respected. We can therefore either more or less amicably work out the fees that I demand; you can remove all quotation; or we can turn the matter over to lawyers, this last solution being the worst of the three, but one which I will use if I need to enforce my rights.
>
> In general, as a matter of principle, and for your own well-being, I urge you to not work on Louis Zukofsky, and prefer that you do not. Working on LZ will be far more trouble than it is worth. You will be far more appreciated working on some author whose copyright holder(s) will actually cherish you, and/or your work. I do not, and no one should work under those conditions. However, if you have no choice in the matter, here are the procedures that I insist upon, and what you must do if you wish to spare yourself as much grief as possible.

Faced with such a notice, many authors will justifiably focus their attention elsewhere, but what this means is that it is possible to shape public discourse and criticism by aggression. The Electronic Frontier Foundation, in conjunction with school of law clinics at Harvard, Stanford, Berkeley, University of San Francisco, University of Maine, George Washington School of Law, and Santa Clara University, have banded together to create an advocacy site called Chilling Effects (www.chillingeffects.org) to advise creators of their rights and to track abuses. However, many publishers err on the side of caution, requiring authors and artists to seek—and pay for—permission to quote even the tiniest section of a copyrighted work. While this requirement provides some assurances about the legality of the new work and puts money in the pockets of other artists, it too is a kind of chilling effect, suggesting there are some subjects that you simply cannot afford to write about.

As unpredictable as the US notion of fair use might seem to be in practice, Canadian fair dealing is an older but weaker principle. The 1921 Canadian *Copyright Act* had a fair dealing provision, but didn't actually define the term, leaving Canadians to sort out the issue as best they could in case law. Fair dealing permits the quotation of "a substantial part" of a copyrighted object, but only for the purpose of news reporting, private study, review, research, or criticism. If someone is quoting less than a substantial part of a copyrighted text, the copyright holder has no say in the matter—but the definition of "substantial" is open to interpretation. Once an act of quotation has been deemed to fall under one of these categories, the question of its fairness arises, with respect to both which section has been copied and how much of it has been quoted. Of course, many of the acts that Canadians do now, such as recording TV shows on a PVR, do not fit into any of these categories, which is one of the reasons that the law needs updating. Nor does Canadian copyright law make explicit provisions for teaching and parody. Various attempts to revise Canadian copyright law have included some provision for educational use and for parody and satire, but the mixed reactions from various segments of the public make it unclear whether they will ever make it into law, or how much of such provisions will change before it is passed.

Many parts of copyright law are deliberately ambiguous, and necessarily so. Copyright law was formulated on the premise that eventually, all ideas should find their way into the hands of the public, so it's actually not in anyone's best interest to define copyright law too precisely. What Vaidhyanathan (2001) calls a *thin, leaky* copyright system "allows people to comment on copyrighted works, make copies for teaching and research, and record their programs for later viewing." A *thick* copyright system that accounts for every possible use of a copyrighted object could all too easily become a tool of censorship (184).

As important as copyright is, it is not the only form of cultural ownership in contemporary culture.

Other Forms of Cultural Ownership

Other cultural objects require other sorts of protection. Whereas copyright protects the fixed forms of expression that ideas take, *patents* protect inventions, a category that can include not only machines, but also processes, art, manufactured articles, and "compositions of matter," which are substances that consist of more than two other substances that have unique properties when combined. Patents have a duration of 20 years, and allow the patent holders exclusive rights over the patented object as long as they disclose its workings.

Sometimes, an individual or a company will deliberately *not* take out a patent to prevent competitors from learning how a product works. *Trade secrets* are information that bestows some economic advantage on a product's owners, and are, well, secret. Such information is generally protected through contracts or non-disclosure agreements. These agreements do not have a fixed expiry date, but the moment that competitors find out a trade secret without violating such an agreement, they can make use of it.

Trademarks are designed to protect the signs and symbols that companies use to identify themselves and their products from others that have the potential to confuse consumers. Trademarks confer on their holders the right to exclusive use of that mark. They can be established through common use or through an official registration process, which provides a stronger degree of protection. Trademarks last for renewable 15-year terms. Because they can be lost if the owner not only fails to renew them, but fails to defend them, they require special vigilance.

Scholarship and academic work operate according to a different system altogether. For example, students own copyright in their work, but teachers and professors sometimes do not: depending on their collective agreements, the institution may in fact own the work that its instructors produce. But it is important to remember, as Murray and Trosow argue, that the academy and the marketplace function according to entirely different economies with different logics. While the marketplace uses copyright to ensure that people have *permission* before quoting a substantial part of an object, an educational institution requires something significantly different: *attribution*. "Copyright infringement is use without permission … and it's a matter of law, whereas plagiarism is use without attribution, and it's a matter of community or professional practice" (Murray and Trosow 2007, 193). The academy, in fact, *rewards* scholars for providing citations; these indicate

The circulation of knowledge is what makes it valuable, and the creation and maintenance of culture require this interchange.

that you have done your research, and have contributed to a conversation that started before you arrived and will continue long after you've moved on to other concerns. In such an environment, the circulation of knowledge is what makes it valuable and useful to others, not hoarding it. It's important to remember that the creation and maintenance of culture require this interchange, and that the role of copyright in it is actually *not* the first priority; producing the conditions under which all people are able to express themselves fully, fearlessly, and productively is.

Indigenous Models of Cultural Ownership

In terms of getting our priorities straight, what if we have to re-examine the very principles upon which copyright is founded? Rosemary Coombe (1998, 209) has argued convincingly that the categories of property that we use unquestioningly all the time—intellectual property, cultural property, and real property—divide peoples and things according to the same logic that historically was responsible for disenfranchising Native peoples in North America. To insist on applying that logic to their ongoing cultural production, then, is a continuation of colonialism. The *traditional knowledge* built up by various groups of First Peoples has no single author, is not always fixed into specific forms (in the manner that an idea may become a photograph, a song, or a poem), and is often very old. Therefore, copyright systems often treat aspects of it, such as traditional tribal designs and motifs, as though they were in the public domain (Murray and Trosow 2007, 187).

So what does it mean when traditional Haida designs can be purchased as automobile decals and anyone can get a Maori tattoo? The answer is complex because, as Coombe explains, when First Peoples lay claim over images, themes, and symbols, they do not do so as either the conventional notion of the "author," insisting on fees and royalties for the circulation of their creative works. Nor do they fall back on an equally stereotypical and essentialist version of themselves as timeless, changeless cultures with claims to special authenticity. Like the rest of us, they are "living, changing, creative peoples engaged in very concrete contemporary political struggles" (Coombe 1998, 228).

Many First Peoples' approaches to copyright are similar to the concept of moral rights. Instead of focusing on protecting the reputation of an individual author as a creative originator, though, they protect the honour of the clan, culture, or nation whose materials the individual transmits. Whether or not the individual is allowed to improvise on or reinterpret the material that is being transmitted depends on the particular tradition (Murray and Trosow 2007, 189).

Increasingly, First Peoples are using the instruments of intellectual property in ways that are effective, and even subversive. For example, the tiny HaidaBucks Café in the village of Masset, in Haida Gwaii (formerly the Queen Charlotte Islands), successfully fended off a trademark infringement lawsuit from the Starbucks corporation (Baldwin 2003). In Haida slang, a "buck" is a young man; the HaidaBucks Café is owned and operated by four young Haida Gwaii men. Visit their website, and you can read all about it, beginning with the joke that "If you're as dull-witted as Starbucks® thinks you are, you may not realize you've reached this site by mistake" (Baldwin 2003).

Figure 10.3 HaidaBucks
View inside the HaidaBucks Café in Masset, British Columbia.
SOURCE: Lane Baldwin. Reprinted by permission.

Public Licensing: The Creative Commons

So if you were concerned about the shrinking public domain and the lengthening terms of copyright, what could you do about it without infringing on the copyrights of others? What if you could use your copyright to encourage sharing and circulation rather than restrict it?

In 2001, a group of cyber-law and copyright experts, including Stanford law professor and author Lawrence Lessig, founded Creative Commons. This group is dedicated to expanding the range of creative work available for others to build upon and share. Its goal is not simply to increase the amount of primary content that is available online, but also to make accessing it easier and cheaper. Drawing inspiration in part from the licensing systems developed by the GNU/Linux Free Software and Open Source communities, Creative Commons has developed a set of tools that help people who have produced creative works (such as websites, scholarship, music, film, photography, literature, and courseware) to make their creations free for certain uses, or to dedicate them entirely to the public domain.

> **KEY CONCEPT**
> New tools for using copyright to ensure the circulation of cultural objects, such as Creative Commons licences, have recently arisen in opposition to traditional uses of copyright laws to restrict the uses of cultural objects.

There are a variety of different Creative Commons licences, each specific to the country in which a person takes it out. Each licence allows the creator to retain copyright, and to announce that other people's fair use, first sale, and free expression rights are not affected by the licence. Each requires licensees to obtain the creator's permission to perform any of the activities that the creator restricts, to keep the creator's copyright notice intact on all copies of the work, not to alter the terms of the licence, and so on. The licences apply worldwide, last for the duration of the work's copyright, and are irrevocable.

The less familiar, and most interesting, aspect of the Creative Commons licence is what it allows people to do with the creator's work: to copy, distribute, perform, or shift media in a variety of ways that the creator can specify from a set of mix-and-match distribution conditions. For example, you might decide that you want to let others copy, distribute, display, and perform your work, and to create derivative works (such as translations or mashups) based upon it, but for non-commercial purposes only. The most interesting of the terms that you can attach to your copyright is the "Share Alike" term, which allows others to distribute derivative works only under a licence identical to the licence that governs your work. The Creative Commons website helps creators design a licence, then presents three different versions: one in everyday prose, one in legal language, and one designed to be read by search engines, which means that the licensed work can be located using Google, Yahoo!, or Flickr. There are now millions of Creative Commons licences in use, on websites, books, music, photographs, and many other objects.

Digital Dilemmas

Faced with the dizzying rate of information exchange on the Internet, many of the people who create things for a living are asking the following question: how many copies of their work will be sold if it's possible to circulate, cheaply and easily, digital copies of that work? The worst-case scenario is that the answer might be one copy—and that everyone else will simply make copies of that first, lonely, legitimately purchased digital file.

In *Being Digital* (1995), Nicholas Negroponte notes that the best way to measure the consequences of digitization for society is to think about the difference between things that are made out of *atoms* and things that are made out of *bits* (the basic unit of digital information) (11). In the physical world of atoms, where making an exact copy of an object is expensive and time-consuming, our economy and culture are driven by the notion of scarcity. When dealing with atoms, sharing something means that you have to give up part of it, so people are more reluctant to share. Digital objects are different, because it is possible to make an infinite number of identical copies of them with little to no effort: click "copy," then "paste," and repeat, or program your computer to do the work for you. Moreover, the advent of

Digital objects are different from non-digital ones, because it is possible to make an infinite number of identical digital copies with little to no effort.

peer-to-peer technologies, beginning with Napster and continuing through BitTorrent, the most popular peer-to-peer protocol in use today, has meant that it is also possible to distribute all those copies with little to no effort.

Peer-to-Peer Systems

Peer-to-peer (P2P) is a network in which each computer that is connected has more or less the same processing power and privileges for the purpose of sharing files as any other. Its opposite is a form of architecture called *client–server*, where large, powerful computers called servers manage resources such as network traffic, file management, and storage and printers for a series of smaller, much less powerful computers or terminals called clients. In the early days of its existence, the Internet functioned as a network of peers, but it has gradually become more client–server focused owing to massive increases in traffic, the introduction of gated systems, and so on.

Today's peer-to-peer applications, such as BitTorrent, basically ignore the powerful, server-based centres of the Internet in favour of establishing small, unstable networks of connected users with minimal resources, in order to accomplish specific short-lived tasks, such as sharing copies of TV programs. P2P doesn't care who you are or which computer you are using. All it cares about is that you want a file, and someone else has it, or vice versa. It's quick and dirty. And it works very, very well: ipoque's annual Internet studies from 2006 to 2009 consistently show that peer-to-peer technologies generate the majority of Internet traffic in many parts of the globe—more than the Web, email, and streaming media (Schulze and Mochalski 2009)! This is partly because more people know how to use the software, and partly because the sizes of the files that are being traded have increased drastically, from single songs to entire full-length movies.

Life After Napster

This situation is a direct result of a near-complete failure over the last decade to deal with the consequences of P2P on any level: technological, legal, governmental, fiscal, or moral. Back in 2001, legal scholar and Free Software Foundation counsel Eben Moglen argued that after the lawsuit that shut down **Napster**, the record companies had an opportunity to retain the 60-million-plus people in the original Napster user base. If they had opted to let people continue downloading music in exchange for a fee collected from their monthly Internet service charge, that money could have been used to establish a pool of funds to pay artists proportionally for the amount that their work had been downloaded. This model is called *voluntary collective licensing*, and it is the mechanism that allows radio stations to function:

Napster
Founded in 1999, this peer-to-peer file-sharing service made MP3 files available outside of copyright protection, and helped usher in a major shakeup of the music industry.

in exchange for being able to broadcast music, the stations pay a fee to organizations that redistribute the fees to the artists and songwriters. Radio makes its money by selling advertisements, not by charging its listeners directly (Electronic Frontier Foundation 2008).

But instead of investigating the possibilities of collective licensing, the labels bet that they could establish their own proprietary networks, and that people would use them. (They didn't, at least until the iTunes music store and Amazon.com MP3 sales began to gain popularity at the end of the first decade of the 21st century. By February 2010, the iTunes Music Store had sold 10 billion songs in less than seven years [Zibreg 2010].) By forcing Napster to shut down and providing no credible alternative, the labels effectively educated Napster's users that there were other places online to get free music. Furthermore, the labels created a situation in which litigation against those people was self-defeating: "Suddenly, instead of a problem posed by one commercial entity that can be closed down or acquired, the industry will be facing the same technical threat, with no one to sue but its own customers. No business can survive by suing or harassing its own market" (Moglen 2001).

> *"No business can survive by suing or harassing its own market."*
> —Eben Moglen

Many Internet service providers (ISPs) have responded to the increase in P2P traffic by throttling bandwidth—that is, imposing speed limits on how fast certain kinds of data will transfer (for example, your ISP might choose to slow down the movement of BitTorrent data packets). Of course, this presumes that the people using the software are infringing on the copyrights of others without actually verifying that this is the case, and it limits the potential of P2P software for legitimate applications, such as the distribution of software upgrades. But at the present moment, we are deadlocked between the desire of people to obtain increasing amounts and kinds of cultural materials online, and no clear path to the creation of a consensus model that can equitably compensate creators for the unchecked copying of their works.

Owning Living Things: Biotechnologies

The state of being impoverished, according to Alexander Galloway and Eugene Thacker (2007), traditionally refers to people who have nothing but their bodies to sell. Until recently, this notion usually meant that the poorest people in a given society survived by selling the power of their physical labour. In contemporary society, selling one's body can be more literal, involving the sale of blood, sperm, or ova, or acting as a surrogate mother. However, these authors argue that to survive today, the poor "are expected to give up not just their body's labour power but also their body's *information* in everything from biometric examinations at work, to the culling of consumer buying habits, to prospecting inside ethnic groups for disease-resistant genes. The biomass, not social relations, is today's site of exploitation" (Galloway and Thacker 2007, 135; emphasis in original).

Legal cases from over the last few decades in the United States suggest that under some circumstances, we do not even have ownership rights to the very cells that we are made of. One of the most famous of these cases involved a surveyor named John Moore, who discovered in 1976 that he had a form of cancer called hairy-cell leukemia. Dr. David Golde, a cancer researcher at UCLA, treated Moore by removing his spleen. Over the next seven years, Golde flew Moore to Los Angeles from his Seattle home to take follow-up cell samples from Moore's bone marrow, semen, and blood. In 1983, several weeks before giving Moore a consent form asking him to agree to voluntarily grant all rights to any potential product developed from his cells to the University of California, Golde filed a patent on a *cell line* ("self-perpetuating clones of the original cells") he had developed from Moore's cells—a patent whose market value at the time was expected to reach $3 billion (Skloot 2006).

Moore sued the following year, and the case went all the way to the Supreme Court of California, where it was finally settled in 1990. The court ruled that although an adult has the right to decide whether to submit to medical treatment, and although doctors have the responsibility to reveal any personal interest in their own research, patients do not own the cells removed from their bodies during a medical procedure. Moore therefore had no rights to Golde's patent, which actually required Golde to physically alter Moore's cells so that they could survive outside his body, a process that was therefore deemed an invention (Evans 2006).

Although both Moore and Golde are now deceased, the repercussions of the *Moore* case are still being felt. One of the arguments against assigning patients the rights to cells removed from their bodies is that doing so would slow down the speed of medical research by creating situations in which patients would demand money from their doctors. Others (including a dissenting judge on the California Supreme Court) argue that "the ruling didn't prevent commercialization; it just took patients out of the equation and emboldened scientists to commodify tissues in increasing numbers" (Skloot 2006). Some hospitals now have specific clauses in the papers that patients sign to ensure that the rights to their cells are waived, but the debate continues, and other lawsuits have been fought over similar issues.

The implications of patenting cells and genes extend far beyond the human body. Jeremy Rifkin (2000) notes that because of the US Patent and

Trademark Office's 1987 decision that genes, chromosomes, cells, and tissues can be patented, some biotechnology critics predict that within 25 years, "much of the genetic commons—the legacy of millions of years of biological evolution—will have been isolated, identified, and enclosed in the form of intellectual property, controlled, for the most part, by a handful of giant transnational life-science companies" (65–66). When farmers pay for genetically modified seeds from such companies, they aren't really "buying" them; they're leasing a single season's use of them, and the harvest belongs to the patent holder. This means that the centuries-old tradition of farmers reserving part of their harvest for later use or emergency food is potentially a crime. Monsanto, a prominent life-science company, has sued hundreds of farmers for patent infringement (Rifkin 2000, 67). The growing dependency of farmers all over the world on a few large seed suppliers, the dwindling of farmers' emergency seed reserves, and the decrease in varieties of seeds being planted are all factors that worry the critics of seed patenting, because of these patents' potentially destabilizing effect on world food reserves.

Conclusion

The examples of how the expansion of intellectual property law is changing our relationship to our bodies, our food supply, and to nature itself point directly to the issue of why these ideas matter. Who controls information, and how, are questions that have life-and-death consequences. And there are no easy answers about how to arrive at an equitable notion of the limits of intellectual property. Some thinkers, such as Marcus Boon (2010), argue that critiquing intellectual property law because it has become more like material property law is beside the point. For Boon, the problem is property itself, and the systems and structures that govern it. He writes that " 'fair use' and 'the public domain' are crippled concepts unless they include, for example, the right to cross national borders (fair use of land), or access to food, hospitals, medicine, and education (all of which have been, to different degrees, part of public domains at some time or other)." From such a perspective, one possible answer to the problem of scarcity in general "is simply to *make more copies* and distribute them freely" (Boon 2010, 246; emphasis in original).

Boon argues that copying is, and has always been, a *practice* rather than a right. Practices are rooted in value and competence rather than ownership. In fact, practices *own us*, reshaping us and inserting us into a community of other practitioners (Boon uses the examples of musicians, yogis, warriors, and lovers) who may well have stolen their knowledge in the first place in order to teach it to others (Boon 2010, 247). Copying as practice can even function within a capitalist economy, as examples demonstrate—ranging from 20th century art (Marcel Duchamp, Andy Warhol, Jeff Koons, Richard Prince) to companies whose business now largely comes from open-source software sales (Red Hat, IBM).

The questions that surround cultural ownership and intellectual property are far more complex than they first appear. Public licensing schemes such as Creative Commons are not a perfect solution to the controversies regarding how we handle intellectual property today, and, as Boon (2010) points out, they do little to address real, lived inequalities unless the entire system in which they are embedded changes. However, they are one positive step in a long journey toward creating a world where it is possible to respect the creative output of others and to have a wide range of materials to work with in the creation of new kinds of cultural objects. An open approach to content, and its result—a rich body of circulating text and images—is crucial to the ongoing viability of culture itself.

NOTES

1. This usage is rare now because of the confusion with pre-digital unauthorized recordings of rock musicians (often live, usually made by fans), which are also called bootlegs.
2. For updated information on Canadian copyright legislation, please visit this book's website at www.emp.ca/intersections.

DISCUSSION QUESTIONS

1. To what extent do your own uses of digital cultural objects (ebooks, music recordings, movies, TV shows) conform to or depart from the existing copyright laws of your country? Explain.
2. Divide the class into two groups. Everyone in one group will write a paragraph that explains why creators should receive maximal protection under copyright law; everyone in the other group will write a paragraph explaining why copyright law should favour the rights of users. Share, discuss, and debate your results.
3. After performing activity 2 above, reflect on how easy it is to favour one side over the other. Try to describe a compromise that recognizes the needs of both positions.

SUGGESTED RESOURCES
Books

Coombe, Rosemary J. 1998. *The Cultural Life of Intellectual Properties: Authorship, Appropriation and the Law. Post-Contemporary Interventions*. Durham, NC: Duke University Press.

Murray, Laura J., and Samuel E. Trosow. 2007. *Canadian Copyright: A Citizen's Guide*. Toronto: Between the Lines.

Vaidhyanathan, Siva. 2001. *Copyrights and Copywrongs: The Rise of Intellectual Property and How It Threatens Creativity*. New York: New York University Press.

Websites

Chilling Effects Clearinghouse. http://www.chillingeffects.org.

Creative Commons. http://creativecommons.org.

Electronic Frontier Foundation. https://www.eff.org.

Michael Geist's Blog. http://www.michaelgeist.ca.

REFERENCES

Baldwin, Lane. 2003. "Starbucks Ends Dispute!" *HaidaBucks*. Accessed April 5, 2011. http://www.lanebaldwin.com/hbc/index2.htm.

Boon, Marcus. 2010. *In Praise of Copying*. Cambridge, MA: Harvard University Press.

Coombe, Rosemary J. 1998. *The Cultural Life of Intellectual Properties: Authorship, Appropriation and the Law. Post-Contemporary Interventions*. Durham, NC: Duke University Press.

dsussman. 2008 (December 10). "*Rolling Stone*'s Top 50 Albums of 2008." *Spike*. Accessed April 5, 2011. http://www.spike.com/blog/rolling-stones-top/71568.

Electronic Frontier Foundation. 2008. "A Better Way Forward: Voluntary Collective Licensing of Music File Sharing." Accessed April 5, 2011. http://www.eff.org/wp/better-way-forward-voluntary-collective -licensing-music-file-sharing.

Evans, Paula C. 2006 (October 1). "Patent Rights in Biological Material: Implications of Principle of Unjust Enrichment Remain Uncertain." *GEN: Genetic Engineering & Biotechnology News*. Accessed April 18, 2011. http://www.genengnews.com/gen-articles/patent-rights-in-biological -material/1880.

Fisher, William. 2003. *The Growth of Intellectual Property: A History of the Ownership of Ideas in the United States*. Boston: Harvard.

Galloway, Alexander R., and Eugene Thacker. 2007. *The Exploit: A Theory of Networks (Electronic Mediations)*. Minneapolis: University of Minnesota Press.

Golijan, Rosa. 2011 (March 1). "70 Percent Find Piracy Socially Acceptable, Says Poll." *Technolog on MSNBC*. Accessed April 5, 2011. http://technolog.msnbc .msn.com/_news/2011/03/01/6162232-70-percent-find-piracy-socially -acceptable-says-poll.

Gordon, Wendy J. 1992. "On Owning Information: Intellectual Property and the Restitutionary Impulse." *Virginia Law Review* 78(1):149–281.

Herreman, S. Todd. 2009. "Audio Mash-ups and Fair Use: The Nature of the Genre, Recontextualization, and the Degree of Transformation." *Journal of the Music & Entertainment Industry Educators Association* 9(1). Accessed April 5, 2011. http://www.meiea.org/Journal/html_ver/Vol09_No01/ Herreman-2009-MEIEA-Journal-Vol-9-No-1-p13.htm.

Illegal Art. 2010. "Girl Talk—All Day Samples List." Accessed April 5, 2011. http://illegal-art.net/allday/samples.html.

Lessig, Lawrence. 2001. "The Future of Ideas: The Fate of the Commons." In *A Connected World* (1st ed.). New York: Random House.

Lessig, Lawrence. 2004. *Free Culture: How Big Media Uses Technology and the Law to Lock Down Culture and Control Creativity*. New York: Penguin Press.

Lessig, Lawrence. 2008. *Remix: Making Art and Commerce Thrive in the Hybrid Economy*. London: Bloomsbury.

Litman, Jessica. 1990. "The Public Domain." *Emory Law Journal* 39:965–1023.

Manganaro, John. 2010 (December 6). "City Councilman Honors 'Gregg Gillis.'" *The Pitt News*. Accessed April 5, 2011. http://pittnews.com/newsstory/ city-councilman-honors-gregg-gillis.

Manovich, Lev. 2001. *The Language of New Media*. Cambridge, MA: MIT Press.

McGranahan, Liam. 2010. *Mashnography: Creativity, Consumption, and Copyright in the Mashup Community*. PhD dissertation, Ethnomusicology, Brown University, Providence, RI.

Moglen, Eben. 2001 (March 12). "Liberation Musicology." *The Nation*. Accessed April 5, 2011. http://www.thenation.com/article/liberation-musicology.

Moore, Adam. 2011 (Spring). "Intellectual Property." Accessed April 5, 2011. http://plato.stanford.edu/archives/spr2011/entries/intellectual-property.

Murray, Laura J., and Samuel E. Trosow. 2007. *Canadian Copyright: A Citizen's Guide*. Toronto: Between the Lines.

Negroponte, Nicholas. 1995. *Being Digital*. New York: Knopf.

Reynolds, Graham. 2009. "A Stroke of Genius or Copyright Infringement? Mashups and Copyright in Canada." *SCRIPTed—A Journal of Law, Technology & Society* 6(3):534–37.

Rifkin, Jeremy. 2000. *The Age of Access: The New Culture of Hypercapitalism, Where All of Life Is a Paid-For Experience*. New York: J.P. Tarcher/Putnam.

Schulze, Hendrik, and Klaus Mochalski. 2009. "ipoque Internet Studies." Accessed April 5, 2011. http://www.ipoque.com/resources/internet-studies.

Skloot, Rebecca. 2006 (April 16). "Taking the Least of You." *The New York Times*. Accessed April 5, 2011. http://www.nytimes.com/2006/04/16/magazine/ 16tissue.html.

Tyrangiel, Josh. 2008 (November 3). "The Top 10 Everything of 2008: 4. *Feed the Animals* by Girl Talk." *Time.* Accessed April 5, 2011. http://www.time.com/time/specials/packages/article/0,28804,1855948_1864324_1864335,00.html.

Vaidhyanathan, Siva. 2001. *Copyrights and Copywrongs: The Rise of Intellectual Property and How It Threatens Creativity.* New York: New York University Press.

Vaver, David. 1983. "*Snow v The Eaton Centre*: Wreaths on Sculpture Prove Accolade for Artists' Moral Rights." *Canadian Business Law Journal* 8:81–90.

Village Voice Contributor. 2008 (November 14). "Interview: Girl Talk a/k/a Gregg Gillis." *The Village Voice.* Accessed April 5, 2011. http://blogs.villagevoice.com/music/2008/11/interview_girl.php?page=2.

Zibreg, Christian. 2010 (February 26). "iTunes in Numbers: No-One Can Beat the Superstore." *geek.com.* Accessed April 5, 2011. http://www.geek.com/articles/apple/itunes-in-numbers-no-one-can-beat-the-superstore-20100226.

Zukofsky, Paul. 2009. "Copyright Notice by PZ." *Z-site: A Companion to the Works of Louis Zukofsky.* Accessed April 5, 2011. http://www.z-site.net/copyright-notice-by-pz.

Alternative Media

What distinguishes alternative media from mainstream media? Must alternative media commit themselves to radical political change? What social, political, and economic goals do most alternative media attempt to achieve?

KEY CONCEPTS

1. Alternative media typically engage in efforts to create social, political, or economic change, and often promote a radical agenda.

2. Alternative media seek to give a voice to the concerns and aspirations of groups that are usually marginalized by mainstream media.

3. Non-professional citizen journalists are considered equally qualified as professional journalists to report on events and tell their stories, and are sometimes more so.

CHAPTER OUTLINE

Introduction 197

What Are "Alternative" Media? 199

Alternative Media as a Tool of Struggle 203

Alternative Media as a Source of Radical Content 206

Alternative Media as a Means of Organizing Cultural Production 209

Alternative Media as a Channel for Expressing Identity and Voice 211

Conclusion 213

Note 214

Discussion Questions 214

Suggested Resources 214

References 215

Introduction

In November 1999, 50,000 people took to the streets of Seattle in a massive demonstration against the World Trade Organization (WTO), an international body that sets and regulates the rules of global trade. Labour activists, environmentalists, students, human rights groups, faith organizations, anarchists, and ordinary citizens arrived in Seattle to protest against the harmful effects of global capitalism. The demonstrators insisted that the WTO privileges the interests of multinational corporations at the expense of indigenous peoples, runs roughshod over international human and labour rights, and poses an imminent threat to the environment, especially in developing countries where existing regulations are either weak or easily ignored. The protest came to be known as the "Battle in Seattle" for the often violent confrontations between protesters and police, and for the millions of dollars in damage to public and private property.

Media coverage of political demonstrations tends to follow a predictable script, and the Battle in Seattle was no exception: activists are the central focus of attention, not the policies they protest against or the corporations and politicians who advance them; businesses and citizens inconvenienced by the demonstrations are framed as the victims, not the communities, citizens, or workers affected by the consequences of global capitalism; and images of violence (smashed windows, tear gas, police "pushing back" the unruly mob) dominate television broadcasts and newspaper front pages.

In advance of the WTO meeting, a group of activists decided they would try to do something about the problems of mainstream media coverage and opened the first Independent Media Center (IMC) in an abandoned building in Seattle. The IMC was established to provide an *alternative* script to the coverage of events by the mainstream media. These stories would be less about the protests than the policy issues that animated them; they would highlight the impacts of global trade agreements on ordinary people in developing countries; and, most importantly, the stories would be shot, edited, and reported not by professional journalists, but by citizens with a connection to the communities that had long been marginalized and ignored.

Although the IMC occupies an important moment in the history of alternative media, this is a history that extends much earlier than 1999. While it is tempting to assess media from the vantage point of the present day, alternative media have emerged under many social and political contexts, and have operated in different ways, at different times, and for different reasons.

This chapter attempts to define alternative media, examines how they are used, and explores the effects that they can have on society and politics. Some of the questions asked include: How are alternative media different from mainstream media? Must alternative media commit themselves to radical political change? What impacts or effects do alternative media have on society, politics, and the people who produce these media? The chapter explores these questions while discussing some real examples of alternative media and the social movements that produce them.

What Are "Alternative" Media?

In the early 16th century, Martin Luther published his *Ninety-five Theses*, a pamphlet that confronted and challenged the established Christian practices of absolution and baptism. Nailed to the doors of a Catholic Church in Wittenberg, Germany, Luther's theses were a radical affront to the religious orthodoxy and became a key component of the Protestant Reformation. In large part, Luther's success was a media triumph because the printing press, invented by Gutenberg a century earlier, had made mass production of the pamphlets possible, ensuring they would be widely distributed and read. As Elizabeth Eisenstein (1980) has argued, the printing press acted as a "precipitant" to revolution, providing "the stroke of magic by which an obscure theologian in Wittenberg managed to shake Saint Peter's throne" (310).

In 1829, the African-American David Walker published his pamphlet *Appeal to the Colored Citizens of the World*. Distributed broadly yet secretly through black communities along the eastern seaboard by sailors, mobile labourers, and charitable societies, Walker's text helped radicalize the abolitionist movement and was pivotal in the antislavery and civil rights campaigns of the 19th and 20th centuries (Downing 2001). The publisher Samuel E.

Figure 11.1 Martin Luther

In one of the earliest and most famous examples of "alternative media," German theologian Martin Luther posted his *Ninety-five Theses* on the doors of a Catholic church in 1517. This challenge to established authority helped spark the Protestant Reformation, one of the great upheavals in the history of Western civilization.

Cornish also demonstrated the importance of alternative media. In 1837 he purchased an existing black newspaper, renaming it *The Colored American*. In his opening editorial, he contended that blacks should not depend on only the white abolitionist press, but should have their own paper because "no class of men, no matter how pious and benevolent, can take our place in the great work of redeeming our character and removing our disabilities" (quoted in Squires 2009, 18–19).

In mid-19th-century Britain, the Chartist movement (arguably the first mass labour movement) was distinguished by the courage of many printers and vendors who faced imprisonment and other punishment for publishing and selling pamphlets that challenged the authority of the state and did not incorporate the government's Stamp Tax, which would have increased the price and made them unaffordable to ordinary people (Downing 2001).

Despite these and other well-known historic examples of alternative media, the field of communication studies suffers from a pervasive inattention to the media of oppositional politics. Although "radical alternative media are by no means latecomers" to society and politics, they are "relative newcomers to the established research and theory agenda" (Downing 2001, v; cf. Atton 2002). As a result, the concept of alternative media remains loosely defined.

Why is the term alternative media so difficult to define? There are several reasons. One important reason is a lack of consistency in terminology. Academics use a number of interchangeable concepts to refer to the same thing. This is partly because "everything, at some point, is an alternative to something else" (Downing 2001, ix). The radical press is an alternative to the establishment (corporate-owned) press. Corporate industry bulletins are an alternative to activist newsletters. Blogs are an alternative to traditional print media and television. Cloud computing is an alternative delivery model for Internet-based IT services. Al Jazeera is an alternative to the CBC and CNN. And SunTV News, a new right-wing news channel in Canada, "aspires to be an alternative" to the nation's so-called left-wing media. The list of alternative media forms is long and illustrates not only the flexibility of the concept, but also how it can mean very different things to different people.

The term "alternative media" can mean very different things to different people.

How, then, may students of media deal with the elasticity of the term "alternative media"? One way of approaching this conceptual problem is to delineate more clearly what we mean by alternative media and why we are using this term. John Downing (2001) assigns the prefix "radical" to capture what he argues should be the politicized nature of alternative media. In other words, it is not enough to offer different or competing topics, voices, and interpretations about issues and events (hate media, for example, also do this). Alternative media should be politically radical and politically progressive—that is, it should offer a vision of social reality that challenges oppression and expands democratic opportunities to economically and culturally marginalized individuals and groups. It should provide a voice for women, visible minorities, youth, the poor, and people living with illness or disease. Furthermore, part of what makes alternative media progressive is its mode of production. For Downing, alternative media should be small-scale, underfunded, sometimes largely unnoticed, and occasionally raise the ire of the establishment. They should seek to "build support, solidarity, and networking laterally against policies or even against the very survival of the power structure" through being organized more democratically (Downing 2001, xi).

KEY CONCEPT
Alternative media typically engage in efforts to create social, political, or economic change, and often promote a radical agenda.

"Community media" is a similar concept that has been used to refer to a range of activities that are intended to challenge or change the operating principles, structures, and practices of mainstream media. Community media are "predicated on a profound sense of dissatisfaction with mainstream media form and content, dedicated to the principles of free expression and participatory democracy, and committed to enhancing community relations and promoting community solidarity" (Howley 2010, 2). Community media often operate as a non-commercial alternative to mainstream media organizations, particularly in countries like the United States that do not have a public broadcaster subsidized directly by taxpayers (like the CBC in Canada). Conversely, in the United Kingdom, parts of Europe, Canada, and Australia, community media are established to challenge the idea that a public broadcaster's primary duty is to construct, sustain, and express a coherent national identity. Community media do so by addressing the many different tastes and interests of ethnic, racial, and cultural minorities that are often misrepresented or underrepresented by official public broadcasters (Howley 2010). Rather than striving for a single national identity, community media celebrate and advocate diversity and the multiplicity of identities.

Community media celebrate and advocate diversity and the multiplicity of identities.

The fact that terms like alternative media, radical media, and community media (among others) are used interchangeably has led some writers to conclude that there can be no clear definition of "alternative media" and we are thus better off without one (e.g., Abel 1997). But is it important or essential to have a clear and distinct definition? Or can we operate with a more flexible framework? The strength of the concept of alternative media may lie in the notion that "it can encompass far more than radical, or 'social change publishing' can" (Atton 2003, 9–10). The variety of formats that are associated with alternative media practice is vast, covering everything from gossip to graffiti, street theatre to performance art, community television to pirate radio, and documentary film to mobile telephony and social media. Not all of these technologies, or the practices of activists and communities who use them, need to be driven by an explicitly political agenda to be considered "alternative." We may therefore be better off using a more general definition of alternative media, provided that we are clear about how we are using it and what we are using it for.

Alternative Versus Mainstream Media

When we talk about alternative media, we are also, by necessity, talking about the **mainstream media**, by which we mean newspapers, radio, television, and even Internet sites that are owned by corporations or supported directly by the state and which produce content for a general audience through technologies of mass dissemination. Because alternative and mainstream

mainstream media Newspapers, radio, television and Internet sites, most owned by corporations, which produce content and widely disseminate it for a general audience.

media are often defined in a negative relationship with each other, it is important to stress the flexibility of both terms, and to emphasize that these concepts are always being redefined. What we might consider alternative media at one time could become mainstream media at another. Blogs can no longer be defined purely as a mode of alternative media, with so many professional journalists now using blogs to publish their work and so many corporations using content management systems (the architecture of blogs) for their own media production. Although blogs are still crucial sites for the construction and distribution of activist messages, they are not defined solely by the cultural labour of this group. Social media sites like Facebook and Twitter are another example. Developed initially as a socializing tool for affluent, college-aged Americans, and a marketing tool for corporations, respectively, these and other social media sites have been redeployed as key tools of political struggle—that is, weapons to be used in the battle against political oppression in many parts of the world (e.g., Shirky 2010).

What, then, do we mean when we talk about the "mainstream media"? Mainstream media are carriers of **dominant discourses**: definitions of events and issues that emphasize the values and interests of powerful groups and do not challenge the political or economic status quo. For example, the dominant discourse in media coverage of homelessness emphasizes the poor choices individuals make that lead to their own misery, and not the political or social structure that produces massive poverty on the back of massive wealth. Mainstream media are also organized according to a large scale of production, and the content is geared toward the broadest possible audience. It is in this sense that mainstream media cannot be provocative for fear of alienating large numbers of readers, listeners, viewers, and the advertisers that seek audience attention. They cannot pursue the difficult questions that challenge audience values because they know that media audiences are more inclined to consume news that reinforces their beliefs than news that challenges them. Mainstream media are profit oriented, vertically structured, and staffed by professionals with specialized training.

Alternative media, on the other hand, take an opposing position in relation to one or more of these features. Alternative media are typically carriers of *subaltern* discourses, that is, the ideas, languages, and arguments of individuals and groups who operate outside the established power structure (visible minorities, the poor, immigrants/refugees, and so on). They are also organized locally with a small scale of production, and are produced by specific audiences for those audiences. They operate independently of the state and market, are not focused on making profits, and are structured in a way that encourages as much access and participation by as many individuals as possible.

Facebook began as a socializing tool for affluent, college-aged Americans, but has been successfully redeployed as a weapon in the battle against political oppression.

dominant discourses
Definitions of events and issues that emphasize the interests of elites, without challenging the political or economic status quo.

However, this distinction between mainstream and alternative media is not without problems. It potentially raises concerns about what we call "definitional determinism" (the idea that social reality gets defined by our concepts, not that reality defines our concepts): just as alternative media are a variegated field, the mainstream media are also pluralistic, not only in editorial orientation (some are more liberal or conservative in their outlook than others), but also in the degree to which they provide access to subaltern voices. Indeed, several studies of social activism have shown that oppositional movements can successfully influence and shift media discourse, and that mainstream media can do more for advancing the cause of oppositional movements than the media of those movements themselves. For example, in their research into the movement for women's suffrage, Hamilton (2006) and Shattock (2007) argue that articles by such leading feminists as Harriet Martineau, Frances Power Cobbe, and others in establishment (that is, mainstream) journals, such as *Westminster Review, Nineteenth Century, Contemporary Review*, and *Fraser's Magazine*, had a measurably greater impact on policy and public opinion than the alternative "specialist press" that was designed by and for the suffragists (see DiCenzo 2011). Studies of media advocacy by activists against homelessness (Greenberg, May, and Elliott 2005) and domestic violence (Ryan, Anastario, and Jeffreys 2005) reach similar conclusions.

All these considerations should lead us to question whether our definition and understanding of "alternative" and "mainstream" media should be fixed (which may be analytically convenient) or fluid (which makes analysis more challenging, if more accurate). Is there such a thing as an "ideal type" when we talk about alternative and mainstream media, or should these categories rather be seen as emergent—that is, always in a process of renewal and change? Does defining alternative media too broadly or too narrowly run the risk of conceptual imprecision? There is no correct answer. However, valuable arguments can be made for both a fixed and a fluid definition.

The sections that follow highlight four recurring themes in research that may be used to define alternative media as (1) a tool of struggle, (2) a source of radical content, (3) a means of organizing cultural production, and (4) a channel for the expression of identity and voice. The discussion of each focal point references actual social movements and their media.

Alternative Media as a Tool of Struggle

In January 2001, the Philippine Congress agreed to ignore crucial evidence against its country's president, Joseph Estrada, during his impeachment trial. Within a few hours of that decision, thousands of angry citizens took to the streets of Manila to protest political corruption and demand Estrada's resignation. Although word of mouth and existing social relationships enabled the protesters to come together, the demonstration was facilitated by the use of text messages reading: "Go 2 ESA. Wear blk." Within a few days, more than a million people had arrived, bringing business and traffic in the capital city to a halt (Castells, Fernandez-Ardevol, Qui, and Sey 2007).

Never before had the Philippines experienced such a sharp and dramatic public response to a political event or issue. So alarmed were the country's legislators by this massive reaction that they allowed the evidence to be presented, leading soon after to Estrada's removal from office (Shirky 2010). Although it is unclear whether the outcome would have been different without the use of SMS, there is no question that new technology was effectively deployed in this example as a tool to coordinate such a massive response. As Shirky (2010) argues, "the event marked the first time that social media helped force out a national leader," leaving Estrada himself to blame "the text-messaging generation" for his fate (Shirky 2011).

fragmentation
The division or splintering of the audience for various media into multiple audiences, primarily caused by the increase in available channels and the rise of new media.

The splintering of audiences and the rise of social media have contributed to, and are reflected in, the **fragmentation** of the mediascape. Opportunities to participate in the coordination of collective mobilization and political action have increased and allowed citizens to demand changes to society and politics in ways that were previously unthinkable. The political revolution in Egypt in 2011 illustrates this argument well. Using a variety of social

Figure 11.2 Protests in Egypt
The ability to share information at lightning speed has allowed political protesters in Egypt and elsewhere to mobilize effectively. In 2011, the Egyptian government responded to the protests by shutting down Internet service for the entire country.
SOURCE: Eric Young Online.

media platforms—in particular, Facebook, Twitter, YouTube, and Flickr—pro-democracy activists (especially youth) in Egypt were able to mobilize mass participation in a popular uprising against the regime of Hosni Mubarak. Because the availability of these technologies reduced the costs involved in sharing information, they allowed citizens opportunities to speak up and to be heard not only within Egypt but the world over, and they increased the rate of coordinating action. Although it is also true that the state responded by using the same tools to conduct surveillance of activists online, and then implemented a complete Internet blackout in an effort to prevent activists from communicating with one another, in this instance it was a case of too little, too late.

During the Egyptian uprising many observers, including some journalists and analysts, mocked the idea that social media might have played an important role in the demonstrations. On *The Daily Show*, Jon Stewart argued that it was not new technology developed in the West but decades of oppression and misery that led to the fomenting of a popular revolution. The essayist Malcolm Gladwell (2011), author of the best-selling books *The Tipping Point* and *Blink*, argued that social media do not support the "strong ties" required for high-stakes political change. And Evgeny Morozov, a Belarusan journalist and blogger based in the United States, has argued that while the Internet played an important role in the Egyptian uprising, this was mostly because "the protesters were blessed with a government that didn't know a tweet from a poke—as illustrated most of all, perhaps, by its desperate (and belated) gambit in temporarily shutting off the country's access to the outside world." Morozov goes on to argue that while activists in other countries may learn a great deal from the case of Egypt, the biggest and most significant lessons will likely be learned by the world's tyrants who will no doubt apprise themselves of "the latest developments in Silicon Valley" (Morozov 2011; cf. Morozov 2009).

While these critical arguments raise important points, they fall short in other respects. In the case of Egypt (and in other recent examples of political revolution), social media and other Internet tools have played an important role in ways these criticisms overlook. Although social media do support weaker ties among people more effectively than other media, this support does not come at the expense of strong ties but rather strengthens both strong and weak ties. Moreover, while authoritarian governments do have the ability to leverage the Internet to increase their repressive capacity, the Internet is also the greatest antidote to anti-democratic forces (Tufekci 2011) because it encourages people to actually talk about events and issues with one another, rather than merely to watch how reporters and other experts are framing it on the nightly news.

Malcolm Gladwell and Mathew Ingram on Social Media

The protests in Egypt in early 2011 sparked a debate about the role of social media during political crises:

> People protested and brought down governments before Facebook was invented. They did it before the Internet came along. Barely anyone in East Germany in the nineteen-eighties had a *phone*—and they ended up with hundreds of thousands of people in central Leipzig and brought down a regime that we all thought would last another hundred years—and in the French Revolution the crowd in the streets spoke to one another with that strange, today largely unknown instrument known as the human voice. People with a grievance will always find ways to communicate with each other. How they choose to do it is less interesting, in the end, than why they were driven to do it in the first place.
>
> —Malcolm Gladwell, "Does Egypt Need Twitter?" February 2, 2011

> [Gladwell] continues to miss the real point about the use of Twitter and Facebook, which is somewhat surprising for the author of the best-seller *The Tipping Point*. ... That's not to say that the question of who is using which social-media tool is inherently more interesting than the actual human acts of bravery and risks that people in Tunisia and Egypt have taken, or are taking. But those tools and that activity can bring things to a tipping point that might otherwise not have occurred, or spur others (possibly even in other countries) to do something similar. Why else would governments like Mubarak's be so quick to shut down the Internet and cellphone networks? And that *is* interesting—or should be—regardless of what Malcolm Gladwell might think."
>
> —Mathew Ingram, "Gladwell Still Missing the Point About Social Media and Activism," February 3, 2011, GigaOM.com

Alternative Media as a Source of Radical Content

What distinguishes alternative media from mainstream media is content that challenges the values and perspectives of the political and corporate elite, police, and other security agents of the state, and myriad experts, from economists to media pundits, think tanks, and even scientists (Harcup 2003, 361). In other words, alternative media confront the biases embedded in established ways of viewing the world and offer possibilities for envisioning different ways of thinking. Bob Hodge and Gunther Kress tell us that "all the major [political] struggles will necessarily be waged in words, through texts that circulate in various ways by virtue of various technologies, in forms of language that bear the traces of these struggles in numerous ways" (quoted in Harcup 2003, 362). By this they mean that the concepts we use, the words that we choose, and the manner of ways in which we make arguments about the world always reflect relations of power.

Alternative media aim to redress a lack of diversity in the content of mainstream media outlets. Whether a community radio station, an NGO blog, a zine for GLBT teens, or a union newspaper, alternative media produce stories about people whose needs and experiences of the world are often ignored or overlooked: the poor, immigrants and refugees, people living with disease or mental illness, women, youth, the working class, and so on. And because the traditional, establishment media tend to be "event-driven" (focusing on *events* that happen, not on what *causes* events to happen), alternative media are more inclined to explore more deeply the issues of social structure: systemic racism and poverty, electoral reform, the consequences of global trade, and more. In many cases, a **progressive** discourse is the defining characteristic of alternative media. Alternative media outlets such as *Democracy Now!*, *SchNews*, and the *Indymedia* network operate with arguably the same professional ethos as traditional news organizations, yet the stories they tell, the focus of those stories, and the language and sources used all differ significantly from news that is reported by the *New York Times*, *CTV News*, or *Time* magazine.

The case of tin miners' radio in Bolivia offers an interesting illustration of the importance of alternative content. When Bolivia was a Spanish colony, many of the indigenous population were forced into slavery in order to mine for silver. In fact, Bolivia's rich silver deposits helped make Spain the wealthiest nation in the world during the 16th century. For the indigenous peoples who actually mined the silver, however, life could only be described as nasty, brutish, and short. By the late 19th century, with almost all of its silver deposits emptied, and now free of Spanish rule, Bolivia's political elite turned to the country's equally rich tin mines to increase exports and its own wealth. While the mineral may have been different, the hardship on those who mined it was the same.

Experiences of suffering and oppression often create the conditions necessary for solidarity and opposition. The hard times experienced by the miners bonded them in a way that could not be shaken, even when the government

Alternative media aim to redress a lack of diversity in the content of mainstream media outlets.

KEY CONCEPT
Alternative media seek to give a voice to the concerns and aspirations of groups that are usually marginalized by mainstream media.

progressive
A political perspective, contrasted to conservatism, that emphasizes social justice, social reform, and an active government role in these efforts.

Protest Music and Social Movements

The political activist and songwriter Phil Ochs famously said of protest music that it is "so specific you can't mistake it for bullshit." There has always been a connection between social movements and music. Music is important not only because it provides a channel for the expression of alternative ideas (through both lyrics and musical form), but because of its capacity to appeal across time and place. Music not only provides a source of entertainment—it can also be instructive, offering new ways of perceiving and speaking about current and historic social and political problems, and provides emotional and spiritual links between movement adherents.

Artists from across genres have woven social and political critique into their music. In 1937, Orson Welles directed the pro-union opera *The Cradle Will Rock*, an allegorical tale about corruption and corporate greed that was set in "Steeltown, USA." In May 1941, on the eve of the US intervention in the Second World War, an ensemble of folk artists called the Almanac Singers released *Songs for John Doe*, which called for non-military involvement and opposed the unequal treatment of African-Americans in the draft. During the civil rights era, musicians became deeply involved in social movements: Bob Dylan and Joan Baez often sang at rallies, including the 1963 March on Washington, where Martin Luther King, Jr. delivered his "I Have a Dream" speech. Soul artists, including Aretha Franklin, Sam Cooke, and James Brown, wrote and performed numerous songs ("Respect," "A Change Is Gonna Come," "Say It Loud—I'm Black and I'm Proud") to honour the civil rights activists who were standing up for equality and social justice.

The ravaging effects of poverty and racism in Jamaica and across the Caribbean provided a source of material for reggae music and helped shed light on centuries of slavery and racial oppression, as well as launching the career of Bob Marley. Bruce Springsteen's "Ghost of Tom Joad," recorded in the mid-1990s during a period of overall economic growth in the United States, pointed to the disproportionate burden that many poor Americans, particularly immigrants, were being forced to shoulder:

> Shelter line stretchin' round the corner
> Welcome to the new world order
> Families sleepin' in their cars in the southwest
> No home no job no peace no rest

Copyright © Bruce Springsteen (ASCAP)

In the early days of the modern anti-globalization movement, hard rock bands like Rage Against the Machine produced protest songs that highlighted the struggles of the Zapatistas, a movement of indigenous people in rural Mexico whose livelihoods were being destroyed by the policies of global trade. The band's lead singer, Zack de la Rocha, once described the band's music as a "bridge" between the Zapatistas and people in the United States: an "alternative medium of communication for young people … to spread the ideas of the Zapatista movement in relationship to the poor, the young, the excluded and the dispossessed in the United States" (Rock & Rap Confidential n.d.).

met their protests with brutal violence. By the mid-20th century, tin miners, far removed from the concerns and interests of the Bolivian elite, set up clandestine radio stations to broadcast news and information specifically to address their own aspirations and interests. Miners' stations were used to broadcast local issues of direct relevance to mining communities. The radio stations aired community messages, called miners to labour meetings, and broadcast union reports. People living in the mining camps used the radio to complain about the abuses of mining companies and to denounce their miserable working and living conditions. While local issues were deemed the most important, stations also provided a different perspective on national news. The most popular station for tin miners, La Voz del Minero, carved out a site of resistance to Radio Fides, the Jesuit-owned national broadcaster (O'Connor 2004). To contest the propaganda of state media, tin miner activists would substitute their own commentary over that of the official broadcaster. It was in many ways an act of theatre: as they "improvised a commentary on what was heard … against the framing voice of the newscast from the capital, a different political voice said firmly: 'we see it differently'" (O'Connor 2004, 29).

Alternative Media as a Means of Organizing Cultural Production

Besides acting as a tool of struggle and providing competing content, alternative media are defined by their organizational structure. Whereas mainstream media outlets are organized vertically (with decision making flowing from the top of the organization hierarchy down), alternative media tend to be organized horizontally because they encourage participation, equality, and openness in decision making. Although there may be a distribution of labour within alternative media organizations, there is not a hierarchy of influence and decision-making authority. Instead, the focus on organization "privileges the processes by which people are empowered through their direct involvement in alternative media productions" (Atton 2004, 17). What this approach emphasizes is the argument that it is not simply the content of a text that defines it as "alternative." Rather, "it is the position of the work with respect to the *relations of production* that gives it this power" (Atton 2004, emphasis added). In other words, what distinguishes alternative media is that they are non-hierarchical, non-professional, and rely on non-commercial modes of production as part of broader efforts to democratize communication. If the goal of a social movement is to eliminate class, racial, or gender hierarchy, its media production should be organized in a way that reflects equality among all participants. Thus, alternative media seek to develop a new social and political order and to design their production activities in accordance with that vision.

Alternative media seek to develop a new social and political order, one that is less hierarchical and more equitable.

What distinguishes alternative from mainstream media is an emphasis on de-professionalization, de-institutionalization, and de-capitalization (Hamilton 2008). Ordinary people without formal journalistic training should be able to be involved in the news-making process without having to invest in professional, broadcast-quality cameras, lighting systems, or highly technical photographic and video editing suites.[1] These three areas of focus make alternative media more amenable to decentralized decision making, resource sharing, and do-it-yourself (DIY) practice as a way of increasing public and member participation. Chris Atton has explained that collective organization "becomes an attempt to include the [audience] in decision-making ... the 'active audiences' of much critical media studies research 'are but one step away from being media creators and producers themselves'" (Downing 1995, 241; quoted in Atton 2001, 50).

KEY CONCEPT

Non-professional citizen journalists are considered equally qualified as professional journalists to report on events and tell their stories, and are sometimes more so.

cultural production
A process of creating myths, images, and symbols through various media (film literature, music, etc.), which help define one's sense of nation, identity, and taste. It is often associated with a struggle for power among groups, and occurs in different social and historical contexts.

James Gillett's research on alternative media and the HIV/AIDS movement illustrates the theme of **cultural production**, its importance to alternative media research, and its pressures and limitations. Gillett examines media projects as "one aspect of a broader strategy" among those involved in the HIV/AIDS movement to construct a space in which infected individuals could exchange ideas and develop a sense of collective identity (2003, 608). He demonstrates how the HIV/AIDS movement provided both an organizational and ideological environment through which infected individuals became involved in media production, from publications and social marketing efforts to television-, radio-, and Internet-based public awareness campaigns. This community-based response to the HIV/AIDS epidemic was effective because it challenged the ideas that only medical experts have control over knowledge of HIV/AIDS and the production of discourse on this topic, and that only the state can control public policy. In many respects, the ability of infected people to become actively involved in the AIDS movement, and in its media projects specifically, provided opportunities to challenge and contest "societal norms and assumptions about what it means to be a person with an infectious, life-threatening disease" (Gillett 2003, 622).

Gillett shows how in the early days of the AIDS epidemic, the lack of public understanding about the virus, and the insufficient attention paid by traditional media, led people who were infected to seek out new ways of gaining control over the environment that defined who they are and what their life chances and opportunities should be. As the issue became more prominent, opportunities to obtain funding for research and advocacy increased. While this was seen as a positive step, it also created unanticipated pressures on the movement to professionalize its media practices. Magazines that were initially conceived to provide alternative content to what could be found in the establishment media were eventually "mainstreamed" in order to appeal to a broader audience of readers and a wider range of prospective advertisers. In particular, some publications experienced enormous pressure to focus more on promotion and publicity. "In many cases, the production of information [became] less collective and more specialized. As a result, participation by those infected with HIV/AIDS has been limited to reading rather than producing" (Gillett 2003, 612). This result was due in no small measure to the "interest among pharmaceutical corporations to advertise" in some of these publications. As treatment options became more widely available, "pharmaceutical corporations discovered that media projects [were] an effective way to promote and market their products—not only to people with HIV/AIDS but also to health care professionals" (619). Thus, Gillett's research shows that new ways of organizing media production may lead to more effective alternative discourses; yet, this result also produces unintended consequences, including pressures to professionalize cultural production in a way that reduces, rather than promotes, participation.

Alternative Media as a Channel for Expressing Identity and Voice

The fourth theme that is central to defining alternative media is that of voice and expression. Although voice is an implicit component of both content and organization, it merits separate discussion. In research on alternative media, there is a commonly held belief that the opportunity to express one's voice is by definition empowering (conversely, the inability to express oneself is seen as inherently oppressive). Producing alternative media content is believed to provide people with opportunities to create their "own images of self and environment" (Rodríguez 2001, 3) and to disrupt how other sources frame who they are and what they stand for. As Rodríguez writes, "it implies becoming one's own storyteller, regaining one's own voice; it implies reconstructing the self-portrait of one's own community and one's own culture" (3).

Alternative media offers opportunities to define oneself, outside of the power structures of mainstream media.

Highlighting the importance of voice in alternative media practice draws attention to power relations. Whereas the mainstream media have a tendency to emphasize the voices and interests of those who are privileged, alternative media set out "to offer a perspective 'from below' and to say the 'unspoken'" (Harcup 2003, 371).

The movement for women's human rights illustrates this theme of expression and voice well. Although the political demands of feminists are often granted because governments recognize the importance of promoting rights in the public arena, challenges remain in making governments accountable for promoting human rights in the private lives of women. Consider the case of gender violence. Many activists argue that existing human rights laws in many parts of the world deal insufficiently with "private-agent abuse"— although governments are not directly responsible, a lack of regulations and the unwillingness of the state to prosecute wife abuse, sexual harassment, rape, and other crimes against women are tantamount to tolerance for gender violence (Friedman 1995). This is an issue that women in the West have effectively vocalized, but it is important to women in every country.

María Suárez, a co-founder and producer of Feminist International Radio Endeavor (FIRE), an alternative radio station in Costa Rica, notes how violence against women was brought to the attention of the international community not only by women in North America, Britain, and Western Europe, but also by women from developing countries, who "had in our minds, our hearts, and our history, and in our bodies and our lives the violence that we have suffered from being imprisoned, from being disappeared, from being shot" (quoted in Friedman 1995, 21). FIRE programs are mostly produced by Latin American and Caribbean women and then broadcast to a global audience. Launched in 1991 on short wave, FIRE later moved to Internet broadcasting in 1998. For the women who are part of the FIRE collective, alternative media help to amplify women's voices and the ideas that mainstream media ignore (Thompson, Anfossi-Gómez, and Suárez 2005, 224). As one FIRE listener explains:

> [FIRE differs] in its courageous approach to challenging themes such as, for example, the war, gringo interventions, and trying to bring in a diversity of women's voices. ... Also it seems great that they are present in a variety

of international spaces, transmitting live. ... This allows women who are not able to participate directly in these spaces to become involved in some manner, and also it benefits those who are able to listen to hear the voices of women involved in those spaces. (Thompson et al. 2005, 224)

The place of voice in studies of alternative media helps overcome the limitations of other research that focuses primarily on alternative media as a tool of struggle, as a source of content, or as a mode of cultural production and organization. These are crucially important to the identity of alternative media; yet, they also narrow the field of inquiry by focusing too heavily on technologies and institutional structures, rather than on social action itself. The inclusion of voice as a component of alternative media shifts our analytical lens to the people involved in these projects, and the ways in which these people engage with others to achieve freedom through their own cultural practices.

Conclusion

The past decade has seen increased interest in and attention to alternative media by communications and media studies scholars. In societies where there are high levels of poverty, inequality, political oppression, and disenfranchisement, it is important to develop alternative channels through which to tell different stories, to express oppositional voices, to construct a sense of shared identity, and even to influence others. This is part of what contributes to the creation of a democratic society.

This chapter has attempted to define alternative media, examine how they are used, and explore the effects that they can have on society and politics. "Alternative media" means different things to different people. It is a form of radical politics for some (a means for challenging the status quo); for others, it is a way of articulating the interests and needs of marginalized communities and groups; and for others still, it is a source of competing information that challenges the stories and events that are told in the mainstream media. Yet, although fixed definitions of alternative and mainstream media can be analytically convenient, they can also be restrictive. What we consider alternative at one time may become mainstream at another. This is why it is important always to look at the people who are using the media and the goals they are trying to achieve, whether that's changing policy, influencing public opinion, experimenting with new modes of production, or developing collective identity.

The chapter has also provided four thematic areas for exploring the application of alternative media. For most social movements, alternative media can be a tool or weapon deployed in political struggle, a site for creating and distributing radical content, a means for envisioning new ways of organizing cultural production (and thus democratic change more broadly), and a channel for the expression of identity and voice.

Examples of how social movements use alternative media include the use of radio in the struggle for indigenous rights and against women's oppression; the development of specialized media for people with potentially life-threatening illness; and the use of social media to fight oppressive political regimes. These are just a sample of the countless, fascinating applications of alternative media that students may explore further.

NOTE

1. Changes in media technology over the past few years, including the rapid introduction of several smart phones with high-quality photography and video, relatively inexpensive and accessible yet professional-grade editing software, and user-friendly, Web-based publishing platforms (such as WordPress) have greatly contributed to the realization of this requirement.

DISCUSSION QUESTIONS

1. Give a "fixed" definition of alternative media and discuss what you think are the strengths and limitations of this definition.
2. In what sense do alternative media seek to challenge or disrupt the event-driven nature of mainstream media coverage? Illustrate your answer with an example.
3. Do you think alternative media are as important in a country like Canada as they are in countries that have a weaker record of democracy? Why or why not?
4. How does Gillett's example of HIV/AIDS media activism reveal the fluid nature of alternative media as a mode of cultural production?

SUGGESTED RESOURCES
Books

Atkinson, Joshua D. 2010. *Alternative Media and Politics of Resistance: A Communication Perspective*. New York: Peter Lang.

Carty, Victoria. 2010. *Wired and Mobilizing: Social Movements, New Technology, and Electoral Politics*. London: Routledge.

Downing, J., ed. 2011. *Encyclopedia of Social Movement Media*. Thousand Oaks, CA: Sage.

Hackett, Robert A., and William K. Carroll. 2006. *Remaking Media: The Struggle to Democratize Communication*. London: Routledge.

Lievrouw, Leah A. 2011. *Alternative and Activist New Media*. Cambridge, UK: Polity Press.

Websites

Alternet. http://www.alternet.org.

Democracy Now. http://www.democracynow.org.

Independent Media Centers. http://www.indymedia.org.

Paper Tiger Television. http://www.papertiger.org.

Schnews. http://www.schnews.org.uk/index.php.

REFERENCES

Abel, Richard. 1997. "An Alternative Press. Why?" *Publishing Research Quarterly* 12(4):78–84.

Atton, Chris. 2002. *Alternative Media*. London: Sage.

Atton, Chris. 2003. "Reshaping Social Movement Media for a New Millennium." *Social Movement Studies* 2(1):3–15.

Atton, Chris. 2004. *An Alternative Internet: Radical Media, Politics and Creativity*. Edinburgh: Edinburgh University Press.

Castells, Manuel, Mireia Fernandez-Ardevol, Jack Linchuan Qiu, and Araba Sey. 2007. *Mobile Communication and Society: A Global Perspective*. Cambridge, MA: MIT Press.

DiCenzo, Maria, with Lucy Delap and Leila Ryan. 2011. *Feminist Media History: Suffrage, Periodicals and the Public Sphere*. New York: Palgrave Macmillan.

Downing, John D. 1995. "Alternative Media and the Boston Tea Party." In J. Downing, A. Mohammadi, and A. Sreberny-Mohammadi, eds., *Questioning the Media: A Critical Introduction*, 238–52. Thousand Oaks, CA: Sage.

Downing, John D. 2001. *Radical Media: Rebellious Communication and Social Movements*. Thousand Oaks, CA: Sage.

Eisenstein, Elizabeth. 1980. *The Printing Press as an Agent of Change*. Cambridge, UK: Cambridge University Press.

Friedman, Elisabeth. 1995. "Women's Human Rights: The Emergence of a Movement." In *Women's Rights, Human Rights: International Feminist Perspectives*, edited by J. Peters and A. Wolper, 18–35. London: Routledge.

Gillett, James. 2003. "The Challenges of Institutionalization for AIDS Media Activism." *Media, Culture & Society* 25:607–24.

Gladwell, Malcolm. 2011 (February 2). "Does Egypt Need Twitter?" *The New Yorker*. Accessed February 21, 2011. http://www.newyorker.com/online/blogs/newsdesk/2011/02/does-egypt-need-twitter.html.

Greenberg, Josh, Tim May, and Charlene Elliott. 2005. "Homelessness and Media Activism in the Voluntary Sector: A Case Study." *The Philanthropist* 20(2):131–52.

Hamilton, Susan. 2006. *Frances Power Cobbe and Victorian Feminism.* Houndmills, UK: Palgrave Macmillan.

Hamilton, James F. 2008. *Democratic Communications: Formations, Projects, Possibilities.* Lanham, MD: Lexington Books.

Harcup, Tony. 2003. "The Unspoken—Said." *Journalism* 4(3):356–76.

Howley, Kevin, ed. 2010. *Understanding Community Media.* Thousand Oaks, CA: Sage.

Morozov, Evgeny. 2009 (March/April). "Texting Toward Utopia: Does the Internet Spread Democracy?" *The Boston Review.* Accessed February 21, 2011. http://bostonreview.net/BR34.2/morozov.php.

Morozov, Evgeny. 2011 (February 19). "Smart Dictators Don't Quash the Internet." *Wall Street Journal Online.* Accessed February 21, 2011. http://online.wsj.com/article/SB10001424052748704657704576150653606688990.html.

O'Connor, Alan. 2006. *Community Radio in Bolivia: The Miners' Radio Station.* Lewiston, NY: Edwin Mellen Press.

Rock & Rap Confidential. n.d. "How America Got Her Groove Back." Accessed March 5, 2011. http://rockrap.com/new/summit.html.

Rodríguez, Clemencia. 2001. *Fissures in the Mediascape. An International Study of Citizens' Media.* Cresskill, NJ: Hampton Press.

Ryan, Charlotte, Michael Anastario, and Karen Jeffreys. 2005. "Start Small, Build Big: Negotiating Opportunities in Media Markets." *Mobilization* 10(1):111–28.

Shattock, Joanne. 2007. "Women Making News: Gender and Journalism in Modern Britain." Review. *Victorian Studies* 49(2):338–40.

Shirky, Clay. 2010. *Cognitive Surplus: Creativity and Generosity in a Connected Age.* New York: Penguin Press.

Shirky, C. 2011 (January/February). "The Political Power of Social Media." *Foreign Affairs.* Accessed March 5. http://www.foreignaffairs.com/articles/67038/clay-shirky/the-political-power-of-social-media.

Squires, Catherine R. 2009. *African Americans and the Media.* London: Polity Press.

Thompson, Margaret E., Katerina Anfossi-Gómez, and María Suárez. 2005. "Women's Alternative Internet Radio and Feminist Interactive Communications." *Feminist Media Studies* 5(2):215–36.

Tufecki, Zeynep. 2011 (January 12). "Delusions Aside, the Net's Potential Is Real." *The Atlantic.* Accessed February 21. http://www.theatlantic.com/technology/archive/2011/01/delusions-aside-the-nets-potential-is-real/69370.

PART FOUR
Media, Culture, and Public Life

CHAPTER 12 / MICHAEL STRANGELOVE
New Media Culture

What is culture? What is old media culture? How "new" are the new media, and do they have a distinct culture? How is new media culture changing audiences and content?

KEY CONCEPTS

1. *Culture* is the process, and the result, of transmitting and reproducing a society's learned behaviours over time.

2. *Old media* were production and distribution systems that were owned and controlled by corporations or the state.

3. *Cultural production* describes the process of creating objects that have meanings and that shape thought and action.

4. *New media culture* is defined by the ability of ordinary individuals, often amateurs, to participate in the production and distribution of shared meanings.

CHAPTER OUTLINE

Introduction 219

Defining Culture 220

Communication and Ways of Thinking 222

The World of Old Media 223

What Is New About the New Media? 225

Factors in the Cultural Shift 226

Shifts in Cultural Production 230

Thinking Critically About New Media Culture 233

Conclusion 235

Discussion Questions 236

Suggested Resources 236

References 237

Introduction

It is a common sight: students carrying new media devices in their backpacks, pockets, on their heads, in their ears, and in their purses. They are, in many respects, masters of the new media. You see them, smart phones in hand, always ready for the next welcome interruption.

Classrooms are packed with new media devices that students bring with them. Next to their books and laptops often sits a cellphone, a symbol of our collective addiction to new media. Students groan when professors ask them to put their phones away. For many, the thought of being disconnected for the duration of a 90-minute lecture is unbearable.

Since the early 1990s, something has changed with our relationship to media. We are communicating through new devices, carrying media with us in new ways, making new social connections, and even making and sharing new content. Communicating, carrying, connecting, making, and sharing—all this has led to the recognition that we have entered into a new media culture. This new culture brings with it new values, enhances old ones, and holds out the promise of better ways of organizing production, consumption, and work. Cultures are distinctive—any particular culture has attributes that distinguish it from other cultures (even though all cultures also share common characteristics). The new media culture that has arisen at the turn of this millennium exhibits distinctive characteristics of productive, expressive, and potentially transformative capabilities that are now extended to billions of individuals.

This chapter will explore these characteristics of new media culture. It offers a perspective on the new culture's promises and potential, which sit somewhere between the **utopian** optimism and dark pessimism that frame speculation on the future of the wired, and increasingly wireless, generation of new media masters.

utopia
An ideal, perfect society or place; *utopian* typically refers to a person or idea that is naively optimistic.

Defining Culture

Before we explore the outlines of new media culture, a brief explanation of culture and its relation to media and communication is in order. The purpose here is not to survey all the major theories of culture, but to present an understanding of culture that is relevant to the study of new media. Theory is a tool that is used for thinking. If a theory helps us understand ourselves and our world, then it can be said to be useful.

A useful theory of culture begins with the recognition that we live in a world filled with shared patterns of thought and behaviour. Culture is the process of constructing shared meaning from a society's available symbolic resources. Our world overflows with symbols that carry meanings—symbolic resources such as flags, television shows, words, clothing, brand names, and gods and goddesses. Culture is both a society's particular constellation of symbolic resources and the process through which those symbols are used to create similarities and maintain differences between people (Geertz 2000).

One writer exploring the relationship between culture and communication oddly observed that the concept of culture is "a

KEY CONCEPT
Culture is the process, and the result, of transmitting and reproducing a society's learned behaviours over time.

weak and evanescent notion in American social thought" (Carey 1989, 19). James Carey partially attributed Americans' "intellectual aversion to the idea of culture" to the "obsessive individualism" that has frequently been identified with American society (19). Ironically, the rejection of culture's influence upon behaviour within America highlights the role of culture as a powerful influence upon thought and action. A highly individualistic society that celebrates individual freedom will have difficulty with the notion that human behaviour is deeply shaped by external forces that are largely beyond control. As another theorist of American culture, Bennett Berger (1995), noted, "people are seldom fully aware of the deepest social sources from which their authentic tastes, feelings, and choices spring, and they often don't even desire that awareness" (132). The study of new media culture brings us closer to understanding how our individual and collective tastes, feelings, and choices are influenced by communication technology.

Culture is one of the most influential forces on thought and action, and has a special relationship with media new and old. Culture is a force that moulds human perceptions, beliefs, and behaviours so that they generally fit with the surrounding society. As anthropologist Ruth Benedict (1934) noted, "most individuals are plastic to the molding force of the society into which they are born" (77). Across all societies, the vast majority of individuals adopt values and goals that fit with the surrounding social order. This is the cultural effect—it provides resources for thought and action that fit the general requirements of already-present collective modes of living.

No society can be all things to all people. Choices are made along the way. By virtue of presenting one set of options, culture filters out other possible worlds. Culture can be an enabling force for innovation and change, but it also restricts behaviour and thought by filtering out other possible ways of living together. For example, a very small percentage of Americans identify themselves as atheists, and a majority of Americans describe their country as "Christian." It is safe to say it would be impossible nowadays for an atheist to be elected president of the United States; a candidate must first publicly declare him- or herself to be a believer in God (and thus far in America's history, every elected president has done so). Thus, the cultural conditions of America dictate the religious belief that candidates must profess if they are to have a reasonable chance at being elected. A society does not present an individual with unlimited options about how to behave and what to believe. As the anthropologist Mary Douglas (1992) has suggested, culture itself is also constrained (136). In effect, we are all born into societies that have already made certain choices for us.

Culture can be an enabling force for innovation and change, but it also restricts behaviour and thought.

Culture: A Communicative Process

Culture is a way of describing the relationship between a society's available meanings and symbols and how those meanings organize individual and group behaviour. The notion of culture provides a partial answer to the question: why do we do and think the things we do and think? Every society has distinct patterns of learned behaviour. The process of transmitting and reproducing these behaviours over time is known as *culture*. Some patterns of behaviour are universal; others are limited to specific societies or smaller groups of people within a society.

Because culture is a communicative process, the specific form it takes (for example, modern North American culture versus 17th-century European culture) depends on the available means of communication within a society (do people use stone, paper, or digital bits?) and the available symbolic resources (what are their common stories and widely shared images?). A society that used paper to communicate stories in a widely shared text such as the King James Bible can be said to have a specific means of expression (the printed book) and specific symbolic resources (the stories contained in the Bible, and the pictures and statues used to represent those stories). This dominant means of expression—printed books—and the shared stock of meanings it communicates—religious stories—will be responsible for shaping patterns of thought and behaviour.

In other words, a culture consists of the ways in which people communicate and the meanings they share through their communication system. If a society changes its way of communicating and its stock of shared symbolic resources (its stories, symbols, and meanings), then it will also change the way people act and think.

Communication and Ways of Thinking

Because anthropology is a social science that specializes in the study of culture, it offers media studies a privileged perspective on new media culture. The fields of media study and anthropology often overlap in their explorations of human behaviour: both are concerned with symbols, meaning, and communication. Media scholars and anthropologists assert that thoughts and actions are constrained and limited by a society's available means of expression. The mind does not operate in a vacuum. What we can think and do is limited by the character of our societies' communication tools and symbolic resources. Different media have different limitations, and therefore allow some patterns of thought and behaviour while disallowing others. In other words, there is a relationship between the structure of communication—the media available to us—and the structure of thought and behaviour. This correspondence between media and mind was also observed and theorized by early media scholars.

The Canadian communication theorist Harold Innis (1951) argued that a society's dominant medium of communication generates a bias within a society. We have just come through a century in which communication and the increasingly global flow of symbols were dominated by corporate media and entertainment industries. Innis proposed that a society dominated by electronic communication, which was largely monopolized by the state and corporations in the 20th century, generated a bias toward ethical bankruptcy in capitalistic social orders. Given the numerous and unending global traumas brought on by unrestrained consumption, the massive inequality in the distribution of wealth, and the looming biocide of environmental destruction, Innis's critique of empire and communication may yet stand the test of time. It took modern electronic communication to create the mindset of the modern consumer.

Mind and media are deeply interconnected. Perhaps the dramatic changes in new media that we are witnessing (and that you are mastering) herald a new type of mind and a new social order. But before identifying the features of new media culture, we might fruitfully remind ourselves of what we are leaving behind. What was the nature of *old* media culture? What is it that new media are surpassing, replacing, or enhancing? An understanding of what old media culture did to create the modern mind sheds light on what new media culture may undo.

Could the dramatic changes in new media that we are witnessing herald a new type of mind and social order?

The World of Old Media

Over the past century, commercial media were responsible for producing much of the shared cultural content—the music, stories, pictures, books, movies, advertisements, and radio and television shows—that most people in North America held in common. Commercial media are our mass media. They are the source of many of our most widely shared stories, and the space where we spend most of our leisure time. Media comprise a vast sector of the capitalist economy, and they are mainly owned and operated by major corporations. Often referred to as commercial, corporate, or mass media, this older media system dominated all Western industrial nations in the 20th century and was, with few exceptions, centralized, privately owned, and funded mainly though advertising revenue. Its main economic function was to "package" different audiences and sell their ears and eyeballs to advertisers. Content was designed to be friendly toward the needs of advertisers and non-threatening to the values of the economic system itself.

manufacture of consent
The transmission to a mass audience of elite opinions, intended to bring voters into line with the interests of those elites.

The main political function of the corporate media system was the transmission of elite opinions to the mass audience (Herman and Chomsky 1988). Old media culture had a distinct bias toward the **manufacture of consent** (Lippmann 1922/1965): bringing voters into line with the interests and the rule of the elite. It did not promote radical political thought—indeed, it actively worked to de-legitimize any challenges to dominant political and economic ideas. Thus, we can speak of our shared belief in dominant political values such as "democracy," and economic values such as "private property," as forces that did not simply come into existence naturally, but rather, were partially manufactured through the media system. Old media culture also manufactured desire for products and services in a marketplace that was dominated by a relatively small number of multinational corporations. Throughout the 20th century, old media became increasingly concentrated in the hands of an ever-smaller number of corporations. This occurred as corporations themselves grew ever larger, more global, and far more influential in shaping the lives of consumers and citizens. Old media effectively functioned as the voice of multinational corporations and a ruling global elite (Schiller 1989).

In the new media culture as well, we also see the concentration of audiences in corporate entities such as Google and Facebook, concentration of content in online services such as YouTube, and concentration in various e-commerce sectors such as online book sales (Amazon) and digital music sales (iTunes). Although competition does exist to varying degrees, sectors such as telecommunications (cellphones), Internet service providers, cable television, computer operating systems (Microsoft and Apple), and chip manufacturers (Intel) exhibit similar trends in market concentration and domination.

The old corporate media system broadcast a relatively narrow selection of content to a vast mass audience. Television was often referred to as the "boob tube" (that is, a device promoting ignorance), and its audience was often characterized in popular culture as "couch potatoes." While these designations underestimated the degree of interpretive and social activity that took place among the broadcast audience of the 20th century, such metaphors are significant. They aptly characterize much about the state and nature of old media culture: commercial content broadcast in a one-way relationship by the few to the many, and audiences who could neither participate in content creation nor provide feedback in any meaningful way. Old media culture could be progressive, as John Fiske (1987) once cogently argued, but it could never provide a sustained voice of resistance or promote an alternative to the values of the corporate and political elite.

Because of their structure, the old media helped create a world in which only corporations or the state could own and control them. The costs, regulatory systems, and physical characteristics of old media determined how they would be used in capitalist social orders. Newspaper printing presses, radio stations, television networks, and film studios all have in common that they are very large and very expensive production systems. Old media thus came to be used to reproduce the values and behaviours desired by the corporate and political establishment. Thus we can say that the dominant available means of expression in the last century was biased toward the needs of the economic and political elite.

> **KEY CONCEPT**
> *Old media* were production and distribution systems that were owned and controlled by corporations or the state.

What Is New About the New Media?

What most distinguishes new media from old media are their economics and their physical characteristics (that is, their structure). Given the anthropological principle that a social order is shaped and constrained by the available means of expression, a dramatically new structure of communication implies the possibility of a new social order. Identifying the characteristics of the new media's structure may help us predict the culture that could be promoted by its rapid infiltration into our daily lives.

A dramatically new structure of communication implies the possibility of a new social order.

The "new" in new media culture designates something that applies to the old corporate media system and something that is, well, new. Telephones, newspapers, television, films, music, computers—all these media have been around for a half century or more, but they have undergone dramatic transformations, particularly since the early 1990s. As old media are transformed into new media, one of the most novel aspects is the fact that we can now carry much of our new media with us in our pockets, purses, briefcases, and backpacks.

In the middle of the last century, situation comedies, soap operas, and evening newscasts were viewed on television sets located in homes. Hollywood films were first seen in theatres. Newspapers provided a daily dose of current events. Radios were found in homes and in cars. But today we can get news, music, and television shows on an increasing variety of highly portable digital devices such as laptops, tablet personal computers (such as iPads), and smart phones. Many students actually get the latest film by pirating it off the Internet before it is in the theatres, and then watch the film on their laptops or tablet PCs.

It is easy to overlook the fact that just a few years ago, the idea of getting news, music, television, books, magazines, and films on a hand-held device that fits in a shirt pocket and can also be used for recording video, pictures, and making phone and video calls was pure science fiction. Now, all this is practically free with a three-year phone contract. Unlike old media, new media are highly portable and can be accessed on a vastly larger range of consumer electronic devices. A typical university student may have at least four such new media devices—one for phone calls and texting; one for taking pictures and videos; one for viewing videos, editing videos and pictures, and composing written texts; and one for listening to music. And it is increasingly likely that each device can do most of what the other devices do. This phenomenon is called *convergence*.

Convergence and Flow

technological convergence
The merging of formerly separate media onto a single platform.

regulatory convergence
The attempt to standardize regulations internationally or across jurisdictions.

economic convergence
Occurs when a media corporation offers a range of interconnected services to its customers (cellphone, cable, Internet, etc.), increasing its efficiency.

The term convergence indicates multiple tendencies within new media. A desktop computer can also be a photocopier, music and movie player, musical instrument, typewriter, film and recording studio, and a library, all rolled into one. This is **technological convergence**. The United States is attempting to dictate how other countries regulate such issues as piracy and other uses of media. This is **regulatory convergence**. Corporations are competing across the entire spectrum of media and telecommunications services, offering cellphone, cable, Internet, and video rental services to their consumers. This competition within the same economic sector is **economic convergence**.

Old media tended to deliver distinct types of content, such as news, dramas, music, and film, through isolated media such as radios, newspapers, televisions, and theatres. In the new media environment, content flows across an increasingly large range of highly portable (and ever smaller) consumer electronic devices. Thus, a dominant aspect of the new media culture is its *flow*. Because of the digital nature of content and the interconnected character of all our media devices (they can "talk" to each other, storing and exchanging content), objects that were once fixed in space, like a paperback novel, are now a series of ones and zeros that can flow between billions of interconnected consumer electronics. This flow creates the problem of content control (piracy) and challenges old media's notion of private property.

The flow of new media creates problems for old media's notion of private property.

Factors in the Cultural Shift

The flow of new media culture is enabled by two key structural changes in the old media system—interconnectedness and digitization. Our new media devices are wired and wirelessly interconnected, and media content itself has been transformed from analogue to digital objects. By 2010 there were over one billion computers connected to the Internet, which in turn connected two billion Internet users. Billions of digital cameras, phones, and hundreds of millions of cars and trucks, along with millions of other consumer devices, are also connected to the global Internet. In total, there are over five billion devices connected to the Internet, and by 2020 it is estimated there will be between 20 and 50 billion.

The anthropologist Clifford Geertz (1973, 5) once described culture as a web of meaning that we have made for ourselves and which defines our existence. We create culture, and are created by our culture. New media culture stems from a web of interconnected devices that we use to create and exchange meanings. It is also a web within which we are collectively entangled.

Media products once existed solely in **analogue** states—a book was made out of paper, music was sold on vinyl disks, and movies were printed on celluloid and stored in big round metal cans. Today, the vast majority of media products are manufactured in digital form. The total universe of all digital media objects exceeds 2,810 billion gigabytes. Old media culture was built upon analogue objects (hard-copy, physical products) that were difficult to copy and pirate, relatively easy to regulate, and awkward to manipulate. This last point refers to the fact that an individual could not easily edit and recombine sections of text, images, television shows, or motion pictures. Cutting and pasting old media involved scissors and glue, not *control+c* and *control+v*. In stark contrast, new media culture is built from digital products that are easy to copy, pirate, and manipulate, but very hard to regulate and control.

analogue
Contrasted to *digital*, and referring to the pre-digital formats for producing, distributing, and consuming music, television, magazines, and so on.

To summarize, new media culture arises out of structural changes in the characteristics of the 20th-century media system. These structural changes include portability, digitization, interconnectivity, and convergence, and they have altered the way content flows. Within the old media system, content flowed from one to many, whereas in the current state of flow, content moves from one to one (for example, a text message), from one to many (a YouTube posting), and from many people to many people (such as a "mashup" video that combines material from multiple sources and is remixed by multiple editors). New media culture has also transformed the audience by giving ordinary people the tools to produce and distribute content across the globe at very low cost. Most of these changes have unfolded since the 1990s, and their social and political consequences are still unclear. Yet we do know this—things have changed.

In a sense, the structural changes of the new media have infiltrated the old media. For example, old media corporations are on the Web, on Facebook, and on our cellphones. Their products are now digitized and portable. Their production systems are converging. The now-defunct Canadian media corporation, Canwest, once had a slogan proclaiming the glory of convergence for consumers: "If you can watch it, read it, hear it, or download it, we want to be the source." This rather Orwellian vision of complete convergence promised consumers that one corporation could fulfill all their media needs. The same media company might produce content; sell cable TV, Internet connections, and cellphones; and even sell consumer products that enable consumers to pirate media products! So new media do not just replace old media with something new; they have transformed the nature of old media's products (analogue to digital) and restructured old media's methods of production and distribution.

The Example of the Music Industry

New media have changed the status of music from private property to a de facto form of public property—the vast majority of the music that consumers download from the Internet is pirated. The new media have also changed *who* sells music online. Neither record labels nor major record stores have captured most of the online music market—a technology company has. Apple's iTunes is responsible for over 66 percent of all online music sales. Here we see the nature of the product change—from physical (packaged) music albums containing multiple songs on compact disks and sold in bricks-and-mortar stores, to individual music tracks sold online. We have seen the de facto status of music change from private property to a new form of uncontrolled (and uncontrollable?) public property. We have also

dis-intermediated
The removal of an intermediary or "middle man" in the distribution process, such as video rental stores or record stores.

seen the retail music sector **dis-intermediated** from the position of being the main seller of music. Dis-intermediation is another characteristic of new media culture, and refers to the way in which the "middle man" in a process tends to be displaced: Amazon displaced bookstores, iTunes displaced record stores, and online news websites displaced newspaper boxes and newsstands. Booksellers, music stores, and newsstands still exist, but they witnessed a dramatic reduction in their sales once consumers began to buy (or steal) from new online sources.

This transformation has had a tremendous economic, but relatively minor political, impact upon our social order. Regardless of the new technological structures of old media, some things about them have not changed. Media and entertainment corporations are still capitalistic enterprises, owned and operated by the very wealthy, regulated (to varying degrees) by the state, and largely serving the interests of the economic and political elite. Yet, "new media culture" describes something far more significant than structural changes in the commercial broadcast and entertainment industries.

New Media in the Classroom

The classroom is a microcosm of the changes being wrought by new media culture. Students are armed with multiple wired and wireless sources of entertainment. Instructors are confronted with a sea of faces all aglow with lights from laptops. Alongside their laptops, students typically place their ever-present cellphones. For an instructor, new media culture represents a culture of distraction. Their students may be masters of these media, but their multitasking habits are often counter-productive: many studies suggest that laptop use in classrooms actually degrades student performance (Fried 2008).

The new media–enabled instructor communicates with students via email, of course, but also increasingly through social networking sites such as Facebook. Instructors are using YouTube to disseminate video lectures and may even require their students to make a video instead of writing a mid-term paper. Many professors who have embraced the new media have begun blogging, tweeting on Twitter, and even using online games as a way to engage their audience.

Yet, some professors have doubts about the efficacy of all this technology, or at least the ways in which it is commonly used. Students have not become better researchers, writers, or thinkers because of new media. Not only has there been no significant increase in student performance, but some studies suggest that new media culture is potentially creating "the dumbest generation" (Bauerlein 2008). Other observers claim that new media culture tends to be the domain of talentless amateurs (Keen 2007).

Ultimately, students themselves may be the best judges of the new media and their effects. Look closely and honestly at yourself, your peers, your courses and instructors, and consider:

- What role do the new media play in my education? Are they having a positive or negative influence?
- Are the new media helping me to learn, become more analytical, and be better informed about the world?
- Are they helping me to develop better research, writing, and presentation skills, or do they just provide shortcuts for completing assignments?
- List three ways in which you feel the new media play a positive role in your studies and education. Then, list three ways in which they may be a negative factor.

Shifts in Cultural Production

Perhaps the most significant aspect of new media culture is the transformation of the mass audience into literally billions of potential content producers who can, at very low cost, create and distribute content across the globe. If new media culture were a series of transformations that affected only media corporations, its social significance would be negligible. Fortunately, it affects much more than media business models.

New media culture represents a transformation in society's available means of expression on a scale never before witnessed in history. As of 2011, two billion Internet users had the ability to create cultural content—words and images, meanings and symbols—and share this content worldwide (Ottawa Citizen). This represents an unprecedented increase in the production and distribution of meaning (the fabric of our cultural web). Whereas the 20th century was characterized by the almost total domination of corporations and states over the production of shared meanings, the 21st century marks the beginning of mass participation in the creation of shared cultural content.

Society is moving from a single dominant mode of cultural production to two modes of cultural production.

Society is moving from an order dominated by one mode of cultural production—the capitalist, corporate system—to an order that has two modes of cultural production: the old system of corporate media, which continues to dominate the economic sector of meaning production, and the new system of amateur cultural production. This new system is based on the two billion potential content producers who are disseminating words, pictures, and videos across the Web and who, for the most part, do so outside of capitalism's system of economic exchange. People are making stuff and putting it up on the Internet for free, usually with little or no expectation of receiving monetary payment in exchange. What does this mean for the new media culture? This new mode of cultural production, epitomized by the online amateur, is not entirely free from the influences of the old production system, but is nonetheless significantly distanced from the economic imperative of the capitalist mode of cultural production. The average Internet cultural producer is making content available on the Internet for free. This is both new and different.

KEY CONCEPT

Cultural production describes the process of creating objects that have meanings and that shape thought and action.

As suggested earlier in this chapter, culture is a collection of shared meanings that organize our perception, thoughts, feelings, and actions. In the 20th century, most shared meanings (the cultural content we collectively consume) came from one source—media corporations. Thus, corporations and their collective agenda had the greatest influence over thought and behaviour in the 20th century. This old system has been absorbed by the new media, but it must, for the first time in its history, compete against another source of cultural content—the amateurs of the Internet. These amateurs are already producing more words, more images, and more motion pictures (videos) than the entire corporate commercial media sector. It is very likely that amateurs will continue to outproduce media corporations.

Amateurs Behind the Camera: YouTube and Barbie

Consider the example of YouTube, a corporate site that provides a point of distribution for amateur videos. Amateur videos depict the world differently from television and Hollywood films. Amateur video allows unscripted representation of ordinary people's lives directly to the world. Within the representational system of commercial media, reality is carefully constructed by professionals working within its institutional framework. Script writing, filming, directing, editing—all these tasks take place with economic concerns in mind. But when amateurs take up the camera to record their world, such institutional habits and economic forces are typically not present. This is one of the fascinating aspects of YouTube—not just because it offers another way to view clips from television shows, but because it provides access to a different point of view, a different style of representation—the amateur style. Online amateur videography demonstrates how new media culture changes the way we produce representations of ourselves and our world.

Consider the Barbie doll. Toy company Mattel has carefully constructed Barbie's appearance: she is the All-American Girl, pretty, wholesome, and sexy (but not too sexy). If you enter the word "Barbie" into YouTube or Google and look through the results, you will see Mattel's official Barbie, but you will also encounter very different representations—images of Barbie as stripper, drug addict, victim of domestic abuse, suicide bomber, and other manifestations too terrible to mention here. A central characteristic of new media culture is the way it enables us to alter corporate media products and consumer goods and transform them so that they mean something different. Needless to say, Mattel's lawyers are not happy about the way amateur and professional artists have represented Barbie online.

Generally speaking, corporations want to control the way their products are represented, and protect their meaning. Yet, new media culture has given rise to a great struggle between corporations and consumers over the meanings and representations of manufactured objects. The Internet has caused corporations to lose some of their control over the distribution of their digital products (think of digital piracy) and over the meaning of their brands and products (as with the Barbie example). This raises the question: is the new media culture a growing form of anarchy, or is it something that will

HISTORICAL HIGHLIGHT

Home Movies and the YouTube Effect

By the time you have finished reading this box, Internet users will have uploaded over 35 hours of video to YouTube. YouTube has commercial media products on it, including complete films and television shows, but it also has millions of videos made by amateurs. This represents something new in media culture—the global dissemination of motion pictures made by amateurs. What are amateurs filming with their camcorders and smart phones? Almost literally, everything and everyone. This is not how amateur filmmaking started out.

By the 1930s, amateur home movies were capturing a very small slice of life, usually using 8-millimetre film cameras. People tended to film family and friends, and then showed those films only to people whom they knew. Typically, the subjects were domestic situations and family vacations. Birthdays, family dinners, weddings, holidays, and vacations were the main subject matter of home movies. Back then, cameras were relatively rare, film was expensive, and home movies were usually shot by the father of the family in middle- and upper-middle-class homes. With the current mass deployment of inexpensive video cameras, all this has changed.

Today, home movies are digital in format, cost nothing to "print," require no time, money, or effort to have processed at a film laboratory, and often end up on the Internet. It is not unusual for thousands and even millions of people to view home videos on YouTube. We are letting complete strangers witness very personal and formerly very private aspects of our lives. The home videos of YouTube are also entering into mass culture. Many of us have seen Charlie bite Harry, David coming home from the dentist, and other widely shared videos of wedding dances, crazy pets, or wild teenagers. Amateur video is transforming the nature of our shared culture. In the 20th century, if we were talking about moving images that we saw on a screen or a television set, they were almost certainly made within the corporate media system. Now, as a result of new media, there is an ever-increasing chance that our shared culture is also coming to us from amateurs and their video cameras.

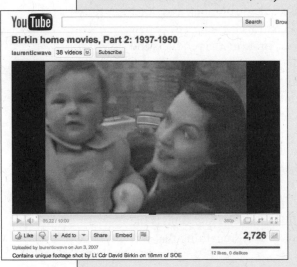

Figure 12.1 Old home movie, now posted on YouTube

Once a very private document of family life, and seen by only a handful of people, home movies now have the potential to reach millions of people around the world thanks to YouTube, and no longer require special equipment or film processing as they did in the pre-digital era.

SOURCE: YouTube.

soon be brought back under tight control by corporations and governments? Or might some sort of balance be achieved in the long term?

New media culture is defined by the fact that ordinary individuals, often amateurs, can participate in the production and distribution of shared meanings—the very stuff that provides society with the raw material for thinking. Individuals may or may not have the same values and agenda as corporations. There are certainly many more individuals than corporations, and (this is the key) there are many more ways of being, of existing, among the vast variety of individuals than there are within the small world of corporations. Media corporations and the marketplace act as a filter that can marginalize anything that threatens their interests. New media culture, as epitomized by the Internet, tends to resist such censorship. This culture represents a transition from a fairly homogenous set of values filtered through commercial media corporations, to a vastly greater diversity of opinions, values, and beliefs that now circulate via the Internet. For this reason, debates are currently raging in many quarters—government, the corporate world, and citizens themselves—over the openness of the Internet, who owns it, net neutrality, and how it will be governed, if at all. (See Chapter 9, Regulating the Media.)

> **KEY CONCEPT**
> *New media culture* is defined by the ability of ordinary individuals, often amateurs, to participate in the production and distribution of shared meanings.

Thinking Critically About New Media Culture

New media culture is *not* a set of cultural values or beliefs that come packaged with all the digital, computerized, miniaturized, marvellous technology that we have in our purses and pockets. It is not necessarily more democratic, more truthful, or more intelligent, and it is certainly not more environmentally friendly. Rather, new media culture is a new way of creating culture itself. It is a new way of creating shared meaning. Exactly what new meanings and new social orders we create with these new media remain to be seen. There are dangerous and contradictory forces that come packaged with the new media. Consider the issue of surveillance.

New media culture is not necessarily more democratic, truthful, or intelligent, but is a new way of creating culture itself.

A Culture of Surveillance

Parents closely watch over their children to teach them and keep them from harm. As adults, we continue to be closely watched, but by the "big brother" of the state and corporations. Walk down the street, go shopping, go to class, and chances are that you will be captured by many cameras. To be watched is a function of power, which is unequally distributed: corporations may record our movements in malls, but the general public cannot use cameras in malls. The people who own Facebook want us to reveal our every secret and be, in the words of founder Mark Zuckerberg, "radically transparent," and yet citizens do not have access to the secrets of corporations, governments, and other influential institutions. New media companies like Google use the Web to gather vast storehouses of data on our surfing habits, but they remain closed to the public. We live in an age where the masses are under constant surveillance, yet the very rich and very powerful remain largely hidden and private. (This helps explain the uproar heard among various elites after Wikileaks' partial exposure of these hidden worlds.)

New media enable the creation of vast collections of data that are used to create profiles about us. These profiles are used to manipulate our behaviour as consumers and citizens, and to discipline us if we are seen as a threat. New media technology has greatly increased the ability of corporations and the state to monitor our daily behaviour, and thus presents the possibility that these institutions will be able to exercise more control over the social order. Fortunately, new media also offer a system of counter-surveillance, wherein those with little power are able to monitor and report on the actions of corporations and political leaders. There are over four billion cameras in consumers' hands; every week, the news—and YouTube—exposes more new stories of the bad behaviour of private and public persons captured on camera. There is a global army of activists who use new media to monitor and report on corporate behaviour. Thus, new media can be said to increase the potential of corporations and the state to monitor and discipline us, while they also increase our ability to monitor and bring to justice those who seek power without accountability (Saunders 2010).

New media can simultaneously be used to report on corporate behaviour, while increasing the potential for corporations or the state to monitor citizens.

All these cameras have the potential to create a world in which we are afraid to be different, afraid to stand out, afraid to protest. The new media might create a stagnant world of conservative social conformists. They might also create a world where we are constantly violating one another's privacy in the name of getting higher viewer counts on YouTube videos. Any predictions about the changes that will come with new media must be cautious; the future has a way of constantly surprising us. Our ability to turn the cameras on the powerful has limits. For example, we have yet to see any dramatic change in Iran's totalitarian regime, even though new media have been widely used to record mass political protests in that country. Democracy does not happen just because a lot of people have cellphones, cameras, and Internet connections.

A New Type of Social Memory

New media affect our culture because they offer a new way of creating and disseminating meanings. They also bring more aspects of formerly private behaviour into the public's awareness (consider the growing number of women who post on the Internet highly graphic videos of themselves giving birth). Billions of people are putting words, images, and videos of themselves and each other on the Internet. These digital bits and pieces of ourselves become part of the raw material for how we and others create a sense of who we are—our identity. The new media are changing how we construct identity by allowing ordinary people to create public profiles of themselves on blogs, on social networking sites like Facebook, and through amateur videography on YouTube.

Identity is related to how we remember. In the not too distant past, our lives were not so intensely recorded. With few exceptions, only the wealthy, famous, and powerful would have left a detailed and accessible record of themselves behind. Now we are all involved, to some degree, in creating extensive public records of our thoughts and actions. The new media culture is a new type of public-ness, a new method of creating social connections, and a new type of social memory. Whereas "what happens in Las Vegas stays in Las Vegas" (as the old advertising slogan claimed), what goes on the Internet usually stays on the Internet. Our productive activity on the Internet creates an indelible record of our acts. We are changing the way we create our personal histories, and as a result, changing our future, as the future is always built upon the past.

When today's young people grow up, they may have to contend with embarrassing words and images on sites such as Facebook. Ironically, the new media may limit a person's ability to change or alter his or her identity. The indelible record of past actions may end up inhibiting change by undermining an individual's freedom to change in the future (Solove 2007).

Conclusion

What, then, is new media culture? It is not a predefined set of values embedded in technology that determines an inevitable future. Rather, it is a vast expansion in society's expressive capabilities. It is a new mode of producing meaning. It deeply affects how meanings are made and distributed. The forces associated with new media culture are highly contradictory. New media culture is a way of living that involves intense interaction with commercial media products, yet it also permits the transformation of privately owned meanings. It turns private property into massively shared public property (as the music and entertainment industry has learned). It expands the individual's freedom of expression, and then binds the individual to what has been expressed. It is power and counter-power.

Perhaps the very thing humanity needs at this moment in history is a new way of creating shared meanings, one that is not controlled by the economic system, one that does not represent the interests of the elite. Capitalism appears to be reaching a state of crisis, as seen in the frequent and severe recessions that have occurred throughout the last century. It has generated enormous disparities of wealth, its mode of production is devastating to the environment, and its social orders often rest on terrible injustices such as exploitation of workers, gender inequality, and racial apartheids. The powerful and privileged few remain unaccountable to the many. We need a new social order, one that corrects the excesses of the past and heals the wounds of the present. It is unlikely that media corporations or dominant political institutions will be the source of new values that correct the excesses of capitalism. Fortunately, amid great suffering and great need, we have stumbled upon a new way of creating shared meanings, one that does not entirely conform to the intentions of those already in power.

For all else that it might be, new media culture is a source of hope.

DISCUSSION QUESTIONS

1. How does the corporate mode of cultural production act as a censor?
2. What does mass involvement in online amateur cultural production imply about the possibility of cultural change?
3. Is the new media culture an inherently progressive force? Explain.
4. What aspects of the "old media" persist in the new media culture?

SUGGESTED RESOURCES

Books

Eisenstein, Elizabeth A. 1983. *The Printing Revolution in Early Modern Europe.* Cambridge, UK: Cambridge University Press.

Jenkins, Henry. 2006. *Convergence Culture: Where Old and New Media Collide.* New York: New York University Press.

Marshall, David P. 2004. *New Media Cultures.* London: Arnold.

Poster, Mark. 2006. *Information Please: Culture and Politics in the Age of Digital Machines.* Durham, NC: Duke University Press.

Strangelove, Michael. 2010. *Watching YouTube: Extraordinary Videos by Ordinary People.* Toronto: University of Toronto Press.

Websites

For Michael Strangelove's video lectures on new media, teaching resources, and blog:
http://www.youtube.com/user/EmpireofMind
http://www.strangelove.com/blog

Some popular websites that cover new media:
Boing Boing. http://www.boingboing.net.
GigaOM. http://gigaom.com.
Wired. http://www.wired.com.

REFERENCES

Bauerlein, Mark. 2008. *The Dumbest Generation: How the Digital Age Stupefies Young Americans and Jeopardizes Our Future (Or, Don't Trust Anyone Under 30)*. New York: Tarcher.

Benedict, Ruth. 1934. "Anthropology and the Abnormal." *Journal of General Psychology* X(2):59–82.

Berger, Bennett M. 1995. *An Essay on Culture: Symbolic Structure and Social Structure*. Berkeley, CA: University of California Press.

Carey, James W. 1989. *Communication as Culture: Essays on Media and Society*. London: Routledge.

Douglas, Mary. 1992. *Risk and Blame: Essays in Cultural Theory*. London: Routledge.

Fiske, John. 1987. *Television Culture*. London: Routledge.

Fried, Carrie B. 2008. "In-Class Laptop Use and Its Effects on Student Learning." *Computers & Education* 50(3):906–14.

Geertz, Clifford. 1973. *The Interpretation of Cultures*. New York: Basic Books.

Geertz, Clifford. 2000. *Anthropological Reflections on Philosophical Topics*. Princeton, NJ: Princeton University Press.

Herman, Edward S., and Noam Chomsky. 1988. *Manufacturing Consent: The Political Economy of the Mass Media*. New York: Pantheon.

Innis, Harold A. 1951. *The Bias of Communication*. Toronto: University of Toronto Press.

Keen, Andrew. 2007. *The Cult of the Amateur: How Today's Internet Is Killing Our Culture*. New York: Crown Business.

Lippmann, Walter. 1922/1965. *Public Opinion*. Glencoe, IL: Free Press.

Ottawa Citizen. 2011 (January 27). "Number of Internet Users Reaches Two Billion: UN." Accessed February 22. http://www.ottawacitizen.com/business/International+Number+Internet+users+reaches+billion/4174906/story.html.

Saunders, Doug. 2010 (December 18). "Imagine a World Without Privacy: The Utopian Dream of Total Openness." *The Globe and Mail*. Accessed February 23, 2011. http://www.theglobeandmail.com/news/technology/just-watch-us-the-utopian-dream-of-total-openness/article1843238/singlepage/#articlecontent.

Schiller, Herbert I. 1989. *Culture Inc.: The Corporate Takeover of Public Expression*. Oxford, UK: Oxford University Press.

Solove, Daniel J. 2007. *The Future of Reputation: Gossip, Rumor, and Privacy on the Internet*. New Haven, CT: Yale University Press.

CHAPTER 13 / SANDRA GABRIELE AND LISA LYNCH

Journalism

What is news? How do journalists sort, select, and frame news stories? How does journalism intervene in public life? How does online news change the ways in which news is produced and consumed?

KEY CONCEPTS

1. News is new information about an event or issue that is communicated in an organized and public way. News forms are historically situated, and thus are constantly changing.

2. The North American and British media systems assume a relationship between journalism and democracy, but that relationship is subject to critique.

3. The rise of new digital delivery platforms for the industry has shifted the ways in which news is produced and consumed.

CHAPTER OUTLINE

Introduction: Journalism's Traditional Role in Public Life 239

What Is News? 240

Forms of Journalism 242

Journalism's Democratic Function: The Ideal 246

Journalism and Democracy? 248

Public Media: Ensuring Journalism's Democratic Role? 254

The Online Transition and the Challenges to Journalism 255

Changing News Presentation and the End of "Fortress Journalism" 257

Conclusion 260

Discussion Questions 261

Suggested Resources 261

References 262

Introduction: Journalism's Traditional Role in Public Life

There has been quite a bit of animosity and heated debate over the potential of citizen journalists and whether or not they're going to replace traditional journalists. And again, I think this question of *who* displaces the question of *what*, which I think is fundamentally more important and interesting. ... By focusing on who is doing it and making that the most important criteri[on], I think we actually lose sight of what journalism is.

—Amanda Michel, editor of "distributed reporting" for the investigative journalism group ProPublica (quoted in Seward 2009)

239

Journalism is traditionally seen as the work that professional journalists do for newspapers, television, or other mass media. But is journalism defined only by professional affiliation, or because it's published by a media organization? Is it defined by the professional standards that govern how journalists collect information—for example, avoiding bias, gaining multiple perspectives? Is it defined by a recognizable style, such as a news story versus an opinion piece? Or is it defined by the timeless nature of gathering information—stories of public interest?

Journalism is defined by the function that news plays in people's lives.

For Bill Kovach and Tom Rosenstiel (2007), journalism cannot be defined by the technologies used to produce or distribute it, who produces it, or the techniques used to produce it; rather, journalism is defined by the function that news plays in people's lives (11). This definition places much of the focus on issues of democracy, and indeed this chapter, like much of the literature within journalism studies, highlights this function. The chapter also discusses other functions of journalism, including its cultural function.

What Is News?

On the most basic level, the *news* has two key characteristics: it is new information about an event or issue, and it is communicated in an organized and public way (Zelizer and Allan 2010, 80). In this sense, news is "limited to events that bring about sudden and decisive change" (Park 1940, 681). *Journalism* is the range of activities that are associated with making the news. It is "the organized and public collection, processing and distribution of news and current affairs material," including the skills, routines, and conventions used in newswork by editors, photographers, reporters, and correspondents (Zelizer and Allan 2010, 62–63). This definition, however, includes only a limited range of what we now consider to be journalism. It favours professional and traditional forms over other, emerging kinds of news. As the opening quotation suggests, journalism is an evolving concept, one that has changed historically and is subject to much debate (Zelizer 2009, 13).

KEY CONCEPT

News is new information about an event or issue that is communicated in an organized and public way. News forms are historically situated, and thus are constantly changing.

Like journalism, news is also a historical category that has changed as media have changed, and that varies across societies (Darnton 2000). In 17th-century England, people gathered in coffeehouses and shared information, much as they gathered around the tree of Cracow in 18th-century Paris, or meet in marketplaces in present-day Morocco (Darnton 2000, 2). In 19th-century Canada, as newspapers grew in popularity and expanded the news they offered, women's pages published content that radically departed from the focus on politics and business that had characterized newspapers previously. In fact, "women's pages" often were not about the latest events at all (although sometimes they were). Women journalists such as Faith Fenton and Kit Coleman, writing as columnists for Toronto papers *The Empire* and *The Daily Mail*, respectively, gave voice to many of women's everyday activities and experiences in a rapidly changing world. Columns and commentary of this nature, although initially disparaged as trivial, became an important addition to our daily news intake. Some scholars even suggest that for much of the 19th and 20th centuries, news was really old stories made new (Rantanen 2009). These features of the news demonstrate that it, and the journalism that produces the news, serves an important cultural function in our society.

The news is always *stories* about news, which are told by *storytellers*, whose voices are "disguised" within news conventions (Adam 1993, 33). Herbert Gans (1979/2004) has highlighted the important role of journalists in the gathering, sorting, and presenting of news. News, he argues, is "information which is transmitted from sources to audiences, with journalists—who are both employees of a bureaucratic commercial organization and members of a profession—summarizing, refining and altering what becomes available to them from various sources in order to make the information suitable for their audiences" (80). Much like other forms of storytelling, journalism is mythological (Bird and Dardenne 1988). **Myths** help create enduring stories that maintain continuity and order over time. As a "first draft of history," journalism is a critical source for future historians to learn about past cultures, ways of life, commodity culture, and belief systems.

myths
Shared beliefs, usually with some basis in truth, that promote certain values and help create enduring stories.

News media, then, are the primary "sense-making practice of modernity" (Hartley 1992); they offer us a vision of reality (not *the* reality). The vision that they offer is ideologically driven and thus always partial (Hall 1980; Van Dijk 2009). The diffusion of information in the contemporary digital world, however, means that news media are not the only way now that we receive information and make sense of the world around us. Any study of the contemporary news world must take account of the broader media environment (Nerone 2009).

Journalism is often thought of as a "first draft of history."

News media are important precisely because they help shape our perception of the world, other peoples, and ourselves. Other scholars have pointed to the ways in which news media also act as a "social glue" (Wahl-Jorgensen and Hanitzsch 2009, 3). As James Carey (1989/2009) observed, media not only disseminate information, they also connect us together ritually. Benedict Anderson (1983/2006) refers to this ritualized connection among readers as an "imagined community." In describing the spread of nationalism, Anderson highlighted the particular role that newspapers played in connecting readers together and creating shared sets of experiences. "The focus on conversation is important for creating spaces in which people can play out the rituals that create communities" (Carey 1989/2009). By consuming news stories, and engaging in conversations with others about them, we construct and understand ourselves as active subjects and citizens within those communities. As Bill Kovach and Tom Rosenstiel (2007) have argued, "the primary purpose of journalism is to provide citizens with the information they need to be free and self-governing" (12).

Forms of Journalism
Print
Largely for historical reasons, much journalistic activity has been limited to print. Journalism "grew up" in the pages of newspapers and magazines across the world. Newspapers were not established immediately after the invention of the printing press because their social potential was not yet apparent. Many historians of journalism have suggested that newspapers gained ascendancy as the societies that read them changed, and as their political systems evolved over time (Barnhurst and Nerone 2009, 18; also see Kaplan 2002; Rutherford 1982; Barnhurst and Nerone 2001). The first newspapers began publication in Europe in the early 17th century. Weekly "corantos" were largely geared toward business culture; a general readership and an investment in political culture didn't emerge as a standard in newspapers until the 18th century.

As a middle-class public sphere emerged in the 18th century, issues of common concern came to be discussed in a public manner. Newspapers were idealized as a venue for such discourse. But well into the 18th century, newspapers were routinely regulated and censored for political or religious reasons. Nor were newspapers impartial; until the mid-19th century in both Western Europe and North America, many were mouthpieces for political parties. But partisanship eventually waned, and newspapers became mass papers.

Popular papers (the "penny press," as it was called in the United States) appealed to a broader range of people and became considerably cheaper. This was the beginning of a shift to an advertising-based, corporate journalism that became the dominant model for print publishing in North America. Although there is much to criticize about this model, the intense competition across the entire print market (newspapers and magazines included) led to the rise of **muckraking**—the earliest form of investigative journalism. Much of the best muckraking journalism emerged in magazines, although newspapers in both America and Britain also had a history of social investigation (Keating 1976; Pittenger 1997).

muckraking
An early form of investigative journalism that typically exposed political or business corruption in the name of serving the public good.

The introduction of the telegraph also changed journalism in significant ways. As information could be transmitted more quickly, the imperative to "scoop" competing papers grew. Telegraphy became essential to achieving this, but because of the cost, news stories were stripped down to the essentials ("just the facts, ma'am") and the inverted-pyramid style emerged as a way to ensure that the most important information arrived first. Cooperative news agencies, in which newspapers pooled their resources to cut down on their telegraphic charges, were also born in the 19th century (Allen 2007; Blondheim 1994).

Print remained the dominant medium for journalism into the first half of the 20th century. Even when film and radio appeared to compete with them, newspapers were keen to adopt and develop these new media in ways that could benefit their print production. Silent newsreels produced by newspaper companies, such as Hearst's Metrotone, were common in film theatres in the 1910s. The immediacy of these media offered interesting possibilities for the papers, especially in times of natural disasters or breaking news of national interest. Moreover, newspapers remained the benchmark for journalism until quite recently. Local television, in particular, relies heavily on the newsgathering of newspapers.

Radio and Television

When both the US and Canadian governments started issuing radio licences for broadcast, newspapers made up a large number of the licensees. Radio was seen as a way to supplement and extend the popularity of the newspaper, and thus, increase sales (Vipond 1992, 44). Entertainment features such as serialized dramas and comedies—borrowed and developed from the comic strips that newspapers were already publishing—and musical programming so dominated the broadcast schedules of these early newspaper–radio stations that news wasn't even a significant part of the programming until the 1930s (Hilmes 1997, 68). It wasn't until the 1930s and 1940s that radio news became a highly developed and sophisticated form, and at that time newspapers began to view them as a threat (Douglas 1999). Newspaper editors, however, were divided in their views on the utility of radio (Hilmes 1997, 69), and many newspapers abandoned broadcasting in Canada by the 1930s (Vipond 1992, 45). Radio remained a major source of news for people well into the 1950s and 1960s, even as television was reaching its ascendancy (Douglas 1999, 12).

Beginning in the 1940s, television news programs began to emerge on public and commercial stations. Like early radio news programs, early television news drew much of its content from existing media forms—in this

Figure 13.1 Edward R. Murrow

Murrow was one of America's most celebrated and uncompromising journalists. As technology and audience habits changed in the mid-20th century, he adapted his radio show to television.

SOURCE: Prelinger Archives Collection.

case, both newspapers and radio; in fact, former radio newsmen were prominent in the first generation of television news presenters. Edward R. Murrow, whose radio broadcasts during the Second World War helped to legitimize radio news, shifted his weekly magazine-format news show *Hear It Now* to television in 1951, retitling the show *See It Now*.

Television news shared with radio news the advantage of instant, simultaneous communication, but added a visual dimension as well, affecting forever the way in which news events were transformed into cultural memories (Sturken 1997). Historic events such as the funeral of Winston Churchill, the war in Vietnam, or the explosion of the *Challenger* space shuttle now became collective memories shared by millions. For the first several decades of television news programming, these collective memories were largely shaped by a few central news outlets. In the United States, commercial television preceded public television by two decades, so television news was long dominated by what were known as the "Big Three" television networks—ABC, CBS, and NBC—with public television emerging in the late

1960s to provide an alternative news source for a minority of Americans. In Canada, where commercial television was prohibited until the CBC had established itself in the late 1950s, the situation was reversed, with the CBC serving as the news provider of choice for Canadians during the 1960s, 1970s, and 1980s. The situation was the same for the BBC, which long held the lion's share of news audiences in Britain.

Cable and Satellite News

Beginning in the 1990s, the audience for television news began to fragment. The first and most striking development in the shifting ecosystem of television news was the rise of CNN (Cable News Network), a 24-hour news channel established by US communications magnate Ted Turner. Although the station's audience share increased steadily from the time of its founding in 1980, dramatically packaged reporting on the 1991 Persian Gulf War drew record audiences and established CNN as serious competition for the networks. Eventually, CNN dominated the US news market and then expanded into the international market as well, establishing such a powerful presence that the term "CNN effect" was coined to describe the influence of CNN's international reportage on both US foreign policy and aid donations during humanitarian crises.

In recent years, CNN's own audience share, as well as the hegemony once enjoyed by public broadcasting in Canada and Britain, has been eroded by the proliferation of satellite television stations. A particular development has been the emergence of further national and international news-only channels, some increasingly geared toward viewers of a specific political bent. In the United States, for example, the conservative Fox Network is complemented by the comparatively liberal MSNBC, while in Canada Sun TV was launched with the intent of attracting conservative viewers. (For more on these issues, see Chapter 8, The Political Economy of Media.) During the "Arab Spring" uprisings in 2011, Qatar-based Al Jazeera became so successful at attracting audiences for both its English and Arabic programming that observers began comparing the network's ascendance with CNN's rise to prominence during the Gulf War.

Even as television audiences themselves have become more divided, television news has increasingly found itself competing with emerging online news media. As audiences have moved online, novel forms of news delivery have brought a new dimension of immediacy to storytelling and changed the relationship between media audiences and media producers. These and further changes have profoundly altered journalism's function, as explored later in this chapter.

The next section discusses the assumed functions of journalism in contemporary liberal democracies: as a tool for democratic governance, as a source of information, and an as an object of cultural representation.

Journalism's Democratic Function: The Ideal

The news media have long been claimed to play a crucial role in a democratic society. By selecting, reporting, and framing the news, journalists are seen to foster a space of communication about important civic matters. Following the work of Jürgen Habermas, social theorists often term this space the *public sphere*. Habermas (1989) argued that such a "sphere" of interaction emerged during the 18th century, mediating between the state and society. Although other factors contributed to the emergence of a public sphere, including the rise of the middle class, and the emergence of leisure and cultural activities that brought relative strangers into social contact, the emergence of the press and a culture of publishing and consuming news played a central role. As Habermas himself noted, the "public sphere" is not so much a historical fact as an idealized way of thinking about the emergence of **civil society** and a media-moulded culture. It is also notably a limited concept when it comes to thinking about contemporary civic life, which no longer consists (if it ever did) of a single "public" apart from the state, but rather competing "publics" vying for consideration (Fraser 1990; Warner 2002).

Still, it is worth considering what it means when we say that the media help to foster a public sphere. First of all, it means that journalism is acknowledged to play a significant role in what we think about and discuss. Media scholars debate whether that is really the case, or whether it is in fact the public who dictates the stories that journalists cover (Muhlmann 2010). There is also much discussion of whether the media's role in shaping public debate ("agenda setting") is a good or a bad thing. If news outlets serve as **gatekeepers** (Shoemaker and Vos 2009), selecting certain kinds of information and discarding other kinds, then it is possible that faulty gatekeeping can lead to important stories being underreported or ignored. After the invasion of Iraq was under way in 2003, there was a public outcry about the misreporting and underreporting of conditions that led to the war. A documentary by US journalist Bill Moyers, *Buying the War* (2007), argues that the Bush administration had essentially performed the agenda-setting function usually ascribed to journalists, manipulating the media into providing pro-war propaganda that enabled the United States to go to war on false pretenses.

This accusation—that the US media had become, in Moyers's words, "indistinguishable" from the US government—called into question not only the media's ability to engender a sphere of debate, but also their ability to

civil society
Groups or institutions, outside of government or business, that contribute to a functioning society (religious groups, unions, etc.).

gatekeeper
An individual or institution that selects what information will be reported, and what will be disregarded.

separate themselves from government and to question government motives. This belief that the press has a distinct role alongside and separate from government can be traced back to the 18th-century concept of the Fourth Estate (the priesthood, the aristocracy, and "commoners" are the other three). This term, coined by British politician Edmund Burke, describes the media's role as a de facto branch of government that reports on the affairs of Parliament. More recently, the "fourth estate" has come to refer to a press that sits apart from a given country's legislative, executive, and judicial branches, serving as a further means to balance the system of governance. In this model, the media may generate debate about matters of civic interest, but they also protect citizens by revealing government's abuse of power.

The effort by journalists to watch for potential government indiscretions is the source of yet another nickname: the "watchdog" press, a coinage suggesting that the press is a faithful servant guarding the interests of its readership. (Ironically, in France, the nickname means the opposite—a

SIDEBAR

News Values and Professional Norms

Traditionally, news has been produced using a set of professional standards that govern how news is collected and presented. Some critics use very broad criteria, such as the classic values of truth, verification, and independence (Kovach and Rosenstiel 2007, 5–6; see also Shapiro 2010). Deuze (2005, 447) suggests a simple though comprehensive list, which includes:

- public service
- objectivity
- autonomy
- immediacy
- ethics

Some of these elements are very familiar, such as the call to objectivity, to remain independent, and to keep news "current." The fact that these elements are familiar is precisely the consequence of professionalization. These conventions, however, are also historically contingent and vary across the world. Comparative media scholars point out that objectivity is not the dominant professional norm in many media systems outside North America, even when formal professionalism exists (Hallin and Mancini 2004).

"watchdog" press watches after the interests of governments, not citizens.) Although investigative work is now generally assumed to be the most important function of the fourth estate, it is a relatively recent form of journalism, emerging only at the end of the 19th century (de Burgh 2008) and becoming popular in the first part of the 20th, when famous American muckrakers such as Ida Tarbell and Upton Sinclair exposed poor labour conditions and shady business practices.

The term "investigative journalism" became popular much later, around 1960. In the United States in the 1970s, the *Washington Post*'s investigation of the Nixon administration's political wrongdoings (known as the "Watergate scandal" after a Washington, DC hotel that featured in the investigation) raised the status of investigative work inside and outside the profession. A film based on the *Post*'s reporting, *All the President's Men* (1976), made heroes of *Post* reporters Bob Woodward and Carl Bernstein, and established Watergate as a cultural touchstone in journalism history that validated the importance of a free press in a democratic society. Although recent scholarship has challenged the degree to which the *Post*'s reporting actually resulted in Nixon's downfall (Feldstein 2004), the Watergate myth still retains tremendous power around the world as a model of the triumph of the press. As sociologist Michael Schudson (1993) writes, the Watergate story "is a myth of David and Goliath, of powerless individuals overturning an institution of overwhelming might. … The press, truth its only weapon, saves the day."

Journalism and Democracy?
Media Convergence

If the *Washington Post*'s Watergate coverage serves as an idealized myth of the watchdog press, it is now often cited as an achievement that cannot be repeated in the current media climate. Media scholars today observe a contemporary paradox: even as journalism is extolled as a beacon of democracy for countries whose media systems are seen as not free, in the United States, Canada, and Europe "free" media systems are said to be losing the respect of their audiences. This is not a new development: the backlash against media reporting during the Iraq War is often cited as a turning point for recent skepticism about the media's watchdog abilities, but the crisis in confidence has deeper roots. Briefly, it can be tied to a debate as to whether news outlets dependent on advertising revenues and broad circulation for profit can truly foster and sustain democratic participation, or represent the diversity of contemporary society in a manner that allows all citizens a voice. As media ownership has become increasingly centralized, media ownership and media diversity are seen to be under threat.

In Canada, debates about the ability of media to fulfill their democratic mandate extend back to 1970, when Senator Keith Davey headed a commission to investigate the increasing centralization of media ownership. Davey was clear that **media consolidation**, a trend that could be traced back in Canada to the 1920s, threatened the civic function of journalism: "this country should no longer tolerate a situation where the public interest in so vital a field as information [is] dependent on the greed or goodwill of an extremely privileged group of businessmen" (Davey 1970). Ten years after the Davey report, a Canadian royal commission headed by Tom Kent expressed similar concerns, noting that in the years since the Davey report, media consolidation had become even more of a pressing concern. "In a country that has allowed so many newspapers to be owned by a few conglomerates," the report noted, "freedom of the press means, in itself, only that enormous influence without responsibility is conferred on a handful of people" (Kent 1981). Despite their dramatic pronouncements, the suggestions of the Davey and Kent reports were largely ignored. A 2006 Senate committee on the status of the media industry in Canada drew similar conclusions, but has had little effect on regulators.

media consolidation
A trend in which fewer and fewer people become owners of a growing proportion of all media outlets.

HISTORICAL HIGHLIGHTS

The Royal Commission on Newspapers (the Kent Report)

In 1981, Tom Kent delivered his report on the status of newspaper consolidation to Parliament. The report focused primarily on the question of concentrated media ownership in Canada. It recommended that corporate ownership of newspapers be subject to limitations, and noted that "industrial conglomerates produce poor newspapers." Commissioners were concerned that the state of Canada's newspaper industry, with its increasing concentration, was no longer clearly serving the Canadian public interest.

> The simple, inescapable fact is that newspapers are *not* like other business ventures. The public's interest in vigorous competition among newspapers is not one that can be quantified in any dollars-and-cents terms. It has to do with the number and quality of individual voices finding expression, voices undaunted and undiminished by dollar concerns. (Kent 1981, 59)

SOURCE: Kent (1981).

In the United States, public concern about media consolidation has been more muted, in part because centralized ownership emerged more slowly than in Canada. In 1983, Ben Bagdikian's book *The Media Monopoly* spurred awareness of increasing concentration of media ownership; still, the legislative trend in the United States has been toward deregulation (in 1996) and the rollback (in 2007) of earlier rules regarding cross-ownership. US media scholar Robert McChesney (1998) has been a persistent critic of both US media consolidation and the lack of public response, noting that "if media are central to the formation of a participating and informed citizenry, and if media organization influences media performance, then issues about ownership, regulation, and subsidy need to be matters of public debate. But such debate has been almost non-existent in the United States."

Despite the lack of public debate about media regulation, US media executives began to express concern by the 1990s that media consolidation was alienating news audiences. In response, the industry experimented with ways to remind the public of journalism's civic role. With foundation support, and with advice from media scholars, newspapers around the country launched "public" or "civic" journalism projects. Such experiments in public journalism included forums hosted by newspapers on controversial topics, the publication of articles that explored civic topics in depth, and reporting that focused on the inclusion of marginalized voices. Although the movement had only limited success in US newsrooms (Nip 2005), it did contribute to an ongoing conversation about the lack of diversity in US media.

Diversity Troubles

Questions of diversity in journalism scholarship tend to focus on three key issues:

1. what's missing from news coverage (underrepresentation)
2. inadequate or predictable coverage (misrepresentation)
3. lack of diversity in news production

The first two issues highlight the ways in which society is ordered and how journalism facilitates, nurtures, and perpetuates dominant value systems, particularly racism and sexism. The lack of diversity in the newsroom is often associated with the first two issues. Many scholars, grounding their arguments on the insights of second-wave feminist and critical race interventions of the 1970s and 1980s, have suggested that one key way to address the problems of misrepresentation and underrepresentation of minorities and women in the news media is to hire more of both, particularly in managerial roles (Steiner 2009, 118).

Figure 13.2 The *Toronto Star* newsroom, 1930

Figure 13.3 The *Toronto Star* newsroom, circa 1964

Traditionally, the newsroom was almost exclusively the domain of white men, as these photos illustrate. Today, the situation has improved, but barriers to female journalists remain. Note how these photos reflect advances in communications technology over three decades, but no corresponding evolution in the employment of female journalists.

SOURCE: City of Toronto Archives (Fonds 1244, Item 2054; Fonds 1244, Item 2056). Reprinted by permission.

There is some cause for concern. The *Global Report on the Status of Women in the News Media* (IWMF 2011), which looked at more than 500 companies in nearly 60 countries, found that 73 percent of top newsroom management jobs are held by men. Two-thirds of the reporters are men, compared with 36 percent women. "Senior professional women" ranked more equally at 41 percent of the news-gathering, editing, and writing jobs. Women hold just 26 percent of the governing jobs and 27 percent of the top management jobs (IWMF 2011). Others have pointed out that the increase in women's presence within newsrooms, and especially on television news screens as anchors, corresponds to the rise in "soft news" (human interest stories) and personality-driven journalism (van Zoonen 1998a, b). Further, the idea that women would (or should) produce a substantially different kind of journalism—one more focused on reader needs, contextualization, and nuance—relies on problematic assumptions about women and places the responsibility for gender balance on women alone (Steiner 2009, 127).

The misrepresentation of women in the news media has been called a "symbolic annihilation" (Tuchman 1981), one that is double-edged: on the one hand, women are routinely excluded as sources for news stories, particularly as experts. On the other, when women are represented in news stories, the reportage tends to follow fairly predictable frames, often reverting to women's traditional roles within family settings (Jiwani and Young 2006). Some scholars, inspired by Tuchman's classic assessment of women's representations, refer to the more general representation of minorities as a "sphere of invisibility" (Sonwalkar 2005, 262).

This invisibility can sometimes, however, translate into misrepresentations that divide the world into "us" and "them" categories. As Sonwalkar (2005) has argued, "journalism is hegemonic; it caters to the 'us' and presents one view as *the* worldview of an entire society or nation" (263). In other words, news values, like proximity, are often reduced to the dictum that "news is essentially about 'us'" (Sonwalkar 2005, 263; see also Gasher and Gabriele 2004). John Hartley (1992) calls these communities of inclusion and exclusion "Wedom" and "Theydom," respectively, and argues that they are formed in relationship to the idealized audience markets created by each news medium. Binaries between "us" (news consumers) and "them" (objects of the news) mean that global flows of news still privilege stories about ourselves (Gasher and Gabriele 2004; Gasher and Klein 2008), with important consequences for racialized others (Bailey and Harindranath 2005).

Although the literature on misrepresentation of minorities in the news media is vast, some scholars have pointed out that depictions of racialized others have specific implications in the context of globalization and the associated migrations of people that are a part of it. For example, ethnic

PRIMARY SOURCE

Journalism and Gender: Women Journalists in the 19th Century

Women entered journalism in greater numbers in the 19th century, but their entry was not an easy one. Florence Finch Kelly (1939) recounts the following story about her start in journalism in the 1880s:

> I was told … that a woman was practically useless in journalism anyway because there was so little she could do. If I asked for specifications of some of the things she couldn't do I always received the same reply, that you couldn't send a woman to a fire, that she would be quite useless if sent on such an assignment and, since there were times when a city editor had to concentrate all his staff on such an event a woman would just be in the way.
>
> Another stone wall against which I was forever butting my head was the conviction universally held that a woman did not have the physical strength to withstand the steady, hard pull of newspaper work; that she would be made ill by it so much of the time that she would be of little use to the paper. (158)

Women during this time were trapped between, on the one hand, conventions that dictated they behave according to a strict definition of femininity, and, on the other, the same rigours of professional work as men. According to one advice book for women wishing to earn a living, the qualification for a woman to be a journalist demanded "the manners of a woman of good society. … Coarseness is unpardonable in a woman who is going out every day to talk with womanly women in the necessary collection of news" (Alden 1904, 174).

Yet at the same time, it was understood that women would lose some of their presumed feminine delicacy in order to become journalists. As one woman journalist humorously stated:

> The newspaper woman is not born, she grows. The process of erection is gradual and—shades of departed martyrs!—is painful. It is death by slow torture and a slow Phoenix-like rising from the dead body's ashes. … [W]hen she has been built over, behold her! one part nerve and two parts Indian rubber … . The girl who has it in her to survive for newspaper work will cry the first time a man swears at her, grate her teeth the second time, and swear back the third time. (McDonald 1889, 13)

Interestingly, women journalists writing at the end of the 19th century and into the early 20th century were some of the last journalists to enter the profession when it was still relatively easy to do so; as the 20th century progressed, professionalization made entry into journalism even more difficult.

communities in Canada have suggested that their representations within the news media are often reduced to "calendar journalism": stories about their communities appear in the news media only when ethnic holidays occur (Mahtani 2008b, 652). Further ethnographic research is needed in order to identify how ethnic communities respond to the news; ethnic groups themselves display great variance, particularly across class and gender lines (Mahtani 2008a, b).

Public Media: Ensuring Journalism's Democratic Role?

Media ownership issues and lack of diversity are persistent problems in journalism. They are also, overwhelmingly, problems of a commercial news industry less interested in serving publics than in cultivating media markets (Carey 1989, cited in Nerone 2009). Strong public media systems, paid for in part through government subsidy and accountable to the needs of a given population, are often said to be the answer to the conflict between commercial journalism and civic interest. Robert McChesney and John Nichols (2010), for example, have suggested that the crisis in the US media industry might best be addressed through government funding, thus expanding the role of tax-funded media. In 2009, following this logic, a "Newspaper Revitalization Act" was introduced in the US Congress that would have allowed all newspapers to become non-profit organizations, much like US public broadcasting stations.

The various national public media systems are shaped by each country's specific history.

But it is difficult to generalize about the corrective possibilities of public media systems, in large part because they vary so much from country to country. Not surprisingly, public media systems are a function of a country's specific history, and of the political and social needs of citizens at the time that a given public medium was first chartered. In Canada, the mandate of the public media system has always been to create a common sense of "Canadian-ness" among people in a vast and sometimes thinly populated landscape. In the United States, in contrast, public media arose as a means of making sure that educational and informational content was available in a landscape dominated by commercial broadcasting. And the BBC, founded in the 1920s when the British Empire was still in full force, was intended equally to foster citizenship inside Britain and represent it favourably abroad. In many countries in Africa and the Arab world, "public media" are state-owned media, often subject to heavy censorship, and often serving the interests of governments instead of citizens.

As well, the reality has been that over the past few years existing public media have been severely affected by funding cuts. In April 2011, the US Committee for Public Broadcasting was almost entirely de-funded by Republican congressmen as the legislature argued over a federal budget. Over the past several years, BBC World Service had its budget slashed by 16 percent, forcing the closure of five foreign-language services that entailed 650 jobs and drew an audience of 30 million listeners. In Canada, the CBC has lost funding since 2009, resulting in layoffs throughout the entire news division. It is probably the case that in the near future journalism's "democracy troubles" will not be compensated by robust interventions from the public media, because public media, like the media industry as a whole, are struggling to keep afloat.

Finally, it is important to consider that the ideal model of journalism's democratic role is just that—an ideal model, one that is grounded on debatable assumptions about the connection between better-informed citizens and direct democratic participation (Gans 2003). As the Watergate myth suggests, perhaps the notion of a watchdog press powerfully serving as David to the Goliath of the state is indeed simply a myth. Moreover, looking back to an impossible "golden moment" in media history will not serve society well in a time when rapid transition in the production and presentation of news is forcing a redefinition of the relationship between news producers and news audiences. That redefinition will challenge our assumptions of what journalism can or should do for us.

> **KEY CONCEPT**
> The North American and British media systems assume a relationship between journalism and democracy, but that relationship is subject to critique.

The Online Transition and the Challenges to Journalism

In *Digitizing the News* (2004), Pablo Boczkowski details the history of newspaper's early experiments with online publication, including Knight–Ridder's expensive and unsuccessful experiments with videotex, USA Today's CD-ROM special publications, and the *New York Times'* partnership with America Online. Most of these endeavours involved the industry's attempt to take advantage of the distribution possibilities offered by computers while in turn restricting access to paying subscribers. By the mid-1990s, however, there was a sudden shift in thinking: newspapers began putting their content on the World Wide Web, where it was freely available. If users were going to migrate online—so the argument went—then advertisers were bound to follow them there, and newspapers would be prepared. Canada's *Globe and Mail* went online in 1995, and the *New York Times* followed in 1996. By the turn of the century, most major newspapers had news websites, and most of these websites had begun not only to repurpose print stories for the Web but also to provide live updates to news stories and other unique online content. As news sites became more attractive to readers, more and more news consumers shifted their news habit online.

> **KEY CONCEPT**
> The rise of new digital delivery platforms for the industry has shifted the ways in which news is produced and consumed.

What happened next, as digital culture scholar Clay Shirky explains in his essay "Newspapers and Thinking the Unthinkable" (2009), was that newspaper publishers made one misstep after another, eventually leading to what most observers agree is a deep crisis in the industry. Shirky argues that the news executives misunderstood the medium's true challenge: while moving online allowed news outlets to distribute information cheaply, it also divorced that information from the revenue structures that kept the news industry afloat—display and (chiefly) classified advertising. In the world of commercial print journalism, the effect has been financially devastating. The industry has seen a wave of layoffs, and several mid-sized US newspapers have closed (one, the *Rocky Mountain News*, was commemorated by its reporters with an emotional video tribute that was published online and widely circulated). Even the *New York Times* has leased out its building in order to remain afloat.

Although print journalism's financial difficulties have other causes, including mismanagement (Meyer 2009), the online transition has brought about not only declining advertising revenues, but also increased competition from non-traditional news sites: weblogs and aggregators. Google News, launched in 2002, is a news aggregator, meaning that it displays on one page the headlines and sometimes the lead sentences of news articles produced by conventional news outlets and wire services. These articles are selected by computer algorithm, and although news outlets are allowed to "opt out" of selection, they were initially not compensated when their copy was included. Despite Google's insistence that Google News drives traffic to legacy news sites, the aggregator inarguably has become the first (and often only) destination for many news consumers searching for breaking news.

Unlike Google News, which does not claim to be a content-creating website, the *Huffington Post* is a weblog-based news site combining linked content from legacy news sites with material written by mostly unpaid writers. Launched by Arianna Huffington in 2005, the site has become hugely popular among audiences in the United States and elsewhere, and by May 2010 had attracted a news audience larger than that of the *Washington Post* and almost as large as that of the *New York Times*. In February 2011, the *Huffington Post* was acquired by the Internet company America Online, leading to speculation that the former might eventually pose a serious threat to the *Times* and other publications.

Among various measures suggested or attempted by media executives to address the industry's economic decline, the idea of charging for online content—establishing a "paywall"—has been the most controversial. There are several reasons for this: first, media scholars argue that the sheer number of free media outlets makes it difficult for any one of them to claim it is offering a service worth paying for. Second, the culture of the Internet has long dictated, in the words of Stewart Brand's popular slogan, that "information wants to be free": many younger media consumers are simply opposed in principle to paying for content. Third, if past experiments are an accurate indication, online media outlets that place their content behind a paywall will likely experience a drastic reduction in the number of readers who visit their sites.

In the face of these challenges, however, newspapers have continued to experiment with paywalls. A recent effort by the *New York Times*, which had been unsuccessful in the past in creating a paid online service, allows users to share a limited number of their stories through social media for free, but charges those who visit the paper's own website to read the news. Even though this version of a paywall is more lenient than many, several key *New York Times* columnists left the paper in the weeks before the paywall was put in place. And in Slovakia, newspapers have partnered together to create a collective paywall, making it more difficult for Slovakian news audiences to find competing outlets willing to provide the news for free.

Another hope of news executives is that the shift of consumers toward more mobile computing devices, such as tablets and smartphones, will revive a paid economy for news. The Amazon Kindle and Apple iPad both have subscription services for some publications, and also allow the purchase of single issues of others. But the high fees collected by Apple, in particular, have left many industry analysts concerned that news outlets that previously controlled their own method of distribution will pay increasing fees to middlemen in charge of content distribution (Doctor 2010).

Changing News Presentation and the End of "Fortress Journalism"

Online delivery has changed the presentation of news with four significant innovations: linking, the solicitation of user-generated content, the inclusion of reader comments at the end of online stories, and weblogging. Taken together, these modifications to traditional news presentation have helped erode what BBC World Service director Peter Horrocks (2009) has described as **fortress journalism**, or the sense that news outlets are the sole gatherers of information and the sole arbiters of truth. The new permeability of online presentation has advantages for news organizations, but it also poses significant challenges to journalistic authority.

The first of these changes has been described by media scholar Jeff Jarvis (2008) as the **link economy**. Online news outlets can place links in their

fortress journalism
A belief in the traditional authority of professional journalists; seen as superior to newer forms of news presentation.

link economy
The value added to news stories or other content by using the Web's ability to link to external information or to share content.

stories that provide the reader with contextual information; in turn, media audiences can share content with one another by linking to a particular news story. Links bring page views and increase the possibility that a news item might be circulated beyond a media outlet's customary online audience. At the same time, however, linking to source material may leave an outlet open to legal challenges if that source material is inaccurate, ethically problematic, or illegally obtained.

The second practice adopted by online news outlets that challenges the fortress model of journalism is the inclusion of reader comments after news stories. Comments allow readers to point out what they believe are inaccuracies or distortions in a story, to debate the issues that a news story might provoke, or, at times, to request additional information that the story fails to provide. Most online comments are moderated to some degree, which means that a staff person—or sometimes, the reporter herself—will remove comments that are inflammatory or off topic. Moderating comments is a labour-intensive process, but necessary: like weblinks, comments are an area of legal concern, as news sites may find themselves responsible for material they did not themselves author. One solution adopted by some outlets has been to make all commenters register on the news website, providing a degree of personal information that will make them less likely to post inappropriate or defamatory remarks.

crowdsourcing
The ability of media outlets to use the Web to directly involve audiences in uncovering news or analyzing information.

Media outlets are also increasingly soliciting reporting and analysis directly from their audiences, a practice known as **crowdsourcing**. In the United States, for example, the *Washington Post* uses materials collected from audiences that are then incorporated into news stories. The broadcast outlet CNN has a portion of its website dedicated to user-generated content, some of which is presented during television broadcasts as well. In Britain, the newspaper *The Guardian* asked readers to scrutinize the expense reports of members of Parliament for financial improprieties, and eventually received assistance from over 20,000 readers. The growing use of crowdsourcing can give audiences a sense of participation and shared ownership in the news-making process: however, critics note that in some cases user-generated reportage has replaced paid journalists.

Yet another way media outlets have changed their practices as a result of the online transition has been the incorporation of the informal weblog format, or blog, as a component of conventional news sites. In the early years of blogging, weblogs were often denigrated by established media as inaccurate and overly opinionated, but the popularity of the form eventually convinced news outlets that professional news blogs might provide an updated news presentation style while maintaining journalistic authority

Chris Tolles: "Journalism Isn't a Profession"

Chris Tolles is the CEO of Topix, a hyperlocal news aggregator website. In the interview excerpt below, he considers the role of the journalist in the digital age (Groupon is an online coupon service):

> Journalists never like to think of Groupon's ad copywriters as journalists, but really they are. As a Silicon Valley person, journalism is just writing copy. Journalism isn't a profession. Journalism is, in fact, merely the pretentious part of the ad copywriter role in some ways. Paying writers to write words—and when they're good they make more money—is kind of the name of the game here. And I think that Groupon is a better model for paying people because it's worth a lot more money than most of the hyperlocal sites at the moment.

SOURCE: Hirschman (2011).

(Hermida 2009). Over time, the blog format has become a common component of news sites: recently, news blogging has also been complemented by microblogging, or the use of services such as Twitter or Facebook to publish short bursts of content or weblinks that are collected in the news feed of subscribers. Microblogging is useful as a means of circulating stories to audiences as they are published; it can also be used by reporters to develop an audience for their work, solicit opinion, or gather information. However, there is still no consensus among media outlets about how much journalists should use this platform.

As news outlets have increasingly adopted the practices of linking, moderating comments, crowdsourcing, and blogging, they have also become less and less distinct from Web publications run by amateur individuals or groups. As the news industry itself faces increasing economic challenges, the number of non-professional journalists continues to rise. Increasingly, amateur images and video have become the lens through which we observe historical events, and citizen reporters have begun to play a significant role in the coverage of political protest, community governance, and natural disasters. This new breed has been described by scholars as "citizen journalists," a term that suggests not just amateur participation but also a civic intention. Media scholar Jay Rosen (2008) argues that "when the people formerly known as the audience employ the press tools they have in their possession to inform one another, that's citizen journalism."

Citizen journalism is created by "the people formerly known as the audience."

Legally Defining the Journalist

The rise of citizen journalism has engendered legal and professional debate about who should be afforded the authority and legal privileges traditionally reserved for journalists who work at established media outlets. Increasingly, citizen journalists are asserting that they should have the same recognition and privileges as conventional journalists, while news professionals continue to draw boundaries that separate journalists from amateurs. In the United States, federal shield law intended to protect journalists from being forced to reveal sources stalled when legislators, with the help of media executives, limited the definition of journalist to someone whose primary income came from journalism—a definition that excluded not only amateurs, but the large number of part-time and freelance journalists currently in the profession. The Supreme Court of Canada, however, established a libel defence suggesting that any writer engaging in "responsible communication on matters of public interest" was reasonably protected from libel, a decision that shifted the definition of "journalist" away from paid professional status and toward the actual content being created.

Conclusion

Interestingly, as the once-exclusive domain of journalism opens up, the citizen journalist reminds us of the haphazard way men and women once entered the profession. Of course, keeping the technological means in mind is essential here. In the 19th century, print was the only game in town: if you wanted to be a reporter, you wrote for either a magazine or a newspaper. In the contemporary world, however, mobile and networked technologies such as smartphones and Web 2.0 mean that the barriers to journalism are substantially lower than they once were. But the plurality of voices also prompts questions about legitimacy, reliability, and sustainability—not to mention finding ways of standing out in a crowded domain.

Journalism, then, continues to be a practice that cannot easily be separated from the functions it serves for its audiences, the technological means used to produce it, and the social and political systems of which it is a part. As this chapter has demonstrated, many of the interesting changes that make up the shifting journalistic landscape today have precursors in the past. Understanding where journalism is going requires us to think carefully about where it came from. It also requires some reconsideration, in this age of changing media forms, about what we need journalism to do.

DISCUSSION QUESTIONS

1. What is the ideal function of journalism in a democratic society? What are the obstacles to this ideal?

2. Chris Tolles offers a polemical statement about journalism's relationship to the advertising industry. Do you think Tolles is justified in this position? Is journalism really no different from copy writing? Explain.

3. What crises is the news industry currently facing? What has been done to address these crises?

4. Consider your own news-consuming habits. What proportion of your consumption time is spent online? How do you view your news: Through individual news sites? A news aggregate, like Google News? A television screen? Or a newspaper?

5. How much of the news do you pay to read? In light of the discussion about the changes in news production, do you think you should be paying for the news?

6. Consider the discussion and quotations in this chapter about the changing role of journalists. What are some of the pitfalls of citizen journalism? What are some of the benefits? In your opinion, do the benefits outweigh the pitfalls? Explain.

SUGGESTED RESOURCES

Books

Bruns, Axel. 2005. *Gatewatching: Collaborative Online News Production*. New York: Peter Lang.

de Burgh, Hugo. 2008. *Investigative Journalism: Context and Practice* (2nd ed.). London: Routledge.

Fenton, Natalie. 2009. *New Media, Old News: Journalism and Democracy in the Digital Age*. London: Sage.

Lang, Marjory. 1999. *Women Who Made the News: Female Journalists in Canada, 1880–1945*. Montreal and Kingston, ON: McGill–Queen's University Press.

Meikle, Graham, and Guy Redden. 2010. *News Online: Transformations and Continuities*. London: Palgrave Macmillan.

Robinson, Gertrude Joch. 2005. *Gender, Journalism, and Equity: Canadian, US, and European Experiences*. New York: Hampton Press.

Rosner, Cecil. 2008. *Behind the Headlines: A History of Investigative Journalism in Canada*. Oxford, UK: Oxford University Press.

Sanderson, Michael. 2008. *Why Democracies Need an Unlovable Press*. London: Polity Press.

Websites

CBC Digital Archives. "Concentration to Convergence: Media Ownership in Canada." http://archives.cbc.ca/arts_entertainment/media/topics/790.

Doctor, Ken. 2010. "Apple and the News Industry: Accommodate, Negotiate, or Litigate?" *Newsonomics Blog.* http://newsonomics.com/apple-the-news-industry-accommodate-negotiate-or-litigate.

International Women's Media Foundation. http://www.iwmf.org.

Kann, Mark E. *Deliberative Democracy and Difference.* http://www.vectorsjournal.net/issues/5/deliberativedemocracy/main.html.

Moyers, Bill. *Buying the War.* http://www.pbs.org/moyers/journal/btw/watch.html.

Newsgaming.com. http://www.newsgaming.com.

Roberts, Matthew. "Final Edition: The Last Days of the Rocky Mountain News." http://vimeo.com/3390739.

REFERENCES

Adam, G. Stuart. 1993. *Notes Toward a Definition of Journalism.* St. Petersburg, FL: Poynter Institute.

Alden, Cynthia Westover. 1904. *Women's Ways of Earning Money.* New York: A.S. Barnes & Company.

Allen, Gene. 2007. "Monopolies of News: Harold Innis, the Telegraph and Wire Services." In *The Toronto School of Communication: Interpretations, Extensions, Applications,* edited by Rita Watson and Menahem Blondheim, 170–98. Jerusalem: Hebrew University Magnes Press.

Anderson, Benedict. 1983/2006. *Imagined Communities: Reflections on the Origin and Spread of Nationalism.* London: Verso.

Bagdikian, Ben H. 1983/1997. *The Media Monopoly.* Boston: Beacon Press.

Bailey, Olga Guedes, and Ramaswami Harindranath. 2005. "Racialized 'Othering': The Representation of Asylum Seekers in News Media." In *Journalism: Critical Issues,* edited by Stuart Allan, 274–86. New York: Open University Press.

Barnhurst, Kevin, and John Nerone. 2001. *The Form of News: A History.* New York: Guildford Press.

Barnhurst, Kevin, and John Nerone. 2009. "Journalism History." In *The Handbook of Journalism Studies,* edited by KarinWahl-Jorgensen and Thomas Hanitzsch, 17–28. London and New York: Routledge.

Bird, S.E., and R.W. Dardenne. 1988. "Myth, Chronicle and Story: Exploring the Narrative Qualities of News." In *Media, Myths, and Narratives: Television and the Press,* edited by J.W. Carey, 67–88. Beverly Hills, CA: Sage.

Blondheim, Menahem. 1994. *News Over the Wires: The Telegraph and the Flow of Public Information in America, 1844–1897.* Cambridge, MA: Harvard University Press.

Boczkowski, Pablo J. 2004. *Digitizing the News.* Cambridge, MA: MIT Press.

Carey, James. 1989/2009. *Communication as Culture*. 1989. New York and London: Routledge.

Darnton, Robert. 2000. "An Early Information Society: News and the Media in Eighteenth-Century Paris." *American Historical Review* 105(1):1–35.

Davey, Keith. 1970. *The Uncertain Mirror: Report of the Special Senate Committee on Mass Media*. Ottawa: Queen's Printer.

de Burgh, Hugo. 2008. *Investigative Journalism: Context and Practice* (2nd ed.). London: Routledge.

Deuze, Mark. 2005. "What Is Journalism? Professional Identity and Ideology of Journalists." *Journalism* 6(4):442–64.

Doctor, Ken. 2010. "Apple and the News Industry: Accommodate, Negotiate, or Litigate?" *Newsonomics Blog*. Accessed May 2, 2011. http://newsonomics .com/apple-the-news-industry-accommodate-negotiate-or-litigate.

Douglas, Susan. 1999. *Listening In: Radio and the American Imagination, from Amos 'n' Andy and Edward R. Murrow to Wolfman Jack and Howard Stern*. New York: Times Books.

Feldstein, Mark. 2004 (August–September). "Watergate Revisited." *American Journalism Review*.

Fraser, Nancy. 1990. "Rethinking the Public Sphere: A Contribution to the Critique of Actually Existing Democracy." *Social Text* 25(26):56–80.

Gans, Herbert. 1979/2004. *Deciding What's News: A Study of CBC Evening News, NBC Nightly News, Newsweek and Time*. Evanston, IL: Northwestern University Press.

Gans, Herbert. 2003. "Journalistic Practices and Their Problems." In *Democracy and the News*, 45–68. New York: Oxford University Press.

Gasher, Mike, and Sandra Gabriele. 2004. "Increasing Circulation? A Comparative News-Flow Study of the *Montreal Gazette*'s Hard-Copy and On-Line Editions." *Journalism Studies* 5(3):311–23.

Gasher, Mike, and Reesa Klein. 2008. "Mapping the Geography of Online News." *Canadian Journal of Communication* 33:193–211.

Habermas, Jürgen. 1989. *The Structural Transformation of the Public Sphere*. Cambridge, MA: MIT Press.

Hall, Stuart. 1980. "Encoding–Decoding." In *Culture, Media, Language*, edited by Stuart Hall et al., 128–38. London: Hutchinson.

Hallin, Daniel C., and Paolo Mancini. 2004. *Comparing Media Systems: Three Models of Media and Poltics*. Cambridge: Cambridge University Press.

Hartley, John. 1992. *The Politics of Pictures: The Creation of the Public in the Age of Popular Media*. London and New York: Routledge.

Hermida, Alfred. 2009. "The Blogging BBC: Journalism Blogs at 'the World's Most Trusted News Organisation.'" *Journalism Practice* 3(3):1–17.

Hilmes, Michele. 1997. *Radio Voices: American Broadcasting, 1922–1952*. Minneapolis: University of Minnesota Press.

Hirschman, David. 2011 (April 18). "Topix CEO Chris Tolles: Community Over Content." *Streetfight*. Accessed April 29, 2011. http://streetfightmag.com/ 2011/04/18/tech-qa-with-topix-ceo-chis-tolles.

Horrocks, Peter. 2009. "The End of Fortress Journalism." In *The Future of Journalism*, edited by David Miller. London: BBC College of Journalism.

International Women's Media Foundation (IWMF). 2011. *Global Report on the Status of Women in the News Media*, Carolyn M. Byers, Principal Investigator. Washington, DC: International Women's Media Foundation.

Jarvis, Jeff. 2008 (July 28). "The Imperatives of the Link Economy." *BuzzMachine*. Accessed April 29, 2011. http://www.buzzmachine.com/2008/07/28/ the-imperatives-of-the-link-economy.

Jiwani, Yasmin, and Mary-Lynn Young. 2006. "Missing and Murdered Women: Reproducing Marginality in News Discourse." *Canadian Journal of Communication* 31(4):895–917.

Kaplan, Richard L. 2002. *Politics and the American Press: The Rise of Objectivity, 1865–1920*. Cambridge, UK: Cambridge University Press.

Keating, Peter, ed. 1976. *Into Unknown England, 1866–1913: Selections from the Social Explorers*. Totowa, NJ: Rowan and Littlefield.

Kelly, Florence Finch. 1939. *Flowing Stream: The Story of Fifty-Six Years in American Newspaper Life*. New York: E.P. Dutton.

Kent, Tom. 1981. *Royal Commission on Newspapers*. Accessed April 29, 2011. http://epe.lac-bac.gc.ca/100/200/301/pco-bcp/commissions-ef/kent1981 -eng/kent1981-eng.htm.

Kovach, Bill, and Tom Rosenstiel. 2007. *The Elements of Journalism: What Newspeople Should Know and the Public Should Expect* (rev. ed.). New York: Three Rivers Press.

Mahtani, Minelle. 2008a. "How Are Immigrants Seen—and What Do They Want to See? Contemporary Research on the Representation of Immigrants in the Canadian English-Language Media." In *Immigration and Integration in Canada*, edited by John Biles, Meyer Burstein, and James Frideres, 231–53. Montreal and Kingston, ON: McGill–Queen's University Press.

Mahtani, Minelle. 2008b. "Racializing the Audience: Immigrant Perceptions of Mainstream Canadian English-Language TV News." *Canadian Journal of Communication* 33:639–60.

McChesney, Robert. 1998 (Summer). "Making Media Democratic." *The Boston Review*.

McChesney, Robert, and Nichols, John (2010). *The Death and Life of American Journalism: The Media Revolution That Will Begin the World Again*. New York: Nation Books.

McDonald, Flora. 1889. "The Newspaper Woman: One Side of the Question." *The Journalist* 26:13.

Meyer, Philip. 2009. *The Vanishing Newspaper: Saving Journalism in the Information Age*. Columbia, MO: University of Missouri Press.

Moyers, Bill. 2007. *Buying the War*. Documentary film. PBS. Accessed April 29, 2011. http://www.pbs.org/moyers/journal/btw/watch.html.

Muhlmann, Géraldine. 2010. *Journalism and Democracy*. London: Polity Press.

Nerone, John. 2009. "To Rescue Journalism from the Media." *Cultural Studies* 23(2):243–58.

Nip, Joyce Y.M. 2008. "The Last Days of Civic Journalism: The Case of the *Savannah Morning News*." *Journalism Practice* 2(2):179–96.

Park, Robert. 1940. "News as a Form of Knowledge: A Chapter in the Sociology of Knowledge." *American Journal of Sociology* 45(5):669–86.

Pittenger, Mark. 1997. "A World of Difference: Constructing the 'Underclass' in Progressive America." *American Quarterly* 49(1).

Rantanen, Tehri. 2009. *When News Was New*. Chichester, UK: Wiley–Blackwell.

Rosen, Jay. 2008 (July 14). "A Most Useful Definition of Citizen Journalism." Accessed April 29, 2011. http://archive.pressthink.org/2008/07/14/a_most_useful_d_p.html.

Rutherford, Paul. 1982. *A Victorian Authority: The Daily Press in Late Nineteenth-Century Canada*. Toronto: University of Toronto Press.

Schudson, Michael. 1993. *Watergate in American Memory: How We Remember, Forget and Reconstruct the Past*. New York: Basic Books.

Seward, Zachary M. 2009 (March 9). "Five Tips for Citizen Journalism from ProPublica's New 'Crowdsorcerer.'" *Neiman Journalism Lab*. Accessed April 29, 2011. http://www.niemanlab.org/2009/03/five-tips-for-citizen-journalism-from-propublicas-new-crowdsorcerer/?=sidelink.

Shapiro, Ivor. 2010. "What's a Good Story? Recognizing Quality in Journalists' Work." In *The New Journalist: Roles, Skills, and Critical Thinking*, edited by Paul Benedetti, Tim Currie, and Kim Kierans, 99–112. Toronto: Emond Montgomery.

Shirky, Clay. 2009 (March 13). "Newspapers and Thinking the Unthinkable." Accessed April 29, 2011. http://www.shirky.com/weblog/2009/03/newspapers-and-thinking-the-unthinkable.

Shoemaker, Pamela, and Timothy Vos. 2009. *Gatekeeping Theory*. New York: Routledge.

Sonwalkar, Prasun. 2005. "Banal Journalism: The Centrality of the 'Us–Them' Binary in News Discourse." In *Journalism: Critical Issues*, edited by Stuart Allan, 261–73. New York: Open University Press.

Steiner, Linda. 2009. "Gender in the Newsroom." In *The Handbook of Journalism Studies*, edited by Karin Wahl-Jorgensen and Thomas Hanitszch, 116–29. London and New York: Routledge.

Sturken, Marita, 1997. *Tangled Memories: The Vietnam War, the AIDS Epidemic, and the Politics of Remembering*. Berkeley, CA: University of California Press.

Tuchman, Gaye. 1981. "The Symbolic Annihilation of Women in the Mass Media." In *The Manufacture of News: Social Problems, Deviance and the Mass Media*, edited by S. Cohen and J. Young (rev. ed.). London: Constable.

Van Dijk, Teun A. 2009. "News, Discourse and Ideology." In *The Handbook of Journalism Studies*, edited by Karin Wahl-Jorgensen and Thomas Hanitszch, 191–204. London and New York: Routledge.

van Zoonen, Liesbet. 1998a. "One of the Girls? The Changing Gender of Journalism." In *News, Gender and Power*, edited by Cynthia Carter, Gill Branston, and Stuart Allan, 33–46. London and New York: Routledge.

van Zoonen, Liesbet. 1998b. "A Professional, Unreliable, Heroic Marionette (M/F): Structure, Agency and Subjectivity in Contemporary Journalisms." *European Journal of Cultural Studies* 1(1):123–42.

Vipond, Mary. 1992. *Listening In: The First Decade of Canadian Broadcasting, 1922–1932*. Montreal and Kingston, ON: McGill–Queen's University Press.

Wahl-Jorgensen, Karin, and Thomas Hanitzsch. 2009. "Introduction: On Why and How We Should Do Journalism Studies." In *The Handbook of Journalism Studies*, 3–16. London and New York: Routledge.

Warner, Michael. 2002. *Publics and Counterpublics*. New York: Zone Books.

Zelizer, Barbie, ed. 2009. *The Changing Faces of Journalism: Tabloidization, Technology and Truthiness*. London and New York: Routledge.

Zelizer, Barbie, and Stuart Allan. 2010. *Keywords in News and Journalism Studies*. Maidenhead, UK and New York: McGraw-Hill and Open University Press.

CHAPTER 14 / SONIA BOOKMAN

Media, Consumption, and Everyday Life

How is consumption organized by media? How do we consume media in everyday life? How do lifestyle media and brands influence the way we consume goods and services? How do we pull together different kinds of media messages to construct our identities and lifestyles?

KEY CONCEPTS

1. Media consumption is characterized by a dual aspect: the mediatization of consumption and the consumption of media.

2. Media such as advertisements or lifestyle television shows increasingly influence our practices and patterns of consumption.

3. We consume media such as mobile phones or brands as we go about our daily lives, integrating them into routines and rhythms of work and play.

4. Media consumption is an integral part of our social lives; it is bound up with the expression of identities or lifestyles, and it marks our belonging to or distinction from various social groups.

CHAPTER OUTLINE

Introduction: A Day in the Life 267

Media and Contemporary Consumer Culture 269

Mediating Consumption and Consuming Media 272

Media and Consumption in Everyday Life 277

Conclusion 284

Discussion Questions 284

Suggested Resources 285

References 285

Introduction: A Day in the Life

Media consumption is an integral part of our everyday lives. We engage with and consume all kinds of media images, objects, and texts as we go about our daily routines. At the same time, media such as fashion magazines or brands increasingly shape our ordinary practices and patterns of consumption. Take, for example, a day in the life of a typical university student.

She wakes up in the morning to the sound of her new favourite tune playing on an iPod alarm clock. She gets dressed, choosing skinny jeans, a

267

sweater, and a leopard-print scarf—just like a photo she saw in a fashion magazine that expressed her sense of style. While eating breakfast, she scans the headlines in the daily newspaper or sometimes on her laptop, for news of what is happing in her city and the world. On the way to class, she encounters a plethora of advertisements vying for her attention, from the streetside advertising built into bus shelters, benches, and wastebaskets, to the giant billboards attached to the sides of buildings. Even the buses are transformed into mobile media, swathed in advertising wraps. Not that our student pays much attention to these. She is occupied instead with her mobile phone, texting friends and updating her Facebook status: "On the bus." In fact, she uses her mobile phone frequently throughout the day to communicate with friends and family, look up information on the Internet, and keep track of time.

At university, our student attends lectures incorporating an assortment of visual media, from digitally projected PowerPoint presentations to educational DVDs designed to enhance her education experience. Between classes she spends time at the library—in its branded Starbucks space—sipping latte while working on her Wi-Fi-enabled laptop. Before heading home, she goes for a snack at the food court, where she finds a vast array of choices, organized and mediated by various fast-food companies. She joins her environmentally conscious friends who, instead of lining up at McDonald's,

Figure 14.1 Media to go

A typical student faces a deluge of various types of media throughout his or her day, from advertising, to in-class educational tools, to personal messages from friends.

purchase fare from a local brand that has a fair-trade, eco-friendly image. After a long bus ride home, our student spends the evening browsing reviews of new "indie" albums on an Internet-based music magazine while down-loading selected songs to her iPod. She lists her new "likes" on Facebook for friends to see and sample, and before going to bed, sets her alarm so that she will wake to her new favourite tune.

Like this fictional but fairly typical student, many of us spend much of our day consuming and interacting with various media as we work, study, and play. The media have also become a significant element in the way we consume such items as food, clothes, and coffee. This chapter focuses on issues of consumption and explores how media are spun into and shape the fabric of everyday life. It will consider both the consumption of media and the **mediatization** of consumption by examining lifestyle media, brands, and mobile phones. The discussion emphasizes the social implications of consuming media: how these processes shape and express our identities or lifestyles, maintain and mark our attachment to social groups, and frame our daily experiences.

mediatization
The process by which society, or an aspect of society (such as consumption), is increasingly influenced by the mass media.

Media and Contemporary Consumer Culture

Consumption is an everyday activity (Paterson 2006). Sociologist Alan Warde (1996) defines consumption as "a process concerned with the acquisition and use of goods and services" (303). He suggests that we should be concerned with the *complexity* of the uses people make of goods and services, pointing out that consumption involves "a set of practices which permit people to express self identity, to mark attachment to social groups, to ac-cumulate resources, to exhibit social distinction, to ensure participation in social activities, and more things besides" (304). Consumption is thus not only about commerce or the utility of goods, but is also a social and cultural process; it is about the meanings, values, and communicative aspects of goods and their use.

Consumption, as it relates to media, has a dual aspect. First of all, we consume a wide range of media—texts, films, mobile phones, and more—putting these to various uses and integrating them into daily life. Second, the media themselves play an important role in how we consume various goods. For example, media such as advertisements or television programs bombard us with images and ideas about commodities and how they relate to our identities or lifestyles. Consider the image of the "Mac Guy" in Apple advertisements. In opposition to the serious, dull, uptight "PC Guy," Mac Guy is presented as creative, youthful,

KEY CONCEPT
Media consumption is characterized by a dual aspect: the mediatization of consumption and the consumption of media.

Lifestyle

David Chaney (2001) states that lifestyles have emerged in the context of modern consumer culture, which provides a broad symbolic repertoire of images and goods from which lifestyle choices are made. In this context, he argues, all aspects of daily life become a matter of style—our choice of clothing, food, furnishings, and entertainment convey our taste or sense of style. Featherstone (1991) refers to this process as the "aestheticization of everyday life," whereby we turn life into art through consumption, taste, and the construction of distinctive lifestyles.

The term *lifestyle* suggests a more fluid notion of style of life, facilitated by the proliferation of cultural goods and meanings people can use to express a particular lifestyle. It implies that individuals are "self-consciously reflexive because actors making cultural choices are necessarily aware that taste could be otherwise" (Chaney 2001, 83). By constructing lifestyles through consumption, we express our identities and mark our membership within particular lifestyle groupings that are connected to and intersect with social structures of class, ethnicity, or gender, for example. In this way, "lifestyle is a matter of cultural belonging and identity" (Thomas 2008, 682). It is also a matter of distinction, because lifestyles mark our difference from social groups to which we do not belong.

intelligent, and hip. Associated with the use of Apple products, this image allows Apple consumers to think of themselves as creative and cool; it is a cultural resource in the processes of identity-making and self-expression.

Brands

The centrality of media in the organization and mediation of consumption raises the issue of whether consumption has been taken over by the stylistic, cultural aspects that media help to convey. A look at brands offers some insight into this issue. Brand names were established in the late 19th century to provide an identity for otherwise indistinguishable products such as oats and soap, which were previously sold as bulk consumer goods. For example, an early proponent of branding, the Pears Company of England, took bars of glycerin soap and marketed them under a brand name to distinguish them from other, similar goods. Using print media and poster advertisements, over time the Pears brand became associated with cleanliness and civilization in the context of colonial Britain (McClintock 1994). In this process, the brand became the main selling point, resulting in a shift from product to brand.

While brands have a long history, they have only recently—from the 1980s—become salient features of contemporary consumer society. As Naomi Klein remarks in her influential book, *No Logo* (1999), the rise of brands occurred when management theorists decided "that successful corporations must primarily produce brands, as opposed to products" (3). Brands such as American Apparel, Subway, or Sony are now everywhere; we take them for granted as part of our everyday experience. Brands today are a powerful mode of communication, drawing on a range of media to convey information and establish a set of brand meanings, or *brand image*. For example, the brand meanings associated with Nike include empowerment, "coolness," and athleticism. These ideas are constructed over time through the coordination of various advertising campaigns that promote the "Just Do It" slogan, as well as the television coverage of Nike-sponsored sporting events, where the brand is displayed on team uniforms and the bodies of sports stars. Thus, when we buy a Nike runner, we are not simply buying a shoe with utilitarian value as footwear; we are buying a whole complex of brand meanings with symbolic significance. Nike is not just selling us a product, but also an image of coolness or success that we use to express our identity and incorporate into our lifestyle.

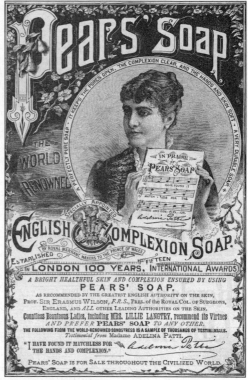

Figure 14.2 Pears Soap

The Pears Company of England was a pioneer in marketing, and was successful in encouraging customers to shift their focus from the product to the brand.

SOURCE: www.maryevans.com. Reprinted by permission.

Consumer Culture

The rise of brands illustrates a growing **aestheticization** of goods and services in contemporary consumer culture. According to leading analyst Celia Lury (1996), consumer culture is defined by a process of stylization (aestheticization) involving "the production, design, making and use of goods, that is, their design, making and use as if they were works of art, images or signs and as part of the self-conscious creation of lifestyle" (77). In other words, stylization or aestheticization involves an intensification of meaning-making in relation to goods and services. In this process, goods are imbued with cultural meanings, values, and symbolic attributes—characteristics such as "sexy" or "exotic"—that they do not inherently possess. This association

aestheticization
The process by which consumer goods are loaded with additional meanings and values.

is achieved partly through the use of visual imagery in the advertising, packaging, and display of goods and services, the use of design, and the presentation or "staging" of consumer goods in specific contexts to create associations with particular events or activities. For example, the energy drink Red Bull is associated with cultural meanings such as vitality, coolness, and youthfulness through extensive multimedia advertising campaigns featuring the slogan "it gives you wings," the sponsorship of extreme sporting events where it is prominently displayed, and its viral, word-of-mouth promotion on university campuses. Through aestheticization, all kinds of goods—from cars, to clothes, to computers—are loaded with meanings that make up "the cultural context of consumption" (McCracken 2005, 164).

cultural consumption
The consumption of goods primarily for their expressive and symbolic properties.

While much consumption is still oriented toward meeting ordinary needs, **cultural consumption**—the consumption of goods primarily for their expressive and symbolic properties—has risen to the fore in contemporary consumer culture (Lury 1996). Cultural goods are consumed for their symbolic attributes, and are put to use as cultural resources in the construction of identities, lifestyles, and shared social worlds. A prominent theorist of consumer culture, Grant McCracken (2005), states that we are constantly "rummaging" in the world of consumer goods for meanings to furnish aspects of our selves and our social worlds: "consumers are looking for something they can use in their construction of new versions of the self, the family, a community. … They are looking for small meanings, concepts of what it is to be a man or a woman, concepts of what it is to be middle aged … concepts of what it is to be a member of a community and a country" (165).

Mediating Consumption and Consuming Media

Mediatization of Consumption

Recall the two aspects of the relationship between consumption and media: the consumption of media, and media-influenced consumption. Discussing the latter, media scholar André Jansson (2002) delineates the growing significance of media in the organization, mediation, and maintenance of consumption as the "mediatization of consumption." This term refers, first, to the way media are increasingly involved as tools in the organization and coordination of consumption practices, including the use of the Internet in the ever-expanding realm of e-commerce, and the use of electronic communications to speed up flows of information between producers and consumers (Förnas et al. 2007; Jansson 2002). It also refers to the expanded role that is played by media in processes of cultural meaning-making related to consumer goods and their use in everyday life. Media industries centrally concerned with the production of social meaning—such as advertising, magazine publishing, and television—have undergone significant expansion in recent decades (Scott 2000; Hesmondalgh 2002). Intricately interconnected with the rise of consumer culture, such media industries and forms such as the brand are considered key aestheticizing agents in shaping the meanings of goods and services. They provide us with ideas and images of various consumer items, informing us of their value and quality, as well as how they might fit into our lives. They provide a cultural framework or context for the use, display, and personalization of goods.

The meanings attributed to a particular product and its consumption are established by media images, not just in advertising but in other kinds of media texts. These texts constantly reference each other and reinforce the meanings associated with a specific product or brand. For example, the meanings established for Apple consumer goods are not only produced by advertisements for Apple merchandise, but are built up by the placement of Apple products in films, television shows, magazines, and on Facebook. Thus, the image of the cool Mac Guy in Apple advertisements is strengthened by magazine articles that discuss the use of Apple software by laid-back "creative types" in California, or the placement of Apple laptops in television shows such as *House*, where they are associated with the maverick doctor who likes to think "outside the box." As media theorist Adam Arvidsson (2006) states, "Goods are connected to the intertextual web of meanings, images and discourses diffused by (mostly commercial) media like television, magazines, film, radio, the internet, and, most importantly perhaps, advertising" (36).

Intertextuality refers to the process whereby meaning is made in connection with other texts. It involves referencing and borrowing from other texts to make meaning, as well as interpreting a given text in light of related texts (O'Shaughnessy and Stadler 2008). Thus, when we read a magazine article about Apple products used by writers, artists, and filmmakers, we are reminded of Apple advertisements featuring the slogan "Think Different" and the image of Mac Guy. The meanings associated with Apple products are established in the interplay between these various texts and the ideas they convey. Through intertextuality, an image is cultivated and inscribed in the commodity. While companies attempt to control this process, their brand images and meanings are nonetheless "never fixed or independent of the dynamics of social life" (Jannson 2002, 26). In processes of consumption, meanings are established in part through everyday practices and processes of interpretation; they are negotiated, adapted, and realized by consumers who are embedded in various social contexts (Förnas et al. 2007, 52).

intertextuality
The process by which meaning is created through connections with other texts.

Jannson (2002) argues that because of mediatization, media and consumption processes are now intricately interconnected. Our knowledge, selection, and use of consumer goods is extensively shaped by the way they are mediated by advertisements, magazines, and other media texts or forms. As a result, the lines between media images and commodities are increasingly blurred; like products and their promotion, goods and images are ever more tightly interwoven in consumer society. In this context, we are being sold not simply commodities but "commodity-signs"—clusters of material things, styles, and meanings.

Consumption of Media

The other aspect of the relationship between consumption and media is the growing consumption of media goods and services in our everyday lives. In *Consuming Media* (2007, 42), cultural studies scholar Johan Förnas and his co-authors point out that the media comprise an increasing share of the products and services that we consume: mobile phones, digital music devices, cameras, computers, advertisements, brands, books, films, CDs, radios, DVDs, Blu-ray players, video games, and more. This list includes both media objects, such as the television set, as well as media texts, such as a television show or series. Media are primarily consumed in the form of marketed commodities—items we select, purchase, use, and dispose of. In consumer culture, media technologies and goods such as iPods, mobile phones, and television series are themselves aestheticized through processes of design, advertising, and branding. For example, Sony Walkman MP3 players are promoted as fashion accessories, available in multiple colours and associated, through advertising, with an innovative music experience. Or consider how the television series *Mad Men* is marketed as cutting-edge television, providing a commentary on advertising itself.

We consume media in a variety of ways, depending in part on the nature of the media commodity (Förnas et al. 2007). For example, we may watch a film, read a newspaper, or listen to the radio. Traditional mass media, such as television or the radio, operated on a broadcast model—transmitting standardized content in a unidirectional manner, from the producer to an undifferentiated mass consumer audience. While these media forms afforded little opportunity for consumer involvement beyond listening, reading, or watching, is this still the case with new media? Unlike traditional, mass media, new media such as digital television or the Internet are organized as multidirectional, non-linear flows of information, offering customized content to fragmented consumer audiences. Based on an interactive model of communication, new media offer more active consumer participation.

Consumers do not simply receive media messages, but are often implicated in the very process of producing the content they consume. For example, we play video games, determining part of the storyline and the outcome of the game. Using the mobile phone, we text our votes to reality television shows such as *Canadian Idol*, shaping the content of media by telling producers which contestants we prefer to see on stage.

In addition to our use of media for entertainment and utilitarian purposes, media consumption is central to the expression of our identities and forms of social belonging. In the context of consumer culture, media objects and texts are important cultural resources used to construct, make sense of, and fashion our selves. Consider the difference between owning a Blackberry mobile phone and an iPhone. A Blackberry enables the expression of a professional, business-like identity, while the iPhone can be used to fashion oneself as playful, creative, and hip. Alternatively, think about how our identities are expressed by the kind of music we consume. Whether we listen to indie or country music indicates something about our self-identity, taste, and style. Significantly, the media we consume not only help to construct our individual identities, but serve as a social marker that indicates group belonging, whether it be to the cool, creative Mac crowd, or country music fans.

Indeed, media consumption indicates our belonging to various social groups, divided along the lines of social class, gender, or ethnicity, for example, as well as myriad forms of lifestyle based on shared interests, tastes, and practices. While the consumption of mass media such as television news can mark belonging to broader, especially national communities, differentiated media—which are targeted toward niche audiences—allow the construction of specialized taste groups with which we can identify (Jansson 2002). For example, the CBC provides its intended mass audience of Canadian viewers with narratives and common cultural experiences that reinforce a shared sense of cultural identity and belonging to the nation. In this sense, the CBC promotes and maintains a broad, national "imagined community" (Anderson 1991) and allows us to identify as national citizens. Our participation in this community is just a matter of watching the evening news; it is less intentional than our involvement with specific media used to mark our belonging to distinctive taste or lifestyle groupings. These can include virtual fan clubs, environmentalist lifestyle groups, or even "brand communities" (Muniz and O'Guinn 2001)—self-selected groups that share an interest in Harley David-son motorcycles, Lego toys, or other brand items and experiences.

Media consumption indicates our belonging to various social groups.

While media consumption is central to constructions of social identity, it also shapes our experiences of everyday life. We consume and interact with media as part of our mundane daily routines of work and play. In

HISTORICAL HIGHLIGHT

The Origins of Imagined Communities

In his book, *Imagined Communities: Reflections on the Origin and Spread of Nationalism* (1991), Benedict Anderson proposes that the modern nation is an *imagined* political community. In his words, "It is *imagined* because the members of even the smallest nation will never know most of their fellow-members, meet them, or even hear of them, yet in the minds of each lives the image of their communion" (6). He highlights the significance of belonging to the imagined community, and indicates that despite existing inequalities, "the nation is always conceived as a deep, horizontal comradeship" (7).

Anderson distinguishes between imagined communities and invented communities, suggesting that they are not invented from nowhere, but are imagined in a particular way. Thus, we need to be concerned with the way in which they are imagined: "[c]ommunities are to be distinguished, not by their falsity/genuineness, but by the style in which they are imagined" (6). He emphasizes the role of the media in the formation of imagined communities, pointing out that the development of the printing press was central to emerging nationalisms in the 18th and 19th centuries. Newspapers, which provided stories about national events and issues, allowed people to imagine the nation and themselves as part of it.

Today, media such as digital television or Twitter allow us to imagine and integrate ourselves into various communities that are not as fixed geographically and socially as the nation. They include communities that revolve around a shared sense of style, taste, or interest, such as vegan food communities who swap recipes through Facebook, online communities such as the people who regularly interact in Second Life, or loose-knit communities of environmentalists who follow eco-reality television shows.

travelling to class or getting the groceries, our individual lives are seemingly invaded by media. For example, our experience of shopping is extensively shaped by the mediated environment we encounter at the mall. Studying the intersection of consumption and communications in the shopping mall, Förnas and colleagues (2007) suggest that "[a]pproaching a shopping centre today immediately places a vast complex of media forms in focus, in a much more intense and complex manner than ever before" (8). The contemporary shopping mall is replete with media texts, technologies, and sounds, including advertisements that guide the processes of acquisition and purchase, music intended to create a relaxing atmosphere, and screens in food courts that project fashion events. There is also an array of media goods for sale, and shops dedicated to media consumption, such as the Virgin store. Our engagement with such media shapes the shopping experience; we are guided by store logos, soothed by music, and enticed by advertisements to buy the latest fashions or phones.

> **KEY CONCEPT**
> We consume media such as mobile phones or brands as we go about our daily lives, integrating them into routines and rhythms of work and play.

Does this mean that our individual lives are taken over by media? While on the one hand, we are bombarded with media images, objects, and texts as we go about our everyday activities, we also actively slip media into our own routines and rhythms. As Förnas and his co-authors maintain, "People develop tendencies to use media at specific times and places and to embed them in different types of social activities and relations" (2007, 53). For example, Janice Radway (1984) has documented how women read romance novels as a way to escape mundane domestic routines and the demands of family; the novels are used to create a "pause" in the 24-hour day. Many people read news media in the morning as part of their breakfast routine. Others make a habit of going to Starbucks and Facebooking friends during their work break. Such routine engagement with media helps us to make sense of and organize our everyday lives, and shapes the way we experience the world around us.

While we have considered each separately, the two aspects of consumption in relation to the media—the consumption of media, and media-influenced consumption—are interrelated. We consume media such as television shows or magazines for information and amusement, while at the same time they provide us with images and meanings about consumer goods that we draw on when we engage in practices of consumption. It is in the interaction between these processes that contemporary life acquires its particular character. The next section will consider this dual aspect of media consumption by focusing on three specific cases: lifestyle media, brands, and mobile phones. Each draws on recent theory and media studies to highlight the complex relationship between media and consumption, and outlines some of the social implications of media consumption.

Media and Consumption in Everyday Life

Lifestyle Media

Lifestyle refers to a particular consumer sensibility wherein "people seek to display their individuality and their sense of style through a choice of a range of goods and their subsequent customizing or personalizing of these goods" (Lury 1996, 80). A prominent feature of contemporary consumer culture, lifestyles are increasingly promoted and constituted by lifestyle

KEY CONCEPT

Media consumption is an integral part of our social lives; it is bound up with the expression of identities and lifestyles, and it marks our belonging to or distinction from various social groups.

media. In the book *Ordinary Lifestyles* (2005), editors David Bell and Joanne Hollows define the term lifestyle media as the different "media products that are centred on ideas of taste and lifestyle." This definition encompasses all radio and television programs, DVDs, books, magazines, newspaper columns, and websites that are concerned with lifestyle topics such as fashion, food and cookery, home and self-improvement, shopping, and travel, among others. While some forms, such as women's magazines, have been in existence for a long time, in recent years we have experienced a proliferation of lifestyle media on television schedules, the Internet, and bestseller lists (Bell and Hollows 2005).

Such media play an important role in the organization of everyday consumption. Various lifestyle media inform us of the cultural value and meanings of such goods as furnishings, music, and fashions, and their "experts" instruct us in how to use and display them in our homes and on our bodies. For example, the lifestyle television show *What Not to Wear* suggests that certain clothing styles and combinations represent good taste, while other styles are "trashy" or in bad taste. In this process, certain clothes and accessories are inscribed with cultural values and attributed meanings, such as *age appropriate*, *professional*, or *frumpy*. In other words, lifestyle media contribute to the aestheticization of consumer goods and services, with the cultural experts acting as aestheticizing agents. The aim is to provide ordinary people with the cultural knowledge they need to select goods that will express a particular style, facilitating the process of "lifestylization."

Lifestyle programs aim to provide ordinary people with the cultural knowledge they need to select goods that will express a particular style.

Lifestyle television has become a particularly popular form, with shows such as *What Not to Wear*, *You Are What You Eat*, and *Rock of Love: Charm School* exerting considerable presence on prime-time schedules. Lifestyle television covers a wide range of subjects, from health to home décor, centred on everyday consumption practices and patterns in mundane settings such as the home. The content tends to "focus on the everyday life of ordinary individuals, together with the accessible dispersal of friendly advice about necessary quotidian [daily] skills and knowledge by program experts" (Craig 2010, 174). Overlapping with the category of reality television, it often includes ordinary folk who are instructed by experts on issues of food consumption, garden design, or femininity (Thomas 2008). The transformation of such individuals is highlighted in make-over programs, which culminate in the spectacular "reveal" when viewers are shown the new and improved participant, home, or garden. Consumerist in orientation, lifestyle television is often accompanied by spin-off products and is linked to product sponsorship.

Analysts have drawn attention to a new subgenre: eco-reality (Thomas 2008) or "eco-makeover" (Craig 2010) lifestyle programs. These programs focus on people who are engaged in the process of adopting more environmentally sustainable lifestyles. Taking the case of *WA$TED*, which is produced in New Zealand but is available on television in Canada and other countries, Geoffrey Craig (2010) outlines the format of the show, which usually focuses on an ordinary family and their everyday consumption practices. Experts evaluate their environmental impact and suggest ways in which participants could consume differently (for example, by using high-efficiency appliances) to achieve a more sustainable lifestyle. In this process, consumer goods—ranging from clothes dryers to take-away food in throw-away containers—are

PRIMARY SOURCE

Mediatization of Consumption

The following is an excerpt from *Brands: Media and Value in Media Culture* by Adam Arvidsson (2006, 39):

Indeed, it is through their connection to media culture that modern consumer goods acquire the horizon of virtuality that is the source of much of the utility that they have for consumers. This also goes for relatively anonymous mass produced objects like cigarettes and chewing gum, that now can acquire deep and complex meanings: through its associations to movies, sports (like baseball) and popular music, chewing gum became an integral element to the myth of the "American dream" ... . [A]s smoked by movie stars like Marlene Dietrich and Humphrey Bogart, cigarettes came to represent an attractive and slightly challenging "modernity" ... . By thus being filled with meaning in media culture, consumer goods can enable their user to think of him- or herself different [*sic*]. By means of cigarettes, it becomes possible to imagine oneself on Marlene Dietrich, or to draw more freely on this ideal to enact a challenging, modern femininity ... . Simmel (1905) has famously argued that the connection between modern consumer goods and individuality has to do with the introduction of choice into what was previously a traditionally determined relation between objects and subjects. But one could add that this probably also has to do with the fact that mediatization extends the capacities of objects themselves. Not only does one now have a choice, but one has a choice between objects that tell different stories.

inscribed with cultural meaning (environmentally friendly or wasteful). The family's successful transformation from "eco-criminals" to eco-friendly consumers is revealed at the end of the program when they win an amount of cash equivalent to their energy savings. As Craig indicates, there is a paradoxical quality to these programs which, while promoting sustainable lifestyles, do so in the context of consumer culture and as a commercially driven product (2010, 176).

While these programs are important in mediating consumption and shaping lifestyles, they are also consumed as part of people's daily routines and rituals of relaxing after work, or spending time with family. They are woven into our everyday life as we watch, listen, and discuss shows with our friends or workmates around the water cooler or on Facebook. They are integrated into experiences of family or roommate bonding, or socializing at the pub. The "everydayness" of lifestyle media texts thus extends from their content and emphasis on mundane practices of consumption to their incorporation into our domestic and workaday lives (Bell and Hollows 2005).

Advertising and Brands

Advertising media and brands play a significant role in the organization and mediation of consumption. Advertisements use images, text, and sound to communicate messages about consumer goods and lifestyles. As McCracken (2005) indicates, advertising is "the conduit through which meanings are constantly transferred from the culturally constituted world to the consumer good" (164). A range of advertising media are used to connect with consumers, including outdoor posters and television advertisements; as well, mobile digital advertising is increasingly pursued as a way of meeting consumers wherever they are and customizing the commercials they receive (McStay 2010). Writing about advertising, William Leiss and his co-authors (2005, 6) suggest that advertising has become a "'privileged' form of social communication" in that its messages are given a place of importance in our everyday lives.

As suggested earlier in this chapter, brands are complex media objects that enable the communication of qualitative information (values such as "environmentally friendly," styles such as "modern," or qualities such as "authentic") through the coordination of advertising and marketing strategies, product design, packaging, and presentation, as well as potential consumer activity, with the aim of establishing a particular brand image or experience (Lury 2000, 2004). Advertising is an important aspect of branding; however, although advertisements create meanings for a particular product or brand, the brand establishes meanings for a whole range of goods and creates a cultural framework for their use: "With a particular brand I can act, feel, and be in a particular way. With a Macintosh computer I can become a particular kind of person and form particular kinds of relations to others" (Arvidsson 2006, 8). In this sense, brands are important cultural resources and tools that facilitate the expression and construction of shared experiences, social relations, and identities (Arvidsson 2006).

Consider the renowned Canadian brand Tim Hortons. In a recent article, Patricia Cormack (2008) states that the prominent coffee–donut brand has become an important source and site of Canadian identity and an icon of Canadian culture. She says that the company's long-standing slogan ("Always Fresh. Always There") "resonates with its claim to be an integral, indispensible, and dependable part of ordinary Canadian life" (370). Tim Hortons' "ordinary Canadian" image is constructed through the use of advertising campaigns and sponsorships, as well as its plain-Jane strategy of store design. Advertising images, in particular, have traded on the hockey fame of Tim Hortons' founder, linking the brand with a popular Canadian pastime. This association is enhanced through brand sponsorship of hockey events and Timbits teams for children. Recent campaigns have featured narratives of ordinary Canadians—including construction workers, fiddlers, skaters, fishers, students, and soldiers—all of whom share a bond with Tim Hortons (Cormack 2008). Often, these commercials employ emotional techniques, evoking feelings of warmth, love, and belonging that are associated with being home, where "home," of course, is Canada. Through these marketing strategies, Tim Hortons is associated with Canadian experiences of work, immigration, and everyday life, positioning itself as not only a purveyor of fresh coffee, but of Canadianness itself.

As mentioned earlier, we use advertisements and brands as cultural resources through which we construct our identities, social relations, and cultural communities. In a recent study of coffee brands in the city of Winnipeg, interviews with Tim Hortons consumers revealed a connection to the Canadianness conveyed by the brand. As one consumer commented: "Tim Hortons give you that local feel but they're everywhere. … Tim Hortons seem like it's that good Canadian company that's been around 'cause you know they've got Tim Horton and they play up hockey and everything like that." Calling Tim Hortons "Canada's coffee shop," another patron suggested that it constituted a common Canadian experience. Consumers especially appreciated the "ordinariness" of the experience mediated by the brand, especially in comparison to the complex, cosmopolitan connoisseur experience and image they associated with specialty coffee brands Starbucks and Second Cup. For its consumers, Tim Hortons enables the expression of down-to-earth, unpretentious attitudes and values, and comprises an important part of their "ordinary" Canadian lifestyle.

At the same time, advertisements and brands such as Tim Hortons are integrated into daily consumption practices. For example, many consumers indicated that Tim Hortons is part of their morning routine of work or socializing with others, and insisted that "it's not the same if it's not Tim Hortons." Many consumers developed a strong connection with the brand through ongoing, routine practices of consumption. In this process, it becomes an important part of the daily experience, providing familiar ways for consumers to orient themselves in their everyday lives.

Mobile Phones

The mobile phone integrates media into everyday life like no medium before.

Mobile phone ownership and use has proliferated around the world from the late 1990s (de Souza e Silva 2006). The mobile phone integrates media into everyday life like no medium before. It is one of the first devices that allow people to communicate without being physically confined to a particular location (Levinson 2006). We can use it on the bus, beach, and busy city streets. The convergence of mobile phones with other technologies, such as digital cameras or portable music players, has transformed the phone into a "mobile device that integrates both communication and multimedia functionality" (Westlund 2008, 444). Its increasingly multimedia nature means that the mobile phone brings all kinds of media—from advertisements to music to video games—into everyday situations and contexts.

mobile commerce and mobile consumption New forms of advertising and consumption made possible by the cellphone, with its connections to Internet-based positioning systems, various apps, and customized marketing.

As media technologies with multimedia capacity, mobile phones are increasingly used as tools to organize processes of consumption. Involved in the mediatization of consumption, mobile phones are central to the expansion of m-commerce (**mobile commerce**), and they provide new mobile environments for advertising communications (McStay 2010). Phones that integrate Internet and positioning technologies, along with proximity and other sensors, enable new forms of **mobile consumption** (Goggin 2009). Not only can we use m-commerce to purchase goods from anywhere at any time, but we can use mobile applications such as Urbanspoon to get information about consumption options (in this case, restaurants) based on our current location.

As consumer goods, mobile phones are invested with meanings by companies and their brands through advertising campaigns and images constructed in film or television media. They are presented to consumers as fashion items or markers of style (the differences in functions of various models are often negligible). Consider how Apple iPhones are marketed as modern, stylish, smart devices, drawing on the broader Apple brand image to establish their cultural meanings as cool, innovative, and associated with imagination. Such media images influence the way phones are consumed.

When the iPhone 4 was launched in Canada, loyal consumers were already lined up at Apple's flagship stores, waiting for a glimpse of the sleek gadget. Having the latest Apple iPhone allows consumers to present themselves as current and on the cutting edge.

Indeed, the consumption of mobile phones as branded commodities is bound up with the expression of identities and the formation of lifestyles. In a study of mobile phone adoption and use by university students in three cultural contexts, Paul Leonardi and colleagues (2006) found that the acquisition of phones was related to safety, style, and symbolism. These authors affirm that mobile phones are consumed by students as a means of creating and maintaining identities; as a way of presenting oneself as modern, fashionable, or technologically savvy. The customization of mobiles is an important feature that permits further self-expression through the selection of "skins," wallpaper, and screen savers. With the introduction of the iPhone, customization has expanded to include variation in screen configuration and applications. Analyzing the potential impact of the iPhone on mobile phone culture, Gerard Goggin (2009) suggests that "the iPhone promises to make the mobile even more customizable and adaptable—identity on the move, made to order" (233). Stylized through customization, mobile phones enable consumers to express and change aspects of their self-identity "on the go" and in diverse contexts. They are central to the construction of new lifestyles premised on mobility and constant communication.

As media devices with conventional communicative capacities, mobile phones are incorporated into our daily routines, shaping the way we organize and experience our everyday existence. In particular, mobile telephones allow us to text, email, or ring and change plans on the move; we can change the location or time of a meeting en route, remind someone to pick up milk when they're at the store, or organize a social event at the last minute via social mobile networks. The coordination of activities "on the fly" via the mobile phone has "led to new ways of organizing everyday life" (Ling 2004, 18). In particular, it provides more flexibility and increased **microcoordination** of everyday activities—"the nuanced management of social interaction" (Ling 2004, 70). The significance of mobile phones in the coordination of daily life is highlighted by Rich Ling (2006) in his study of mobile phone use among couples in Norway. He found that mobile phones were used by these couples to facilitate and maintain daily routines and cycles of work, school, child care, and evening leisure activities. Phones were integral to what he terms the "flexible routinization" of activities such as making dinner, taking children to school, or food shopping, which are flexibly adjusted and rearranged throughout the day (2006, 72). For example, information about

microcoordination
The managing of minor details of our daily social interactions, made possible by mobile phones.

what food is needed for the household can be conveyed while someone is in the process of food shopping. In addition, Ling found that mobile phones allowed couples to maintain emotional balance in the "folds" of daily life (2006, 79). Couples could catch up with each other and converse during commutes on the train or while waiting for appointments, engaging in what Ling calls "expressive maintenance" (2006, 82).

Conclusion

Media consumption is an integral part of our daily lives, so commonplace that we take it for granted. However, it is important to think about the ways in which media shape everyday processes and practices of consumption by inscribing goods with cultural meanings or coordinating new forms of m-commerce. At the same time, we should be concerned with how we consume media in processes of constructing identities and expressing lifestyles, or creating shared meanings and social relations. How is media consumption integrated into daily routines and rhythms of work, school, and play? How does it shape our experiences of everyday life and the contexts in which we are situated?

This chapter has described both the consumption of media and the mediatization of consumption, focusing on three specific media forms: lifestyle media, brands, and mobile phones. It delineated how practices of consumption and processes of lifestylization demonstrate membership in or distinction from various social groupings. The discussion considered how lifestyle media, such as the television show *WA$TED*, provide us with cultural resources for fashioning ourselves as environmentalists through our consumption choices. It highlighted how brands, as complex media forms, enable expressions of national identity and ordinariness. In the case of mobile phones, we consume and use these aestheticized media objects to express our style, flexibly coordinate our routines, and maintain social networks and relations. In addition to lifestyle magazines, brands, and mobiles, however, we consume a wide range of media. It is vital that we continue to observe, analyze, and critique the ways in which these are implicated in processes of consumption and the roles that they play in shaping our lives and social worlds.

DISCUSSION QUESTIONS

1. Think of a lifestyle television show. What consumption practices does it advocate? What lifestyle does it promote? How does it involve or address ordinary people in everyday contexts?

2. Consider an advertising campaign for a particular brand of mobile phone. What cultural meanings does it evoke? How can these meanings be used to express self-identity?

3. How do you use mobile phones to organize and coordinate your routines and activities? Does the mobile phone allow you to flexibly "microcoordinate" plans with friends, family activities, or social events? Explain.

SUGGESTED RESOURCES

Chaney, David. 1996. *Lifestyles*. London: Routledge.

Goggin, Gerard. 2006. *Cell Phone Culture: Mobile Technology in Everyday Life*. London: Routledge.

Kellner, Douglas. 1995. *Media Culture: Cultural Studies, Identity and Politics Between the Modern and the Postmodern*. London: Routledge.

McCracken, Grant. 1988. *Culture and Consumption: New Approaches to the Symbolic Character of Consumer Goods and Activities*. Bloomington, IN: Indiana University Press.

McMillan, Divya. 2009. *Mediated Identities: Youth, Agency, and Globalization*. New York: Peter Lang.

Moor, Liz. 2007. *The Rise of Brands*. Oxford, UK: Berg.

REFERENCES

Anderson, Benedict. 1991. *Imagined Communities: Reflections on the Origin and Spread of Nationalism*. London: Verso.

Arvidsson, Adam. 2006. *Brands: Meaning and Value in Media Culture*. London: Routledge.

Bell, David, and Joanne Hollows. 2005. *Ordinary Lifestyles: Popular Media, Consumption and Taste*. Maidenhead, UK: Open University Press.

Chaney, David. 2001. "From Ways of Life to Lifestyle: Rethinking Culture as Ideology and Sensibility." In *Culture in the Communication Age*, edited by James Lull, 75–88. London: Routledge.

Cormack, Patricia. 2008. "'True Stories' of Canada: Tim Hortons and the Branding of National Identity." *Cultural Sociology* 2(3):369–84.

Craig, Geoffrey. 2010. "Everyday Epiphanies: Environmental Networks in Eco-Makeover Lifestyle Television." *Environmental Communication: A Journal of Nature and Culture* 4(2):172–89.

de Souza e Silva, Adriana. 2006. "Interfaces of Hybrid Spaces." In *The Cell Phone Reader: Essays in Social Transformation*, edited by Anandam Kavoori and Noah Arceneaux, 19–44. New York: Peter Lang.

Featherstone, Mike. 1991. *Consumer Culture and Postmodernism*. London: Sage.

Förnas, Johan, Karin Becker, Erling Bjurström, and Hillevi Ganetz. 2007. *Consuming Media: Communication, Shopping and Everyday Life*. Oxford, UK: Berg.

Goggin, Gerard. 2009. "Adapting the Mobile Phone: The iPhone and Its Consumption." *Continuum* 23(2):231–44.

Hesmondalgh, David. 2002. *The Cultural Industries*. London: Sage.

Jansson, André. 2002. "The Mediatization of Consumption: Towards an Analytical Framework of Image Culture." *Journal of Consumer Culture* 2(1):5–31.

Klein, Naomi. 1999. *No Logo*. Toronto: Knopf Canada.

Leiss, William, Stephen Kline, Sut Jhally, and Jacqueline Botterill. 2005. *Social Communication in Advertising* (3rd ed.). London: Routledge.

Leonardi, Paul, Marianne E. Leonardi, and Elizabeth Hudson. 2006. "Culture, Organization, and Contradiction in the Social Construction of Technology: Adoption and Use of the Cell Phone Across Three Cultures." In *The Cell Phone Reader: Essays in Social Transformation*, edited by Anandam Kavoori and Noah Arceneaux, 205–26. New York: Peter Lang.

Levinson, Paul. 2006. "The Little Big Blender: How the Cellphone Integrates the Digital and the Physical, Everywhere." In *The Cell Phone Reader: Essays in Social Transformation*, edited by Anandam Kavoori and Noah Arceneaux, 9–18. New York: Peter Lang.

Ling, Rich. 2004. *The Mobile Connection: The Cell Phone's Impact on Society*. San Francisco: Morgan Kaufmann.

Ling, Rich. 2006. "Life in the Nomos: Stress, Emotional Maintenance, and Coordination via the Mobile Telephone in Intact Families." In *The Cell Phone Reader: Essays in Social Transformation*, edited by Anandam Kavoori and Noah Arceneaux, 61–84. New York: Peter Lang.

Lury, Celia. 1996. *Consumer Culture*. Cambridge, UK: Polity Press.

Lury, Celia. 2000. "The United Colours of Diversity." In *Global Nature, Global Culture*, edited by Sarah Franklin, Celia Lury, and Jackie Stacey, 146–87. London: Sage.

Lury, Celia. 2004. *Brands: The Logos of the Global Economy*. London: Routledge.

McClintock, Anne. 1994. "Soft-Soaping Empire: Commodity Racism and Imperial Advertising." In *Travellers' Tales: Narratives of Home and Displacement*, edited by George Robertson, Melinda Mash, Lisa Tickner, Jon Bird, Barry Curtis, and Tim Putnam, 131–55. London: Sage.

McCracken, Grant. 2005. *Culture and Consumption II: Markets, Meaning and Brand Management*. Bloomington, IN: Indiana University Press.

McStay, Andrew. 2010. *Digital Advertising*. Basingstoke, UK: Palgrave Macmillan.

Muniz, Albert, and Thomas O'Guinn. 2001 (March). "Brand Community." *Journal of Consumer Research* 27:412–32.

O'Shaughnessy, Michael, and Jane Stadler. 2008. *Media and Society* (4th ed.). Oxford, UK: Oxford University Press.

Paterson, Mark. 2006. *Consumption and Everyday Life*. London: Routledge.

Radway, Janice. 1984. *Reading the Romance: Women, Patriarchy, and Popular Literature*. Chapel Hill, NC: University of North Carolina Press.

Scott, Allen. 2000. *The Cultural Economy of Cities*. London: Sage.

Simmel, Georg. 1905. *Die Probleme der Geschichtphilosophie* (Problems of the Philosophy of History). Leipzig: Duncker & Humblot.

Thomas, Lyn. 2008. "Alternative Realities." *Cultural Studies* 22(5):680–99.

Warde, Alan. 1996. "Afterward: The Future of the Sociology of Consumption." In *Consumption Matters*, edited by Stephen Edgell, Kevin Hetherington, and Alan Warde, 302–12. Oxford, UK: Blackwell.

Westlund, Oscar. 2008. "From Mobile Phone to Mobile Device: News Consumption on the Go." *Canadian Journal of Communication* 33(3):443–63.

CHAPTER 15 / ALEXANDRA BOUTROS
Media, Representation, and Identity

Do media reflect reality—or do they construct it?
What role does culture play in constituting our
identities? Do the unique characteristics of
particular media shape practices of representation?

KEY CONCEPTS

1. Media, as vehicles of *representation*—or signifying practices—are central to the process of identity formation.

2. Social difference becomes *naturalized*—that is, accepted and established—through ideology.

3. People, media, and technology co-constitute one another in the context of social and cultural practices, simultaneously expanding and limiting the ways in which we think and act in the world.

CHAPTER OUTLINE

Introduction 289

Essentialism 290

Oppositional Identity Formation 291

Ideology 294

Identity and New Media 297

Rise of the Prosumer 298

Participatory Media 300

The Digital Divide 303

Conclusion 304

Notes 305

Discussion Questions 305

Suggested Resources 306

References 306

Introduction

The intersection of media and representation is such a part of our everyday lives that it can be difficult to step back in order to understand how particular representations are constructed through media. Representations are constructed or constituted not simply by media production practices, but by the ways in which media production is situated in social and cultural conventions, ideology, and history, and how it intersects with our own subjective positions or identities.

Because representation is always mediated by these factors, analyzing representation is challenging and requires attention to who the intended audience is; what the purpose, motivation, or intent is behind the production of a given representation; and how that representation is shaped by what has come before. Even more challenging, perhaps, is unpacking how, if, and when identity is shaped by what we see (on TV, in films, and in advertisements), or by what we experience (when we role-play in video games or construct social networking profiles for ourselves).

Essentialism

Identity, be it gender, race, sexuality, or ethnicity, can seem intrinsically tied to our bodies. When we reduce our differences to biological or genetic factors, we are drawing on a belief that our differences are natural, determined solely by our genetic code. This belief is called *essentialism*, and it is problematic not only because it leads to the naturalization of differences, but because it fails to account for the social or cultural roots of difference. The naturalization of the differences between men and women, for example, has been deconstructed by post-structuralist theory in general and post-structural feminist scholarship in particular. Feminist philosopher Marion Iris Young famously untangled assumptions about gender differences in her influential essay, "Throwing Like a Girl" (1990/2005), in which she challenged the idea that girls inherently lack physical coordination, strength, and comportment because of an innate or essential feminine quality. Young, like other post-structuralist theorists of identity, reminds us that "[e]very human existence is defined by its situation; the particular existence of the female person is no less defined by the historical, cultural, social and economic limits of her situation" (29).

Theorists of identity construction suggest that identity is not innate, but is constructed by social and cultural norms. Such theorists tend to disavow any connection between cultural identity and the biological body because they see this connection as inevitably leading back to essentialist assumptions. Other thinkers argue that identity categories can be understood to constitute solidarity, community, or belonging (Karlyn 2003). Still others contend that although identity is always culturally determined, it still intersects with the physical body. For example, Judith Butler argues that while gender cannot be equated with sex, gender is nonetheless inscribed upon the body (Butler 1990). Even in this latter view, biology may be understood as defining our sex as male, female, or somewhere in between, but culture assigns gender roles to those biological differences. It is these culturally constructed gender roles that may have us wearing fishnets or ties, shaving our faces or our legs.

Michel Foucault (1988) also disputed ideas of identity as fixed or innate; he argued that we produce our own identities through practices of self-disclosure, contemplation, and self-discipline. Foucault called these practices "technologies of the self," and they are fundamentally communicative practices. Self-disclosure, for example, is something we articulate in the form of diaries, blogs, Facebook profiles, and countless other autobiographical practices often mediated through various technologies. Network and social media make particularly visible the "technologies of self" that go into the identities we present to the world. For example, new media scholar danah boyd (2010) points out that social networking sites are places where "participants actively and consciously craft their profiles to be seen by others. Profile generation is an explicit act of writing oneself into being in a digital environment" (43). How we edit and refine our various online profiles is very much about controlling and shaping the face we present to the world. But our identities are not entirely within our control, nor are they entirely shaped by our own practices.

Social media make particularly visible the "technologies of self" that go into the identities we present to the world.

Oppositional Identity Formation

One of the key intersections of media, representation, and identity can be found in the articulation of social difference, such as race, gender, class, sexuality, physical ability, language, ethnicity, or religion. Identities are frequently articulated through a language of polarization. Geopolitical strife is often framed in the context of schisms between identity groups. Recent discord between Bosnians and Serbians, Tamils and Sinhalese, or Tutsis and Hutus have complex histories, but are often represented as struggles between communities distinguished by religious, ethnic, or cultural difference. Even in everyday life, identity is often defined through difference and oppositional categories: male or female, queer or straight, black or white, rich or poor. These oppositional categories, some argue, define post-Enlightenment Western thought and culture (Bordo 1993). Binary oppositions can become laden with cultural values that position one part of each pair as privileged, the other as subjugated.

For example, Western literature—from Shakespeare's Caliban to Conrad's *Heart of Darkness*—has historically aligned whiteness with rationality and civilization and blackness with savagery and primitiveness, perpetuating recognizable racial hierarchies. Similarly, Victorian-era soap advertisements—by companies such as Vinolia, Pears, and Fairy Soap—carried these value-laden dichotomies into the realm of visual culture by depicting white children "educating" black children on the ways of cleanliness and hygiene. Images of black skin being scrubbed "white" encapsulate the stark racism of the advertisements. Appearing at a time when the material wealth generated by British empire expansion triggered a rising commodity culture and the advent of mass marketing campaigns, these soap advertisements embodied emergent middle-class values. Anne McClintock explains that through the depiction of racial difference, these ads represented "class control ('cleansing the great unwashed'), and the imperial civilizing mission ('washing and clothing the savage')" (2006, 757). While oppositions like "white is to black as clean is to dirty" may seem overly simplistic, these examples demonstrate the pervasive privileging of whiteness as a representation of goodness and purity, and a devaluing of darkness as sinful and contaminating.

Working in the area of critical race theory, Stuart Hall (2006) proposes an understanding of cultural identity that allows explanation of not only how social difference is constructed, but how it is perpetuated. Hall, like Young, argues that identity is constructed in part by historical forces. "Historical," in this case, does not imply a fixed or **reified** story, but a constantly changing narrative: "Identities are the names we give to the different ways we are positioned by, and position ourselves within, the narratives of the past" (Hall 2006, 394). Hall suggests that the meaning of identity is fluid, something that can change over time. What it means to be a woman or queer in North America today is not the same as what it meant to be a woman or queer in North America 100 years ago. Women's suffrage movements (which gave women the right to vote in the United States in 1920 and in Canada in 1916) and the gay liberation movement (often said to have arisen out of the Stonewall riots in New York in 1969) are just some of the multiple social factors that have reconstituted what we have meant by these labels over time.

Similarly, Hall points out that blackness signified differently in the precolonial era than it does today. The colonization of Africa and the Caribbean and the trauma of the Middle Passage, which brought slaves to the "New World," is part of the history that constitutes post-colonial conceptualizations of blackness. Hall suggests that we need to pay attention to the historical conditions that shaped (and continue to shape) the "ways in which black people, black experiences, were positioned and subjected in the dominant regimes of representation" (Hall 2006, 394). In other words, every representation is historically contingent, even as history evolves, changes, or is even widely forgotten. When thinking about identity, representation and media, we need to account for these "dominant regimes of representation." This means coming to terms with the ways in which identity is shaped, not

reify To make an abstract idea more concrete or real.

Hall suggests that the meaning of identity is fluid, something that can change over time.

just by representations themselves, but by the ways those representations are situated in social, cultural, and economic systems of power.

Who Is Representing Whom?

Hall's work on identity and representation draws on the work of Edward Said, who explored the powerful impact of representation on geopolitical relationships. Said examined how Western representations of the Orient, and more specifically "Arab" cultures, has shaped Western ideologies about and representations of people from the Middle East.[1] Western media are rife with negative images of Arabs in general and Islam in particular. From daily newscasts to Hollywood films such as *Raiders of the Lost Ark* (1981) and *Aladdin* (1992), viewers in the West are bombarded with images that depict Islam as a dangerous and barbaric religion and Arabs as villainous (Shaheen 2001). Said argued that the complexity and heterogeneity of Islam is often overwritten by simplistic stereotyping, which pits the supposedly civilized and modern West against the apparently primitive and backward-looking "Arab World." Speaking of news media reports, Said observed that "[i]t is only a slight overstatement to say that Muslims and Arabs are essentially covered, discussed, apprehended, either as oil suppliers or as potential terrorists" (Said 1981, 26).

PRIMARY SOURCE

Edward Said on the Clash of Ignorance

In his essay "The Clash of Ignorance," Edward Said wrote (2001):

> How finally inadequate are the labels, generalizations and cultural assertions. At some level, for instance, primitive passions and sophisticated know-how converge in ways that give the lie to a fortified boundary not only between "West" and "Islam" but also between past and present, us and them, to say nothing of the very concepts of identity and nationality about which there is unending disagreement and debate. A unilateral decision made to draw lines in the sand, to undertake crusades, to oppose their evil with our good, to extirpate terrorism and, in Paul Wolfowitz's nihilistic vocabulary, to end nations entirely, doesn't make the supposed entities any easier to see; rather, it speaks to how much simpler it is to make bellicose statements for the purpose of mobilizing collective passions than to reflect, examine, sort out what it is we are dealing with in reality, the interconnectedness of innumerable lives, "ours" as well as "theirs."

Western media and popular culture have a long history of framing the Arab as "other." Systemic and problematic representations of the Middle East, situated in history, have a contemporary impact on geopolitical relations between Western and Arab nations. And yet these negative images do not simply go unanswered. The emergence of the international Al Jazeera news network has been seen as an alternative to hegemonic Western views of the Middle East (El-Nawawy and Iskander 2002). The work of both Hall and Said—whether focused on the colonial and the post-colonial, or the Occident and the Orient—rests on an awareness of intercultural communication as central to the project of shaping not only identities themselves, but the systems of power that privilege some identities and disenfranchise others. Identities, whether acquiesced to or resisted, are forged through representation. And media, as vehicles of representation, are central to this project of identity formation.

Ideology

Representations, disseminated via media, structure and articulate the unequal power relations often embedded in ideology. Ideology, in the Marxist tradition, encompasses all the conventions of a society (Marx and Engels 1845/2001). These conventions and ideas become naturalized over time. Ideology legitimizes certain social relations and hierarchies and renders certain power imbalances or inequalities almost imperceptible. These power imbalances are usually kept in place not through overt violence or force, but by subordinate groups' acceptance of their social position as natural, normal, or commonsensical. When subordinate groups accept the dominant discourse that insists on their subordination, we call this condition **hegemony** (Gramsci 1971). Marxist theory is particularly concerned with how ideology stratifies society. Marx was interested in the role of the proletariat, or the working class, in capitalist society. In Marxist theory, the proletarians are those who do not own the means of production (such as factories and machines), but who nonetheless labour to produce goods. The best interests of these labourers (for example, to have high-paying jobs) are always inevitably at odds with the best interests of those who own the means of production (to keep costs of production, including workers' wages, as low as possible). Sometimes the working class struggles to define workers' needs and act to have those needs met (by going on strike, for example). At other times, the working class accepts exploitative conditions imposed upon them by capitalist ideology.

Although the working class are sometimes depicted as hard-working, salt-of-the-earth types, representations of them are often rife with negative

hegemony
Acceptance by subordinate groups of the dominant discourse that insists on their subordination.

PRIMARY SOURCE

Marx and Engels on "Ruling Ideas"

In *The German Ideology* (1845/2001, 64), political economists Karl Marx and Frederick Engels coined the phrase "ruling ideas":

> The ruling ideas are nothing more than the ideal expression of the dominant material relationships, the dominant material relationships grasped as ideas; hence of the relationships which make the one class the ruling one, therefore, the ideas of their dominance.

PRIMARY SOURCE

Barbara Ehrenreich on "The Silenced Majorlty"

In her essay "The Silenced Majority" (1990), US sociologist and political activist Barbara Ehrenreich commented on the apparent "disappearance" of the American middle class:

> [W]hen I say the working class is disappearing I do not mean just a particular minority group favored, for theoretical reasons, by leftists. I mean the American majority. And I am laying the blame not only on the corporate sponsors of the media, who undoubtedly prefer to have us think that everyone is either a capitalist or a "consumer," but on many less wealthy and powerful people. Media people for example. ... [I]t is possible for a middle class person today to read the papers, watch television, even go to college, without suspecting that America has any inhabitants other than white-collar operatives and, of course, the annoyingly persistent "black underclass."

---

stereotypes. On television, for example, the character of Homer Simpson self-consciously exemplifies the portrayal of the working-class man as uneducated and unrefined, crude, lazy, and unskilled. Such stereotypes of working-class people perpetuate the social stratification necessary to maintain the subordination of this social group. In a capitalist society, which fosters a strong belief in the possibility of economic upward mobility, stereotypes about the lower classes serve to lay blame for a failure to achieve that upward mobility on the individual, rather than on the workings of systemic class hierarchy. This system devalues the labour of the working classes in the interests of raising the profits of those who own the means of production. In Canada, class distinctions are sometimes drawn along regional lines. The Maritimes, for example, are often seen as the home of the working class (particularly those whose labour is tied to natural resources such as fishing or logging).

While media can perpetuate stereotypes, they can also call attention to them. The television series *Trailer Park Boys*, which is set in Halifax, Nova Scotia, plays upon traditional class stereotypes (Hughes-Fuller 2009): the characters are uneducated and lazy (they spend much of their time consuming alcohol and drugs and scheming about ways to make money without really working), yet the show exploits these stereotypes, generating a humour and affection that challenges and subverts the assumed dominance of the upper or bourgeois classes by validating the unapologetic values and practices of an often-marginalized social group.

Countercultural Representation

Although the signifying practices of media play a role in perpetuating hegemonic ideologies by reflecting and reproducing oppressive stereotypes, examples such as *Trailer Park Boys* show that media representations can also work to subvert dominant ideologies. It is too simplistic to assume that media only reflect dominant ideologies. Representations can be **countercultural** as well as cultural; they can resist dominant ideologies as well as perpetuate them. Representations can become sites of debate on and struggle around conflicting beliefs about race, gender, sexuality, and class. Individuals and audiences sometimes reappropriate stereotypes as cultural resources, making new meaning out of media images. Fan fiction—the creative works generated by fans of literature, film, and television—is one particularly visible example of how audiences create new meaning out of mediated representations. Whether Harry Potter fans are writing new romantic storylines for Harry and Hermione, or fans of the television show *Supernatural* are cutting and pasting video clips of main characters Dean and Sam into video mashups that can be found on YouTube, fan creations transform the original representation into something new. Scholar John Fiske (1989) explains that audiences can transform a popular representation "into a cultural resource, pluralize the meanings and pleasures it offers, evade or resist its disciplinary efforts, fracture its homogeneity and coherence, raid or poach upon its terrain" (28).

Although an analysis of how negative stereotypes and representations affect identity formation may seem straightforward, the complex intersections of media and identity can be difficult to untangle. If identity seems closely tied to ourselves (and our bodies), media can seem entirely separate from those same selves. Broadcast media, in particular, tempt us to imagine

counterculture
The values and practices of a social group, or subculture, that run counter to those of the mainstream.

ourselves simply as witnesses to the stream of audio and visual material that emanates from our TVs and radios.

Identity and New Media

The intersection of identity, media, and representation is particularly visible when we are confronted with the emergence of new media. Recent adoption of networked, digital, and mobile media has elicited debate about how such media change not only our everyday lives but our very selves. We can see concern with how new media seem to be changing us in news reports on how video games lead to violence, or the rise of the term "digital natives" to refer to a young generation so accustomed to digital technology that their use of it appears "natural."

Discussion of the intersection of media, identity, and representation is often framed in simplistic or deterministic ways: advertisements that use skinny female models lead to poor self-and body image in young girls; violent

---

HISTORICAL HIGHLIGHT

The Brownie

Anxiety about the impact of emergent forms of media and communication on identity isn't particularly new. For example, current concerns about loss of privacy through social networking sites such as Facebook parallel in many ways the moral panic that arose in 1888 with the introduction of Kodak's Brownie Camera. These cameras were inexpensive (a mere 25 cents when first introduced) and so put photography, for the first time, in the hands of ordinary people. The sudden pervasiveness of this new medium led many at the time to feel as if they were losing control of their own image. The camera was seen not just as a way to capture or memorialize happy events, but as an intrusive "eye" that could catch people unawares in private, embarrassing, or even compromising acts. Brownies were banned in some public places, including beaches. The *Hartford Courant*, a Connecticut-based newspaper, expressed concern that "the sedate citizen [could no longer] indulge in any hilariousness without the risk of being caught in the act" (quoted in Brayer 2006, 71) by the new, lightweight cameras.

Similar concerns about privacy and loss of control over self-image pervade discussions about social networking sites today. As we tag and untag images of ourselves online, we find ourselves wondering what impact online sharing of photos may have on us down the road. Underlying many discussions about the impact of new media is a concern that it may be changing how we understand ourselves and our location in the world.

images on TV lead to violent behaviour. Reducing these representations to simple cause and effect fails to account for the multitude of social factors that contribute to self-image problems or violence. The argument that technologies determine social change, called technological determinism, tends to be overly **reductionist**. A reductionist approach implies that new forms of technology or media arrive fully formed in society, where we have no choice but to learn how to deal with their effects. Focusing on the deleterious effects of texting on literacy, or the distractions caused by pervasive digital screens (laptops, smart phones, PDAs), implies that new media are simply foisted upon us and that we have no control over how we use them.

reductionist
The tendency to reduce the understanding of a complex issue or phenomenon to a single or simpler explanation.

Like identity, media and technology are socially constructed. The creation of culturally specific or subcultural forms of production illustrates how identity is constituted by specific histories and discursive formations (statements necessarily understood in relation to each other). **Discourse**—or the constitution of knowledge and social practices as well as the power relations that govern them—works in conjunction with the materiality of media and technology to produce representations circumscribed by particular material and historical conditions. A variety of factors, including social access, economics, and cultural mores, govern how we adopt and adapt to new media and new technologies. Not only does society play a significant role in determining how new media will be taken up and used, but also, the ways in which media are appropriated can vary from one social group to another.

discourse
The constitution of knowledge and social practices, as well as the power relationships that govern them.

Rise of the Prosumer

Encompassing music, dance, clothing style, and visual art (such as graffiti), hip hop culture originated in the late 1970s in New York's South Bronx neighbourhood among economically and socially disenfranchised African-American and Latino youth. Influenced by the reggae music brought to the Bronx by Jamaican immigrants to the United States, hip hop was (and continues to be) characterized by intertextuality (Rose 1994). Early hip hop pioneers repurposed the almost obsolete sound technologies of vinyl and turntables to cut up existing music into samples, which they then remixed into new musical forms. These artists generated a participatory culture that required neither high-tech equipment nor specialized knowledge to access.

In many ways, the inception of hip hop, with its blurring of distinctions between music producers and artists, foreshadows the contemporary concept of the "prosumer"—a consumer whose versatility with production technology allows him or her to become an active producer rather than simply a passive consumer (Tapscott and Williams 2006, 124). Prosumers are often imagined to be the result of new digital technologies and media that make participation and DIY (do-it-yourself) production easy. Like participants in fan culture, prosumers transform pre-existing mainstream cultural products into new texts or products that better reflect their own desires and experiences (Jenkins 2006). In the same way, pre-digital-era hip hop artists resuscitated older and arguably fading technologies such as vinyl and turntables, largely for the purposes of self-representation. Hip hop became a mode of self-expression for a segment of the population that was not only disenfranchised, but that was underrepresented in mainstream media. When Chuck D famously quipped that "rap is CNN for black people" (Decurtis 1992, 227), he was alluding to both a failure of mainstream US news media to accurately reflect the lived worlds of African-American citizens and the power of hip hop (and rap lyrics) to offer a corrective to chronic under- and misrepresentation.

As individuals come to identify with and through the subcultural practices of hip hop culture (or punk, heavy metal, grunge, and multiple other musical and non-musical subcultures), cultural production can constitute communities of belonging. Often, we perform our affiliation with certain groups through our consumption of cultural products. But this **performativity** can give rise to fraught strategies of identification when belonging is constituted around cultural products and practices that signify particular identities. While hip hop has a particular situated history, rooted in the conditions of the black US inner city, the genre has gained popularity (and commercial viability) with American youth who have no experience of the ghettos so often the topic of hip hop lyrics (Kitwana 2005). This popularity raises issues of authenticity and authority. Many US hip hop artists perform what some argue is a hyper-masculinized, hyper-materialistic black identity (Rose 2008) generated by the conditions of commercial hip hop, which lifted production out of the hands of the black communities and placed it in the hands of (predominantly white) record executives who sold the stereotype of black masculinity to suburban youth.

performativity
An aspect of creating affiliations with certain groups through consumption of cultural products.

What does it mean when hip hop, a genre with strong ties to American black history and culture, is consumed by white suburban youth? Does this change the communities of belonging that hip hop constitutes? There are no simple answers to these questions, but the history of hip hop, from grassroots production to commercial success, illustrates how cultural production and consumption are closely tied to issues of identity and representation. The confluence of identity, representation, and popular music is also visible in the global hip hop movement. Groups such as Palestine's DAM and Kenya's Kibera Kid take up hip hop's political and resistive impetus when they rap about conditions they face in their home countries, creating a transnational

What does it mean when hip hop, a genre with strong ties to American black history and culture, is consumed by white suburban youth?

platform for their concerns. Inevitably, each group (or audience) that encounters hip hop approaches it through a unique interpretive framework. Engagement with media and representation is always a situated activity. As we explore how media constitutes identity through representation, we need to take into account the cultural specificity and social locations of both media producers and consumers.

Participatory Media

Media representations portray a range of possible selves, arguably allowing us to witness the roles or identities we may occupy within society. This is the reason underrepresentation or misrepresentation of a particular group is often seen as a social problem that merits attention. For example, the It Gets Better Project, launched in the United States in 2010 after a rash of suicides by gay youth, was designed to inspire hope for young people facing bullying in their everyday lives. The project takes the form of an online video channel (first hosted on YouTube, then moved to its own website) initiated by Dan Savage and his husband, Terry Miller.

In a call for representation, the project's home page invites positive accounts of LGBT (lesbian, gay, bisexual, and/or transgendered) lived experiences:

Figure 15.1 It Gets Better

Popular sex columnist Dan Savage and husband Terry Miller (pictured above) launched a participatory website designed to present positive narratives to gay and lesbian youth who are struggling with their identity or experiencing bullying.

SOURCE: Image/logo/screen shot reprinted with permission from the It Gets Better Project. Copyright 2010 by the It Gets Better Project.

"Many LGBT youth can't picture what their lives might be like as openly gay adults. They can't imagine a future for themselves. So let's show them what our lives are like, let's show them what the future may hold in store for them" (It Gets Better Project 2010). The It Gets Better Project has been criticized for perpetuating an overly simplistic message that suggests the systemic issues that support and perpetuate bullying and homophobia somehow (magically) disappear as one grows up (Veldman 2010). While this may be a valid critique, the very form of the project—its networked, participatory digital video platform—allows the project to absorb and encompass criticism. Because anyone can upload a video, even one critical of the project, a diversity of experiences and perspectives can be represented.

While broadcast media are generally understood as unidirectional, ill equipped to receive messages from their audience directly, digital networked media (such as YouTube) are generally understood to be participatory. Because digital media blur the boundaries between producers and audiences (or consumers), some see digital media as creating an all-access democratic public sphere where all participants have the opportunity to have their voice heard, to contribute to both the formation of knowledge and the discussion about issues of general concern (much like the discussion engendered by the It Gets Better Project).

But although broadcast media appear to disallow the participatory practices associated with networked digital media, Stuart Hall (2000) reminds us that even mass media practices engage what he calls a "circuit of communication," in which messages and meanings encoded in production are decoded in diverse ways by different audiences (2000). Unlike some forms of mass media, reality TV is a genre that seems to exploit and highlight audience participation. Some programs, such as *American Idol* and *Big Brother*, allow viewers to directly influence the outcome of the show. Other reality TV shows, such as *Survivor* or *The Amazing Race,* offer the possibility of viewer participation for a limited few contestants. Still others, such as *Jersey Shore, The Hills,* or *The Real Housewives* series, seem to offer only voyeuristic engagement. Although the level of audience participation may vary, these programs (like other forms of mass media representation) encode certain social identities into their narratives. Some viewers may identify with the individuals they see on these shows, while others may reject, or partially reject, any identification with them. Stuart Hall (2000) would argue that those who identify with the social identities encoded in mass media are engaging in a hegemonic "reading" of mediated representation, while those who reject what they see employ a counter-hegemonic interpretation. However, determining what constitutes a hegemonic reading of something like a TV show can be difficult. While reality TV seems to portray everyday (or "real") characters with which audiences can readily identify, some scholars argue that audiences engage with these programs not because they expect to see reflections of their own identities, but out of a fascination with representation itself. As Mark Andrejevic (2004) explains, "the promise of reality TV is coupled with an erosion of faith in representation itself—in the ability of mediated symbols to provide access to reality" (197).

Perhaps this skepticism is a result of the fact that reality TV brings viewers into close contact with the mechanics of production. *American Idol* takes us "behind the scenes," and *Big Brother* reveals and even highlights the ever-present cameras and microphones that allow us to witness every moment of the housemates' lives. But more than these technical aspects of production, reality TV highlights the construction of "reality" in representation. The pretty, young, and privileged individuals on MTV's *The Hills*, for example, seemed to be engaging in "real-life" scenarios—fights with close friends and roommates, awkward first (or last) dates, fabulous house parties. As the series gained fame and its cast gained notoriety, speculation spread on fan sites and in the blogosphere that the show wasn't as "real" as it pretended to be. Reports emerged that highly emotional scenes were often shot (and thus enacted) multiple times, revealing that "reality," in this case, was as highly manufactured as any television soap opera (Stack 2008).

Such revelations did not hurt the popularity of *The Hills*. On the contrary, the producers appeared to welcome the controversy around the show's production, on occasion exploiting the ambiguity that this engendered. In the series finale, after two of the show's main characters bid each other a tearful goodbye, the camera tracked outward from the empty Los Angeles street scene, revealing it to be nothing more than the backdrop of a Hollywood set (Fallon 2010). The controversial ending reflects the self-consciousness of the genre and suggests that viewers are " 'hip' enough to understand the constructedness of television's 'realism' " (Hearn 2009, 169). Stuart Hall's argument, that media representations are decoded differently by those occupying different social positions, is one that analysts of media need to address. The skepticism and self-consciousness that seem to be emerging around the reality TV genre remind us that even the most seemingly passive and voyeuristic audience plays a role in meaning-making processes that can, in turn, influence the production of representations.

Participatory media, whether in the form of networked digital media or genres such as reality TV, seem to permit new, more direct, participation in the public sphere. Although the story of Eastman's Brownie Camera is an example of how the advent of new media may be framed negatively, much emerging discourse about new media relies heavily on utopian ideas about participatory democracy. Such utopian ideas imply that the proliferation of individual citizen voices online (via participatory platforms such as blogs, YouTube, and Twitter, to name only a few) can only enrich the public sphere (Jenkins 2006). And certainly, digital participatory media—unlike broadcast media—seem to allow every representation to be shaped as much by bottom-up decisions as by top-down forces. Those immersed in social media live in a world where there are multiple opportunities to engage, re-contextualize, appropriate, transform, and recirculate messages.

The Digital Divide

Although new media facilitate participation, there are many who do not have access to a digital public sphere. Jürgen Habermas's (1991) definition of the **public sphere**—as a realm of social engagement equally accessible by all—has been criticized by some scholars who argue that Habermasian definitions of the public sphere are founded on a number of social exclusions (the term emerged, for example, at a time when women in most Western countries were barred from voting, and so from participating in the democratic public sphere). Nancy Fraser (1993) points out that the public sphere has never been a unified entity and suggests instead that there are multiple public spheres and counter-spheres. If we are going to analyze the possibilities opened up by new media and digital technologies, we also must acknowledge how issues of access constrain participation in the digital public sphere. As Fraser explains, in the context of seemingly increasingly borderless transnational flows of media, "[i]t matters who participates and on what terms" (Fraser 2007).

public sphere
According to Habermas, a realm of social engagement equally accessible by all.

The gap between those who have access to digital technology and infrastructure and those who do not is called the **digital divide**. Statisticians show that access to digital technologies varies according to race, gender, age, economic situation, and geographic location. While almost three-quarters of the population in North America has access to the Internet, only around 11 percent of the population in Africa has Internet access (with percentages ranging from approximately 1 percent to 40 percent in different African countries). What such statistics are less likely to demonstrate is how these factors of access intersect with the characteristics and materiality of new media, making adoption in certain locales, or among certain groups, more or less likely or desirable. For example, the lack of telephone and cable lines limits the spread of the Internet in many East African countries. At the same time, a rapid adoption of mobile cellular technology (such as the cellphone) in that region opens up possibilities for new forms of communicative practice.

digital divide
The gap between those who have access to digital technology and those who do not.

As a case in point, cellphone use in Kenya increased from 9 percent in 2002 to 65 percent in 2010 (similar to rates in Canada). The adoption of the cellphone opens up possibilities for a transformation of social, cultural, and economic practices. A recent study shows that "roughly one-in-five Kenyans participate in [digital] social networking" (Pew Research Center 2010). Cellphone users in Kenya now have the opportunity to utilize M-PESA, a unique money transfer system that allows users to pay for cab fares, school fees, utilities, and more via their cellphones (Hamza 2010). So while Internet adoption in Kenya has been slow, cellphones have been quickly adapted to suit the specific needs of a society where many people in rural areas don't have easy access to formal banking networks. Many factors—decisions made during research and development, the conditions of commercial release, and how products are used and reused—affect the spread and impact of new media and digital technology.

Technological Affordances

While media adoption is shaped by a variety of social and cultural factors, the unique characteristics, or *affordances*, of media also influence how we interact with and through them. An examination of technological affordances encourages us to take into consideration the material nature of technology and media, and come to terms with the possibilities and limits of new communicative practices.

The social networking site Facebook offers an example of how a technological affordance can circumscribe our interaction with new media. Early in its history, Facebook's status update template included the word "is" immediately following the member's profile name. This meant that status updates had either to include the "is" or ignore the verb, rendering updates grammatically nonsensical.[2] Facebook users successfully lobbied to have the "is" removed from the status update (in 2007), but the word's brief tenure demonstrates how the technological affordances of participatory media can constrain the way users present themselves to the world, even as new media provide possibilities for participation in digital public spheres.

KEY CONCEPT

People, media, and technology co-constitute one another in the context of social and cultural practices, simultaneously expanding and limiting the ways in which we think and act in the world.

Conclusion

We choose how we engage with media. At the same time, our choices are influenced by issues of access, the affordances of the media we engage with, and our social position. Media, as transmitters of representation, offer us a range of possible selves that shape our identities even as we shape representations through cultural and countercultural practices. It is helpful to think of media and identity, or self and technology, as part of a network in which our participation is vital, but circumscribed by ideological, historical, material, and cultural forces. Media, identity, and representation co-constitute one another, simultaneously expanding and limiting the ways we think and act in the world.

NOTES

1. Like the designation "Arab," which Said problematizes, the term "Middle East" (and its variants, "the Arab World" and "the Muslim World") has also been criticized as Eurocentric.
2. An example of a grammatically nonsensical status would be, "Alexandra is … My dog just destroyed my cellphone!," where "Alexandra is" is part of the unchanging Facebook status template and "My dog just destroyed my cellphone!" is the user-generated status.

DISCUSSION QUESTIONS

1. How do you define your own identity? How do you know what it means to occupy that identity position? Can you identify a representational moment (a character in a film, something you see in the news, a magazine advertisement) that has defined your identity position in a particular way? Do you agree or disagree with the messages about your identity that you have encountered? Do you think representations in media have shaped your perception of your own identity or that of others? Explain.
2. John Fiske argues that audiences do not have to buy in to the dominant, or hegemonic, meanings of representations in media and popular culture, but can instead produce a countercultural response. Can you identify a countercultural response to a mainstream media representation (a film, a television show, a novel, a news report)? What are the elements that define something as a countercultural response?
3. Can you identify the *technological affordances* of the social networking site you are most familiar with? How, for example, does a social networking site such as Facebook dictate the way in which you present yourself to others? Is your social networking limited or enhanced by online social networking sites? Explain.

SUGGESTED RESOURCES

Books

Gross, Larry. 2001. *Up from Invisibility: Lesbians, Gay Men, and the Media in America*. New York: Columbia University Press.

Lipsitz, George. 1994. *Dangerous Crossroads: Popular Music, Postmodernism and the Poetics of Place*. London: Verso.

Parker, Andrew, and Eve Kosofsky Sedgwick. 1995. "Performativity and Performance." In *Performativity and Performance*, edited by Andrew Parker and Eve Kosofsky Sedgwick, 1–18. New York: Routledge.

Said, Edward. 1981/1997. *Covering Islam: How the Media and the Experts Determine How We See the Rest of the World*. New York: Vintage.

Spigel, Lynn. 2004. "Theorizing the Bachelorette: 'Waves' of Feminist Media Studies." *Signs* 30(1):1209–21.

Websites

Flow. 2011. Online journal of television and media studies, published by the Department of Radio, Television, and Film and the University of Texas at Austin. http://flowtv.org.

In Media Res: A Media Commons Project. 2011. http://mediacommons.futureofthebook.org/imr/.

REFERENCES

Andrejevic, Mark. 2004. *Reality TV: The Work of Being Watched*. Lanham, MD: Rowan and Littlefield.

Bordo, Susan. 1993. *Unbearable Weight: Feminism, Western Culture, and the Body*. Berkeley, CA: University of California Press.

boyd, danah. 2010. "Social Network Sites as Networked Publics: Affordances, Dynamics, and Implications." In *Networked Self: Identity, Community, and Culture on Social Network Sites*, edited by Zizi Papacharissi, 39–58. New York: Routledge.

Brayer, Elizabeth. 2006. *George Eastman: A Biography*. Rochester, NY: University of Rochester Press.

Butler, Judith. 1990. *Gender Trouble: Feminism and the Subversion of Identity*. New York: Routledge.

Decurtis, Anthony. 1992. *Present Tense: Rock and Roll and Culture*. Durham, NC: Duke University Press.

Ehrenreich, Barbara. 1990 (January/February). "The Silenced Majority: Why the Average Working Person Has Disappeared from American Media and Culture." *Utne Reader* 37:46–47.

El-Nawawy, Mohammed, and Adel Iskandar. 2002. *Al-Jazeera: How the Free Arab News Network Scooped the World and Changed the Middle East*. Boulder, CO: Westview Press.

Fallon, Kevin. 2010 (July 14). "'The Hills' Series Finale's Unexpected Genius." *The Atlantic*. Accessed March 9, 2011. http://www.theatlantic.com/culture/archive/2010/07/the-hills-series-finales-unexpected-genius/59755.

Fiske, John. 1989. *Understanding Popular Culture*. London: Unwin Hyman.

Foucault, Michel. 1988. "Technologies of the Self." In *Technologies of the Self: A Seminar with Michel Foucault*, edited by Luther H. Martin, Huck Gutman, and Patrick H. Hutton, 16–49. Amherst, MA: University of Massachusetts Press.

Fraser, Nancy. 1993. "Rethinking the Public Sphere." In *The Cultural Studies Reader*, edited by Simon During, 518–36. London: Routledge.

Fraser, Nancy. 2007. "Transnationalizing the Public Sphere: On the Legitimacy and Efficacy of Public Opinion in a Post-Westphalian World." *Theory, Culture, Society* 24(4):7–30.

Gramsci, Antonio. 1971. *Selections from the Prison Notebooks*. London: Lawrence and Wishart.

Habermas, Jürgen. 1991. *The Structural Transformation of the Public Sphere: A Inquiry into the Category of Bourgeois Society*, translated by Thomas Bruger. Cambridge, MA: MIT Press.

Hall, Stuart. 2000. "Encoding/Decoding." In *Media Studies: A Reader*, edited by Paul Morris and Sue Thornton, 51–61. New York: New York University Press.

Hall, Stuart. 2006. "Cultural Identity and Diaspora." In *Theorizing Diaspora*, edited by Jana Evans Braziel and Anita Mannur, 233–46. Malden, MA: Blackwell.

Hamza, Isaac. 2010 (November 26). "M-PESA Transforms Way Kenya Does Business." *African Business Review*. Accessed March 10, 2011. http://www.africanbusinessreview.co.za/tags/m-pesa/m-pesa-transforms-way-kenya-does-business.

Hearn, Alison. 2009. "Hoaxing the Real: On the Metanarrative of Reality TV." In *Reality TV: Remaking Television Culture*, edited by Susan Murray and Laurie Ouellette, 165–78. New York: New York University Press.

Hughes-Fuller, Patricia. 2009. "Wild Bodies and True Lies: Carnival, Spectacle, and the Curious Case of Trailer Park Boys." *Canadian Journal of Communication* 34(1):95–108.

It Gets Better Project. 2010. The IOLA Foundation. Accessed March 10, 2011. http://www.itgetsbetter.org.

Jenkins, Henry. 2006. "'Worship at the Altar of Convergence': A New Paradigm for Understanding Media Change." In *Convergence Culture: Where Old and New Media Collide*, 1–24. New York: New York University Press.

Karlyn, Kathleen Rowe. 2003. "Scream, Popular Culture and Feminism's Third Wave: 'I'm Not My Mother.'" *Genders Online Journal* 38:1. Accessed March 10, 2011. http://www.genders.org/g38/g38_rowe_karlyn.html.

Kitwana, Bakari. 2005. *Why White Kids Love Hip Hop: Wankstas, Whiggers, Wanabees and the New Reality of Race in America*. New York: Basic Civitas Books.

Marx, Karl, and Frederick Engels. 1845/2001. *The German Ideology*. New York: International Publishers.

McClintock, Anne. 2006. "Soft-Soaping Empire: Commodity Racism and Imperial Advertising." In *Media Studies: A Reader* (2nd ed.), edited by Paul Marris and Sue Thornham, 745–63. New York: New York University Press.

Pew Research Center. 2010 (December 15). "Computer and Cell Phone Usage Up Around the World: Global Publics Embrace Social Networking." Pew Global Attitudes Project. Accessed March 10, 2011. http://pewglobal.org/2010/12/15/global-publics-embrace-social-networking.

Rose, Tricia. 1994. *Black Noise: Rap Music and Black Culture in Contemporary America*. London: Wesleyan University Press.

Rose, Tricia. 2008. *The Hip Hop Wars: What We Talk About When We Talk About Hip Hop—And Why It Matters*. New York: Basic Books.

Said, Edward. 1978. *Orientalism*. New York: Pantheon.

Said, Edward. 2001 (October 26). "The Clash of Ignorance." *The Nation*. Accessed March 13, 2011. http://www.thenation.com/article/clash-ignorance?page=0,1.

Shaheen, Jack. 2001. *Reel Bad Arabs: How Hollywood Vilifies a People*. Ithaca, NY: Olive Branch Press.

Stack, Tim. 2008 (August 19). "The Hills: They Shoot, Lauren Conrad Scores." *Entertainment Weekly*. Accessed March 10, 2011. http://www.ew.com/ew/article/0,,20215857,00.html.

Tapscott, Don, and Anthony D. Williams. 2006. *Wikinomics: How Mass Collaboration Changes Everything*. New York: Portfolio.

Veldman, Michael. 2010 (October 19). "Opinion: 'It Gets Better' Needs to Do More." *The Tech* 139(46). Accessed March 10, 2011. http://tech.mit.edu/V130/N46/veldman.html.

Young, Iris M. 1990/2005. *On Throwing Like a Girl and Other Essays*. Oxford, UK: Oxford University Press.

CHAPTER 16 / BEVERLEY BEST

Speed, Sensation, and Stimulation

In what ways has speed become a prominent aspect of modern life? What changes has it brought to our economy, our society, and our culture? How has our sense of space been challenged or reshaped by the speed of modern communication?

KEY CONCEPTS

1. The acceleration of communication media has shaped every aspect of society.

2. The annihilation of space through time is a central theme in the history and modernization of capitalism.

3. The modern compression of space and time has had a profound impact on the way people perceive the world and their own lives.

CHAPTER OUTLINE

Introduction: Communicating at the Speed of Light   309

Speed, Commerce, and Communication   310

Media, Globalization, and the Political Economy of Speed   312

Speed and Space   314

The Regime of "Real Time": Immediacy and Instantaneity   317

Stimulation, Distraction, and the Tempo of the City   320

Speed, Spectacle, and the 24-Hour News Cycle   324

Conclusion   327

Discussion Questions   327

Suggested Resources   328

References   328

Introduction: Communicating at the Speed of Light

Speed has become a guiding principle of modern life in societies in the global North, and increasingly throughout the world. In our modes of transportation and communication, work, and entertainment, speed is assumed to be a fundamental value, a goal, an end in itself. We may readily think of speed as an economic imperative, or as a technological force, but speed is equally a *cultural* logic. In other words, speed has become one of society's dominant cultural ideologies: the virtue and utility of speed, in almost all societal contexts, are accepted as self-evident and commonsensical. As Paul Virilio, theorist of speed and modern society says, "speed is the hope of the west" (Virilio 2006, 78).

To a large extent, the pace of modern life is set by the speed of our communications media. In the era of digital communications technologies, where information can travel at the speed of electromagnetic impulses, it is a challenge for the popular imagination even to keep pace with what is "technologically" feasible, never mind to understand the meaning of these developments. The acceleration of the movement of information reorganizes all spheres of society and all forms of human association typically faster than we can become aware of the changes taking place.

> **KEY CONCEPT**
> The acceleration of our communication media has shaped every aspect of society.

Meanwhile, the high-speed movement of information characteristic of modern media also requires us to confront a staggering *abundance* of information. Today, movies, music, books, magazines, and personal communications are delivered directly to our homes both by "old" media (TV, radio, telephone, mail) and by "new" (wireless and fibre-optic networks). Our media are now designed to increase our mobility as well: we are plugged into MP3 players, read newspapers on the metro, email on laptops in cafés, use cellphones to locate our kids, update our Facebook sites throughout the day, watch movies on planes, send text messages while walking, listen to audiobooks while driving, and sort out our weekly agendas on our personal digital assistants over lunch. As media scholar Todd Gitlin (2002) argues, our popular culture is a frenzy of communication: "never have so many communicated so much, on so many screens, through so many channels, absorbing so many hours of irreplaceable human attention" as in the "swarming enormity" of our media environments (4).

This chapter will look at the way the social imperative of speed, and in particular the acceleration of our communication media, has shaped our society from top to bottom, from our political and economic organizations, to the way we produce and consume our news and entertainments, to our leisure and social activities, to our own psyches and imaginations.

Speed, Commerce, and Communication

One sphere of social life where speed has always been a fundamentally organizing logic is the economy. In capitalist societies, profits for business owners are realized at the end of the cycle of production, distribution, and consumption. For example, businesses manufacture a product or offer a service; the product or service is made available to consumers; consumers purchase the product or service; and the profits from that sale are directed back to the business owner. The faster the cycle of production, distribution, and consumption, the faster profits are delivered to business owners. For this reason, the question of speed and, in particular, how to increase the speed of this cycle, has been a central concern of business owners from the earliest days of capitalist societies to today. As Gitlin (2002) says, "capitalism loves speed" (76). One way to increase the speed of the production–distribution–consumption cycle ("the PDC cycle") is to increase the speed of the movement of information required to carry out the cycle.

"Capitalism loves speed."

—Todd Gitlin

The movement of information between various parties has always been a central component of commerce and economic activity. For this reason, the history of the development of communication media is inextricably intertwined with the history of economic development throughout the world. Furthermore, the logic that links these two histories together is speed: on the one hand, communication media have generally developed toward an ever-greater velocity of movement of information; on the other hand, an increasing ease and velocity of information circulation has been a principal means by which economic activities, such as the production, distribution, and consumption of goods and services, have been revolutionized from the mid-19th century to the present.

The histories of technological achievements, modalities of communication, and commercial practices all converge around advancements in moving messages and information faster across distances. In the 19th century, the railway system dramatically sped up the movement of people, raw materials, and finished goods, as well as messages and information across geographical distances, representing, simultaneously, revolutions in transportation, communication, and commerce. The large scale and complexity of the railway system, together with the fact that its transportation functions were multiple and not concentrated on information delivery alone, meant that it was not necessarily the most practical and efficient mode of communication in all circumstances. Authors Howard Rosenberg and Charles Feldman (2008, 33) recount how in 1850, Paul Julius Reuter, a journalist, media owner, and eventually a pioneer in using the telegraph to gather and deliver news, found that trained pigeons could

Figure 16.1 Carrier pigeon

In the past, trained pigeons were often the fastest and most reliable way to share information, and were used by journalists and businesspeople, and in wartime.

fly news and stock prices from Germany to Belgium in just four hours, whereas the railroad took six hours to cover the same distance.

The invention of the telegraph made it possible for the first time to sever the functions of transportation and communication. It introduced to the world a technology and an industry whose sole focus was on the movement of information. But what was even more astounding in its day was the speed of this movement: information could now travel at the speed of an electric current, leaving trains and carrier pigeons far behind. In 1861, Western Union erected the first transcontinental telegraph line, ushering in the electric age of communication and dramatically speeding up the movement of information between North America's burgeoning commercial hubs and extending the regulatory reach of the increasingly centralizing forces of government.

However, whereas the telegraph and the telephone carried signals on cables, the invention of radio realized the sending of signals over airwaves, making it possible for masses of people to receive those signals together simultaneously, revolutionizing yet again modalities of both communication and commerce. In 1913, the first radio signal was beamed around the world from the Eiffel Tower, becoming an iconic moment of a 20th-century revolution in broadcasting that would shrink once prohibitive global distance to "an instant in universal public time" (Harvey 1989, 266). This awesome power of radio, and subsequently television, to overcome global geographical distance through speed (in this case, the speed at which electronic signals can travel on airwaves) and assemble national and international audiences in "real time" would become the greatest gift to manufacturers and advertisers of consumer goods and facilitate the formation of what we now call "consumer society."

Media, Globalization, and the Political Economy of Speed

Today, in advanced consumer societies, we are experiencing another revolution in the ease and acceleration of information delivery that, since the end of the 1980s, has been reorganizing modes of communication and commerce. The broadcast revolution of the 20th century has been followed by what Paul Virilio calls the "transmission revolution" of the 21st century, brought about by new digital technologies (Virilio 1997, 12). **Digitalization** is the technological process characterizing "new media," or computer-mediated forms of communication and information collection, storage, and delivery. When new media are introduced, older media do not disappear; instead, the uses of old media are restructured in the new media environment. It is the combination of older modes of transportation (shipping, the railway, air travel)

digitalization
The technological process that characterizes new media, or computer-mediated forms of information collection, storage, and delivery.

and older communication technologies (cable and cellular telephony, satellites) with the tremendous new facility of computer technologies for gathering, storing, and processing data and information that ushered in the era of economic reorganization known as **globalization** in the late 1980s. As political economist David Harvey (1989, 285) explains, this stage of economic reorganization, as much as any before it, expresses a logic of speed:

> Imported systems of communication and information flow coupled with rationalizations in techniques of distribution (packaging, inventory control, containerization, market feed-back, etc.), made it possible to circulate commodities through the market system with greater speed. Electronic banking and plastic money were some of the innovations that improved the speed of the inverse flow of money. Financial services and markets (aided by computerized trading) likewise speeded up, so as to make, as the saying has it, "twenty-four hours a very long time" in the global stock markets.

Once again, digitalization has reorganized communication and commerce by accelerating the movement of information. This time, however, as communication technologies become cheaper, lighter, and more mobile, we have witnessed a vast multiplication of the number of people communicating (that is, the points from which information is sent and received) and a subsequent multiplication of communicational channels and directionalities. The multiplication of channels of communication is illustrated in the increasingly complex movement of information in the PDC cycle in the era of globalization. For example, in the context of production, a CEO of a company must communicate with other company executives who, in turn, communicate with various department managers who, in turn, communicate with suppliers of raw materials and with those who oversee factory production, who must then communicate with factory workers. In the context of distribution, information must be communicated among company executives, managers, marketers, accountants, advertisers, wholesalers, retailers, and consumers. Finally, information about consumers' satisfaction (or not) with the product must travel back to company executives. Manufacturers and retailers aggressively pursue as much information as they can gather concerning consumer likes and dislikes, desires, habits, valued conveniences, and patterns of behaviour in order to anticipate and influence future consumer behaviour. Computers have made it possible to collect and process consumer data at the point of sale, representing the movement of enormous amounts of information from consumers back to companies while requiring only the passive, and often unwitting, participation of consumers themselves.

globalization
The recent reorganization and integration of the world's economies, driven in part by advances in computer technology.

This complex movement of information in the contemporary communication environment has led many to describe globalization as a society of vast information "networks" composed of accelerated and multidirectional information "flows." Digitalization offers new ways of organizing commercial activity around the increased flow of information between consumers and manufacturers. Manufacturers can now take stock of, and process, consumer demand almost immediately, delaying the production of goods until after they have been ordered and purchased. This inventory system is called **just-in-time production**, and it allows manufacturers to reduce their production costs by minimizing stockholding and eliminating the risk involved in producing a product that may not successfully find a buyer. In 1993, in an effort to represent the speed, expanse, and utility of these new information networks and flows, digital applications such as the Internet and the World Wide Web were dubbed by political leaders in the United States as "the information superhighway." This metaphor is an example of how the collective imagination could not keep up with the pace and scope of the material reality of information, the speed of which had already far surpassed that of vehicles on a highway.

just-in-time production
An industrial inventory system, driven by computerized networks, that allows manufacturers to be more efficient in producing and warehousing products.

Speed and Space

The information superhighway metaphor is also insufficient at capturing the most distinctive feature of the globalizing thrust of digital modes of communication, namely the way in which, by the 1990s, they had virtually obliterated geographical distance as an obstacle to commercial activity. The ease of communicating over great distances (one can now communicate as quickly and easily with someone on the other side of the world as with someone down the hall) means that the activities that constitute the PDC cycle, even those that are internal to a single enterprise, can be scattered all over the globe. Manuel Castells (2001), a theorist of the role of information technology in social and economic life, calls this phenomenon the global space of information flows. These, in turn, have created a new international division of labour and production, where "even small and medium-sized enterprises connect directly or indirectly to the world market through linkages in the [information] networks" (155). For example, without leaving Montreal, a person can purchase a product that is manufactured in China, from a store in New York, whose head office is in London. A person who seeks technical support for a computer system in Canada may link up with a technician in Atlanta, Georgia or Mumbai, India. As David Harvey (1989) points out, it is now possible for large multinational corporations to coordinate their operations—financial decisions, input costs, quality control,

By the 1990s, digital communication had virtually obliterated geographical distance as an obstacle to commercial activity.

Figure 16.2 A globalized economy

Information networks allow for the coordination of complex business operations on a global scale. Moving something with more *speed* means that *space* becomes less of an obstacle for transporting it.

SOURCE: NOAA photo library/Creative Commons.

factory working conditions, and so on—in more than 50 different locations, around the world, simultaneously (293).

The manner in which the accelerated movement of information allows the elements of the PDC cycle to be delocalized and dispersed around the globe illustrates the inherent interconnection between speed and *space*: the greater the speed of movement of something (or, the less time required to travel a distance), the less space is an obstacle to its transportation or transmission. In other words, the faster and easier the means of communication, the more negligible is the geographical distance between communicating parties. With respect to the movement of information, new transmission capabilities negate the space between point A and point B, whether that is the distance of a hallway, across an ocean, or that between Earth and Mars. David Harvey (1989) describes this dynamic as the "annihilation of space through time," or as the *time–space compression* that occurs with each revolution in transportation and communication (205, 240). Paul Virilio (1997) calls this same phenomenon "critical space" (mimicking the term "critical mass"), referring to the shrinking of geophysical space "due to

KEY CONCEPT
The annihilation of space through time is a central theme in the history and modernization of capitalism.

the acceleration of communication tools that *obliterate the Atlantic* (Concorde), *reduce France to a square one and a half hours* across (Airbus) or *gain time over time* with the TGV [high speed trains]" (9; emphasis in original). The annihilation of space through time is one of the central narratives of the history of capitalist modernization.

SIDEBAR

The Global Village

When David Harvey spoke of a "global village of telecommunications," he was building on a concept made famous by media scholar Marshall McLuhan. McLuhan coined the term "global village" to describe a new collective sense of intimacy and proximity created by our electronic communication technologies. McLuhan argued that these technologies, which network the world and allow us to bear witness to the ins and outs of lives far away from our own, are causing the world to *implode* or contract, turning the experience of global space into something akin to the older experience of village life:

> The stepping-up of speed from the mechanical to the instant electric form reverses explosion into implosion. In our present electric age the imploding or contracting energies of our world now clash with the old expansionist and traditional patterns of organization. Until recently our instructions and arrangements, social political and economic, had shared a one-way pattern. We still think of it as "explosive," or expansive. ... In fact, it is not the increase in numbers in the world that creates our concern with population. Rather, it is the fact that everyone in the world has to live in the utmost proximity created by our electric involvement in one another's lives. (McLuhan 1964, 35)

Some readers mistake McLuhan's concept of the global village for a utopian image of a worldwide togetherness, mutual accountability, and reciprocity. However, for McLuhan, this term resonates even more with the negative connotations of village life: with the anxiety of being under constant surveillance and with a suffocating lack of anonymity. This spatially implosive character of social life is another aspect of the phenomenon referred to above as globalization. Globalization is equally a case of the technologized shrinking or condensing of global space as it is a case of the acceleration and explosion of communicational and economic networks and flows.

Contemporary dynamics of time–space compression have a profound impact on the way people perceive the world and the dimensions of their everyday lives. According to Harvey (1989, 240), one consequence of space–time compression is that "the world seems to collapse inwards upon us," shrinking to a "global village" of telecommunications:

> Mass television ownership coupled with satellite communication makes it possible to experience a rush of images from different spaces almost simultaneously, collapsing the world's spaces in a series of images on a television screen. The whole world can watch the Olympic Games, the World Cup, the fall of a dictator, a political summit, a deadly tragedy. (Harvey 1989, 293)

KEY CONCEPT
The modern compression of space and time has had a profound impact on the way people perceive the world and their own lives.

The Regime of "Real Time": Immediacy and Instantaneity

That modern society both creates the conditions for, and is shaped by, an ideology of speed was evident long before the digital revolution. Philosopher Friedrich Nietzsche wrote in *The Gay Science* (1882/1974), "One is ashamed of resting, and prolonged reflection almost gives people a bad conscience. One thinks with a watch in one's hand, even as one eats one's midday meal while reading the latest news of the stock market; one lives as if one might 'miss out on something.' … Virtue has come to consist of doing something in less time than someone else" (259). However, Nietzsche's suspicion of this new regime of speed and his sense of the collective anxiety that it engenders were not shared by all of his contemporaries. Some greeted the frenetic pace of modern industrial society with a sense of exuberant wonder and excitement over how the acceleration of everyday life was reinventing human existence and perception. For some, this new speed represented the possibility of infinite change and rejuvenation. The avant-garde poet F.T. Marinetti wrote in *The Futurist Manifesto* (1909), "We declare that the splendor of the world has been enriched by a new beauty: the beauty of speed."

Canadian media scholar Marshall McLuhan (1964, vi) wrote that all media introduce "new perceptual habits" into the adopting community and that an important challenge was to try and "recognize the very large structural changes in human outlook that [were] occurring" in the electronic age of the 20th century. Paul Virilio (2001, 24) refers to a society organized by the speed of its transport, the speed of its weapons, and the speed of its means of communication—what he calls a "dictatorship of speed at the limit"—as a "dromocracy" (Virilio 2006). Like McLuhan, Virilio argues that

Figure 16.3 A different sense of time

The increased speed of our world altered our collective sense of time, and introduced "new perceptual habits," but *recognizing* these large-scale changes represents a significant challenge for society.

SOURCE: melhi/iStockphoto.com.

profound changes in human outlook have accompanied the emergence of "dromocratic" society, in particular, our collective sense and experience of time. The sense of time that dominates dromocratic society is the perspective of "real time." For example, cellphones or computers allow us to communicate with loved ones in real time; radio and television broadcasts allow advertisers to make pitches to vast, dispersed audiences in real time; satellite signals allow us to watch the big game from wherever we are in real time; video cameras and live cable feeds allow us to follow the police chase in real time; and so on.

Real time expresses the twin logics of **immediacy** and **instantaneity** (Virilio 2001, 23). Immediacy is the time of our contact with the world and with one another. Digital and cellular technologies offer us immediate contact-at-a-distance, or "telecontact" (Virilio 2001, 23). We may come into immediate telecontact with victims of a natural disaster half a world away and take immediate "teleaction" in response. The regime of real time has made such disasters, once geographically remote, immediately present; it has become "our" disaster, wherever we may be, delocalized because, in the era of instant and immediate images, sounds, and information, it is "local" to everybody. Instantaneity is the time perspective of our telecommunications.

immediacy
The sensation of "real-time" contact with the world and one another, now possible virtually anywhere in the world through digital communication.

instantaneity
The quick-time perspective created by telecommunications, which animates our culture of instant gratification, and instant obsolescence.

It is the logic of consumer society: it animates the culture of instant meals, instant weight loss, instant gratification, and instant obsolescence and disposability—making it also the cultural logic of our present ecological crisis.

According to Virilio (2001, 23), when a society reaches absolute speed—namely, the speed of electromagnetic waves, the velocity of our communication technologies—it creates the collective perspective of real time that comes to supersede the perspective of real space. In the regime of real time, time takes primacy over space and geographical distance; the imperative of time management comes to replace the imperative of space management. Politics no longer revolves around the management and organization of geographical expanse, of distances, of regions, of national or international space, or of centre–periphery relations. Real time dissolves the consequential

SIDEBAR

Dromocratic Versus Democratic Society

Paul Virilio's fear for real-time society is that its inhabitants inevitably undergo a fundamental social and historical disorientation. He states, "[In dromocratic society] a total loss of the bearings of the individual looms large. To exist, is to exist *in situ*, here and now … . This is precisely what is being threatened by cyberspace and instantaneous globalized information flows" (Virilio 2001, 24). What Virilio means here is that all individuals exist in a particular place and in a particular historical time. To understand one's own place and time is to understand them in relation to other particular places and other particular historical times.

The ideology of immediacy–instantaneity, the dominant sense of time in dromocratic or real-time societies, recognizes only the present moment. Virilio refers to the outlook of the present-as-the-only-time as "dromology," and argues that it comes to supersede "chronology," or a linear sense of time, a sense of historical time, of time as a trajectory of "before, during and after"—the perspective of a pre-electronic age. In other words, the dynamics of real time create a "civilization of forgetting," a "live-coverage society" without past or future, without extension or duration (Virilio 1997, 25).

According to Virilio, this popular historical disorientation has dire consequences for society's democratic aspirations. Because democratic societies require a citizenry that is capable of reflecting on the character of its own place and time, and of understanding decisions and actions with respect to future consequences, dromocratic processes eventually edge out democratic ones in the era of absolute speed.

reality of space, distance, region, and the particularities of regional cultures or localities (Virilio 1997, 79). Politics now involves synchronizing all local and regional time—the timeframes of our cities and neighbourhoods (Virilio 2001, 25)—with "worldwide time" (Virilio 1997, 83), the time of global commerce, the time of our tele-present moment, the temporal homogenization of the planet to a universal multimedia time.

Stimulation, Distraction, and the Tempo of the City

The new urban environments of the early 20th century, dominated by the pace of industrialism and the increasing circulation of the images, texts, and sounds of a burgeoning consumer society, offered what scholars of the day observed as an overwhelming barrage of external stimuli. The chaotic activity, frenzied tempo, and growing population densities of city life offered excitement and stimulation to city dwellers and, at the same time, demanded profound adjustments to their sensibilities. Georg Simmel (1903/1971), an early analyst of urban life, argued that in response to the potentially overpowering and disorienting inundation of sensation and spectacle in the new metropolises, people develop what he called a "blasé attitude" (330). The blasé attitude is a psychological comportment (behaviour) of disengagement; it is an emotional mechanism that protects the city-dweller by numbing her nerves to the torrent of sensory stimuli. The blasé attitude creates an artificial mental distance between the individual and her socio–technological environment (including the swarm of her fellow urbanites), preventing her from being swallowed up by its intensities (Simmel 1903/1971, 324).

Walter Benjamin observed in the 1930s that everyday life in the city is constituted by a succession of sensory shocks.

Susan Buck-Morss, writing a century after Simmel, looking back on the early modern experience of urban society, comes to a similar conclusion. Buck-Morss elaborates on an observation made by Walter Benjamin in the late 1930s that everyday life in the city is constituted by a succession of sensory shocks. In order to withstand the trauma of this chronic assault to the nervous system, Buck-Morss argues that individuals developed strategies of anaesthetizing themselves to their environments—behaviours such as drug use, for example, that would inure them to the frenetic pace of urban life:

Anaesthetics became an elaborate technics in the latter part of the nineteenth century. Whereas the body's self-anaesthetizing defenses are largely involuntary, these methods involved conscious, intentional manipulation of the ... [senses]. To the already-existing Enlightenment narcotic forms of coffee, tobacco, tea, and spirits, there was added a vast arsenal of drugs and therapeutic practices, from opium, ether, and cocaine to hypnosis, hydrotherapy, and electric shock. (Buck-Morss 1992, 18)

Georg Simmel argued that as the metropolitan personality becomes distracted and disengaged in response to the sensory shocks of modern urban life, the resulting fatigue and ennui of disengagement cause her, paradoxically, to seek out more of the speed, intensity, and stimulation that was the source of nervous and psychological discomfort in the first place: "[modern life] impels us to search for momentary satisfaction in ever-new stimulations, sensations and external activities" (Simmel 1907/1978, 484). As McLuhan pointed out, "The effect of electric technology had first been anxiety. Now it appears to create boredom" (McLuhan 1964, 26). Todd Gitlin also describes this paradoxical texture of our contemporary media flows as simultaneously "disposable and essential, distracting and absorbing, sensational and tedious, emotional and numbing" (Gitlin 2002, 7). The turnover of taste, fashion, and opinion, moving at the velocity of the flows of capital (Gitlin 2002, 51), supports this oscillation between seeking out the latest, scintillating amusements and seeking out ways to escape them. As if we were evolving an increasingly high metabolism for media spectacle, our amusements become more violent, salacious, voyeuristic, scandalous, and gory, while the impressions they leave on us seem to evaporate ever more quickly.

Our fast-paced, technologized environments are also characterized by a paradoxical dynamic of reversal. New technologies may accelerate one aspect of everyday life, and simultaneously slow down another aspect of it. Highways and vehicles have sped up the movement of goods and people across land while simultaneously creating the routine gridlock known as the daily commute, slowing down this same movement and extending the average working day by up to several hours. Our new digital technologies allow us to gather, store, and process information and data with tremendous speed and ease, creating ever-growing mountains of paperwork on desks and inboxes as the time required to make meaningful sense of these data increases in step. Work slows down in proportion to the increased speed of data flows. The ease and speed of communicating over email creates a tidal wave of correspondence, requiring many new hours of sorting, reading, and responding to messages as well as deleting reams of electronic junk mail. Walkers with their heads bowed slow down to a zombie-like pace as they divert their attention from the city streets to their digital phones and PDAs. Texting while driving can bring life to a sudden halt, permanently.

McLuhan recognized, quite early in the era of emerging "time-saving" devices and appliances, that these new technologies were creating and routinizing new tasks as much as they were speeding up old ones. For instance, the washing machine may have sped up the task of washing clothes, but it also conventionalized new standards of cleanliness that required washing

PRIMARY SOURCE

Marshall McLuhan and the Outering of Our Senses

Marshall McLuhan argued that society's ongoing adoption of new media is our unconscious attempt to numb ourselves to the overpowering effects of technologized society. McLuhan's argument proceeds from his observation that each new technology or medium of communication is an extension of one of our human faculties. The introduction of the wheel, for instance, extended the human foot and the faculty of walking and transporting. The telephone extended the ear and our faculty of hearing so that we can now hear the voices of people halfway around the world as easily as we can those next to us. Television extends our faculty of sight and gives us an eye on the whole world from the comfort of our homes.

For McLuhan, electricity and electronic media represented the technological extension of consciousness itself. With electronic networks, human society has extended its central nervous system. Our extended and "collectivized" sensory and nervous system makes us part of a technologically enhanced collective consciousness and therefore more deeply interconnected with our fellow community members, even on a global scale, than ever before. McLuhan called this the "tribalizing" dynamic of electronic media; radio, TV, and now the Internet allow us to forge globally dispersed tribes of people:

> In the electric age, when our central nervous system is technologically extended to involve us in the whole of mankind and to incorporate the whole of mankind in us, we necessarily participate, in depth, in the consequences of our every action. It is no longer possible to adopt the aloof and dissociated role of the literate Westerner. ... As electronically contracted, the globe is no more than a village. (McLuhan 1964, 4–5)

This dynamic plays out when the media allow us to watch a popular uprising unfurl in a country far away from our own, or when we watch the aftermath of a natural disaster visit devastating consequences on people on the other side of the world. In these situations, even from our relative safety and comfort, we emotionally participate in the events, sympathize with the grief and hardship of others, and are often moved to various forms of action in response. As McLuhan (1964, 47) said, "In the electric age we wear all mankind as our skin."

This deep, sensory participation in one another's lives is one aspect of what McLuhan believed was also intolerable about our modern world. The flipside of deep participation is a suffocating and burdensome responsibility for others. The requirement of living through and sharing the pain and hardship of all others is a situation from which McLuhan argued we would eventually need to distract, distance, and numb ourselves for psychic survival. Instead of enhancing a collective spirit of sympathy and mutuality among members of the global community, McLuhan argued that bearing witness to the suffering of others creates the need to anaesthetize oneself to the experience, producing a static and politically conservative culture: "As we begin to react in depth to the social life and problems of our global village, we become reactionaries. Involvement that goes with our instant technologies transforms the most 'socially conscious' people into conservatives" (1964, 34).

This dynamic of reversal, where the experience of deep involvement produces a distracted and aloof sensibility, speaks to the dual nature of the extension of our senses through media and technology. When we extend our senses we are also, as McLuhan said, "outering" them, or moving them outside our bodies; when we outer one of our senses we are simultaneously and consequently *numbing* that sense. The telephone may extend our collective faculty of hearing by moving it outside our bodies, but it also numbs or diminishes the "pre-technological" or bodily form of that sense. The drive to numb our senses, expressed in the invention and social integration of new technologies, is, in part, an unconscious collective strategy to adjust to overwhelming pressures or irritations presented by our social environments and, in particular, by the pace and intensity of everyday life:

> [Outering is a strategy] resorted to by the body when the perceptual power cannot locate or avoid the cause of irritation. ... [M]an [is] impelled to extend various parts of his body by a kind of autoamputation or isolation of the offending organ, sense, or function. Thus the stimulus to new invention is the stress of acceleration of pace and increase of load. ... [A] mplification is bearable by the nervous system only through *numbness or blocking of perception*. (McLuhan 1964, 42; emphasis in original)

If the collective outering of the senses (through the social integration of new media and technologies) gives relief to our central nervous system, overstimulated from the pace and intensity of the modern world, then our electronic communication networks represent the final stage of this process, through the outering of our collective central nervous system itself. McLuhan did not live long enough to see our contemporary accelerated world of digital communications and, therefore, could not appreciate just how prescient his words would be:

> With the arrival of electric technology, man extended, or set outside himself, a live model of the central nervous system itself. To the degree that this is so, it is a development that suggests a desperate and suicidal autoamputation, as if the central nervous system could no longer depend on the physical organs to be protective buffers against the slings and arrows of outrageous mechanism. It could well be that the successive mechanizations of the various physical organs since the invention of printing have made too violent and superstimulated a social experience for the central nervous system to endure. (McLuhan 1964, 43)

clothes much more frequently than before. As McLuhan pointed out, "[t]his reverse pattern appeared quite early in electrical 'labor-saving' devices, whether a toaster or washing machine or vacuum cleaner. Instead of saving work, these devices permit everybody to do his own work. What the 19th century had delegated to servants and housemaids we now do for ourselves" (McLuhan 1964, 36).

As a way of offsetting the frenzied pace of everyday life, people cultivate habits, rituals, and other practices, intentionally or unintentionally, to slow things down; as Gitlin (2002) suggests, in a "hyperkinetic society ... pockets of deliberate slowness are cultivated" (110). The slow food movement, for example, has been one such cultivated practice responding to the increasingly global dominance of the fast-food industry. The idea of the importance of spending "quality time" with one's children, an idea put forward both by churches and by the discourses of family and childhood psychology, is elevated as a value in an era when people are working longer hours than at any other time since the turn of the 20th century. Wellness practices such as yoga and meditation, Pilates or tai chi, circle through cycles of fashion and popularity. Those with enough money visit spas and fitness clubs, literally buying time out from harried schedules. Facebook, Twitter, and other digital social networks may speed up and facilitate communication among masses of users, but they are equally as much strategies for slowing down the relentless pace of the day. Taking the time to craft one's public profile, sifting through the public diaries, photos, and "updates" of others, reading and sending "tweets"—the outering of our internal monologue—is a strategic "waste of time," a more-or-less deliberate strategy to slow things down.

Speed, Spectacle, and the 24-Hour News Cycle

One practice that has been thoroughly transformed in the context of the contemporary regime of speed and spectacle is the production and dissemination of news. On the one hand, news production has always been informed by the principle of speed. As James Compton (2004) points out, from the very beginning, the publishing of daily newspapers was tied to the business community's need for up-to-date information—hence, the imperative to produce news as quickly as possible (61–62). When it comes to news commodities, the logic of "the newer, the better" has always dominated the industry (Compton 2004, 62). However, in the 1980s, news production underwent a significant transformation and reorientation. At this time, the growth of cable and direct-broadcast satellite technology—together with the advent of the digital era, which greatly expanded the means and channels by which to gather information and disseminate it as "news"—thoroughly consolidated the principle of immediacy and instantaneity in the news business.

HISTORICAL HIGHLIGHT

The Age of Newsreels

The medium of film was the first method of delivering news to mass audiences in the form of moving images. In France, in 1911, Charles Pathé created the first silent film newsreel. At first, newsreels were screened in theatres weekly. However, as transportation became more efficient and film technology improved, the amount of time it took for a newsreel to reach an audience after an event was filmed diminished. Consequently, newsreels increased in number and were screened more and more frequently over the next few years. In 1914, Pathé launched the first daily newsreel. Daily newsreels were made possible by the invention of non-flammable film, called "safety film," which could be sent through the mail. During the First World War, this daily newsreel service had to be stopped because it became too dangerous to ship the newsreels from around the world on a daily basis.

The Embassy theatre in New York City was the first theatre to screen newsreels exclusively. Launching the service on November 2, 1929, just three days after the great stock market crash, the newsreels provided much desired political and economic news throughout the 1930s and 1940s—the years of the Great Depression and those leading up to the Second World War. The newsreel theatre was so popular that many others proceeded to open in major cities across the United States. Precursor to the 24-hour news format, the Embassy screened 45-minute newsreels continuously throughout the day and night, charging an entrance fee of 25 cents. As Howard Rosenberg and Charles Feldman (2008) describe, "[n]ever before had images and sounds of distant places and foreign intrigues been available so quickly—weeks, if not days, after being filmed" (37). The end of the Second World War also marked the end of the era of the newsreel, as the popularity of this medium became sidelined by the rapidly growing adoption of television.

SOURCE: Rosenberg and Feldman (2008).

One expression of this principle was the creation of the Cable News Network, more commonly known as CNN, in 1980 and, even more so, the launch of their 24-hour news service, CNN Headline News, in 1983 (Compton 2004, 73). On the one hand, CNN's 24-hour programming cycle—soon copied by BBC World News, MTV, ESPNews, MSNBC, Fox News Channel, Al Jazeera, and CBC Newsworld and CTV News in Canada—reflected what was made possible by certain "integrated technological efficiencies," such as the way the "latest computer and satellite technologies [allowed broadcasters to] integrate newswires, the assignment desk, producers, graphic rundowns, tape lists, and anchor scripts," thereby creating the 24-hour format (Compton 2004, 81). On the other hand, these developments both reflected and helped to crystallize even more significant changes that were taking place in the character of the news commodities themselves, and in ideas about what the role and purpose of news production and delivery is or should be.

The ideology of the 24-hour news format is that the faster news can be delivered to audiences, the more "newsworthy" and valuable it is. Within this logic, "live coverage," the instant and apparently unmediated transmission of events, is the model form of news commodity. The form of the 24-hour news cycle is the constant high-speed flow of images, data, information, and opinion; the imperative is to broadcast a story as fast as possible. This form, however, clashes with the mandate of journalists to provide citizens and audiences with news stories that are accurate, balanced, considered, clearly narrated, and thoroughly sourced (Rosenberg and Feldman 2008, 3). Criticizing what they describe as the "speed-for-speed's-sake mania" of contemporary news media, Rosenberg and Feldman quote Keith McAllister, former executive vice-president and managing editor of CNN's national new gathering: "every mistake that's made in the news business is made because of speed" (Rosenberg and Feldman 2008, 4). If the immediacy imperative of live coverage makes it difficult to provide audiences with even basically accurate information, more thoughtful and examined reflection on, and analysis of, the issues and events being reported becomes even more of an anachronism. As these authors argue, with the "rush-to-report herd instinct," there is "no time for cool, deliberate, thoughtful discourse" (Rosenberg and Feldman 2008, 14, 17). In this context, considered reflection on issues and events is practically abandoned in favour of delivering something more suited to a regime of speed: spectacle.

Competition among broadcasters, and an obsession with reporting information immediately, has resulted in journalism that replaces thoughtful reflection with spectacle.

Competition among broadcasters for a finite resource, namely audience attention, together with the practical challenge of filling 24 hours' worth of programming, steers news producers toward stories that are dramatic, visual, sensational, and emotionally charged. The drama of war, political scandal, a celebrity's fall from grace, a devastating natural disaster, a high-profile trial, or a gruesome accident promise solid ratings. Such stories often have the added benefit for broadcasters of being "never-ending recombinant stories" (Compton 2004, 73), or stories that continue to unfold day after day. These stories provide a great deal of reaction but little considered opinion.

Politicians and commentators who are called upon by the news media to offer explanation of issues or events are required to tailor their contributions to fit high-speed, ever-shrinking news segments, preferably as "sound bites." Unfortunately, the possibility of saying anything meaningful about a complex topic in the few seconds that a sound bite allows is practically nil. A recent US study found that the average weekday news sound bite from a presidential candidate shrank from 42.3 seconds in 1968 to 9.8 seconds in 1988. By 2000, the average was 7.8 seconds (Gitlin 2002, 96). Of course, the point is not to say anything meaningful in the sound bite at all. Politicians know that the point of the sound bite is not to explain but to convey an image, to make an impression, to strike an emotional cord with the audience.

Conclusion

Should people be concerned that high-speed media environments offer little time for sustained collective reflection and, instead, give priority to spectacular images and impressions of current events? Paul Virilio (2006) reminds us that Joseph Goebbels, Minister of Propaganda in Nazi Germany from 1933 to 1945, had this to say about strategic communication: "Propaganda must be made directly by words and images, not by writing" (31). In other words, reading implies reflection; the slowing down that reading and reflection entail destroys a mass's dynamic momentum (Virilio 2006, 31). In the case of Nazi Germany, such a slowing down of mass momentum would have been desirable. And yet, we would be hasty to pronounce that speed is inevitably a destructive social force. At the time of writing, social revolutions in Tunisia (January 2011) and Egypt (February 2011) have succeeded in deposing the respective authoritarian regimes that held those countries in stasis for decades. Digital communication media, and social networking applications in particular, played an important, instrumental role in these civil resistance campaigns, as they did in the Iranian social uprising of 2009. In all these instances, the speed of digital media greatly enhanced people's ability to mobilize and coordinate their voices and activities *en masse*—a requisite of any viable social or political entity.

These examples illustrate that speed is not an inherently positive or negative force in society. It is a significant and powerful force, but it is one of many. Its social character will be determined by the nature of the other social forces—political, economic, cultural, technological—with which it comes into play in the larger, complex movement of history.

DISCUSSION QUESTIONS

1. How is your movement through the day structured by your communication devices (your cellphone, PDA, or laptop)? With whom do you communicate in your everyday life and for what purposes? Can you imagine spending a day without your devices? How would this change the movement and pace of your day?

2. Do you think that compressed, speedy, and ephemeral modes of communication (such as text messaging, Twitter, or Facebook) have induced a shortening of attention spans among their users? Explain. Do those who are more immersed in these modes of communication see the world differently from those who are not?

3. Does the speed and ease of communication in present-day society facilitate community building among people, or does it encourage and facilitate people's isolation from one another? Imagine a scenario where the first case applies, and one where the second scenario is the case.

SUGGESTED RESOURCES

Books

Crary, Jonathan. 1999. *Suspensions of Perception: Attention, Spectacle and Modern Culture*. Cambridge, MA: MIT Press.

Hansen, Mark. 2004. *New Philosophy for New Media*. Cambridge, MA: MIT Press.

Kavka, Misha. 2008. *Reality Television, Affect and Intimacy: Reality Matters*. New York: Palgrave Macmillan.

Van Dijk, Jan. 2006. *The Network Society* (2nd ed.). Thousand Oaks, CA: Sage.

Websites

Debord, Guy. 1967. *Society of the Spectacle*. Translated by Ken Knabb, 2002. Bureau of Public Secrets. http://www.bopsecrets.org/SI/debord/index.htm.

Major, William. 2011 (January 16). "Thoreau's Cellphone Experiment." *The Chronicle of Higher Education*. http://chronicle.com/article/Thoreaus -Cellphone-Experiment/125962/.

REFERENCES

Baudrillard, Jean. 1988. *America*. New York: Verso.

Buck-Morss, Susan. 1992. "Aesthetics and Anaesthetics: Walter Benjamin's Artwork Essay Reconsidered." *October* 62:3–41.

Castells, Manuel. 2001. "The Information Economy." In *Reading Digital Culture*, edited by David Trend, 154–58. Oxford, UK: Blackwell.

Compton, James. 2004. *The Integrated News Spectacle: A Political Economy of Cultural Performance*. New York: Peter Lang.

Gitlin, Todd. 2002. *Media Unlimited: How the Torrent of Images and Sounds Overwhelms Our Lives*. New York: Henry Holt.

Harvey, David. 1989. *The Condition of Postmodernity*. Oxford, UK: Blackwell.

Marinetti, Filippo Tommaso. 1909. *The Futurist Manifesto*. Accessed February 23, 2011. http://einar_garibaldi.lhi.is/manifesto_futurista.pdf.

McLuhan, Marshall. 1964. *Understanding Media: The Extensions of Man*. New York: McGraw-Hill.

Nietzsche, Friedrich. 1882/1974. *The Gay Science*. New York: Viking Press.

Rosenberg, Howard, and Feldman, Charles. 2008. *No Time to Think: The Menace of Media Speed and the Twenty-four Hour News Cycle*. London: Continuum.

Simmel, Georg. 1903/1971. "The Metropolis and Mental Life." In *On Individuality and Social Forms*, 324–39. Chicago: University of Chicago Press.

Simmel, Georg. 1907/1978. *The Philosophy of Money*. Translated by Tom Bottomore and David Frisby. London: Routledge and Kegan Paul.

Virilio, Paul. 1997. *Open Sky*. New York: Verso.

Virilio, Paul. 2001. "Speed and Information: Cyberspace Alarm!" In *Reading Digital Culture*, edited by David Trend, 23–27. Oxford, UK: Blackwell.

Virilio, Paul. 2006. *Speed and Politics*. Los Angeles: Semiotext(e).

PART FIVE
Researching the Media

Thinking About Methods

What are the first steps when beginning to study a topic? What does it mean to "think methodologically"? What sorts of truth or knowledge can media research reveal?

KEY CONCEPTS

1. Thinking methodologically means paying attention to how a particular study was done.

2. Thinking methodologically can make you a better critical thinker.

3. The way you choose to research a topic will influence your results.

4. We not only *study* communications, but we also need to learn *how* to communicate.

CHAPTER OUTLINE

Introduction 333

Quantitative and Qualitative Methods 334

The Researcher's Toolkit 336

A Methodological Approach 337

Messy Worlds: Seeking Truth, Wisdom, Knowledge, and Understanding 338

Paradigms and Concepts 339

Literature Reviews and Research Problematics: Reading 340

Considerations for Your Study 341

Conclusion: Back to Method 346

Note 348

Discussion Questions 348

Suggested Resources 348

References 349

Introduction

When they first hear the phrase "research methods," many students immediately assume it is a synonym for "boring." It need not be so. In fact, many students later discover that undertaking a research project can be a very creative process. The goal of this paper is to instill a passion for methods, and offer some suggestions on how to *think* methodologically.

Research methods are the techniques and strategies that one selects in order to investigate a topic. "Thinking methodologically" means that you pay attention to how a particular study was designed and produced. This

research methods
The techniques and strategies that one selects in order to research a topic.

approach considers research methods and methodology to be more than simply a set of techniques that we learn, a template that we follow, or an "apparatus" that we choose and then apply to some media institution, technology, or communications practice.

Even if a method isn't made explicitly clear in an article or a text that you read—and too often, it isn't, as Jane Stokes (2003) argues in her book on methods in media studies—every author has still gone through a set of procedures or steps in order to analyze the media practice or communicative act he or she is researching. By thinking methodologically, you will learn to be aware of how the establishment of a research process necessarily influences research outcomes or results. You will be prepared to ask how that author constructed his or her study. Thinking methodologically should make you a better critical thinker, and hopefully open new potentials for your own creative research projects. As C. Wright Mills (1967) once wrote, method is not only about being rigorously scientific; it is also about learning a craft.

> **KEY CONCEPT**
>
> Thinking methodologically means paying attention to how a particular study was done.

> **KEY CONCEPT**
>
> Thinking methodologically can make you a better critical thinker.

This chapter cannot possibly do justice to any one method. Communications, media studies, and cultural studies are three intertwining fields replete with researchers who engage in a multiplicity of methods and approaches to research. We study texts and media genres; we study institutions and regulations. We research the past in order to understand the present. We understand relationships of power and ownership. We examine what people do with media and how our identities are formulated in, by, and through media. We look at representations. We listen. We observe.

The majority of the work in this field is conducted from within the social sciences and the humanities, the two dominant areas that are a part of the unique composition of communication and media studies in Canada (Shade 2009). Rather than discuss any one method, this chapter offers a series of practical tips on researching. You may find these tips very basic, rudimentary, and commonsensical. Perhaps. They are intended to speak to beginning students doing their first research project, although they may also be helpful to more advanced students.

qualitative methods
Research approach that emphasizes human interactions and processes, as opposed to numerical or statistical information.

Quantitative and Qualitative Methods[1]

The phrase "research methods" implies research as a *process*, particularly for those who practise **qualitative methods**. As Norman Denzin and Yvonne Lincoln (2000) write in their introduction to a highly recommended book on methods, the word "quality" is key: "The word qualitative implies an emphasis on the qualities of entities and on processes and meanings that are not experimentally examined or measured (if measured at all) in terms of quantity, amount, intensity or frequency" (8). In other words, qualitative methods emphasize human interactions and processes, and do not seek to reduce or translate our understanding of these processes into numerical or statistical information.

Quantitative methods, by contrast, tend to emphasize the "measurement and analysis of causal relationships between variables, not processes. … Proponents of such studies claim that their work is done from within a value-free framework" (Denzin and Lincoln 2000, 8). Although many researchers in the field do employ statistics, numbers, and data, they often use these to support an argument or claim rather than as an end in itself.

quantitative methods
Research approach that typically emphasizes measurement and data.

In the field of communications and cultural studies in Canada, the majority of work is conducted within the tradition of qualitative research. The main emphasis falls on methodologies that examine practices, processes, meaning construction, experience, and relationships of power and control. While much is often made of the distinction between quantitative and qualitative methods, in actuality researchers need to understand both.

As Darroch and Darroch (2010) argue in their critique of the demise of the long-form census survey in Canada, data are not only political but may offer important contextual information for researchers in communications. Even if you do focus on human interactions, textual forms of analysis, historical research, or institutional analysis, you should be comfortable with numbers and learn to unravel the language of statistics. It helps to see patterns and trends. Further, qualitative researchers often use statistical information in their research, and statistics are often used to make "claims." Conversely, the best in quantitative research always involves an interpretation, analysis, and contextualization of the data presented. On their own, numbers are just numbers; what matters is how numerical information is collected and presented in the analysis, and the arguments being put forth in a given article or book.

PRIMARY SOURCE

Intellectual Craftsmanship

In his classic text *The Sociological Imagination*, C. Wright Mills discusses the importance of what he calls "intellectual craftsmanship." He begins "by reminding you, the beginning student, that the most admirable thinkers within the scholarly community you have chosen to join do not split their work from their lives." They use each for the "enrichment of the other." Mills explains how he uses files to "loosen up" his own sociological imagination. Keeping files of ideas for studies you would like to carry out are a means to bring together what you are doing as a researcher and what you are observing based on your experience.

What this means is that you must learn to use your life experience in your intellectual work: continually to examine and interpret it. In this sense craftsmanship is the center of yourself and you are personally involved in every intellectual product upon which you may work. To say that you can have experience means, for one thing, that your past plays into and affects your present, and that it defines your capacity for future experience. As a social scientist, you have to control this rather elaborate interplay, to capture what you experience and sort it out; only in this way can you hope to use it to guide and test your reflection, and in the process shape yourself as an intellectual craftsman. But how can you do this? One answer is: you must set up a file, which is, I suppose, a sociologist's way of saying: keep a journal. Many creative writers keep journals; the sociologist's need for systematic reflection demands it.

In such a file as I am going to describe, there is joined personal experience and professional activities, studies under way and studies planned. In this file, you, as an intellectual craftsman, will try to get together what you are doing intellectually and what you are experiencing as a person. Here you will not be afraid to use your experience and relate it directly to various work in progress. By serving as a check on repetitious work, your file also enables you to conserve your energy. It also encourages you to capture "fringe-thoughts": various ideas which may be byproducts of everyday life, snatches of conversation overheard on the street, or, for that matter, dreams. Once noted, these may lead to more systematic thinking, as well as lend intellectual relevance to more directed experience.

SOURCE: Mills (1967, 195).

Methods
Broad theoretical frameworks researchers use to inform their analysis, such as "political economy of media," or the "isms" (feminism, for example).

The Researcher's Toolkit
Methods and Theory

On the subject of "approach," it may be useful to distinguish between a Method (with a capital M) and a methodology. **Methods** are the broad frameworks for analysis that researchers use and that inform their analytic perspective. For example, the method of political economy of the media orients us toward issues of work and labour, to relationships of power and economies, and to the dynamics of social class. Feminism, as a theory and in practice, methodologically draws attention to issues of gender and sexuality and relationships of power within communications and media. Rhetoric, or discourse, brings researchers to studies on languages, to the construction of meanings in texts, to the processes of interpretation, and the symbolic dimensions of communications, as well as to the genres and forms that they take in the print media, television, radio, or in exchanges between people on a blog site. Methods, with a capital M, are often identifiable when researchers, in writing of their method, speak of "isms." Each of these terms is a universe of concepts and a point of fervent argument and debate among academics. Methods, with a capital M, are *theoretical* in focus and tie research practice to different theoretical traditions in the field of communications or media studies.

Methodologies

In contrast to Methods, **methodologies** may be understood as much more precise and specific. There are particular techniques that become a part of the knowledge-building "toolkit" that will be acquired, expanded upon, and transformed as the researcher gains experience. For example, if we speak of *observational analysis*, we are thinking about a specific methodology that involves close listening to a community or paying close attention to a particular set of practices for a given period of time. *Interviewing* is another example of a methodology. If we engage in individual or group interviewing, we are thinking of specific ways of "gathering data" for a project through conversations that may be recorded or transcribed. Researchers who are interested in the past engage in another set of practices: historians of communications often do primary research in archives or scour very old newspapers looking for traces of information. Semioticians—those who study various types of signs, symbols, and their cultural significance—may do close readings of an advertisement, television show, or film. These are examples of methodologies for the study of communications or media. Methodologies may cross the boundaries of our paradigmatic (conceptual) frameworks that orient our research and guide our methods.

methodologies
The particular techniques that become part of the researcher's knowledge-building toolkit (such as interviewing or observational analysis).

A Methodological Approach

This chapter uses the term "approach" deliberately. Saying that one must develop and understand the methodological approach signifies the tentative footsteps we make, as researchers and perpetual students, as we move toward identifying the subject of our research, and as we ponder how best to approach it. Sometimes we move

KEY CONCEPT
The way you choose to research a topic will influence your results.

toward it in a beeline. At other moments, we might seem to circle around it; at other times, we move in a complicated to-ing and fro-ing, toward and away, as we assess and reassess a particular topic. For most of your beginning papers you will want to test and practise your craft by focusing on what one method has to offer. However, for many studies, researchers in the field often use a combination of methods. In fact, many books on qualitative methods suggest that researchers should practise what is known as **triangulation**—examining a phenomenon using three different methods, or three different points of view, to compare the results and determine whether these are the same or different. As you read through the materials on offer, ask yourself at what level the author is being explicit about her or his Method or methodology. Is the author describing a general approach? Is he naming a specific set of techniques he will follow? Does she actually do this, and does she reflect upon it?

triangulation
Examining a phenomenon using three different methods, and then comparing the results.

Messy Worlds: Seeking Truth, Wisdom, Knowledge, and Understanding

As suggested earlier in this chapter, there is a close relationship between theory and Method, but as well, between theory and methodologies. As Thomas Lindolf and Bryan Taylor (2002) point out: "Although it may not be immediately apparent to a novice, research methods form the practical technologies of larger systems of belief about the nature of reality (ontology) and about how that reality may be known (epistemology)" (7). Ontology and epistemology: these are two words that are critical for the communications researcher. Indeed, one of the key ontological assumptions in the field of communication studies is that communications, in and of itself, *matters* and is a key aspect of what we experience and perceive as reality. We tend to hold the belief that our reality, and our very being, is constituted in acts of communications. Meanwhile, epistemology asks us to ponder the basic question of what we think is knowable, and how we might come to know it.

There is an easy way to understand the importance of epistemology. Ask yourself what you think your research will reveal: the "truth" about a given practice? Knowledge of a given practice? Wisdom? Understanding? Each of these terms points to the different ways that researchers conceptualize the end-results of their research, the possibility of making generalizations and claims, and what we think is knowable. In the social sciences and humanities, we tend not to make claims that our research will reveal a particular "truth" about all human beings and for all times. The world is a messy, ever-changing place, and hence what we might claim as real for one moment or in one context may not be true for all human beings.

We tend not to claim that our research will reveal a particular "truth" about all human beings and for all times.

In the difficult but fascinating book *After Method* (2004), John Law comes to a prescient conclusion regarding methods and the limits of what is knowable. As researchers engaged in the study of communications and cultural processes, we are facing a dilemma. We are constantly stopping the flow of events and activities, and as soon as we write about a given subject, it already seems out of date. Further, we are very much a part of the processes we are studying. If language, images, and so on are a part of communications and culture, then we are not standing outside of whatever it is we seek to study and describe.

John Law (2004) suggests that the chaotic messiness of the social world demands not just one method, but a knowledge of a set of methods, or rather a set of methodological approaches, that will allow researchers to write about their subjects intelligibly, creatively, and rigorously. For students who must find an approach and an appropriate way to conduct research, methods are not just a messy business. According to Law, methods are a *delightfully* messy business that asks us to take pleasure in uncertainty and to confidently learn to be accountable, even if we are not revealing a truth that will hold for all people, at all times, in all places.

> *The messiness of the social world demands knowledge of not just one but of multiple methods.*

Paradigms and Concepts

Theory is often discussed in terms of "frameworks" or "paradigms." Theoretical paradigms, as discussed by Thomas Kuhn (1962), are systems of thought that have been developed over time. For the first-year student, paradigms are often large and difficult to grasp, so a professor might advise students to think of the concepts that are key in their own research, then ask themselves how they understand or place those concepts. A student should be prepared to *interrogate* a concept (such as democracy, for example) and see how it varies widely, depending on the paradigmatic assumptions of an author.

The "public" in Jürgen Habermas's theory of communicative action (1989) is very different from the idea of the public in the work of Nancy Fraser (1993) or the sociology of C. Wright Mills (1962), even though the concept is central for all three scholars. Likewise, the term "sign" found in Wilber Schramm's (1954) positivist framework is very different from the same term as used in the semiotics of Roland Barthes (1972). Culture, technology, media, even communications itself—these are not just dictionary terms, but concepts found within different ways of understanding, as John Durham Peters wonderfully charts in the introduction to his book, *Speaking into the Air* (1999). Understanding the key concepts in an article is key to deciphering the methodological approach of the author; articulation of key concepts is critical for any research project. Identifying the key concepts that interest you in communications will connect theory to methods. As you read through a communications text or article, ask yourself: what are the author's theoretical vocabularies and commitments? Are they sustained? Is this a theory-building project? What are the concepts? If you need help understanding a concept, a paradigm, or a method, check out keyword texts (instead of Wikipedia!). Some of the most useful reference sources in the field are keyword dictionaries, which give expanded discussions of terms from experts in our field (Williams 1996; Ambercrombie and Longhurst 2007).

Literature Reviews and Research Problematics: Reading

Once you identify a potential topic (video games and youth, for example) and a set of concepts or ideas that interest you, then reading what has been written in this area is essential. And it is important not simply to go to Wikipedia or do a Google search, but to use a library and to learn to identify credible online sources. In this respect, librarians are your best friends—they can often point you to the right databases to look in, indexes to research, or journals to search through.

If you are setting up a research project, you need to know whether the study has been done before, any debates about the research you have, and how the topic has been researched. Therefore, you must review the literature. Build a bibliography and start your reading. Even if you are not doing a research project, having a sense of the literature out there will help you to assess the quality of the article you are reading, its claim to originality or innovation, or its intervention in a set of debates.

Articles that appear in refereed books or peer-reviewed journals go through a process of assessment by others who have expertise on a subject or theory, or on methods. But when these articles are assessed, they are done so according to their contribution to the field at the time they were written. Ask yourself: when was the article written? What else has been written about this topic? What debates are the authors engaged in? In other words, the authors of a text must be able to assert with confidence that their work is "original" because the subject has not been written about, has been inadequately studied, or must be understood from a different perspective. To make this claim, we, as researchers, must read widely.

Literature reviews are often confused with theory. These areas may overlap, but they are not the same. A *literature review* is a descriptive overview pertaining to your research topic. Researchers who write in the tradition of the social sciences and humanities must often engage in a debate, dialogue, or discussion with other authors—not directly, but through the ideas in their texts. Learn what a literature review is, and how to do it. When you do a literature review, you are taking the step of defining a topic that interests you, and you are seeing what others have written about it.

Planning a literature review allows you to set up this dialogue and debate. You can do a literature review of the theories, or of a set of methods. This means surveying the work that has been done, and what is most up to date. Literature reviews tend to be more descriptive and cluster research together into ways that enable you to detect patterns. Without an adequate literature review, you cannot come up with a thesis statement, or a tentative hypothesis.

Considerations for Your Study

Which Method for Which Topic?

Researchers in communications, media studies, or cultural studies engage in a number of activities that Thomas Lindolf and Bryan Taylor (2002) name quite simply as:

- observing, learning, and reporting
- asking, listening, and telling
- reading, analyzing, and interpreting.

It is paramount that you pay attention to how and where an author has "collected" his or her information: was it by watching people? If so, who? Was it by asking questions? If so, were the questions asked to an individual or a group? Was information collected by reading about this group in a particular medium? If so, then by what methods has the group been represented? By researching its history? If so, in what archive, using which documents and sources? If you are looking at types of films or television shows, what source materials will you have access to: the shows themselves? The reviews written about them? Pay attention to how a researcher has gathered his or her information. Knowing where information was collected, and how it was collected, will help you to assess the quality of an article that you are reading.

The Politics of Ethics

Ethics in media research is too vast and important a topic to be covered adequately in an introductory chapter like this one. But even beginning students should be aware of this dimension of research.

Researchers who study or interview people must acquire the formal, written consent of their "human subjects" when undertaking a project. Research practices are governed, in the academic setting, by a set of protocols that try to ensure that researchers do not exploit their subjects, or misuse or abuse the information they gather. As researchers, we are under an obligation to ensure that we do not put our subjects "at risk"—that no harm comes to a subject because of our research. For these reasons, researchers must negotiate how they will represent their subjects in a study. For example, as a point of confidentiality, subjects may request that their real names not be used in a published study to protect their privacy.

If you are going to embark on a pilot interview in a class or for an honours thesis, be very aware that you will need to know the ethics protocols that your university department has in place. These rules and protocols are particularly important when studying populations—for example, subjects who are young or who have historically experienced oppression or subjugation by those who have power. For example, in the Canadian context, a history of domination and racism means that many First Nations people are rightfully concerned about who gains access to their information and how researchers represent First Nations communities.

"How" Questions and "Why" Questions

How we ask questions is crucial.

Setting up a research question is a crucial aspect. What are the things that you want to know, and how will you ask them? How we ask questions is crucial. Gaye Tuchman (1994) makes a crucial distinction between a "how" question and a "why" question. For example, if you are interested in online journalism, you may ask *why* journalists use a cellphone. However, you may also ask *how* they use a cellphone, when they use it, and under what circumstances. The first question leads to a causal explanation: "I use it because it is convenient." "How" questions lead to a discussion of process: "I use it in the field to send photos, and to transmit a story. I don't compose on my cellphone, but I use it to be in contact with those who give me an assignment, to make appointments, or to arrange meeting times." A "why" question leads to answers that explain motivation or causality; a "how" question leads to a discussion of practices and processes.

One pitfall is to ask a question that invites only a yes-or-no answer, or a single-word answer. For example: *Do journalists use cellphones or wireless mobile media?* Such a question leaves no room for research or subtlety, and thus should be avoided. When you are reading an article, ask: have the authors been explicit about their research question or questions? How do they ask their questions? Do they answer them? What "evidence" or support do they provide to build an argument and answer their questions?

The Thesis Statement as a Provisional Guess

As writers and scholars, when we develop an article we often begin with a set of questions. But by the time we have done our research we also start to

PRIMARY SOURCE

"How" and "Why" Questions

Gaye Tuchman writes that in "historical research, as in all kinds of research, the data to be used depend on the question the researcher wishes to answer and the information the researcher can find to answer questions." She advises that we also need to consider how we ask a question.

> Often it is more difficult to discern patterns in qualitative data, but qualitative data are richer: They are likely to be meaning-ful(l)—more likely to let a researcher see how a social world seemed and felt to a variety of its members. They are more likely to reveal process. Some scientists believe that the key scientific question is how, not why. For instance, evolutionary biologists believe that *why* tends to devolve into a search for origins, whereas *how* enables comments about process.

SOURCE: Tuchman (1964, 312).

find some answers, make claims, or build an argument. We develop what is known as a **thesis statement**—an articulation of a position or point of view that will serve as a theme throughout an article or book. The proposition by McLuhan (1964), for example, that the "the medium is the message" is not only a theory about the media; it acts as a thesis statement for his book *Understanding Media*, a theme that is explored in different ways in each of the chapters. Developing a thesis statement is vitally important. It articulates how you, as the author of a particular piece of writing, understand your position, whether you are able to summarize your main point and argument, and whether you are clear about the contribution or intervention of your research into a set of debates.

thesis statement
An articulation of a position or point of view that will serve as a theme throughout an article or book.

Scope

We all make decisions about how extensive our study will be. Will we look at one story of the media coverage of disasters, or will we compare how these stories changed over time in one newspaper? Will we compare how a particular news event was covered in the Canadian press with how it was covered in European newspapers? Any project involves defining its scope, for example, the range of locations studied and the number of people.

The scope of a project depends on your timeframe and your resources. If you have a three-year project and unlimited funds, then the scope can be large. But if you have two weeks or a month to do your research, then you must narrow the scope of your study. All studies are limited, and all researchers must make decisions. The most important point is that you are aware of the limitations of your study and that you are able to articulate to your readers a rationale for those limitations. The scope of your research may also be related to the genre in which you are writing: a book is, of course, longer than an article and will allow greater depth and coverage of your topic.

Evidence

Thinking about communications can involve formulating an argument and suggesting that you have found some type of "evidence" to back up your assertion or claim. First-year students will largely rely on the research of experts in the field who have done studies. Here it is important, again, to be able to assess what has been said about a given subject. In other words, you will mainly rely on what is known as *secondary sources* to make claims—for example, about corporate concentration in the Canadian media. And here, again, the important point is to be able to identify the source of the information, as well as the perspective from which the source's research has been gathered, developed, and written up. In the field of mobile communications, for example, the wireless industry generates one set of data, while researchers studying ownership and access may question the industry's figures. If you are making a claim, you must know how to back it up with some evidence to support or to refute it.

In assessing the claims of others, you must ask: What does the author take as evidence? And how does that evidence relate back to the central claim?

Write Now

One essay that all students of media should read is Laurel Richardson's "Writing: A Method of Inquiry" (2000). In it, Richardson talks about how she has yawned her way through articles. She points out that in writing we actually learn what we might have to say. We clarify our thoughts, come up with new ideas. Writing is not a mopping-up project after the research is done. It is part of the procedure for qualitative methods. Richardson gives tips for writing exercises. She distinguishes between types of note-taking (theoretical notes; observational notes; methodological notes; personal notes), and suggests you go through your own work and see what kind of observations and intuitions you are making about a given subject.

Richardson's primary recommendation is not to leave the writing until the end of a project, after the research has been done. The research is never done; as John Law (2004) suggests, you are always in the middle of something.

When we try to write our work, we begin to generate our own thoughts and ideas. We become aware of what we know and do not know. And to go back to C. Wright Mills (1967), writing is a craft that must be learned and must be practised. It is only by doing it that you will improve. This point is particularly important for communications: we not only *study* communications, but we also need to learn *how* to communicate.

PRIMARY SOURCE

Field Notes for Media Studies

In her essay, "Writing: A Method of Inquiry," Laurel Richardson advises that writing up your field notes is an opportunity to expand your writing, vocabulary, habits of thought, and attentiveness to your senses. It is how to develop your "voice."

Building on work in *grounded theory* by Glaser and Strauss (1967), Richardson identifies four categories of notes that are of value. Even if you are not conducting field research but are simply scouring the secondary literature, you may find her discussion of these useful. Try using her approach to go through your notes for a research paper you have written. Can you identify whether you have made an observational, methodological, theoretical, or personal note?

Observational notes (ON): These are as concrete and detailed as I am able to make them. I want to think of them as fairly accurate renditions of what I see, hear, feel, taste and so on. I stay close to the scene as I experience it through my senses.

Methodological notes (MN): These are messages to myself regarding how to collect "data"—who to talk to, what to wear, when to phone, and so on. I write a lot of these because I like methods, and I like to keep a process diary of my work.

Theoretical notes (TN): These are hunches, hypotheses, poststructuralist connections, critiques of what I am doing/thinking/seeing. I like writing these because they open my field note texts to alternative interpretations and a critical epistemological stance. They provide a way of keeping me from being hooked on one view of reality.

Personal notes (PN): These are uncensored feeling statements about the research, the people I am talking to, my doubts, my

> anxieties, my pleasures. I want all my feelings out on paper because I know they are affecting what/how I lay claim to know. I also know they are a great source for hypotheses; if I am feeling a certain way in a setting, it is likely that others might feel that way too. Finally, writing personal notes is a way for me to know myself better, a way of using writing as a method of inquiry into the self.
>
> SOURCE: Richardson (2000, 941).

If you are having trouble writing, start with what you know. Do not worry about starting from the beginning. Start with a description of your project, your ideas. Work on outlines. Keep your thesis statement in front of you so that you can keep track of it, and revise it as you begin to cobble together your notes into a paper. Write up imaginary scenarios and think where they might take you. Whom do I imagine my interlocutors to be? How do I use evidence and make claims? How do I integrate the text? How do I imagine its structure? Finally, you must consider the question of "audience": whom do I imagine as my ideal reader?

Thinking methodologically also means that you pay attention to how the authors you are reading practise the craft of writing themselves. Do they use the first person? Do they write poetically? Do they rely on description? Do they use metaphors—if so, what are they? How do these authors structure their papers or books? Do they write in a way that convinces you? If so, what is it about their writing that persuades you?

Conclusion: Back to Method

A student once asked, "What is a method?" The simplest answer is that in thinking about a method, we pay attention to *how* we do *what* we do. Writing up a method is about making decisions early on about how you will do something. A methodological account means that you are prepared to be accountable—intellectually, ethically, and politically—for the choices you have made and will make. No method will ever fully explain everything we do as communications scholars. Method is, at its core, about being accountable for our research process, to our research subjects, and to our community of peers. It involves, perhaps, not the pursuit of ultimate truths, but at a minimum, it will lead us to a better understanding of the world of media, communications, or culture. It can remind us that knowledge isn't out there for us to find, but that we are complicit in its creation. Method can be an

> **SIDEBAR**
>
> ## Thinking Methodologically: A Checklist
>
> Thinking "methodologically" means learning to analyze and understand how a program of research generates knowledge. When reading any article or text in terms of method, you may ask yourself some of these questions:
>
> 1. What methodology or methodologies are used?
> 2. Is the methodology stated explicitly and discussed in detail, or is it implied by the work?
> 3. Was it employed in a consistent and rigorous fashion?
> 4. Was it appropriate for the study?
> 5. What kind of information or knowledge does the method give us about the phenomenon under study?
> 6. For whom was this work written?
> 7. What theoretical and epistemological assumptions are implied by the use of this method?
> 8. What are the political or ethical questions raised by this research?
> 9. Was the information interpreted and analyzed in an effective manner?
> 10. Are the claims following the argument supported by the evidence?
> 11. Is the work persuasive? Consistent? Coherent?
> 12. What are the researcher's conclusions, and are they consistent with the interpretation?
> 13. What further research could be conducted in light of the approach developed by the researcher?
> 14. What strategies of writing does the researcher use?

inventive intellectual act. It demands that we be rigorous, yet flexible, in our approach to research in communications.

Method can be an inventive intellectual act.

Thinking methodologically asks us to be aware not only of what we find, but how we collect, organize, and analyze our data; how we represent, communicate, and configure our research; how we make arguments and muster evidence to make a claim. We must also acknowledge that in choosing a methodological approach, or set of approaches, we are necessarily involved in an act of pointing out to our readers what is, or may be, significant.

Thinking methodologically is essential for the production of our own research. But being attuned to questions of methods is also essential for engaging in the task of assessing the validity of the research that we are reading. Even if you never embark on your own study of methods, paying attention to how a study has been set up—asking what its aims and scope might be, who it is written for, what its sample was—engages us in the politics of knowledge and knowledge production. Research results do not just exist; they are made in collaboration, and as a result of the methods chosen.

NOTE

1. For more on the methods in media studies, please consult the Suggested Resources at the end of this chapter.

DISCUSSION QUESTIONS

1. Before you read this chapter, what did the term "research methods" mean to you? What does it mean to you now that you have read the chapter?
2. Identify an incident or event from your personal experience that you might wish to turn into a research paper. How would you go about researching it?
3. Select two articles from peer-reviewed journals that appeal to you. One must be a social science article, the other from a more humanities-oriented journal. Using the checklist on page 347 in this chapter, compare the articles. What are your findings?

SUGGESTED RESOURCES

Baxter, Leslie, and Earl Babbie. 2004. *The Basics of Communication Research.* Toronto: Thomson/Nelson.

Baxter, Lorraine, Christina Hughes, and Malcolm Tight. 1999. *How to Research.* Buckingham, UK: Open University Press.

Deacon, David, Michael Pickering, Peter Golding, and Graham Murdock. *Researching Communications: A Practical Guide to Methods in Media and Cultural Analysis.* New York: Oxford University Press.

Descombe, Martyn. 1998. *The Good Research Guide for Small-Scale Social Research Projects.* Buckingham, UK: Open University Press.

Devereux, Eoin. 2003. *Understanding the Media.* Thousand Oaks, CA: Sage.

du Gay, Paul, Stuart Hall, Linda James, Hugh Mackay, and Keith Negus. 1997. *Doing Cultural Studies: The Story of the Sony Walkman.* Buckingham, UK: Open University Press.

Hearn, Greg, Jo Tacchi, Marcus Foth, and Jane Lennie, 2009. *Action Research and New Media: Concepts, Methods, Cases.* Cresskill, NJ: Hampton Press.

Merrigan, Gerianne, and Carole L. Huston. 2009. *Communication Research Methods* (2nd ed.). New York: Oxford University Press.

O'Sullivan, Tim, Brian Dutton, and Philip Raynar. 2003. *Studying the Media* (3rd ed.). Oxford: Oxford University Press.

Scannell, Paddy. 2008. *Media and Communication.* Thousand Oaks, CA: Sage.

REFERENCES

Ambercrombie, Nicholas, and Brian Longhurst. 2007. *Dictionary of Media Studies.* London: Penguin.

Barthes, Roland. 1972. *Mythologies,* translated by Annette Lavers. New York: Hill and Wang.

Darroch, Michael, and Gordon Darroch. 2010. "Losing Our Census." *Canadian Journal of Communication* 35(4):609–17.

Denzin, Norman K., and Yvonna Lincoln. 2000. "Introduction: The Discipline and Practice of Qualitative Research." In *Handbook of Qualitative Research* (2nd ed.), 1–30. Thousand Oaks, CA: Sage.

Fraser, Nancy. 1993. "Rethinking the Public Sphere: A Contribution to the Critique of Actually Existing Democracy." In *The Phantom Public Sphere*, edited by Bruce Robbins, 1–32. Minneapolis: University of Minnesota Press.

Habermas, Jürgen. 1989. "The Public Sphere." In *Jürgen Habermas on Society and Politics: A Reader*, edited by Steven Seidman, 231–36. Boston: Beacon Press.

Kuhn, Thomas. 1962. *The Structure of Scientific Revolutions.* Chicago: University of Chicago Press.

Law, John. 2004. *After Method: Mess in Social Science Research.* New York: Routledge.

Lindlof, Thomas, and Bryan Taylor. 2002. *Qualitative Research Methods* (2nd ed.). Thousand Oaks, CA: Sage.

McLuhan, Marshall. 1964. "The Medium Is the Message." In *Understanding Media: The Extensions of Man*, 7–21. Toronto: McGraw-Hill.

Mills, C. Wright. 1962. "The Mass Society." In *The Power Elite*, 298–324. Oxford, UK: Oxford University Press.

Mills, C. Wright. 1967. *The Sociological Imagination.* London: Oxford University Press.

Peters, John Durham. 1999. *Speaking into the Air: A History of the Idea of Communication.* Chicago: University of Chicago Press.

Richardson, Laurel. 2000. "Writing: A Method of Inquiry." In *Handbook of Qualitative Research* (2nd ed.), 923–49. Thousand Oaks, CA: Sage.

Schramm, Wilbur. 1954. "How Communication Works." In *The Process and Effects of Mass Communication*, 3–26. Urbana, IL: University of Illinois Press.

Shade, Leslie Regan, ed. 2009. *Mediascapes: New Patterns in Canadian Communication* (3rd ed.). Toronto: Nelson Canada.

Stokes, Jane. 2003. *How to Do Media and Cultural Studies*. Thousand Oaks, CA: Sage.

Tuchman, Gaye. 1964. "Historical Social Science: Methodologies, Methods and Meanings." In *Handbook of Qualitative Research*, edited by Norman K. Denzin and Yvonna S. Lincoln, 306–23. Thousand Oaks, CA: Sage.

Williams, Raymond. 1996. *Keywords: A Vocabulary of Culture and Society*. London: Fontana Press.

Index

3D cinema, 130
3D IMAX, 130
3G networks, 85
9/11, 143
24-hours news service, 324–26
1984, 46
2001: A Space Odyssey, 107

A

ABC, 244
Aboriginal culture, 56, 58, 186–87
Access Copyright, 154
accounting, 58
Adorno, Theodor, 21, 22, 54, 64, 66, 138, 166
advertising, 280–82
aestheticization, 271
After Method, 339
agenda setting, 59, 246
Aird Commission, 124, 164
Al Jazeera, 144, 200, 245, 325
All Day, 173–74
All the President's Men, 248
Allen, Mark, 89
Almanac Singers, 208
alternative media
    as a channel to express identity, 211–13
    as a means of organizing cultural production,
        209–11
    as a source of radical content, 206–9
    as a tool of struggle, 203–6
    defined, 199–201
    differentiated from mainstream media,
        201–3
    empowerment, and, 80
Althusser, Louis, 118
Amazing Race, The, 301
Amazon.com, 190, 224
American Idol, 65, 301, 302

analogue format, 227
Anderson, Benedict, 14, 241, 276
Andrejevic, Mark, 302
Angry Birds, 79
annihilation of space, 309, 316
AOL, 140, 256
Appeal to the Colored Citizens of the World, 199
Arcade Fire, 155
Archaeology of Knowledge, 26
Arnold, Matthew, 165
Arvidsson, Adam, 273, 279
ASCAP, 158
attribution, 185
aura, 22
Avatar, 130

B

Baez, Joan, 208
Bagdikian, Ben H., 145, 250
Bakhtin, Mikhail, 93, 94, 95, 105
Barthes, Roland, 22, 32, 339
bastard pop, 174
Battle in Seattle, 198
Bazin, André, 125
BBC, 41, 105, 163, 164, 254, 255, 257, 325
Beatles, The, 61
Being Digital, 188
Bell, David, 278
Bell Media, 140
Bellour, Raymond, 60
Benedict, Ruth, 221
Benjamin, Walter, 22, 125, 320
Berger, Bennett, 221
Bernstein, Carl, 248
bewildered herd, 29
Bias of Communication, The, 27, 117
big brother, 233
Big Brother, 301, 302

binding spaces, 37, 47–51
biotechnology, 190–92
BitTorrent, 189, 190
BlackBerry, 85, 275
blasé attitude, 320
Blink, 205
Bliven, Bruce, 102
blog, 63, 79, 80, 143, 151, 202, 205, 259, 291, 303
Blondheim, Menahem, 48
BMI, 158
Boczkowski, Pablo, 255
body language, 79
Bolter, Jay David, 67, 83
boob tube, 224
Book-of-the-Month Club, 40
Boon, Marcus, 192, 193
bootleg, 174
bourgeois public sphere, 26
Bowling Alone, 13
boyd, danah, 291
brand community, 275
brands, 270–71, 280–82
Brands, 279
Broadcasting Act, 154, 159, 165
Broken Social Scene, 156
Brown, James, 208
Brownie Camera, 297, 302
Buck-Morss, Susan, 320
Burke, Edmund, 247
Bush, George W., 144
Butler, Judith, 290
Buying the War, 246

C

cable television, 224, 245
calendar journalism, 254
Camera Lucida, 22
Canada Music Fund, 156
Canada Radio-television and
    Telecommunications Commission, 160, 161
Canada–US Free Trade Agreement, 155
Canadian Association of Broadcasters, 154
Canadian Broadcasting Act, 124
Canadian Charter of Rights and Freedoms, 162
Canadian culture, 163

Canadian Idol, 275
Canadian Newspaper Association, 140
Carey, James, 23, 103, 120, 221, 241
Carpenter, Edmund, 99
carrier pigeon, 311–12
Castells, Manuel, 314
cave analogy, 7–9, 31–32
CBC, 81, 82, 124, 142, 146, 167, 200, 275, 325
CBS, 157, 244
cease and desist letter, 183
cellphones, 224, 304, 318
centre–periphery relations, 319
Chaney, David, 270
Chartist movement, 199
Cherry, Don, 147
Chicago School, 28
children's rhymes, 97
chilling effect, 183, 184
chip manufacturers, 224
Chomsky, Noam, 23, 145
Chuck D, 299
CHUM Group, 140
CHUM Radio, 140
cinema, 126–31
    see also film
cinematic apparatus, 60
citizen journalist, 259
civil society, 246
Clarke, Arthur C., 107
"Clash of Ignorance, The," 293
client–server, 189
cloud, data, 17
CNN, 41, 200, 245, 299, 325, 326
Cobbe, Frances Power, 203
code-switching, 104
Cognitive Surplus, 33
Coleman, Kit, 241
Coleridge, Samuel Taylor, 67
Colored American, The, 199
comic book, 42
comics, 54
commodity-signs, 274
commons, 176, 177
Communication as Culture, 23, 120
Communications, 33

communications, *see also* media
    accounting, and, 58
    biases, 78–80, 117–18
    cultural practice, 115, 120, 222
    media, effect on, 3–18
    mediation, and, 73, 74–76
    political economy approach to, 23, 30
    raw material of, 76
communicative function, 74, 78, 85
Communist Manifesto, The, 30
community media, 200–1
computer operating systems, 224
concentration, 138, 140–41
consumer culture, 271–72
consumer society, 312
Consuming Media, 274
Contemporary Review, 203
content analysis, 59
content producer, 137
Contribution to a Critique of Political Economy, 30
convergence culture, 68
convergence, 138–39, 226, 227, 248–50
Cooke, Sam, 208
Coombe, Rosemary, 186
copyright, 158, 174–85
Copyright Act (Can.), 180, 184
Copyright Act (US), 179
Copyrights and Copywrongs, 176
Cornish, Samuel E., 199
couch potatoes, 224
counterculture, 296
Cradle Will Rock, The, 208
Craig, Geoffrey, 279
Creative Commons, 187, 188, 193
creative workers, 66
critical space, 315
critical theory, 21, 26, 30
crowdsourcing, 258
CTV, 65, 139, 207, 325
cultural consumption, 272
cultural divide, 50
cultural industries, 64–65
cultural logic, 310
cultural materialism, 33
cultural ownership, 173–93

cultural production, 209–11
cultural sovereignty, 164
culture
    communication, and, 222–23
    defined, 219, 220–22
    new media, and, 225–26, 233–35
    old media, and, 223–25
    Quebec, 49–51
    shifts in, 226–33
culture industry, 54, 64
culture production, 64, 219, 230–33

D

Daily Mail, The, 241
Daily Show, The, 61, 205
Darnton, Robert, 58
Das Kapital, 30
data cloud, 17
Davey, Keith, 249
decoding, 27
definitional determinism, 203
Democracy Now!, 207
Department of Homeland Security, 158
Derakhshan, Hossein, 151, 152
Des Moines Register, 125
Detroit Free Press, 128
Dewey, John, 24, 165
Dialectic of Enlightenment, 21, 138
dialogism, 89, 93–94, 98
digital divide, 303
Digital Millennium Copyright Act, 180
digital natives, 297
digital platform, 144
digital projection, 130
digitalization, 44, 226, 227, 255–57, 312, 313, 314
Digitizing the News, 255
DiNucci, Darcy, 62, 63
dis-intermediated, 228
Discipline and Punish, 26
discourse, 25, 165, 202, 207, 298
Discourse Networks 1800/1900, 101
disempowerment, 81
dissemination, 56
distance, abolition of, 46
dominant discourse, 202

dominant reading, 27
Douglas, Mary, 221
Douglas, Susan, 24, 123, 159
Downing, John, 200
dromocratic society, 318, 319
DVDs, 80, 268
DXing, 123, 124
Dylan, Bob, 208
dystopian society, 13

E

eBay, 44
eco-makeover, 279
eco-reality, 279
economic convergence, 226
economies of scale, 139
Edison Manufacturing, 126
Edison, Thomas, 126–28, 129
Egyptian uprising, 63, 81, 204–5, 206
Ehrenreich, Barbara, 295
Eiffel Tower, 312
Eisenstein, Elizabeth, 14, 25, 100, 115, 116, 199
electronic age, 63
Electronic Frontier Foundation, 183
elitism, 147, 165
Ellul, Jacques, 62
embedded reporters, 144
Empire, The, 241
empowering function, 74, 80, 85
encoding, 27
Engels, Friedrich, 30, 295
Enlightened Sexism, 24
epistemological approach, 53, 338
essentialism, 290–91
Estrada, Joseph, 203–4
ethics, politics of, 341–42
evidence formulation, 344
expressive maintenance, 284

F

Facebook, 4, 14, 41, 44, 45–47, 61, 63, 81, 83, 84,
   135, 136, 158, 202, 205, 224, 227, 233, 269, 273,
   276, 291, 297, 304, 324
FACTOR, 156
fair dealing, 181, 183

fair use, 181, 183
famille Plouffe, La, 50
FAN 590, The, 139
Federal Communications Commission, 157, 161
Feed the Animals, 175
Feist, 106
Feldman, Charles, 311, 325, 326
feminism, 24, 25, 290
Feminist International Radio Endeavor, 212
Fenton, Faith, 241
field notes, 345–46
film, 60–61, 101
      see also cinema
Fiore, Quentin, 30
First World War, 163, 325
Fisher, William, 177
Fiske, John, 224, 296
Flickr, 188, 205
Flight Stop, 182
floppy disk, 116
flow, 226, 314, 321
Fluxus movement, 67
form of medium, 53, 55–61, 68, 116
formal analysis, 54, 60
format, 53, 54, 55, 63–66, 68
Förnas, Johan, 274
fortress journalism, 257
Foucault, Michel, 25, 153, 165, 291
fourth estate, 247
Fox News Channel, 325
fragmentation, 204
"Fragmented Future," 62
Franklin, Aretha, 208
Fraser, Nancy, 303, 339
Fraser's Magazine, 203
Free Culture movement, 175
Free Software Foundation, 189
Friends of Canadian Broadcasting, 141
Friendster, 63
Futurist Manifesto, The, 317

G

Galloway, Alexander, 190
Gans, Herbert, 241
gatekeeper, 246

Gates, Bill, 136
Gay Science, The, 317
Geertz, Clifford, 227
German Ideology, The, 295
Gillett, James, 210–11
Gillis, Gregg, 173–75
Girl Talk, 173–75
Gitelman, Lisa, 115
Gitlin, Todd, 310, 311, 321
Gladwell, Malcolm, 205, 206
Global Media Monitoring and Analysis
    Laboratory, 141
*Global Report on the Status of Women in the News
    Media*, 252
global village, 63, 316, 317
globalization, 138, 141–42, 312, 313, 315, 316
Globe and Mail, The, 139, 255
GNU/Linux Free Software, 187
Goebbels, Joseph, 327
Goggin, Gerard, 283
Golde, David, 191
Gone with the Wind, 131
Google, 14, 188, 224, 231, 234, 340
Google News, 256
Gordon, Wendy J., 178
gramophone, 101
Gramophone, Film, Typewriter, 101
Gramsci, Antonio, 26
graven image, 10
Great Depression, 325
Grebe Tone radio, 113, 114, 128
Gregg Gillis Day, 175
grounded theory, 345
Grusin, Richard A., 67, 83
Guardian, The, 258
Gutenberg, Johannes, 14, 98–99
gutter press, 79

H

Habermas, Jürgen, 13, 14, 26, 58, 246, 303, 339
HaidaBucks Café, 187
Haitian earthquake, 14
HAL 9000, 107
Hall, Stuart, 26, 30, 60, 292, 293, 294, 301
Hamilton, Sheryl, 158

Harley Davidson motorcycles, 275
Hartford Courant, 297
Hartley, John, 252
Harvey, David, 313, 314, 315, 316, 317
Havelock, Eric, 15, 96, 103
Hear It Now, 244
Hebdige, Dick, 57
hegemony, 26, 294
Here Comes Everybody, 33
Herman, Edward, 23, 145
Hesmondhalgh, David, 64
heteroglossia, 94
Higgins, Dick, 67
Hills, The, 301, 302
hip hop, 298–300
historical materialism, 30, 33
historicize function, 83, 85
History of Sexuality, The, 26
Hockey Night in Canada, 147
Hodge, Bob, 207
Hollows, Joanne, 278
home movies, 232
Hooked on Classics, 174
Horkheimer, Max, 21, 138, 166
Horner, George, 126
Horrocks, Peter, 257
Howsam, Leslie, 101
Huffington Post, 140, 156

I

iconoclasm, 10
ideology, 114, 117, 118, 119, 289, 294
ideology of immediacy–instantaneity, 319
ideology of progress, 119–20
idiolect, 95
Illegal Art website, 173
illegal literature, 58
Indymedia, 207
image
    intercession of, 10
    mediated, 31
    suspicion toward, 9–10
imagined community, 241, 275, 276
immediacy, 318, 319
Imperial Copyright Act, 180

Independent Media Centre, 198
individuated purposes, 123
information
    flows, 226, 314, 321
    processing, 43
    storage, 43
    transmission, 43
information superhighway, 314
Ingram, Mathew, 206
Innis, Harold, 23, 27, 30, 31, 78, 116, 117, 118, 131, 138, 152, 156, 223
instantaneity, 318, 319
instrument of communication, 29
intellectual property, 158, 177–78
interactivity, 157
interconnectedness, 226
interface, 53, 54, 61–63, 68
intermedia, 67
Internet, 44, 62, 63, 64, 65, 80, 103, 104, 148, 157, 158, 160, 161, 205, 227–35, 272, 282, 303, 314
Internet service provider, 190
intertextuality, 273, 298
interviewing, 337
investigative journalism, 248
iPad, 113, 114, 128, 257
iPhone, 85, 106, 275, 282, 283
iPod, 61, 78, 267, 269
Iraq War, 144, 145, 245, 248
It Gets Better Project, 300, 301
iTunes, 61, 80, 106, 190, 224, 228

J
Jackson, Janet, 157
Jansson, André, 272
Jazz Singer, The, 129
Jenkins, Henry, 67, 68
Jersey Shore, 301
Jobs, Steve, 136
journalism
    defined, 240
    democratic function, 246–55
    diversity in, 250–54
    forms of, 242–46
    fortress journalism, 257–60
    news, defined, 240–42

online transition, 255–57
profession of, 259, 260
traditional role, 239–40
women, 19th century, 253
just-in-time production, 314

K
Kellner, Douglas, 139
Kelly, Florence Finch, 253
Kent, Tom, 249
Kindle, 105, 257
kinetoscope, 126, 127
King James Bible, 222
King, Martin Luther, 208
Kittler, Friedrich, 15, 16, 18, 28, 43, 101, 104, 105
Klaehn, Jeffrey, 146
Klein, Naomi, 143, 271
Kovach, Bill, 240, 242
Kress, Gunther, 207
Kuhn, Thomas, 339

L
Labov, William, 95
langue, 91–93, 107
Lasswell, Harold, 28, 76, 163, 165
Law, John, 339, 344
Lazarsfeld, Paul, 59
LCD Soundsystem, 3
Leiss, William, 280
Leonardi, Paul, 283
Lessig, Lawrence, 175, 177
liberal media, 142
lifestyle media, 267, 277–80
Lindolf, Thomas, 338, 341
Ling, Rich, 283
lingua franca, 105
linguistic competence, 92
linguistic performance, 92
linguistic universality, 105
link economy, 257
Lippmann, Walter, 24, 29, 163, 165
Listening In, 24
literature reviews, 340
lonelygirl15, 12–13
long tail, media, 43

Lowenthal, Leo, 5, 6, 11
Luhmann, Niklas, 17
Lury, Celia, 271
Luther, Martin, 199

M

M-PESA, 304
Mad Men, 274
Madness and Civilization, 26
mainstream media, 201–3
Manovich, Lev, 176
manufacture of consent, 29, 224
Manufacturing Consent, 23, 145
Marinetti, F.T., 317
Marley, Bob, 208
Martineau, Harriet, 203
Marvin, Carolyn, 29, 83
Marx, Karl, 30, 294, 295
Marxism, 33, 118, 294
Marxism and Literature, 33
mashup, 174, 175, 227
mass media, 73, 75
Massey Commission, 167
McAllister, Keith, 326
McChesney, Robert, 137, 140, 142, 144, 250
McClintock, Anne, 292
McCracken, Grant, 272
McLuhan, Marshall, 16, 23, 28, 30, 31, 51, 62, 63,
    83, 91, 96, 97, 98, 116, 118, 131, 156, 316, 317,
    321–24
media, *see also* communications
    alternative, *see* alternative media
    as an industry, 136
    binding effect, 37, 47–51
    consumption habits, 41, 267–84
    cultural ownership, and, 173–93
    culture, *see* new media culture; old media
        culture
    forgetfulness of, 42
    form, 53, 54, 55–61, 68
    format, 53, 55, 63–66, 68
    functionality, 73–86
    historicity of, 83, 85
    instrumentality, 74
    interface, 53, 54, 61–63, 68
    language as, 89–108
    long tail of, 43
    mainstream, *see* mainstream media
    news, *see* journalism; news media
    paradox of, 14–15
    political economy approach to, 23, 30, 135–48
    preservation role, 42
    public service function, 81–82
    regulation of, 151–68
    representation, and, 289–305
    research, *see* media research
    space/time biases, 27, 37–51, 79, 117
    spatiality aspect, 37, 45–47
    studies, approaches to, 77
    technologies, changes to, 113–31
    temporality aspect, 37, 38–45
media bias, 27, 28, 37–51, 79, 117
media consolidation, 249–50
Media Control, 23
media effects paradigm, 38, 77
media history
    de-familiarization, and, 114
    old and new technologies, relationship, 114,
        116
    remediation, 114
Media Monopoly, The, 250
media policy, 153
media research
    ethics, and, 341–42
    evidence formulation, 344
    literature reviews, 340–41
    methodological approach, 337–38
        checklist, 347
    methodologies, 337
    note taking, 344–46
    qualitative methods, 334–35
    quantitative methods, 334, 335
    questions, use of, 342, 343
    research methods, 333–34, 336–37, 346–48
        choice of, 341
    scope of, 343–44
    theoretical paradigms, and, 339–40
    thesis statement, 342
Media Studies 3.0, 66
mediated images, 31

mediation, 73, 74–76, 91, 115
mediatization of consumption, 269, 272–74
Medium Is the Message, The, 30
methodological notes, 345
methodological thinking, 334, 337–38
methodologies, 337
Metric, 156
Metz, Christian, 60
Meyrowitz, Joshua, 116
microblogging, 259
microcoordination, 283
Mill, John Stuart, 59
Miller, Terry, 300, 301
Miller, Toby, 66
Mills, C. Wright, 334, 335–36, 339, 345
miscommunication, 73, 79–80
mobile commerce, 282
mobile consumption, 282
mobile phones, 282–84
mobile technology, 103, 104
Moglen, Eben, 189
monoglossia, 95
Monsanto, 192
Moore, John, 191
moral rights, 181, 182
Morozov, Evgeny, 205
Morse code, 23
Mosco, Vincent, 148
movable type printing, 25
Moyers, Bill, 246
MSNBC, 245, 325
MTV, 325
Mubarak, Hosni, 205, 206
muckraking, 242, 248
Mulvey, Laura, 60
Murdoch, Rupert, 142
Murrow, Edward R., 244
Music Entrepreneur Program, 156
music, 56–58
MySpace, 63
Mythologies, 22
myths, 241

N
Napster, 189–90
NBC, 244

Necessary Illusions, 23
Ned's Atomic Dustbin, 10
negotiated reading, 27
Negroponte, Nicholas, 188
Nesbitt-Larking, Paul, 144
net freedom, 161
net neutrality, 144, 160–61
Netflix, 80
network economy, 148
"New Languages, The," 99
new media, 29, 61, 84–85, 116, 148, 157, 219,
    225–35, 297, 312
New Media Monopoly, The, 145
New Republic, The, 29
New York Sun, The, 39
New York Times, 89, 128, 166, 207, 255, 256, 257
new technology, *see* new media
News Corporation, 142
news media
    24-hour services, 324–27
    cable/satellite, 245–46
    characteristics, 240–42
    defined, 241
    print, 242–43
    radio/television, 243–45
news networks, 137, 142
newspaper, 39, 54, 58, 137, 225
newsreels, 243, 325
Nietzsche, Friedrich, 317
Nineteenth Century, 203
Ninety-five Theses, 199
No Logo, 143, 271
non-communication, 79
North American Free Trade Agreement, 155
NPR, 147

O
Obama, Barack, 142
observational analysis, 337
observational notes, 345
obsessive individualism, 221
Ochs, Phil, 208
off the grid, 81
old media, 223–25, 310
Old Testament, 6, 9
On Liberty, 59

Ong, Walter, 31, 56, 96, 98, 100, 103, 116
ontology, 338
open source software, 187, 193
opinion leaders, 59
oppositional reading, 27
oral–aural culture, 98
Orality and Literacy, 31
orality, 89, 96–98, 100
Ordinary Lifestyles, 278
ordinary thought, 120
Orientalism, 32
Orwell, George, 46, 153, 228

P

Palin, Sarah, 142
paradigm, 38, 339
Paris, John, 126
parole, 91–92
participatory media, 300
patents, 185
Pathé, Charles, 325
Payne Fund Studies, 8
Pears Soap, 271, 291
peer-to-peer systems, 189
penny press, 242
perfect communication, 119
performativity, 299
perpetual present, 44
personal notes, 345
Peters, John Durham, 5, 6, 18, 31, 76, 85, 119, 339
Phaedrus, 11, 13, 32
Phantom Public, The, 24, 29
phantoscope, 126
phenakistoscope, 126
phonetic alphabet, 96–97
Plateau, Joseph, 126
platforms, 77, 144
Plato, 6–18, 31–32
political economy approach, 23, 30, 135–48, 312
political theatre, 79
political tracts, 58
Politics, 28
Pony Express, 23, 121
post-colonial theory, 32
post-structuralism, 25, 32
Powell, Michael, 161

PowerPoint, 268
pre-cinema, 126
Presse, La, 39
primary orality, 96
Prime Time Sports, 139
print, 25, 48, 55, 58–59, 98–101, 242–43
printing press, 25, 98, 99, 199
Printing Press as an Agent of Change, The, 25
Printing Revolution in Early Modern Europe, The, 25
Privacy Commissioner, 158
production–distribution–consumption cycle, 311, 313, 314, 315
progressive discourse, 207
propaganda, 153, 327
propaganda model, 24, 145
Propaganda Technique in the World War, 28
prosumer, 298
protest music, 208
Protestant Reformation, 199
Province, 140
Psychopathology and Politics, 28
Public and Its Problems, The, 24
public domain, 177, 179
Public Opinion, 29
public service function, 81–82, 154, 165
public sphere, 26, 58, 246, 303
punctum, 22
Putnam, Robert, 13

Q

qualitative methods, 334–35
quantitative methods, 334, 335
Quebec culture, 49–51
Quebec sovereignty, 167
Queen Elizabeth II, 164
quipu, 58
QWERTY keyboard, 85, 102

R

radio, 24, 40, 42, 49, 81, 120, 123, 124, 157, 225, 243–45, 312
Radio Act of 1912, 124
Radio Fides, 209
radio movies, 128
Radway, Janice, 277
Rage Against the Machine, 209

rail, 23, 311, 312
Ramones, The, 57
Real Housewives series, *The*, 301
real time, 312, 317–20
reductionist approach, 298
regulatory convergence, 226
reified story, 292
Reith, John, 165
remedial function, 74, 82–85, 114
Remediation, 83
Remix, 175
representation, 32, 60, 78, 289–305
Republic, The, 6–9, 11
research methods, 333–34, 336–37, 346–48
Reuter, Paul Julius, 311
rhetoric, 32
rhythm effect, media, 38
Richardson, Laurel, 344–45
Rifkin, Jeremy, 191
de la Rocha, Zack, 209
Rock of Love, 278
Rockwood Foundation Research Unit, 175
Rocky Mountain News, 256
Rogers Media, 139
Rolling Stone, 175
Rosen, Jay, 259
Rosenberg, Howard, 311, 325, 326
Rosenstiel, Tom, 240, 242
Royal Commission on Newspapers, 249

S
safety film, 325
Said, Edward, 32, 293, 294
satellite television, 245
de Saussure, Ferdinand, 22, 32, 91–93, 95, 105, 107
Savage, Dan, 300, 301
SchNews, 207
Schramm, Wilber, 339
Schudson, Michael, 248
Sconce, Jeffrey, 123
scoop, 243
Scorsese, Martin, 43
Second Cup, 281
Second Life, 276
Second World War, 208, 244, 325
secondary sources, 344

See It Now, 244
semiotics, 22, 89, 91–93, 337, 339
SESAC, 158
Sex Pistols, The, 164
Shirky, Clay, 256
Shrek, 67
Shrek: The Musical, 67
sign, 32, 92
signified, 32, 92
signifier, 32, 92
"Silenced Majority, The," 295
Silverstone, Roger, 85, 86
Simmel, Georg, 320, 321
Sinclair, Upton, 248
Skype, 104, 161
Smythe, Dallas, 138
Snow, Michael, 182
SOCAN, 154
social construction of technology, 115
social glue, 241
social media, 206, 291, 324
	see also blogs; Facebook; Twitter
social memory, 234
social movements, 208
soft news, 252
Songs for John Doe, 208
Sony Walkman, 274
sound bite, 326
space–time compression, 309, 315, 317
spatiality, 37, 45–47
Speaking into the Air, 31, 119, 339
spectacle, 138, 139
spectrum scarcity, 158–60
speed
	commerce, and, 310–12
	political economy of, 312–14
	space, and, 314–17
	spectacle, and, 324–27
spin, 79
Split Enz, 164
Sportsnet Radio, 139
Springsteen, Bruce, 208
Stamp Tax, 199
staples thesis, 27
Starbucks, 281
Statute of Anne, 179

Stewart, Jon, 205
Stiegler, Bernard, 16
Stokes, Jane, 334
stories, 241
storytellers, 241
Straw, Will, 156, 167
Street, John, 153
Structural Transformation of the Public Sphere, The, 26, 58
structuralism, 22, 25, 32
studum, 22
Suárez, Maria, 212
subaltern discourses, 202
Subculture and the Meaning of Style, 57
substantial part, 184
Sun, 140
SunTV News, 200, 245
Supernatural, 296
surveillance, 233
Survivor, 301
symbolic annihilation, 252

T

tabula rasa, 16
talkies, 129
Tarantino, Quentin, 43
Tarbell, Ida, 248
Taylor, Bryan, 338, 341
technical protection measures, 181
technological affordances, 304
technological convergence, 226
technological determinism, 118
Technological Society, The, 62
technologies of the self, 291
Technology and Cultural Form, 33
TED lectures, 33
teleaction, 318
telecontact, 318
telegraph, 23, 48, 84, 103, 120, 121, 122, 243, 312
telephone, 312, 322
television, 61, 78, 80, 85, 128, 157, 243–45, 276, 322
temporal homogenization, 320
temporality, 37, 38–45
textuality, 57
Thacker, Eugene, 190

thaumatrope, 126
theoretical notes, 345
thesis statement, 342–43
thick copyright system, 184
thin, leaky copyright system, 184
Thompson, John, 14
tickertape, 84
Tim Hortons, 281–82
time-saving devices, 321–24
time–space compression, 309, 315, 317
Time, 62, 175, 207
timetable effect, media, 38
Tipping Point, The, 205
Tolles, Chris, 259
top-40 radio stations, 40
Topix, 259
Toronto Sun, 142
total cinema, 125–31
Toy Story, 67
trade secrets, 185
trademarks, 185
traditional knowledge, 186
traffic shaping, 161
Trailer Park Boys, 296
transliteration, 97
transmedia, 67
transport mechanism, 62
triangulation, 338
tribalizing dynamic, 322
true communication, 5, 11
TSN, 147
Tuchman, Gaye, 342, 343
Tunisian uprising, 14
Turner, Ted, 245
Twitter, 4, 14, 39, 41, 63, 67, 79, 81, 103, 202, 205, 276, 303, 324
typewriters, 85, 102

U

unacknowledged revolution, 25
Understanding Media, 30, 343
US Patent and Trademarks Office, 191–92
USA Today, 255
user interface, 54
uses and gratifications approach, 77
utopian optimism, 220

V

Vaidhyanathan, Siva, 176
Vaver, David, 182
video home system, 130
videocassette recorder, 130
Vietnam War, 244
Village Voice, 175
Virgin, 277
Virilio, Paul, 310, 312, 315, 317, 319, 327
visual telegraphy, 128
vitascope, 126, 127, 128
"Voices in the Air," 89
voluntary collective licensing, 189
Vote Compass, 142

W

Warner Brothers, 68, 129
Warde, Alan, 269
Warner Brothers Animation, 68
Washington Post, 248, 256, 258
WA$TED, 279, 284
watchdog press, 247, 248
Watergate scandal, 248, 255
Weaver, Warren, 105, 106
Web 2.0 technologies, 61, 62, 63, 66, 260
Western Union, 312
Westminster Review, 203
What Not to Wear, 278

When Old Technologies Were New, 29
Where the Girls Are, 24
Wi-Fi access, 45, 268
Wiener, Norbert, 152
Wikipedia, 63, 340
Williams, Raymond, 26, 30, 33, 61, 74
Winnipeg Tribune, 125
Wizard of Oz, The, 42, 131
women's pages, 241
Wonderful Writing Machine, The, 102
Woodward, Bob, 248
World Intellectual Property Organization, 180
World Trade Organization, 197–98
World Wide Web, *see* Internet
worldwide time, 320

Y

Yahoo!, 188
You Are What You Eat, 278
Young, Marion Iris, 290
YouTube, 39, 44, 63, 116, 205, 227, 229, 231–35, 296, 300, 303

Z

Zapatistas, 209
zoetrope, 126
Zuckerberg, Mark, 83, 136, 233
Zukofsky, Paul, 183